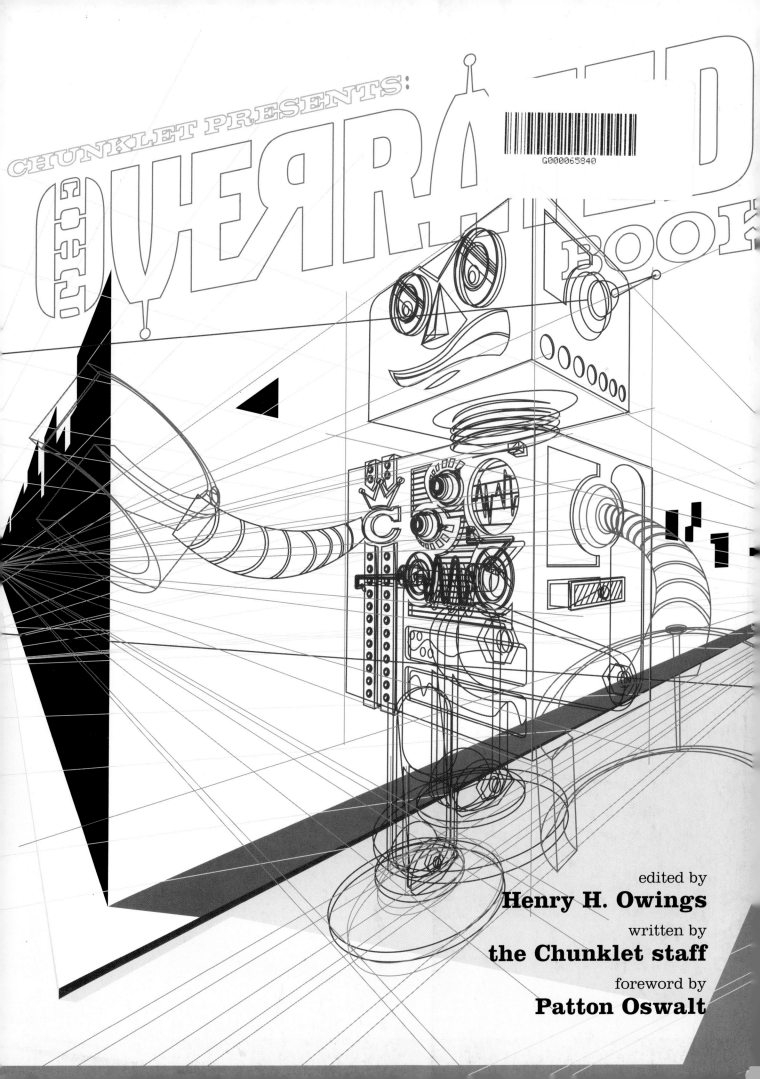

CHUNKLET PRESENTS:
THE OVERRATED BOOK

G000065840

edited by
Henry H. Owings

written by
the Chunklet staff

foreword by
Patton Oswalt

The Overrated Book: The Only Book You'll Ever Need
Edited by Henry H. Owings

© 2006 Chunklet Magazine

Published in 2006
Last Gasp, 777 Florida Street, San Francisco, CA 94110
www.lastgasp.com

Contributors: Mike Appelstein, Adrienne Arambula, Ben Arnold, Tom Bagby, Dave Batterman, Ron Bell, Chris Bilheimer, Steve Birmingham, Ben Blackwell, Nick Blakey, J. Bowers, Stuart Braithwaite, James Brubaker, Hugo Burnham, Rob Carmichael, Merrilee Challiss, Marina Chavez, David Cho, Papa Crazee, David Cross, Emerson Dameron, Silas Dameron, John Darnielle, John Davidson, Thomas Davies, Ben Davis, Chris Davis, Timothy Den, Antonio Depietro, Jason DiEmilio, Andrew Earles, Neil Eber, Mike Elliott, Colin English, Brett Essler, evildesign.com, Michael Faloon, Fat Bobby, Justin Fitterman, Gary T. Flom, Russ Forster, Mike Fournier, Adam Fuchs, Jerry Fuchs, Joe Garden, Daniel Gill, Dag Luther Gooch, Patrick Gough, Toby Halbrooks, Chris Hamrin, Ron Hart, Randy Harward, Andrea Herman, Heath K. Hignight, Jim Hayes, Ben Hellmann, Tim Hinely, Jef Hoskins, Patrick Hughes, Chris Iseli, Cup Iwata, Seth Jabour, Alan Jacobson, Sarah Jacobson, Benjamin Johnson, Garth Johnson, Tim Kabara, Logan Keese, Dryw Keltz, Tony P. King, James Korba, Jesse LeDoux, Aaron Lefkove, Matt Loomis, Seth Losier, Elina Mabe, Neil Mahoney, Jordan Mamone, Sam McAbee, Chris McGarvey, Jeff McLeod, Brian McManus, Anthony Melita, Kid Millions, Aye Jay Morano, Amanda Nichols, Brian O'Neill, Bob Odenkirk, Patton Oswalt, Chris Ott, Henry H. Owings, Sarah Hayes Owings, Joe Peery, Paul Poison, Neal Pollack, Brian Posehn, Andrew Quinn, Jim Raymond, Ted Rall, Benn Ray, Davis Rea, Jon Resh, Rock Action, Pablo A. Rockafucker, Ryan Russell, Jay Ryan, Michael Ryan, Robert Schriner, Abraham Scott, Michael Seghini, James Seizure, Joe Selby, Julianne Sheppard, Eryc Simmerer, Jim Slade, Jeff Smith, Scott Sosebee, Ryan Stacy, Dave Steiner, Alexander Stimmel, Brian Teasley, Matt Thompson, Rich Tommaso, Kevin Trowel, William Tyler, Johnny V., Blaine Vanderbilt, Eric Vazquez, Brian Walsby, Mark Wasserman, Curt Wells, Carrie Weston, Terry White, Jon Whitney, Pete Wilkins and Jon Wurster.
Proofing: Ben Arnold, J. Christopher Arrison, Ana Balka, Ben Blackwell, Jeff McLeod, Henry H. Owings and Benn Ray.
Legal: Stephen Pedersen
Jacket illustration and design: Scott Sosebee ©2006 Reprinted with permission.
Interior layout: Henry H. Owings with Scott Sosebee

ISBN 0-86719-657-2

Printed in China

First edition

For my mom.

She bought me my first Bill Cosby and Steve Martin records.

She always encouraged me.

She never questioned my decisions.

And yes, she's entirely to blame.

Dare to fail, Mom.

ADVANCE PRAISE FOR "THE OVERRATED BOOK"

From a few famous dead people

"The new socialist manifesto, but with better illustrations. The *Chunklet* staff is my only hope to kill Billy Bragg and Wilco for stealing my lyrics…assholes!" —*Woody Guthrie*

"If I had read 'The Overrated Book' in '66…'67, I'd probably be alive today, and hopefully without that goofy-ass Dutch boy haircut!" —*Brian Jones, The Rolling Stones*

"I can't read me one of them fancy books like 'The Overrated Book,' but I can't wait to get me the audio-book when it be a'comin' out." —*Blind Lemon Jefferson*

"All Glocks down! *Chunklet* is the new voice of black youth in America—end of story." —*Tupac Shakur*

"I always thought our little make-up smeared Rolling Stones rip-off band was underrated…that is, until I read 'The Overrated Book' and learned otherwise!" —*Johnny Thunders, The New York Dolls*

"I basically drowned at Marina Del Ray because I thought I had thrown the latest issue of *Chunklet* in the water, so I jumped in after it. I couldn't swim that well then…thanks, Quaaludes…well, you know the rest. Regardless, the book is still a gem. Manson always loved it." —*Dennis Wilson, The Beach Boys*

"Does 'The Overrated Book' make me look fat?" —*Karen Carpenter*

"Dear frat boys, quit doing shitty impressions of me, and buy this book!" —*Rick James*

"If only 'The Overrated Book' had been around to let me know that my white-boy, wanky-ass guitar playing was so fucking lame, I would have probably just stuck to being a coke addict." —*Stevie Ray Vaughan*

"This book has some fucking funny-ass shit in it. Take it from me—don't try to read it while driving a motorcycle." —*Duane Allman, The Allman Brothers*

"A big Mancunian hi-five to 'The Overrated Book.' My band was definitely overrated. I mean, one decent album and a few random bits? C'mon! Brooklyn really needs to get over itself." —*Ian Curtis, Joy Division*

"Ben, Jerry…hey man, give these dudes their own ice cream already, bro! They really deserve it." —*Jerry Garcia, The Grateful Dead*

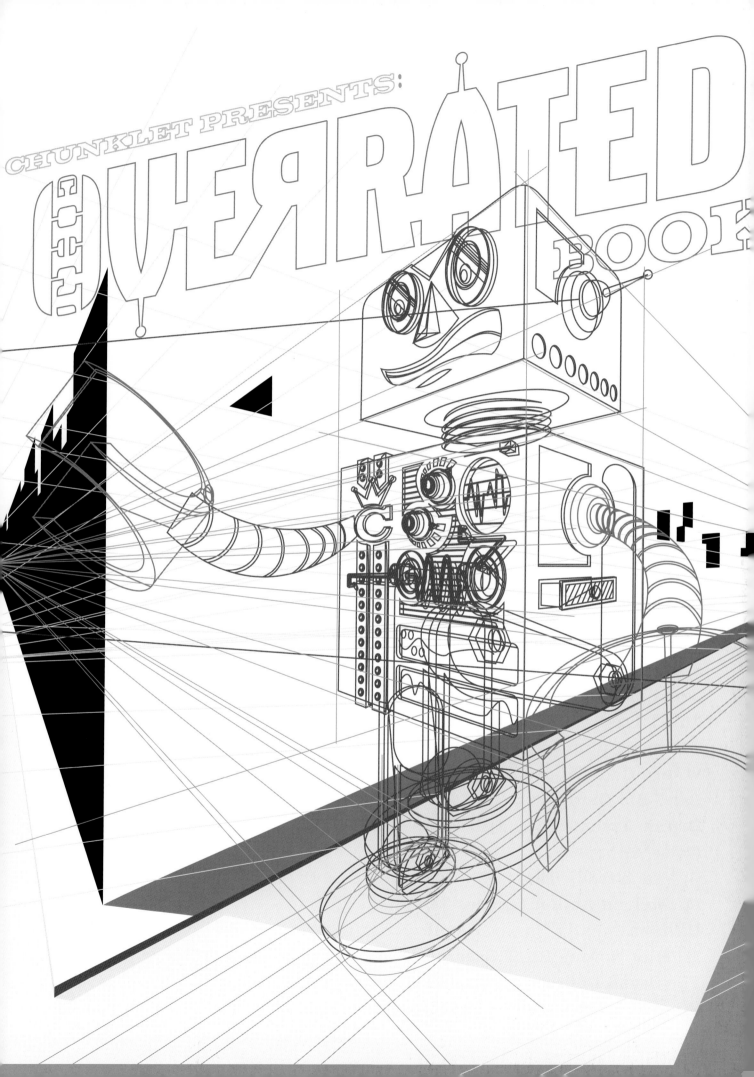

TABLE OF CONTENTS

PART ONE OVERRATED HILARITY

PART TWO OVERRATED: THE MUSICAL

PART THREE OVERRATED 2: ELECTRIC BOOGALOO

FOREWORD

by Patton Oswalt

photo by Chris Bilheimer

Do you have cancer? This book will cure it.

Are you illiterate? Open this book to any page—those funny little squiggles that used to make you punch your spouse and enjoy *American Idol* will suddenly make perfect sense.

If you're a fan of Shakespeare, Dickens, Nabokov or Borges, get ready to build a bonfire made of their works. This book—this *miracle*—that you hold, will make you clear a lot of space on your shelves. You will find a copy of *War and Peace* and punch it. You will pee on *Pride and Prejudice*. Spit on Seneca. And do something that starts with "u" on *Ulysses*.

That's how good the writing is. In fact, the layout and execution by themselves are at such a pitch of perfection that many people can't even get to the point where they can read this book. They're that dazzled by its inherent brilliance.

The tome you hold in your unworthy hands is like holding a sheaf of shavings from the gold pillars of paradise, inscribed with ink made from an angel's tear and bound with threads made from the shorn locks of martyrs. You do not deserve it, yet the editors, in their superhuman graciousness and giving, have deigned to allow its existence.

You will find it necessary to read this book while on your knees. And you'll notice, after reading each sentence, you'll whisper, "I'm sorry".

Don't judge yourself. You are beneath judgement.

Patton Oswalt is the greatest introduction writer in the pre- and written history of the Universe. His name, uttered aloud, can reverse the Doomsday Clock.

INTRODUCTION

by Henry H. Owings

photo by Ryan Russell

This introduction is totally unnecessary. Anybody with have a brain has already moved on to see what this book holds in store. Don't believe me? Well, you've made it four sentences into this so you must be wanting something from this. So here it is...

Chunklet Magazine finally has its first book, and it answers to nobody. *Chunklet*—the only magazine that doesn't care about the music it loves, but ridicules it anyway—has been around for thirteen years and has me as its attendant/janitor/bill payer. Nice to meet you, my name's Henry. Please don't call me Hank. I cut the checks. I lay the magazine out. And, of course, I annoy record labels for advertising. Yes, I lead a charmed life. *Chunklet* is a magazine that is available (for a small price) all over North America, Europe and other parts of the world. Many publications that you see at the newsstand shamelessly steal from us. It also seems like now is a good time to mention that if you're not actively creating music and "work" in the "industry," please know that your continued existence is destroying music. I'm an expert on this. Trust me.

"The Overrated Book" is a collection of the two overrated-themed issues of *Chunklet* plus heaps of additional material that old fans and new readers alike demand. There's many people that are responsible for this book, but there's several that deserve special mention. First is our publisher Last Gasp, and namely Colin, Ron and especially our all-'round go-to guy Bucky. They were the first (and only) publisher I called when I came up with this idea. So please, don't blame them for any pages herein*. Secondly, each and every writer, illustrator, designer and proof reader is priceless to *Chunklet's* continued operation, but I'd specifically like to single out Brian Teasley for keeping me on my toes with countless prank calls, obligatory bar-b-que runs and reams of material that he inspired. Also, Brian has also singlehandedly kept my editing and proofreading skills razor sharp. Finally, and most importantly, I'd like to thank my wife, my mother, my sisters, my niece and nephew, and all notable in-laws for not disowning me for my continued inability to grow up.

I'd tell you to enjoy "The Overrated Book," but I'm sure you're already doing that.

Now go out, publish your own magazine and maybe one day you can have your face as big as mine is (see right),

Henry

P.S. Oh, you music industry types that thought I was joking about your existence. I wasn't.

*I'd like to take this moment to suggest that you e-mail me directly at henry@chunklet.com with any comments and/or complaints.

HUNKLET PRESENTS:

OVERRATED

BOO1

PART ONE

OVERRATED HILARITY

ROCKTOIDS

The on-going Chunklet index of what's going on

by Brian Teasley & Henry H. Owings

Worst teeth in rock: Roky Erickson

Rap star most likely to be worshiped as the new savior of man in the year 4017: Tupac

Artist who got sexier as s/he approached death: Warren Zevon

Video director most likely to spontaneously grow an arm out of his ass in order to pat himself on the back: Spike Jonze

Guy most likely to be there videotaping the arm coming out of Spike Jonze's ass: Lance Bangs

Christian emo label who named itself after a Dokken song: Tooth & Nail

Artist most likely to have a magician in their video to procure a sword out of thin air: (tie) Ronny James Dio and Tenacious D

Activity that artists like Ani DiFranco, Moby, Mike Patton, et. al. who are commercially successful do to try to validate themselves: Surround themselves by touring with — or releasing records by — artists who are actually good

Drummer last in line to catch on to the distorted, overly ringy piccolo snare sound: Lars Ulrich

Most self-congratulatory documentary by a bad frat-rock joke band: *Gigantic—Tale of Two Johns* (They Might Be Giants)

Two things Neil Young supported in the 1980s: Ronald Reagan and nuclear energy

ZZ Top song most likely to be about cumming on a woman's tits: "Pearl Necklace"

Least believable line to get to the band's complimentary beer: "Man, you guys were awesome"

Musician's passing interest in photography parading as art that is really just a sad disguise for being a pompous socio-phobe: Nick Zinner from the Yeah Yeah Yeahs

Least ironic band name: Something Corporate

All-star jam band we'd actually pay to see: Eric Bachman Mick Turner and Hooch Overdrive

Content most likely to be found on a band's bonus DVD: A couple of shitty non-sequitur videos shot haphazardly by a friend along with painfully boring one-camera live footage, again shot by a friend

Label waiting to pull the trigger on this whole internet craze: Touch & Go

Hip hop album that your lame, out-of-touch coworker got as a Christmas present: Outkast *Speakerboxxx/The Love Below*

Television show that we embarrassingly weep during: VH1's "Band Reunited"

Winner of the wait-around-long-enough-and-kids-will-be-naive-enough-to-buy-my-melodramatic-pap-again award: Morrissey

Most overrated date activity for a hipster couple: Talk about starting an electronic duo

Best current way to describe taking a shit that is especially effective in new age stores: "Having bad energy"

Most worshiped still-active band who hasn't written a decent song in nearly fifteen years: The Cure

Person your songwriting truly has nothing in common with: Bob Dylan

State that has created more shitty hardcore bands than Ethiopia has famines: New Jersey

What friends should never do for each other: Put out each other's records

Only band that still can't even be helped by adding Nels Cline on guitar: Wilco

Music that should never be covered: Nintendo game music

Aging rocker most likely to put central air in his house by selling his own records on eBay: Robert Pollard

Thing that British people think is part of actual record collecting: Reissues

Actual number of Hot Topic abortion escapees who vote: 17

What being on the road since you were fourteen will do to your mind: Convince you to rock with a meglo-maniacal dreadlocked Axl Rose on the G'n'R comeback (ck. Tommy Stinson)

Type of bag people who write for the *NME* couldn't write their way out of: Paper

Artist most likely to play his CD and check his e-mail on stage instead of 'performing' on his laptop: Jim O'Rourke

Torture tactic that Abu Ghraib prisoners should be damn thankful they weren't exposed to: Repeated viewings of Neil Young's *Greendale*

Rock club that had the honor of reaffirming to Kathleen Hanna that she couldn't sing: Cat's Cradle

Band with highest ratio of members that wear shorts: Built to Spill (100%)

Artist most mistaken for Ron Jeremy: Har Mar Superstar

Club where you're most likely to bust your ass while loading out: Gabe's Oasis, Iowa City, Iowa

Worst new genre name: "Intelligent Metal"

Most overdone rock fashion: *(tie)* Leather arm band watch & Belt with holes all the way around the belt

Smelliest stretch of US Interstate: Midway on I-5 between LA and San Francisco (aka The Poo Zone)

Band who are still bigger fans of themselves than their fans: Red Kross

Only rock magazine bad enough to put Me First and the Gimme Gimme's on the cover: *Rockpile*

Person most likely to destroy press photos of former band: Jack White

Only publication that thinks Matador's best band is still Chavez: *Chunklet*

Person most likely to be seen performing in a "Canadian Tuxedo" (aka double denim): Anton Newcombe (Brian Joneston Massacre)

Worst current genre name: Folktronica

Least accurate album title in relation to actual album artwork: Quasi's *Hot Shit*

Definitive proof that zombies walk among us: Mark E. Smith

Artist whose brilliant-to-embarassing post-'86 output ratio is 1 to 33: Robyn Hitchcock

Band least likely to send Sonic Youth their deserved royalty check: And You Will Know Us By The Trail of Dead

Worst part of a Pixies reunion: Interfering with David Lovering's burgeoning Mr. Wizard-style magic career

Worst band makeover: The Dandy Warhols

Band with best fake English accents: Black Rebel Motorcycle Club

Most unfuckable Canadian band: Broken Social Scene

Artist whose name most sounds like a bad new "Star Wars" character: Scout Niblett

Least-noted, overdone genre : Fucked-up, heavily effected, Texas acid-punk

Worst record store logo: Amoeba Records

Most collected collected item on a European tour: Kinder Eggs

Musician who should not be allowed to do own artwork: Bill Callahan from Smog

Most overrated party idea: *Zaireeka* listening party

Person most likely to say while having sex, "Prepare to accept the seed of Rollins": Rollins

Band most likely to seem less scary because you can see their Timberland boots: Slipknot

Person most likely to yell at his musicians for not loading out quickly: Mike Watt

Lamest form of self-promotion for profit: Stuart Murdoch from Belle & Sebastian selling car on Ebay as a celebrity owned collector's item.

Worst band championed by Lester Bangs: *(three-way tie)* Black Oak Arkansas, J. Geils Band & White Witch

Most obvious choice for a record store name: Earwax

Most common current idea for naming a band: Geographical reference

Most common words in current new bands: Black, Star(s) and Space. If you put "Super" in your name, please have the decency to kick your own ass.

Most uncommon idea for naming a band: Naming after pouch-packaged fruit drinks

Lamest inside joke naming trend: Naming band after state motto or license plate catch phrase (e.g. The Good Life)

Most tired live stage tactic: *(tie)* Setting stuff on fire & Smashing equipment

Worst comedy album of new millennium: Jimmy Fallon's *The Bathroom Wall*

Worst album title of all-time: *(tie)* Wonderstuff *Eight Legged Groove Machine* / REO Speedwagon *You Can Tune A Piano But You Can't Tunafish*

Thickest neck size for old fat old fucks who still make music: Steve Earle

Worst small venue in the United States: The Nick, Birmingham, Alabama

Most irrelevant music scene for a metropolitan city: Dallas, Texas

Most useless and desperate tactic for an indie band to promote itself: The in-store

Most erroneous nostalgic statement by people who still call "Alternative" a genre: "Dude, do you remember when *120 Minutes* used to actually show good videos?"

Least employable session drummer: Damon Che

Artist whose music instantly becomes good due to his death: Jeff Buckley

Band who should never have put out a DVD which basically shows what a shitty live band they were: Pavement *[Slow Century]*

ROCK SNIGLETS

sniglet (n.): a word that should be in the dictionary, but isn't

by Colin English

AIR GUITARDED (adj.)
Term used to describe anyone in an audience who plays air guitar along with the band.

"CAN YOU SMELL ME NOW? GOOD!" (exp.)
Expression used to describe any gutterpunk who begs change in between taking calls on his cell phone.

CANADIORITY (adj.)
A state of thinking one is of a higher nature or kind due to being in a band from Canada. *Example: Bob wondered why the band from Toronto, in the midst of their Canadiority, continued to release records in the States and tour America in order to seek support from the lowly American youth.*

CELLDUMB (adj.)
Any person who tries to talk on their cell phone during a show, especially when standing right in front of the band or PA.

CELLPHISH (adj.)
One who talks on their cell phone during a Phish concert. May also apply to Galactic, moe., String Cheese Incident, Leftover Salmon, Grateful Dead, Widespread Panic and Lefthand Smoke fans.

CIGAPROP (n.)
The use of a cigarette by a musician to appear "cool" rather to actually smoke it as a means of satisfying his/her need for nicotine.

COCK-N-BALLS (n.)
Any band that is known as being a central core of two people who have a revolving line up and/or hired guns playing to fulfill the band's needs. *Example: I made the mistake of going to the record store to find that Cass McCombs was playing in the parking lot. As it turns out, cock-n-balls have a new record out.*

CONCERT CALL (n.)
The transmission of a live show via a cell phone held up above the audience.

COOL-SIGHTED (adj.)
People who wear eye glasses not because they need to correct their vision but because they think they look cool. *Example: We ended up seeing Lisa Loeb last night doing coke in the bathroom, fronting her cool-sighted specs.*

DUSTAINTER (-s (pl.) n.)
Any dude who rocks a goatee. *Example: Martin pondered as to why so many people showing up to the show in pick-up trucks were dustainers.*

EMOPHELIAC (-s (pl.) n.)
Any guy or guys who form or join an emo band in order to score with under-age chicks. *Example: Not only is Tom a Jimmy Eat-All he is also a confessed emopheliac.*

FAINTDOM (n.)
The saddening process during which a normal alternative rock band changes its sound to become "electroclash" in the hopes of being cool. Usually involves firing the drummer and buying a drum machine. (a.k.a. Electrificlashion, a.k.a. The Tastefaker)

FOREGOFLUFF (v; -in, n.)
[when talking to a musician who is not local] the act of lying to them and as a result reinforcing their feeling that he/she plays their instrument well or produces likeable music. *Example: Since I had no money left for booze I gave the guitarist in the band A-Set a foregofluffin to get him to slide me some free drinks.*

GERIROCKTIC (adj.)
A branch of the rock scene containing old and aging people, namely ones who were in "hip" rock bands 10+ years ago.

GUITAR CENTRIFUSION (n.)
Used to describe the sound of any band made up of Guitar Center employees.

HOMEGOFLUFF (v., -ing, n.)
[when talking to a local musician] the act of lying to them and as a result reinforcing their feeling that he/she plays their instrument well or produces likeable music. *Example: Dude, what the fuck where you thinking with that homegofluff you just gave the drummer of the Mazarin?*

INCOGLAME-O (n.)
The adaptation of a look, attitude, musical style, etc. by a musician as a means of trying to fit in with the audience for that particular evening.

INFLATIFACE (n.)
The condition experienced by rock club employees, bar hags and true rockers in which one's face is constantly bloated and puffy due to life-affirming alcohol and cocaine abuse.

JIMMY EAT-ALL (n.)
1. Emo bands that are made up of portly 30 something ex-alt-rockers who prey upon 14-year olds. *Example: Dude, my kid sister is dating some dude who works at Tower Records and is in one of those Jimmy Eat-All bands.* 2. Any 30 something and/or obese person who fronts tight fitting thrift store t-shirts and or high waters. Also may dye hair black to cover up graying hair. *Example: What would the Jimmy Eat-Alls do should Urban Outfitters forever close their doors tomorrow?*

MACHISMO-SCOPE (n.)
When the guy in front of you at a show turns his back to the stage to scan the audience as a means of checking out the chicks in the crowd.

MANISTROKEWITZ (n.)
In any environment: the state of multiple dudes dressed like Blondie meets the Ramones with long, shaggy curly hair (i.e. skinny ties with blazer, leather jackets with thrift t-shirt and sneakers, or any resemblance to a member of the Strokes). *Example: We went out last night to get a burrito and found ManiStrokewitz there en masse.*

MESHROPOLITAN (n.)
Urban hipsters who wear mesh hats, most of them bought at Urban Outfitters.

MONOROCKER (–s (pl.) n.)
see *Unirocker.*

NEOHOMOPOLITAN (n.)
A person or group of people who are over 30 and wear a wardrobe consisting of black jeans, black t-shirt (preferably Calvin Klein) and black leather jacket. When not designing websites or other dotcom-type duties they can be found at coffee shops or driving SUV's entirely too fast. When at a show they pretend to not be paying attention to the performing group and will usually discuss John Cusack films. *Example: The audience at the Air show was pretty neohomopolitan.*

NIGHT PAINGER (n.)
When the drummer in a band sings. (a.k.a. the Phil Collinsist)

OLYSBIANS (n.)
Term used to describe the scene of nouveau lesbians who can easily be confused for any member of Sleater-Kinney, Le Tigre, Bikini Kill or any Olympia, Washington band.

OMAYAWN (n.)
The belief that Omaha, Nebraska (or any music scene for that matter) is of any significance to the real world.

PEEWEE PHONE (n.)
The look of annoyance people get when they try to use their cell phones during a show, as if to say, "I AM TRYING TO USE THE PHONE!!"

PICKHEAD (n.)
Any guitarist who needs a pick holder on his mic stand to hold his guitar picks.

PREDESLEEPER (n.)
During a show, the band member that takes on the soporific task of explaining what his/her band's next song is about as if anyone in the audience really cares.

RACLONES, THE (n.)
see *Unirocker.*

RASHOKRAVITZ (n.)
In a rock club: the state of (multiple) dudes dressed like rock stars (i.e. scarves, 'Charlies' Angels' sunglasses, make up, feathered hair, 'Elvis' sunglasses, or any resemblance to Lenny Kravitz). *Example: Not only was the Crocodile a sausage fest last night Rashokravitz was in full effect too.*

SCRAPPER BAND (n.)
A musical group that has both a screamer and a rapper.

STATUTORY ROCK (n.)
The occurrence of autobiographical songs written by a songwriter about, his/her being a teenager when in fact he/she is in his/her 30's.

SYNTHNOTIZE (v.)
To add a synthesizer to a band's line-up as an attempt to convince the audience that the band is actually good.

TANDEMONIUM (n.)
The occurrence of "scene" or "genre" specific wardrobe(s) worn by an entire audience at a concert.

THREEPEAT (n.)
When rock stars have the same threesome multiple times.

UNIROCKER (- s (pl.) n.)
Members in a band that all look the same or front the same image or genre. *Example: If I had a nickel for every local band that was made up of unirockers I would be a millionaire.*

URLOSER (-s (pl.) n.)
Mostly male, but any person who by day designs web pages, and by night frequents rock clubs/bars covered in tattoos, rocking a wallet chain, and overflowing with testosterone drenched machismo. Preferred shirt is a wife beater. Male variety commonly found sporting a goatee.

WHAT WOULD JESUS SPIN? AKA WHERE WOULD JESUS MOSH? (adj.)
The act of Christian religious freaks in justifying using a once "unholy" form of music (something previous Christians burned lp's and people alive for) as a means of expressing their beliefs. *Example: Aw man, the show tonight was a total disappointment; all the bands were shitty Where Would Jesus Mosh? hardcore bands.*

WHOFLUNGDUNG (n.)
the osmotic processes in which one local band copies another local band's sound.

WOOLIE STINKETH, AKA HARRY AND THE ACNE-SONS (n.)
The look of a musician who does not bathe or shave while on tour. *Example: Is it just me or does the new guitarist from Man...Or Astroman? seem to be a Woolie Stinketh?*

GREAT MOMENTS IN TELEVISED SHOW BUSINESS HISTORY!

Van Halen at the US Festival, 1983

by Henry H. Owings • transcription by Sarah Jacobson

As many of you will remember, Apple Computer threw a weekend festival called the US Festival '83 at the Glen Helen Park in Southern California. Among televised highlights (at least as far as I remember) were The Pretenders, The Clash and an overly-theatric U2 with Bono climbing the stage's scaffolding, almost breaking his neck in the process. What a goon!

Well, as luck would have it, Van Halen closed ceremonies on the middle night. They were paid $1.6 million for their performance, which was, at the time, the most a group had ever been paid for a gig. As legend has it, they insisted on being paid more than David Bowie in order to play. Bowie was paid $1 million. Not bad for a night's work. Now, David Lee Roth is a man who conjures up equal amounts of sheer amusement and respect around the *Chunklet* offices, but on this particular night, he couldn't have been more whacked out of his mind. Here's the deal....

WHAT WE SAW ON TELEVISION: Right before Van Halen went on stage, millions of viewers saw a pre-taped (read: staged) skit go on backstage involving Diamond Dave, a piano, two groupies and a bottle of Jim Beam. However, the reality of the situation was far more rock (read: hilarious).

WHAT REALLY HAPPENED: Moments before going out on stage in front of 670,000 fans (not to mention all of the viewers on then-two-year-old MTV), DLR was barely able to stand up after a day of rocking and/or rolling. As the rest of the band went on stage to earn approximately $200,000 per hour per person, their soon-to-be-shit-canned lead singer puked, then followed *that* up with two lines of cocaine, *then* rushed on stage! Now, that, dear reader, is rock'n'roll!

Below is the transcript of the "stage banter" after the second song. Elapsed time? *Five minutes*! The time was necessary to get Roth to sober up, but what transpired was nothing short of hilarity! Please keep in mind that Roth is performing in front of what *The Guinness Book of World Records* called the largest attendance for a concert. Let's take a look at the damage:

("Runnin' With The Devil" ends) Well, hello, Glen Helen Regional Park! Look at all the people here tonight! Oh, man! I've got to make an announcement right here. Can you hear me out there? *(screams from crowd)* Hey, man, don't be squirting water at me! I'm gonna fuck your girlfriend, pal! I just wanted to say that as of right now, this time tonight, more people have been arrested today than the entire weekend last year, man! You a rowdy bunch of motherfuckers! *(extensive screaming, 48-second pause)* Who likes rock'n'roll? Yeah! Yeah! I'll tell ya, this is the time of the evening when the band gets to have a drink, right here. Ooooohhh-ohh. *(Roth's midget assistant comes out and hands him a bottle of whiskey.)* Is everybody having a good time so far right here? *(screams, whistles and cheers, 40-second pause)* I want to take this time to say that this is real whiskey here. The only people who put iced tea in Jack Daniels bottles is The Clash, baby! *(segue into "Jamie's Crying")*

FUN THINGS TO DO AT THE MALL OF AMERICA

Minneapolis, Minnesota

by Henry H. Owings • photos by Elina Mabe

If you have been there, no explanation is necessary. If you haven't, there's not one that would suffice....

These four boxes feature Philadelphia's Enon (top left), Brooklyn's Les Savy Fav (top right), Baltimore's Oxes (bottom left) and Brian Teasley and me (bottom right) and were all made at Cereal Adventureland. For $12, you were allowed to make your own personalized Wheaties box along with your own "home-brew" of breakfast cereal which Brian and I ate during our 3-day drive from Minneapolis to Los Angeles on the Mr. Show tour.

Regretably, we have found out that General Mills has shut Cereal Adventureland's doors, but these boxes will always remind me of what used to be.

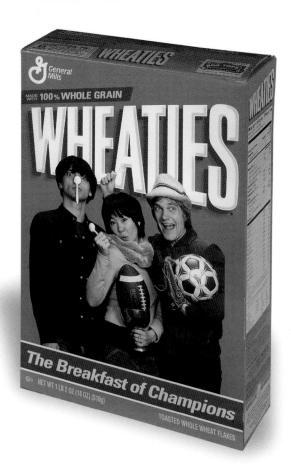
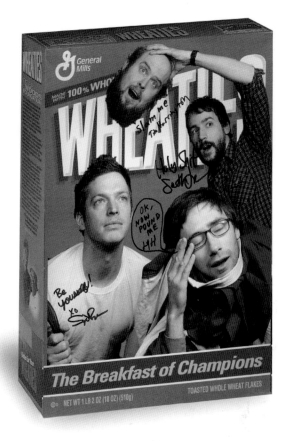
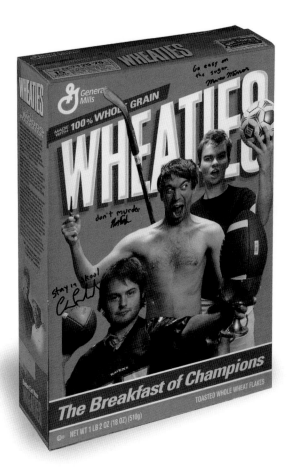
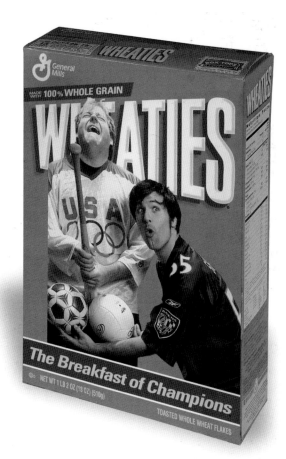

OFFENSIVE BUMPER STICKERS

...and the need for new professional bumper sticker writing

by Brian Teasley & Henry H. Owings with Bob, Garth, Mark, Quinn, Sarah and Scott

Bumper sticker writing has been an isolated, unacknowledged art form. Many of the gifted, early writers got little or no recognition in spite of having authored the catch phrases that would encapsulate modern opinion and culture. Lamentably, we may never know who authored some of the brilliant sayings like "My Other Car is a Broom."

Only "The Ventura Blvd. Boys" of the mid-70s—a Tin Pan Alley-like bumper sticker think-tank—got their fair share in the annals of the art form. Writers such as Zeb Washington, B. Manley and Artie Sanchez, who were often in need of paying bills in between novels, would literally sit around an "almost round" table, and just "riff" on slogans, quips, and sayings of the day. It is here that phrases like "Metaphors be with you," and "I owe, I owe, it's off to work I go," were born. All three writers were awarded the National Prize For Fiction (Under Ten Words in Length) on multiple occasions, and were honored by President Carter for their "Succinct Cultural Contributions." Alas, all have retired with the torch never passed.

Sadly, airbrush t-shirts, fortune cookies, novelty hats, and especially cable television, all but wiped out the need for bumper sticker think tanks like The Ventura Blvd. Boys. Throughout the '80s and the early '90s, very little innovative thought was brought to bumper sticker writing. Most were simple "Where's the beef!"-style regurgitations of the TV advertising world or manipulative religious propaganda such as "Get to church or the devil's gonna get ya!"

Of course, it was neither the hackneyed television commercial tags nor moral majority mottos that killed the craft of bumper sticker writing, rather it was the internet. Allowing the average Joe to "create" his own bumper sticker is the greatest tragedy of the short fiction canon. These days, anyone from a sixteen-year-old high school student to a concerned grandparent, from a new age-cult zealot to an amateur porn entrepreneur can turn a sloppily-written, often offensive quip into a mini-banner for the mainstream consciousness. Simply, this is a license the layman should never have been given.

The following are examples we found. We hope that you find them as repugnant as we do, and that your indignation will send a shockwave through the media, eventually putting bumper sticker writing back into the surgically precise hands of professional writers who slave over the one-line-highway-horse sense that may just remain with you the rest of your life. Honk if I'm horny? You bet your ass I will!

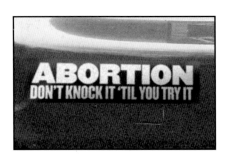

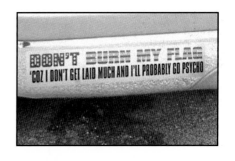

WHAT I CALL CHILDREN'S MUSIC

by Andrew Earles • illustration by Brian Walsby

I love my underground metal. I love it when it's good. But when some band bolts out of the underground wearing Smiths, Cure or Echo and the Bunnymen t-shirts, styling them around a black shirt/red tie or a dilettante mohawk, further invalidating Swedish melodic death metal with a constant raping—and is nothing more than totally dumbed-down pop metal with screaming and blast beats—it is not good.

But this is what many people believe should fly under the banner of metal. It sells metal magazines...otherwise you wouldn't see the pages of *Terrorizer* or *Decibel* soiled with cover and full-page shots of complete and total man-pussies molded by the same highly-productive machine. If the "I-can't-add-anything-original-to-the-'80s-so-let's-just-connect-the-dots" hair and indistinguishable sound doesn't raise a flag, the t-shirts will. The Cure and The Smiths have sadly become the visual dumbshit marquee, the audible moron mantra. But why not rock a Mighty Mighty Lemon Drops, Close Lobsters, Wedding Present, Jesus and Mary Chain, Chameleons or Church t-shirt? It's all good stuff from roughly the same era, since it's "late-period" all the way with these losers anyway. Oh, that's right, you don't know about these bands. You don't know about these bands because you own the same 100 albums as that done-up shithead standing next to you...and the only albums that you do own that carry a pre-1997 release date were FUCKING MADE BY THE SMITHS AND THE CURE.

Now I have moved into a writing style in which I am openly addressing "you," the bands. The new nü-metal. I enjoy the counteractive approach utilized by you "extreme" lemmings: the "I know a lot about good, classic underground metal" one. Go get fucked. Then play like it, if you're so into it. I guess you can't go all the way with real, classic underground metal because then your pussy would vanish. At least you can win some bootleg, tight-fitting Destruction, Thin Lizzy and Morbid Angel t-shirts[1] off of eBay for appearances. Still, tat sleeves and long hair—for the more ballsy of the bunch—will never hide that YOU ARE NOT METAL. If all of this interchangeable vanilla wasn't enough, you soon-to-be-gang-tagged-by-the-music-biz douche bags can't even come up with original names. How in the hell is some fog-headed tart or, uh, guy that looks just like you going to keep from getting shot as he relays the names back and forth in some chain store? Names like As I Lay Dying, A Life Once Lost, Every Time I Die, Bane, On Broken Wings, Haste The Day, The Red Chord, Light This City, Playing Enemy, The Agony Scene (good God, have you laid eyes on these idiots?!), Embrace The End, Embrace Today, The Red Death, Paint It Black. Did I just predict the titles from the upcoming Lifetime "Movies For Women" series? If optimism were to prevail right now, all this at least could be looked at as a helpful combination of awful art: the uniting of hardcore's stupidity, emo's overall banality, indie rock's mediocrity, with textbook nostalgia lifts from the '80s. That would be easy, but then they rip riffs and start calling it metal.

---

[1] *These shirts were not form-fitting backing the day. They were XXL and they hung-off of ugly dudes.*

BAND BIO DICTIONARY

by Brian Teasley

What do publicists really mean in those irritatingly patronizing scraps of toilet paper known as "the one sheet?" Well, not much of anything really. Their job isn't to translate any authentic information about a specific band; their job is to get you "pumped" about a record, so you will either write a favorable review about it, play it on radio or TV (or as pathetic as it may be, possibly even on the internet), stock it in your store, or maybe just actually buy it—at least that was the case when people actually bought music.

They're basically well-paid bullshit artists having to hype bands that they never choose to work with. I do concede you can't blame someone for having to write about a shitty band when it's simply their job. I do, however, blame someone for taking an utterly despicable job in the first place. If being a publicist is a record label's version of a prostitute, then writing a hype sheet is certainly the equivalent of a facial.

What I've done here is run their dim-witted, amateurish prose through the bullshit decoder and gotten to the really distasteful orangey, stale Butterfingery-like center in their den of lies. Dear publicists, you can't help bands; you can only hurt them. You've gotten way too used to your own stanky shit piles and have forgotten that some people can actually smell it. I guess what I'm saying is "Fuck You, You Pathetic Ass Puppets."

If a one sheet's bio describes their latest album to be a "mature work," it really means...

...it's a slapped-together, shit-dribbled menagerie of slow songs for people over thirty who don't go to rock shows any more.

If a band's one sheet relates all the awesome bands that they have toured with, it really means...

...that they still can't headline their own shows, and have all but failed in developing their own fan base.

If a band's one sheet reveals the fact that their record was home-recorded, it really means...

...that their last record didn't sell dick and didn't get enough of a budget from their label to record at a real studio.

If a band's one sheet describes their music as being "whiskey-soaked," it really means...

...the band can't play together for shit and most likely plays some fake country crap.

If band's one sheet claims that their chops are "dexterous," it really means...

...that the dudes in said band were pimple-faced, D& D playing nerds who grew up on Rush and practiced for several hours a day. Thankfully, they still mostly only hang out with other guys.

If a band's one sheet claims that they "deliver" something, it really means...

...that they did as little as they could to keep their skinny necks above the sewage that contains all other bands that they are compared to, or often steal from.

If a band's one sheet labels their record as "experimental," it really means...

...the band is lazy and can't really compose authentic music, but has enough money to buy expensive samplers and computers.

If a band's one sheet describes their demeanor as being "enigmatic," it really means...

...the band sucks at doing interviews and are sad, sour bastards.

If a band's one sheet overloads you with parentheses relating what everyone involved with the record has done, it really means...

...that although this record, by no means, can stand on its own merits... oh shit, did you see who the guest vocalist plays with?

If a one sheet describes a songwriter's music as being "introspective," it really means...

...he uses the fine backdoor art of subtlety to get pussy from girls who work at vintage clothing shops.

If a band's one sheet terms their career as "long-time," it probably means...

...they probably have just been together for far too long and rock like two old Jewish men playing chess in Washington Square Park.

If a band's one sheet says their sound is "idiosyncratic" (or worse, "quirky"), it really means...

...they're sucking with such a special kind of suck, and that no one is anywhere near the same league of suckiness as they are.

If a band's one sheet calls their music "cathartic," it really means...

...you'll probably have to take a big dump after listening to the first few songs.

If a band's one sheet says that they're "challenging," it really means...

...their record has absolutely no fucking hooks on it.

If a band's one sheet says their singer is a "chanteuse," it really means...

...she's a frumpy alt-country singer who has drooping breasts and a flair for the ironic.

If a band's one sheet describes their music as "ambitious," it really means...

...that the band spent way too much money in the studio ordering take-out and recording out-of-key harmony vocals that they'll never use, because of the great expense of making the record (not finished).

If a band's one sheet alleges that a record is a "return to form," it really means...

...the band has sold out and compromised enough to recreate a watered-down version of what they were when everyone really liked them, otherwise known as the SOMPTfP* game.

If a band's one sheet describes their sound to be sometimes "jazzy," it really means...

...their guitar player and/or drummer wasted a lot of money majoring in music and will punish their audience with whacky chords and jerky rhythms whenever possible.

If a band's one sheet credits someone as having played a "Mellotron," it really means...

...there was a non-functioning Mellotron at the studio where they did their basic tracking, but they used a Midi sample of a Mellotron on one or two songs, and most likely mixed it so low you couldn't even hear it.

*Sad Old Men Parodying Themselves for Profit

Drunk Assholes Can Still Write (Sort of)

The only enterprise I've participated in at clubs as much as actually playing shows is "droppin' a deuce." The following is my highlight reel from about six years of partaking in some of the globes finest shitholes. Originally, this was intended for issue twelve many tours ago, but I forgot about turning in my homework. I recently came back across this list, and thought that enough stench had past between myself and the crappers that the world could finally take a whiff of its own.
BY BRIAN TEASLEY ARTWORK BY MARK WASSERMAN

SMASH THE ← STATE!

IF IT WASN'T FOR CAPITALISM, NO ONE WOULD MAKE MAGIC MARKERS THAT MORONS LIKE YOU USE. [1]

FAT GIRLS WORK FOR IT. ONCE YOU'VE HAD FAT, YOU'LL NEVER GO BACK. [2]

OH, THE BITCHES... THEM CHAPEL HILL BITCHES... [3]

BEATING YOUR MEAT IS MURDER [5]

$E=MC^2=+3DB$ [4]

IN ONE END, OUT THE OTHER. I JUST LOVE A CLEAN TOILET SEAT. WARM, CLEAN, QUIET, IT'S TIMES LIKE THESE WHEN TOURING SEEMS O.K. I'M EASY TO PLEASE, IT COULD BE WORSE YOU KNOW. I COULD BE TOURING AMERICA. PLASTIC LAND, HOME OF TELEVISION FED FAT AND HAPPYS; HOME OF MACHO SEX STARVED MORONS, INTERESTED IN NOTHING ELSE THAN GETTING RICH, GETTING LAND AND COMPETITION — I KNOW BECAUSE I AM ONE. I'M SURE GLAD I LIVE IN EUROPE. OCT '96 [6]

HUMAN BEINGS ARE FUCKHEADS NERDS BORING STUPID ALL OF THE ABOVE. [7]

NOT ONLY DOES JIMMY WORK THE DOOR. HE WORKS IT ALL OVER ME. [8]

SEAMUS EATS PUSSY LIKE IT'S HIS MOM'S COOKING. [9]

WHAT ARE YOU GOING TO DO WHEN YOUR SHITTY BAND BREAKS UP? TAXI DRIVER? TEACHER? DOLE? HAS BEEN? DOPE MANIAC? [10]

The exotic blow jobs, suck! [11]

IT'S NOT WHAT YOU GOT. IT'S WHAT YOU GET. - BIKINI KILL [13]

ROADIE RULES I. IF IT'S GREEN: SMOKE IT. II. IF IT'S LIQUID: DRINK IT. III. IF IT'S WALKING: FUCK IT. IV. IF IT DON'T MOVE: PUT IT IN THE VAN. [12]

Mom, Dad... I use drugs. [14]

MORNING DAWNS WITH THE HANGOVER, OBSCURING THE NAME OF THE IMPOTENT LOVER LYING NEXT TO ME. [15]

FOUND AT THE FOLLOWING ROCK ESTABLISHMENTS: 1. Biograph (Richmond, Virginia), 2. JR's Light Bulb (Fayetteville, Arkansas), 3. The Lizard and Snake (Chapel Hill, North Carolina), 4. Zürich, Switzerland, 5. Tivoli (Utrecht, Holland), 6. Star Club (Dresden, Germany), 7. Doornroosje (Nijmegen, Netherlands), 8. Galaxy Club (Dallas, Texas), 9. JR's Light Bulb (Fayetteville, Arkansas), 10. Paard (Den Haag, Netherlands), 11. Marquee (Hamburg, Germany), 12. Doornroosje (Nijmegen, Netherlands), 13. The Subway (Karlsruhe, Germany), 14. Second Story (Bloomington, Indiana), 15. Club Toast (Burlington, Vermont), 16. Kerosine (Ausburg, Germany), 17. Komm (Nurnberg, Germany), 18. The Underground (Göteborg, Sweden), 19. Bottleneck (Lawrence, Kansas), 20. The Underground (Göteborg, Sweden), 21. Christiana, Denmark, 22. Christiana, Denmark, 23. Cow Haus (Tallahassee, Florida), 24. Sluggo's (Pensacola, Florida), 25. Cat's Cradle (Chapel Hill, North Carolina), 26. Exit/In (Nashville, Tennessee), 27. Komm (Nurnberg, Germany), 28. Conne Island (Leipzig, Germany), 29. Galaxy Club (Dallas, Texas & deEffenaar (Eindhoven, Netherlands), 30. ESC Club (Bern, Switzerland), 31. Cat's Cradle (Chapel Hill, North Carolina), 32. Rockafella's (Columbia, South Carolina), 33. Vera (Groningen, Netherlands), 34. Concert Cafe (Green Bay, Wisconsin).

'D RATHER BE WITH MY GIRLFRIEND - TOUR '96 [16]

KILLING FOR PEACE IS LI...
FUCKING FOR VIRGINITY [17]

Hammerhead is a dancing queen. [18]

Eat beans, fart in a crowd
and get more out of life... [19]

FUCK FASHION. FUCK DISCO. FUCK YOU. [20]

You say you're gonna kick my ass, well I'm
gonna suck your dick. Whadda think of that? [21]

TED DANZIG "ANOTHER DAY,
ANOTHER COUNTRY" TOUR '96 [22]

LOVE IS A RUMOR CREATED BY GOVERNMENT TO SPREAD VERY
VERIOUS (SP?) VENEREAL DISEASES. SORRY ABOUT THE SPELLING,
I'M QUITE DRUNK. [23]

MY ASS IS RAW,
BUT AT LEAST I CAN
STILL ENJOY THE SMELL. [24]

ALL-WHITE REGGAE BANDS ARE LIKE
AN ALL-JAPANESE ROOTS COUNTRY BAND -
It's just not in their genes. [25]

TIME FLIES LIKE THE MIND.
FRUIT FLIES LIKE BANANAS.
MY FLY'S OPEN TO ANYTHING. [26]

WHEN WILL IT END
- UNSANE [27]

KIDS WHO SKATE ARE HOMOSEXUAL. [28]

Never trust a band
that has to leave
its own graffiti.
Sincerely, The Sex Pistols [30]

I HATE THIS PART OF TEXAS. [29]

There are two kinds of people in this world:
Those who think that there are two kinds
of people, and those who don't. [31]

IF YOU CAN PLAY AN INSTRUMENT
AND WRITE A FEW GOOD RIFFS
WHY DO YOU NEED A GIRLFRIEND? [32]

GEFFEN RECORDS CONTRACT.
PLEASE TAKE ONE.

↓
[33]

ANYONE CAN PISS ON THE SEAT.
BE A HERO, SHIT ON THE CEILING. [34]

NOISE ANNOYS

by Andrew Earles • illustration by Jesse LeDoux

When Thurston Moore writes (and this is my best impersonation of his writing style and taste) that some sax and drums duo is going to "blow your asshole up through your lungs," you can bank that he has no idea what he is talking about. Nope. Not even Thurston. Around thirty people the globe over care about the "wailing," bush-league, limited-edition caterwaul Thurston wants you to know he knows about. You see, when people claim to feel something other than nervousness, irritation, or boredom while listening to free improv or noise, they are, with *minimal* exceptions, lying.

First, let's dispense with the exceptions:
John Coltrane probably felt something when he switched over to free jazz. Religion, dope and insanity will do that. Mike Watt probably feels something when he listens to latter period John Coltrane because, well, when Mike Watt believes he feels something, he probably feels something. Otherwise his head would explode. That's all I can think of. Noiseniks like to dismiss pop and rock music under some ill-constructed ideals. Funny. When these blinder-wearing sycophants *do* like something with structure, it has to be self-consciously "fucked-up," like Bobby Conn, who is a pop aficionado, or Gary Wilson.

Anyone can make a Wolf Eyes record. Anyone can make a Black Dice record. Granted, "the emperor wears no clothes" argument is a predictable one. But it is also a reliable one and carries weight. Bringing Throbbing Gristle, Whitehouse or Non into the '00s is not an admirable feat. It's a prolonging of tired negativity.

It's also unfair to the toiling, dead-end efforts of someone like Tom Smith. Having Terry Richardson photo-fodder trot around making noise must be frustrating to a guy that's been using his "edgy" noise to entertain the same 50 people for the last 20 years. When noiseniks do have a sense of humor (very rare), it tends to be acutely pedestrian, like Smith's. Naming your one "known" vehicle after an already stupidly-titled porn movie, *To Live And Shave In LA*, or choosing "biting" album monikers like *Vedder, Vedder, Bed-Wetter* only strikes hot with the numbest of miscreants. If he had an ounce of topicality,

Smith would attack the new wave of noise. Fake "outsiders" that dress up as furries or sentient machines must certainly be easy targets.

Noise has been here all along. It just currently looks like a scrappy fashion spread. Just as *Vice* magazine added vomit, doo-doo, crackhead and overdose humor to the base qualities of *Big Brother*, *Grand Royal* and *Answer Me!* magazines, the new noise adds visuals—both in the forms of cute guys and urban psych outfits—to get the cool kids looking, and get the act-right-juice flowing with the ladies, all while adding nothing to a 2-step sonic recipe.

No one cares when you throw on an Albert Ayler album, because you're only throwing on an Albert Ayler album so that people will know you're throwing on an Albert Ayler album. The best Beefheart albums are *Safe As Milk, Blue Jeans and Moonbeams* and *Unconditionally Guaranteed*. Those claiming to understand or enjoy over 30 collective minutes of the Jandek output are nothing more than heartless, insincere showoffs. If perusing eBay, you end up spending over ten dollars on a handmade, limited-to-12" record that features some sociopath running a bunch of pedals from a mic'd generator and plucking some anti-notes as dressing, you deserve to remain unlaid. The world remains shiftless when the No Neck Blues Band talks a homeless wino onto a roof to "wail" on clarinet. No one is shocked. No one is blown away. Nothing new has happened.

Le Doux

IT WAS ALREADY THERE

An example of how Jackass and CKY served it to you easy and contrived

by Andrew Earles • illustration by Jay Ryan

The now-tired-yet-venerable antics of the *Jackass/CKY* carnival are admittedly addictive, entertaining and sometimes brilliant. However, something should be known about this phenomenon: no matter how many stupid kids imitate what they see on *Jackass* or one of its spin-offs, the bored youth of today are not shaped by any of it. The bored youth of *Jackass/CKY*, on the other hand, were shaped by a vandalistic drive and culture that I sincerely believe reached them right before or right as video cameras became a widespread toy. I believe that stories abound from the proto-sprawl stretches that haloed moderately-sized cities approximately 15 to 17 years ago. I have one of these stories.

Though he may likely be dead or the worst kind of MIA, the protagonist of this non-fiction account will nonetheless have his true identity hidden. He will be referred to as the Sarge[1]—a very real, self-appointed and encouraged nickname. The period I'm documenting here is roughly '86 to '90, the end of junior high and much of high school for both he and I.

Sarge was a blue-blooded sociopath with inventive, tragic, bullying, hilarious and predictably dangerous tendencies. He was of the common vandalistic, abusive stripe that always needed one thing: an audience. Despite the fact many members of the audience were treated badly by the Sarge, most of us came back for more, being ravenous gluttons for punishment in the name of entertainment. We always strolled into the backyard where the Sarge would fire broom handles from his father's deer bow, or chase us with a pellet gun that shot wet wads of toilet paper.

The Sarge lovingly dubbed one member of our group "Beefhead." Beefhead, by no stretch of the truth, received the brunt of the Sarge's wrath, probably due to his status as a latchkey kid living with a single mom. Beefhead's home was a macro example of what happened to most of us at one point or another. If the Sarge was heard laughing maniacally and running out of the front door, one could bank on finding a steaming pile of shit in the middle of the hallway. Letting the Sarge dwell unaccompanied in a section of the home was a reliable mistake. The Sarge once located a twelve-gauge shotgun in Beefhead's house, discharged it into the back wall of a closet, and then sat down in the den area to resume watching a porno. Food items were taken from the freezer or fridge and hidden behind couches to rot. Things were put in the microwave for thirty minutes.

---

[1] *The nickname can be traced back to fourth grade, and specifically to a lunch ritual, in which empty Jungle Juice or milk cartons were filled with food/drink leftovers, inserted with a straw, and moved around the table like a toy tank. "Who's going to get the Sarge today?!" was repeated until an unlucky soul "got the Sarge." They wound up on the receiving end of the carton being smashed, its contents spewing through the straw.*

But there actually were those less lucky than Beefhead. They could be counted amongst the motorists, pedestrians, homeowners, food service and retail workers of our extended neighborhood. While prowling on Mischief Night (Oct. 30) one year, we approached a lone porta-potty sitting in the middle of a construction site. A voice came from inside: "Ken, is that you?" The Sarge turned to us with a shushing motion and then, single-handedly, tipped the plastic outhouse over onto its door. Though the screams would indicate death or serious injury, the kid eventually escaped. The next day, the potty was on its side, door swung open, dried contents all over the place.

A turning point came when the Sarge's already embattled parents allowed him a driver's permit and full use of a 1986 Ford LTD named "The L." It was a predictable catalyst for an elevated stage of cruel hi-jinks. The Sarge was constantly yelling obscenities from ''The L's'' window. Couples strolling down the sidewalk were treated to a bellowed "start fucking!!!" A pump-fueled, .22 caliber pellet pistol was kept under the driver's seat. Men mowing their yards were shot in the bare legs as "The L" slowly rolled through nearby subdivisions. Random "fucking assholes!!!" were fired upon as they arced past in the turning lane. Drive-thru workers were drenched with squeeze chocolate syrup as the Sarge feigned a soft-drink order.

I lived at the corner of a cove and a moderately busy two-lane road, an approximate one and a half minutes from where the Sarge resided. Like me, he was an only child living with both parents. My bedroom afforded a vast view of the immediate neighbors, and my bedtime in ninth grade was around 10:30 or 11. I often slipped through the house, offing the ringers on each phone barring the one in my bedroom. One night, the Sarge called to notify me that "The L" was being surreptitiously taken out, and that I should be looking out the window in 10 minutes. Obeying, I watched the Sarge pull into the yard of my neighbors across the street, floor "The L," destroy the yard, and take out a mailbox in the process. Minutes later, the phone rang. Under heavy breathing and giggling, I was asked, "Did you see that?"

Once mobile, a regular after-school activity consisted of small gatherings in the Sarge's kitchen before his parents arrived home from work, where the arsenal was conceived for his daily 2 hours of terror. One hot afternoon, he mixed cat feces and litter, human urine, mayonnaise, mustard, ketchup, chocolate syrup, toilet water, pickle juice, milk and toothpaste into a 64-ounce Big Gulp cup. The concoction was delicately transported around an adjacent neighborhood until the Sarge located his preferred target: kids playing in a yard. Stopping "The L" and motioning a kid closer, the short conversation went like this:

"Excuse me, I'm lost, can you tell me where Winchester Avenue is?"

"Yeah, it's right over... AAAAAYYYYYYYHHHHHHPPPHH-HH!!!!!!"

There were things I wasn't present for; though I harbor no doubt they occurred. Like the time the Sarge brazenly walked into a stranger's unlocked apartment, snatched some car keys from the kitchen countertop, and absconded with a Ford Escort. Hiding the car behind a warehouse until nightfall, he then snuck out of his bedroom window and drove the car into a golf course pond. Strangely, this one was done solo.

Another time, we were in a 1987 Buick Century, I was doing the driving while the Sarge rode shotgun. He made it known he was going to hook a nearly-full carton of chocolate milk into the open window of an also nearly-full school bus traveling next to us. Thrown with excessive force, the carton cleared the bus. A minute later, while we are stopped at an intersection, the Sarge looked in his rearview mirror and began to laugh.

"Roll 'em up! Lock the doors!" he warned.

In my mirror, a man was running between the stopped automobiles. He was covered in chocolate milk, and soon wanted me to "get out of the fucking car!!!" I ran the red light, leaving chocolate milk fist streaks down the side of the Buick. To this day, I'm convinced that I'm paying for this one offense...or for all of them.

It should come as no surprise that the Sarge also played a large part in introducing me to pornography, N.W.A., drugs, Too Short, amateur explosives, The Accused, esoteric self-defense, homemade weaponry, the nuances of shoplifting and prank calling. I outgrew some of these things, but I'm going to venture a guess the Sarge's future was different. After all, the class eventually graduated (and every class has one of these guys), the audience left, and so the Sarge's urges most likely went in the directions hinted at by the years of red flag behavior. Aside from a chance grocery store encounter in the mid-'90s, I last spoke with the super-vandal in '91 or '92. There's the chance that the Sarge retreated and embarked on a nondestructive adulthood; then there's the chance the following rumor, told to me years later by a random couple of school friends, holds water. The Sarge may have gotten drunk and unloaded a 9mm skyward before stumbling back into his apartment, where he was later ripped from his bed by the police. Not so meaty, but then again, I didn't want to hear meaty.

We were just slightly-off kids that knew, and were morbidly attracted to, one very fucked-up kid. Though it presents us as no better than a DVD-documented, blatantly homoerotic, ham-fisted skater culture, we were not born of that. We had no more than word-of-mouth as a preserver.

MUSIC ICON ACTION FIGURES

by Brian Walsby

HE WALKS! HE TALKS! HE PLAYS BASKETBALL! HE SUES! AND ONCE IN AWHILE, HE PLAYS GUITAR! YES, IT'S THE...

GREG GINN ACTION FIGURE!

THE GREG GINN ACTION FIGURE COMES WITH A PULL STRING WHERE YOU CAN HEAR SOME OF GREG'S MOST UNFORGETTABLE QUOTES:

- "HEY, SST RECORDS IS DOING GREAT!"
- "THE LAST LINE-UP OF BLACK FLAG WAS THE BEST ONE!"
- "IT WASN'T A TOOLSHED.. IT WASN'T A TOOLSHED!!"
- "WITH THIS REUNION, WE WERE ABLE TO TAKE OUT THE GREED FACTOR...IT'S ALL ABOUT THE CATS." - PLUS MORE!

BREIFCASE OF LAWSUITS:

THIS STURDY REPLICA BRIEFCASE COMES COMPLETE WITH DETAILED MINI-LAWSUITS FROM THE LIKES OF MEAT PUPPETS, SONIC YOUTH, RAYMOND PETTIBON, CASEY KASEM, NEGATIVLAND, KEITH MORRIS, HIS MOTHER, THE BASS PLAYER FROM DAS DAMEN, THE CITY OF HERMOSA BEACH, JESUS CHRIST, GOD, AND YOU!

COMES WITH GRAYING TEMPLES AND JARHEAD HAIRCUT!

CRUZ RECORDS T-SHIRT! (ALSO COMES WITH "CORPORATE ROCK STILL SUCKS" T-SHIRT!

AUTHENTIC LOOKING BASKETBALL!

BRIEFCASE FULL OF LAWSUITS!

SECOND BRIEFCASE FULL OF MARIJUANA!

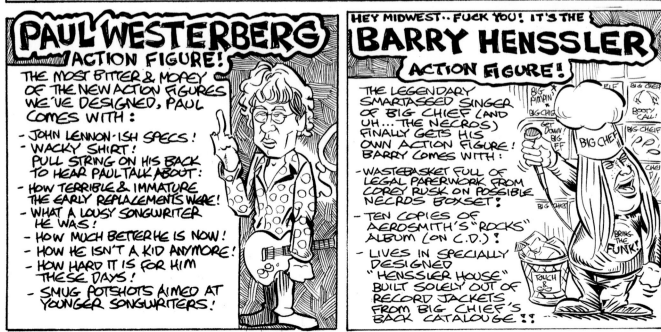

PAUL WESTERBERG ACTION FIGURE!

THE MOST BITTER & MOPEY OF THE NEW ACTION FIGURES WE'VE DESIGNED, PAUL COMES WITH:

- JOHN LENNON-ISH SPECS!
- WACKY SHIRT! PULL STRING ON HIS BACK TO HEAR PAUL TALK ABOUT:
- HOW TERRIBLE & IMMATURE THE EARLY REPLACEMENTS WERE!
- WHAT A LOUSY SONGWRITER HE WAS!
- HOW MUCH BETTER HE IS NOW!
- HOW HE ISN'T A KID ANYMORE!
- HOW HARD IT IS FOR HIM THESE DAYS!
- SMUG POTSHOTS AIMED AT YOUNGER SONGWRITERS!

HEY MIDWEST.. FUCK YOU! IT'S THE

BARRY HENSSLER ACTION FIGURE!

THE LEGENDARY SMARTASSED SINGER OF BIG CHIEF (AND UH... THE NECROS) FINALLY GETS HIS OWN ACTION FIGURE! BARRY COMES WITH:

- WASTEBASKET FULL OF LEGAL PAPERWORK FROM COREY RUSK ON POSSIBLE NECROS BOXSET!
- TEN COPIES OF AEROSMITH'S "ROCKS" ALBUM (ON C.D.)!
- LIVES IN SPECIALLY DESIGNED "HENSSLER HOUSE" BUILT SOLELY OUT OF RECORD JACKETS FROM BIG CHIEF'S BACK CATALOUGE!!

WATCH OUT! IT'S THE... H.R. ACTION FIGURE!

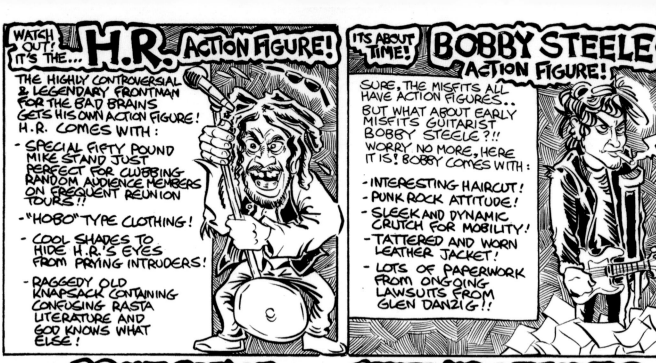

THE HIGHLY CONTROVERSIAL & LEGENDARY FRONTMAN FOR THE BAD BRAINS GETS HIS OWN ACTION FIGURE! H.R. COMES WITH:

- SPECIAL FIFTY POUND MIKE STAND JUST PERFECT FOR CLUBBING RANDOM AUDIENCE MEMBERS ON FREQUENT REUNION TOURS!!

- "HOBO" TYPE CLOTHING!

- COOL SHADES TO HIDE H.R.'S EYES FROM PRYING INTRUDERS!

- RAGGEDY OLD KNAPSACK CONTAINING CONFUSING RASTA LITERATURE AND GOD KNOWS WHAT ELSE!

IT'S ABOUT TIME! BOBBY STEELE ACTION FIGURE!

SURE, THE MISFITS ALL HAVE ACTION FIGURES... BUT WHAT ABOUT EARLY MISFITS GUITARIST BOBBY STEELE?!! WORRY NO MORE, HERE IT IS! BOBBY COMES WITH:

- INTERESTING HAIRCUT!
- PUNK ROCK ATTITUDE!
- SLEEK AND DYNAMIC CRUTCH FOR MOBILITY!
- TATTERED AND WORN LEATHER JACKET!
- LOTS OF PAPERWORK FROM ONGOING LAWSUITS FROM GLEN DANZIG!!

BRIAN BAKER ACTION FIGURE!

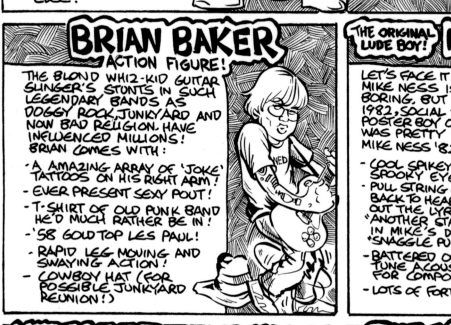

THE BLOND WHIZ-KID GUITAR SLINGER'S STUNTS IN SUCH LEGENDARY BANDS AS DOGGY ROCK, JUNKYARD AND NOW BAD RELIGION, HAVE INFLUENCED MILLIONS! BRIAN COMES WITH:

- A AMAZING ARRAY OF 'JOKE' TATTOOS ON HIS RIGHT ARM!
- EVER PRESENT SEXY POUT!
- T-SHIRT OF OLD PUNK BAND HE'D MUCH RATHER BE IN!
- '58 GOLD TOP LES PAUL!
- RAPID LEG MOVING AND SWAYING ACTION!
- COWBOY HAT (FOR POSSIBLE JUNKYARD REUNION!)

THE ORIGINAL LUDE BOY! MIKE NESS '82 ACTION FIGURE!

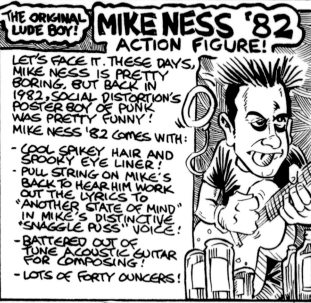

LET'S FACE IT. THESE DAYS, MIKE NESS IS PRETTY BORING, BUT BACK IN 1982, SOCIAL DISTORTION'S POSTER BOY OF PUNK WAS PRETTY FUNNY! MIKE NESS '82 COMES WITH:

- COOL SPIKEY HAIR AND SPOOKY EYE LINER!
- PULL STRING ON MIKE'S BACK TO HEAR HIM WORK OUT THE LYRICS TO "ANOTHER STATE OF MIND" IN MIKE'S DISTINCTIVE 'SNAGGLE PUSS' VOICE!
- BATTERED OUT OF TUNE ACOUSTIC GUITAR FOR COMPOSING!
- LOTS OF FORTY OUNCERS!

MIKE WATT ACTION HEADBUST!

THE LEGENDARY MIKE WATT HEADBUST WAS BUILT WITH A SPECIAL STRING YOU CAN PULL TO HEAR ONE OF TEN THOUSAND DIATRIBES UTTERED BY WATT HIMSELF! PULL THE STRING A LITTLE HARDER AND ALL OF THEM WILL PLAY IN ONE LONG RAMBLING SESSION! JUST TRY & STOP HIM! MIKE IS DECKED OUT IN HIS TRADITIONAL FLANNEL SHIRT & CASTRO-ISH BEARD! COMES WITH EARPLUGS!

MIKE WATT

BILLY ZOOM ACTION FIGURE!

THE JESUS LOVING AGELESS GUITAR HERO OF X GETS HIS OWN ACTION FIGURE!

- THE BILLY ZOOM ACTION FIGURE COMES IN HIS CLASSIC ONSTAGE PLAYING STANCE! HE CANNOT BE MOVED IN ANOTHER WAY AT ALL!
- WHAT CAN YOU STICK IN BILLY'S HAND? IT'S UP TO YOU!:
- SILVER GRETSCH GUITAR!
- TOOLS FOR FIXING AMPS!
- THE BIBLE FOR PRAYING!
- ASSORTED VEGETABLES!

CARROT!

HOLY BIBLE

...WATCH OUT! IT'S THE DAVID YOW ACTION FIGURE!

THE ENTERTAINING AND USUALLY INTOXICATED FORMER FRONTMAN FOR SCRATCH ACID & THE JESUS LIZARD, DAVID MAKES ONE GREAT FIGURE!

- SPECIAL 'STRETCH ARMSTRONG' BODY CLAY LETS YOU PUT DAVID IN ANY BODY CONTORTION YOU CAN THINK OF!
- SHIRT OPTIONAL!
- COOL UNDERWEAR!
- PANTS PERMANENTLY AROUND HIS ANKLES!
- THE COMPLETE OUTPUT OF THE BIRTHDAY PARTY!
- EMPTY BEER CANS!

THE BRAND NEW THERAPY-FREE JASON NEWSTED ACTION FIGURE!!

THE HAPPIEST & MOST CONTENT ACTION FIGURE EVER CREATED, THE JASON NEWSTED IS A CLASSIC EXAMPLE OF A FAMOUS MUSICIAN CUTTING HIS LOSSES IN THE NICK OF TIME! COMES WITH:

- PEACE OF MIND!
- HAIR FRESHLY GROWN OUT ONCE AGAIN!
- T-SHIRT OF THE MUCH BETTER AND WELL RESPECTED BAND HE HAS HOOKED UP WITH!
- AMAZING BANK ACCOUNT OF LIMITLESS FREEDOM!
- REGULAR PANTS & SHOES!
- SIGHS OF RELIEF!

CHUCK BISCUITS ACTION FIGURE!

ONE OF THE GREATEST DRUMMERS OF ALL TIME, THE HORRIBLY MISUSED AND POORLY DOCUMENTED CHUCK BISCUITS HASN'T SEEN A LOT OF ACTION LATELY BUT HE MAKES FOR AN INTERESTING ACTION FIGURE! CHUCK COMES WITH:

SIGH...

- CHUCK'S DUST & COBWEBS COVERED DRUM SET!
- COMFY CHAIR!
- TELEVISION THAT BROADCASTS ANY SHOW OF CANADIAN CONTENT TO CURE HOMESICKNESS!
- ASSORTED PENS AND PAPER FOR DRAWING!

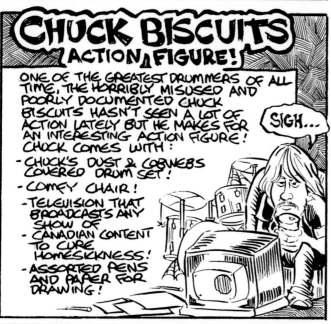

GOOO!! IT'S THE... RAY CAPPO ACTION FIGURE!

THE ONE-TIME INFLUENTIAL GOD OF POST-EIGHTIES HARDCORE, YOUTH OF TODAY'S PIED PIPER OF STRAIGHT EDGE 'BREAKS DOWN THE WALLS' WITH HIS OWN ACTION FIGURE! RAY COMES WITH:

- SHAVED HEAD & BUG EYED STARE!
- MICROPHONE GLUED TO HAND & POISED PERFECTLY FOR MASSIVE SING-A-LONGS!
- THE RAY CAPPO FIGURE ALSO COMES WITH A BUSLOAD OF FOURTEEN YEAR OLD ITALIAN & JEWISH BOYS, ALL READY TO SING ALONG!
- KRISHNA CLOTHING AND LITERATURE ALSO INCLUDED!

YOUNG AND STRAIGHT TILL I GET OLD AND DRUNK

KIM GORDON ACTION FIGURE!!

"...I DON'T WANNA...... ..I DON'T THINK SO..."

IS THIS CHOICE OR WHAT? THE KIM GORDON ACTION FIGURE COMES WITH:

- TRUNK FULL OF WACKY CLOTHING ON LOAN FROM REDD KROSS!
- SCHOOL BUS SCHEDULE FOR PICKING UP COCO!
- SIX MONTHS WORTH OF GUITAR LESSONS!
- SMALL COLLECTION OF MUSIC BY CURRENT GLUT OF WORTHLESS "DIVAS" (FOR THE IDEA OF FINDING ARTISTIC INSPIRATION!)
- NANNY AND/OR SENSE OF HUMOR SOLD SEPERATELY!!

RUN AND DUCK! IT'S THE... DAMON ("CHE") FITZGERALD ACTION FIGURE!

...FUCK THIS! I QUIT!

THE TITANIC "ALL DRUM FILLS AT ALL COST" DRUM LEGEND COMES COMPLETE WITH:

- ALIENATING ATTITUDE!
- HIS OWN ECONOLINE VAN (WHICH HE CAN TAKE HOME AT ANY GIVEN MOMENT!)
- STURDY DRUM SET MADE FOR EASY TOSSING!
- DETACHABLE DRUMSTICKS!
- ALSO COMES WITH EIGHTEEN INTERCHANGEABLE BAND MEMBERS!!

by Steve Birmingham, Nick Blakey, Emerson Dameron, Michael Faloon, Ben Hellmann, Cup Iwata, Benjamin Johnson, Tony P. King, Henry Owings & Brian Teasley
illustrations by Brian Walsby
layout by Sosebee

Howard Zinn
James Lipton
Ross Perot
Peter Hook
Jon Benet Ramsey
Bud Dwyer
Rodney King
Billie Jean King
Marlon Brando
Richard Dawson
Bob Seger
Sharon Tate
Charlton Heston

Unintentionally

Chuck Norris

Okay, an easy target in this day of winking cynicism, but lately Conan O'Brien has mounted a lever that, when fitfully pulled, shows a clip from "Walker: Texas Ranger." Just showing them can stand alone in spite of Conan's quips.

The Girl from the Overstock.com Commercials

Not sure if anyone's seen these, but her acting is so awful, her delivery so wooden, that I find myself transfixed by it. In one ad, you could swear she's about to crack herself up.

Yellowcard

Great. Safety Punk with a hyped up diddler, er, *fiddler*. What's next, acne-core with a pogoing sax player?

William Shatner

I cannot put my finger what exactly it is about him that tickles me. Maybe because he looks so confused and like he just woke up.

David Caruso

The last man on Earth still doing Quaaludes. Despite his resurrection status as the truly living dead, it still hasn't made up for his leaving *NYPD Blue*.

Benny Hill

I know, another comedian, but not for why you'd expect. Mugging, fat lotharios aren't really funny anymore (well, except maybe in South America) but any time one of the characters encountered something violent that happened to their bodies, the camera would splice from a shot of the real person, to a shot where a dummy had been put in their place. Watching a prop dummy flail straight into the air, consequently land, and then splice back to the real person getting up never fails to keep me in wheezing stitches. Somewhere out there, Comedic Science might have an explanation as to why.

Glenn Danzig

So big he's little, so manly he's gay, so evil he's cute.

Stephen Baldwin

Hardcore born-again Christian instruction and militant boosterism for the Bush junta from a D-level actor whose sole previous claim to fame was making brothers Daniel and William's cinematic output and drunken buffoonery seem slightly less appalling. But bless our 'lil evangelical Rumplestiltskin for spinning fundamental delusion into pure comedy gold.

John Ashcroft

a) Hey, he lost to a *dead* man!
b) Ever notice how he looks like Louis Farrakhan?
c) You just *know* he pays underage hookers to dress up as Catholic schoolgirls and shit big ones into his mouth.

W. Axl Rose

Awlright! Rick James' worst hair days *are* immortal!

Louis Farrakhan

Ever notice how much he looks like John Ashcroft?

The Entire State of Florida

They're *still* paying for 2000! Payback's a bitch, ain't it?

Courtney Love

A haunted house mixed with a 24-car pile-up with no survivors. Attempts to be so legitimate, you can't help but guffaw. Even with all her plastic surgery, nothing can make her a beautiful person. Ever.

George W. Bush

See Courtney Love.

Laura Bush

See Courtney Love minus the rehab attempts.

The Bush Twins

See Courtney Love x 2.

Alan Keyes

Quite possibly the scariest black man ever.

Ozzy Osbourne

He also gets points for being unintentionally sad.

Dalai Lama
Timothy Leary
Jackie Robinson
Roy of Seigfried and Roy
Margaret Mitchell
Lord Mounteban
William Howard Taft
Merlin Olsen
Wolf Blitzer
Tom Greene
Magic Johnson
Garrett Morris
Malcolm X
Perry Farrell
Liza Manelli
Celine Dion
Ray Manzarek
Skip Stevenson
John Wilkes Booth
Harey Carey
Jeff Foxworthy
Dennis Kucinich
Pol Pot

Janet Reno
The Rock
Sammy Hagar
Bill Buckner
Carrot Top
David Brooks
Richard Branson
Ayn Rand
Zell Miller
Jello Biafra
Miles O'Brian of CNN
Noam Chomsky
David Blaine
The Baldwins

John Stossel
Richard Simmons
Andy Rooney
Quentin Tarantino
Mumar Quadafi
Lenny Kravitz
Judy Garland

funny people

Vincent Gallo

When the DSM-V comes out, the section about narcissistic personality disorders will be replaced by the text from Gallo's website.

Arnold Schwarzenegger

Truth is indeed stranger than fiction; and you never thought California had a sense of humor?

Ronald Reagan

His post-death brainwashing of America proves just how fucked we really all are.

Dick Cheney

The only politician in America you could assassinate with a large steak and cheese sub with extra mayo!

The Entire Staff of Rolling Stone

See the entire post-*Tattoo You* catalog by The Rolling Stones.

Anna Nicole Smith

Although originally a beacon to show women that being a skeleton isn't sexy, years of downers and pathetic reality show fodder have morphed this dumb-as-a-post Texan to hilarious Texan.

Mike Tyson

"I want to eat your babies." He really said that. And he wasn't joking. He's really a baby-eater.

General Wesley Clark

Did anyone else see him on the cover of *The Advocate* in leather making claims about doing more for gay rights than anyone else has previously? Where *was* this hunk when we needed him most?

Bobby Fischer

More fucked than Jacko? More screwed than Drew? Every reason why you should never force your kids into stardom, period. Also, takes the phrase "Big in Japan" to new heights/lows.

Bill O'Reilly

The master of the sweeping generalization. My favorite O'Reilly tactic is linking two unrelated, unprovable and offensive assertions, then steamrolling past the outrage of the first with the phrase "we all know that." I find this endlessly fun to imitate: the retarded in this country are defrauding the health care industry with false insurance claims, we all know that. Now the liberal elite in Washington want you to foot the bill for providing these people with such "necessities" as pornography on demand and pizza-kebabs.

Conan O'Brien

Most bullies are, by their nature, unintentionally funny. (Anger is hilarious, so long as it's stupidly directed.) So sometimes, in the privacy of my own domicile, I like to imagine I'm a bully. I pour a stiff drink, flip on Conan O'Brien (a defiantly unfunny man) and imagine I'm in the studio with him, launching paper airplanes toward his nose, putting duct tape in his hair, sowing general discord. And he always seems to be bothered by it — the bullying, that is. If I saw him in person, I'd leave him alone. But I like to pretend it's me that's fucking up his composure, causing his utter lack of showmanship.

ISOURMOVIERU

YOU BET. HERE'S WHY.

BY BOB ODENKIRK

AS TOLD TO HENRY H. OWINGS / PHOTOGRAPHY BY MARINA CHAVEZ

{Run *Ronnie Run*} was written by David Cross and myself with Scott Auckerman, BJ Porter, and Brian Posehn — most of the writers of the last season of "Mr. Show." The goal of the script was this strange kind of hybrid between telling a linear story with a single character as our focal point — it included telling something you would see in a typical big-budget studio comedy, say your Rob Schneider, Adam Sandler, David Spade-type comedy — [and] something that would, on the poster and in the preview, look like a traditional comedy, a typical mall theatre comedy with one very funny crazy main character and his story, so that we wouldn't scare away [the audience]. Our goal was to

really distant from us, and then when it came time to edit, he asked us to leave. He came to us after the film was shot, and asked, "Is it okay if I do the first cut?" We said, "Sure, you worked so hard, go ahead and do the first cut. Just do us a favor and don't overcut it, so you don't mind changing anything." He assured us he wouldn't, but of course he did. He cut like crazy. He was extremely proud. He thought he'd made a perfect film. And then when we went in and started giving notes, he immediately got really frustrated and angry, and on the second day of our effort at editing, he kicked us out. And from that day on, we were not allowed to call him directly anymore, only talk to his assistant; we were never

moments, but it's not a great movie. But he still thinks it's fucking awesome. And secondly, I think he'd had enough of doing whatever we told him, over the six years of "Mr. Show." Everybody has an ego, and in this case, his ego finally decided, "That's enough. I'm not going to listen to anybody anymore." And it was a horrible, horrible experience. The worst experience I've ever had in my career by far. It was a nightmare!

If you rent the DVD — and I encourage people to rent, not buy — what you see is a much slower, less focused, much less funny movie in its first edit. We basically polished a turd; we didn't do any alchemy. So as the editing

IRONNIE RUN OVERRATED?

reach out to those who don't know "Mr. Show," which is a lot of people. Our goal was to present a movie to them that, on the face of it, looked like a typical comedy that they would seem very willing to take a chance on.

Our further goal was to very cleverly skip off our little linear story and do little scenic bits that would be more like "Mr. Show," and that would hopefully enhance the story, and make the movie a more interesting experience, and yet not intimidating, because you return to the story that you're used to. We thought we could gently prod people into seeing a movie with an alternative sensibility, but mask it in a kind of traditional structure. That was our high-minded goal.

I would argue that the script was not airtight, or perfect, and I never thought it was. I thought it was just the best we could do in the time we had, and good enough to go shoot and try to make work. The only thing that matters in that little formula is [that] in order to make it work, you need David and I in the editing room, just like we edited "Mr. Show." David and I were the executive producers of "Mr. Show," and we oversaw the directors, the writing, and all the editing.

Well, what happened with *Run, Ronnie, Run*, was [that] the director, who was somebody we'd known for six years — I'll refer to him as Jack Frost — had been very cooperative and willing to execute our vision, and pretty much give it up to us at any time in the process, whether it was in the editing, or even in the directing. However, in this film, he got

allowed to see dailies of the movie; we could only make suggestions based on cuts that he had already made, or on our memory of the shooting from weeks before. We had no recourse, and he knew it.

Michael De Luca — who was the executive at New Line who helped get the movie made — was a huge "Mr. Show" fan, and he understood that it was David's and my sensibility that made "Mr. Show" great, but he'd been fired in the course of shooting our movie. So Jack Frost knew that we had nowhere to go over his head. On top of this is the fact that we'd given up our producer credits in this movie—at Jack Frost's request before it was made. He came to us and said, "In order to get these two guys, Warren Burgin and Mark Coolis, to help—to be producers on the movie, and to help get it made, we need you guys to give up your credit, 'cuz there's too many producers on the banner." And we immediately agreed, because at that point, Jack Frost had been nothing but friendly and cooperative and great to us, and we never foresaw that he would be anything else.

I think the reason he did it was twofold. One, I think he walked away from the shooting thinking, "There's no way I can fuck this up." David Koechner, David Cross, everybody had been so funny in their parts. I think he was grinning ear to ear when it was over, and he pretty much felt like, "I don't need anyone to tell me how to make this funny." And just so you know, he still thinks it's a great movie. It may have some good

process went on, we basically influenced it with arguments, begging, kissing ass, and long emails thanking Jack Frost for putting jokes in that had been cut, and begging him to try other things that we thought would work. I feel like there's a chance that, based on the weaknesses of the script, and let's even point out my own weaknesses as a performer, maybe there's no great movie there. But I can't say that unless I get a chance to edit it first. The things that are wrong with the movie are that it shifts gears between being kind of dry and funny and a little bit harsh, which is very Mr. Showy, to being saccharin-sweet and strangely emotionally cloying, and begging for your sympathy in a very weird way with this music and these shots that have no sense of irony to them at all. So it's this really weird gearshift that happens constantly throughout the movie. It's one of the reasons the movie feels so long. It's a very short movie, but it feels really long.

I was talking to somebody about it, and it occurred to me that there's a lot of comedies that come out where people like only four or five scenes. I remember the last Austin Powers. You know, you'd talk to people about it and they'd go, "Oh, it's great! I didn't like Goldmember, but I liked this, and that, and this!" And they name, like—everybody names, like, three things. And it's like, "So you liked three things and that makes it a great movie?" And the difference between that movie, which I do think is a good comedy, and *Run, Ronnie, Run*, which I think is a bad comedy, is that when there's a weak joke in *Goldmember*, it still belongs in the movie. When there's a weak moment in the movie, it's not from another movie; it's just an attempt at an Austin Powers joke that maybe isn't the best, but somehow it all works together, and when you're done, you're thinking only about the parts that work. But with *Run, Ronnie, Run*, the parts that don't work and don't fit are so wrong in tone, they're like from a different movie, and they weigh the movie down. They drag it down. You can't just dismiss them and forget they happened after they're over.

The thing that's missing is the gap that exists between our reputation and movie studio executives' awareness. To "Mr. Show" fans and people who know us, it's ludicrous that we would get kicked out of the editing room of a movie that I wrote. But movie executives have never heard of "Mr. Show." Ever. None of them. Except for the lower-level execs at pretty much all of the studios — they've heard of it and are fans. But all the top guys, these 50-year old German billionaires, they don't know "Mr. Show." And they do pay attention to what goes on their networks, and they do pay attention to what movies they put out, and they've just now started to hear about, you know—they're barely gonna become familiar with Jack Black in the next year. He's a new face to them that just has never done anything before until this new movie comes out. They live in Aspen, they live in Europe, they live in, you know—they go to Japan and Australia, they just aren't living anywhere near the level that you and I live, and when these younger executives who are so excited

done this, and college kids like it..." "Well, I'm not a college kid, and I've never heard of it, so you can't have $8 million. No." There is a major disconnect there. It's a strange thing, but it's really true.

And the reason the movie is so overrated is because it was buried by New Line, which was a relief to David and I. It was a very strange situation, because we were under the impression that it was going to get released, so we fought like crazy to champion the movie, to be on its side, so we could have as much influence as possible over the content of movie. If we were seen to be slagging the movie off before the edit was done, nobody would've even read our e-mails, or our long memos that begged for changes and jokes and all of these moments to be protected, or put back in, or discovered. So we had to fight for the movie. And people say, "Why did you seemingly change your opinion on your movie?" For months on the website, we were fighting for the movie, but we had no choice. We very quickly sized up our situation. We could tell everybody, "the movie's gonna suck and we hate it and we're angry," but then the movie was planning to come out. So our effort was to have as much influence on it as we could, and the way to do that was to appear to be championing the movie and hoping for the best. The day that we found out they weren't going to release it was a huge relief for David and I. We were even deluded by our own efforts to go, "Yeah, yeah, it's gonna be good, we're gonna try and make it good!" And then we find out they're not gonna be releasing it, this strange feeling of joy descends, like, "Oh, wow, I don't have to lie anymore! I can just tell people it's just not good."

nobody in the upper echelon, who has ever heard of "Mr. Show." Never heard of us at all! People in the movie business don't watch TV. They barely know the top movie stars. They're very busy going to parties and flying around on private jets. They really have a lot to do. So in New Line's defense, they didn't know who we were, and they just saw a movie that was sluggish, slow, oddly offbeat and unpleasant, and that didn't test that well. And I agree with them. They would've lost their fucking shirts if they'd put that movie out and spent another $12 million on promotions. On the other hand, the person to blame is the director, who knew us, and knew how important we were to our own comedy, and chose to freeze us out, hold us at arm's length and not let us influence the movie nearly on the scale that we should have.

Movies can be made and broken in editing. Everybody knows that. Let me re-edit *Casablanca* for you and turn it into a big fat piece of shit. The raw comedy is so much about little moments, playing the tone just so, and taking a scene and just hanging on it a little bit longer than you would normally, and giving it that awkward moment that makes it human and raises the level of humor. It's all about tone, and the person editing it has to have a sensitivity and a sensibility to that. It's overrated because it was shit on by the studio. It's [considered] this "lost gem" when

LET ME RE-EDIT CASABLANC FOR Y
AND TURN IT INTO A IG FAT

about us and want to work with us, go to them, the guy who writes the check, and say, "I want to do a movie with this guy," they say, "No fucking way, I've never heard of him." "Well, he's got this TV show, and he's

Look, people are angry at New Line. Don't be angry at New Line. The only thing New Line did "wrong" was not defend us. But in their defense, they didn't know who we were! There's nobody at New Line, and certainly

really it's a lost fucked-up gem. ❑

ECE OF SHIT.

Neil relaxing inside the Pit Pat costume.

IS WORKING FOR BOB & DAVID OVERRATED?

It's been pretty awesome, so I have never stopped to consider it. Not because "it's just a job" and not because I'm such a fan-boy that I have never questioned my career path. I just can't imagine that the general public would spend the energy to develop any preconception accurate or otherwise. I guess I'm saying that I need to know the agreed upon rating before I can determine if it's overrated. The long and short is, I graduated college and wanted to sit on a couch and make my friends laugh for a living, and Mr. Show and Co. were the only people who laughed at the same stuff we did. Is working with Bob and David a non-stop party train of comic insanity? No. Do Bob and David

. . . "IT'S JUST A JOB" . . .

hang out together? More than Regis and Kelly and less than Siegfried and Roy. Instead of fantasizing about what it would be like to work intimately with your comic heroes, spend the time wisely and look for my skin-flute joke in *Run Ronnie Run*, and listen for my laughter in the background of the Season 3 DVD commentary. Oh, and David Cross introduced me to Henry, so that was cool too. — *Neil Mahoney*

THE SEVEN DEGREES OF WINONA RYDER

by Merrilee Challiss, Sarah Hayes Owings & Henry Owings • introduction by Brian Teasley
illustration by Terry White

"You're no one in music until you have feuded with me or until you sleep with Winona!" —Courtney Love

If there is one undeniable truth in the universe, it is that, over the years, more pipe has been laid in Winona Ryder than New York City's entire sewage system. Ever since Winona (real name: Winona Laura Horowitz) starred in *Heathers* (1989), white, heterosexual, self-loathing geeks have found her jean-creamy in an approachably sadistic way: As only a rare, semi-beautiful, half-goth movie star can be jean-creamy. If not for most states' statutory rape laws, most would have gladly banged her as Rina, the ignored dork in love with Corey Haim, in 1986's Nerd-Pièce De Resistance, *Lucas*. Such desire makes sense in retrospect—just think of all the man-jelly up in that mess since '86!

Our 5'4", 104 lb. nympho-virtuoso is certainly bed-worthy, but the fact that she has maintained the title of "Obligatory Celebrity Trophy Fuck" for over a decade is a bit head-scratching. Winona's pump-priming backstage visits have replaced the Sirens of Greek myth as a zeitgeist metaphor for modern man's sexual downfall. What is it about our "Interrupted Singles Girl" that makes modern day axe-wielders swoon like high school football players fighting over who goes first at a post-victory gang bang? And will scientists of the future even know?

In 1990, John Waters' favorite jerk fantasy, Johnny Depp, had "Winona Forever" tattooed on his right bicep. Unable to tame Winona's wild dogs of lust, Depp parted ways with her after three years — which now seems unfathomably long. In a cheap attempt at irony, Mr. 21 Hump Street later had the tattoo changed to "Wino Forever." Sorry, Johnny, but you might as well have gotten "Betamax Forever" tattooed on your forehead in 1981 than to get a tat that professes the faith of Winona's love.

C'mon, man! More people have visited that Crazy Cooter's Garage than the entire population of Hazzard County; more balls have been unloaded through that hair-lined basket than the Chicago Bull's goal during the height of Michael Jordan's career; Jesus Christ Almighty, she's dispensed more melted vanilla cones than a Florida Dairy Queen during a mid-summer brownout; hell, I bet that girl has bitten into more Oscar Meyer wieners than a packed Yankee stadium on free hot dog day...okay, I know; I should stop before this becomes crude.

Included in this piece, "The Seven Degrees of Winona Ryder: Rock 'n Roll's Jizz Jar," are just a few of the forgettables that have dipped their schnitzels into Hollywood's favorite chuff-box. Other sausage warriors receiving honorable mentions for spilling their bowls of cookie crisp inside the "Furry Entrance Gate of Cult Star Status" include rockers: Ryan Adams, Beck and Jay Kay; wannabe rockers: Jimmy Fallon and the aforementioned Depp (P, anyone?); and thesbos: Colin Farrell, Matt Damon, Christian Slater, David Duchovny and Daniel Day Lewis. This list could go on like chorus refrains in the "It's a Small World" ride at Disney World.

Completing a full Winona fuckography would be a task for much more dedicated Bible-copying monks than us, but we hope this does shed some dim light on the elfin star-fucker-supreme who has hung out with more hot nuts than Dave Clark. If you see her at a show, please pay her proper respect, and remember that no one has done more to make "Bobbing for Rock Cock" an Olympic event than Wah-moan-ahh! Being able to trace fictional beings like the Tooth Fairy back through the endless chasm that is Ms. Ride-Her's Middle Earth says it all.

So heed this, aspiring young rock star fancying Ms. Whorowitz...ENTER AT YOUR OWN RISK...at least, that's what I imagine on a hand-painted sign hanging over her hairy bush, as if to lure meddling teenagers and an unspecified talking animal companion through the door of a funhouse in a mid-'70s Hanna-Barberra cartoon.

AQUAMAN
Swims around talking to fish and is stuck in Freud's aquaeously ambiguous "polymorphous perverse stage," which is prior to sexual assignation.

DR. FREUD
Father of psychoanalysis. Hated by Nabokov, author of *Lolita*, who also hated Pasternak.

DR. ZHIVAGO
1965 movie based on the novel by Boris Pasternak stars Julie Christie.

ROBERT EVANS
Infamous producer (*Rosemary's Baby* and the *Godfather* movies, etc.) has recently been the star of his own Comedy Central animated series, "Kid Notorious."

ROSEMARY'S BABY
Polanski's classic, in which the devil chooses the willowy Mia Farrow to be the mother of his child, was filmed at the Dakota.

THE DAKOTA
The hotel where John Lennon was murdered in 1980. Named in 1884 for its Uptown location, which was considered to be as remote as the Dakota territory.

BART SIMPSON
Nancy Cartwright (who is infinitely less fuckable than Winona) is Bart's voice; told *The Washington Post* that she credits Scientology with enriching her life.

SCIENTOLOGY
Celeb adherents include Kirstie Alley and Issac Hayes; makes use of such terms such as "engram" and "demon circuit."

CHRIS SALVO
Flight Engineer at NASA's Jet Propulsion Laboratory, cites L. Ron Hubbard's *Battlefield Earth* as one of the inspirations for his career in space research.

SAN ANDREAS FAULT
A 1989 earthquake there resulted in over $6 billion in damages, not unlike Winona's shoplifting spree, where she received over 200 hours of community service.

WIDENING CRACKS
The forces of plate tectonics arise from rising magma squeezing through widening cracks. No need to spell this one out.

MAE WEST
Deserving of Winona's admiration for being the original pussy-peddling floozy, was one the biggest cracks to come from California.

THE TOOTH FAIRY
Santa Claus's perennial, slightly off, new-agey cousin, collects baby teeth and deposits money under the pillows of millions of non-Muslim children around the world.*

MUHAMMAD ALI
Former heavyweight boxer whose 1976 story record promoting oral hygiene featured the line: "We gotta whoop Mr. Tooth Decay."

DON KING
SNL ritually parodies Don King, the ex-con, promoter and activist who is honored every year on "Don King Day" in cities like Newark, New Jersey.**

RAGNAR THE VIKING
Current Minnesota Vikings mascot; has taken it upon himself to learn sign language to communicate with his hearing impaired fans.

NORSE MYTHOLOGY
J.R.R. Tolkein, a staunch Roman Catholic, borrowed extensively from pagan Norse mythology in the fantasy fiction trilogy, *Lord of the Rings*.

LEIF ERICSSON
Renowned Viking sailed to the New World in the year 1001 (almost 500 years before Columbus), where he reportedly pillaged and killed Indians.

FREEMASONS
A fraternal order bound together by vows of morality and public service, now an elitist secret society that manipulates the music industry.

MATTHEW BARNEY
Artist that uses tapioca as a sculptural material and also makes use of Masonic symbols such as the square and compass in his film cycle, the Cremaster series.

BUBBLE TEA
Another refreshing, if trendy, beverage, features pearls of tapioca, which is a gelatinous root starch derived from the cassava or yucca plant.

DOLLY THE CLONED SHEEP
(b. 1996, d. 2003)
The first mammal to be cloned from an adult cell. Like Winona, sheep are often shagged.

ORGONE ENERGY
He and William Reich pioneered research based on the Orgone Energy Accumulator Kit, which includes layers of sheep's wool batts as insulators.

SANSKRIT
Nikola Tesla, influenced by Vedic philosophy, frequently used Sanskrit-inspired terminology, such as "free energy" to describe natural phenomena.

*To indulge in a "brief analysis in critical thinking" debunking the myth of the tooth fairy, by someone whose foster parents didn't dish out the green for the baby toofers, check out this site: www.abarnett.demon.co.uk/atheism/tooth.html
**There is no known public record of Winona sleeping with a brother.

DR. MARJORIE GREENFIELD
Expert in pregnancy and birth (ck. drspock.com); advises couples with fertility problems against swimming after intercourse.

DR. JOSEF MENGELE
Experimental "Dr. Death" for the Nazis died of a stroke while swimming off the coast of Brazil in 1979.

DR. SEUSS
aka Dr. Theodore Geisel, won an Academy Award for the propaganda piece *Your Job In Germany (aka Hitler Lives)*.

JAMIROQUAI
Wears a Dr. Seuss hat.

YOKO ONO
Also a member of Fluxus; was the inspiration for one of Al Hansen's seminal acts, "Yoko Ono Piano Drop."

AL HANSEN
Beck's grandaddy. Member of Fluxus — an avant-garde movement characterized by a strong Dadaist attitude.

GRANDADDY
Performed with Beck at the 2003 Reading Festival which boasts an annual "usage" of more than 800 Port-O-Lets.

BECK HANSEN
Born in 1970 in Los Angeles. Author of the post-alternative explosion 'hit' "Loser."

A PLASTIC BUBBLE
The Boy in the Plastic Bubble, played by Scientologist John Travolta, lived inside a NASA-produced space suit.

THE GRADUATE
1967 film where one family guest preaches to Dustin Hoffman's character about the virtues of "plastics."

LEMONHEADS
It's A Shame About Ray album featured a cover of Simon and Garfunkel's "Mrs. Robinson," from *The Graduate* soundtrack.

EVAN DANDO
Sometimes-former lead singer of Lemonheads; was the subject of a fanzine called "I Hate Evan Dando."

WARREN BUFFETT
World's second richest man, and Nebraska native. Often quotes Mae West.

OMAHA
Nebraskan Chip Davis gave birth to such gems as "Convoy." Later formed Mannheim Steamroller.

SADDLE CREEK
Conor's Omaha based record label. Also, a golf course in the foothills of the Sierra Nevada mountains.

CONOR OBERST
The great white hope of Saddle Creek, uses uninspired post-revisionist Nick Drake-isms to get all kinds of pussy!

HAPPINESS
A film that follows the lives of three highly dysfunctional sisters in New Jersey.

MICHAEL STIPE
Singer for R.E.M., and co-producer of *Happiness*, a 1998 dramedy directed by Todd Solondz.

R.E.M.
Yorn went on tour with R.E.M. a couple years ago, making R.E.M. actually appear to still have some energy on stage.

PETE YORN
Lonely troubadour from suburban New Jersey; cites Peter Buck of R.E.M. as an early influence.

LEIF GARRETT
Also a *Behind the Music* subject; once killed a friend by means of good ol' fashioned vehicular manslaughter.

WEIRD AL
Parodied Devo, and also did a Nirvana parody. Had his own VH1 *Behind the Music* special.

NIRVANA
Covered Devo's "Turnaround." If Cobain were alive, he would have slept with Winona by now.

DAVE GROHL
Played in the punk band Freak Baby, and would eventually fish for dollars with Kurt Cobain in Nirvana.

ICED TEA
A Southern, Don Meredith-endorsed refreshing beverage, served with stultifying, seizure-inducing amounts of sugar.

ICE CUBE
A gangsta rapper praised for his raw portrayal of "ordinary" life in South Central Los Angeles in *Predator 2*.

SOUL ASYLUM
Wrote a song titled "Black Gold" which touched a nerve in the wake of the race riots in Los Angeles that same year.

DAVE PIRNER
The hair-challenged guitarist for Soul Asylum.

WAR
The Sanskrit word for it translates as "desire for more cows."

BETTY GRABLE
The original pinup girl entertained troops in World War II. 20th Century Fox insured her legs for a million dollars.***

HELMET
Band that practically invented nü metal and breech-birthed squadrons of sub-par copycats by the time their album *Betty* was released in 1994.

PAGE HAMILTON
Guitarist/songwriter for Helmet. Claims his main interest is jazzzzz!

***The number of Russian soldiers that died in WWII is just short of the number of quasi-celeb dudes thave have given Winona a beef-job.

STUDENT LOANS ARE FOR SUCKERS

The fleecing of our young

by Ted Rall • illustration by Joshua Krause

Five years ago, I wrote a story called "College Is For Suckers." I argued that the costs of tuition, dorms and fees had risen so high that the additional income you'd earn as a college graduate—compared to going straight to work after high school—wouldn't make up for the massive student loan debts you'd acquire.

The magazine that ran my piece is no more. Both books that published it are out of print. But the problem of crippling student loan debt has gotten worse.

[illegible] Servicing
P.O. BOX 9500
WILKES BARRE PA 18773-9500

(888) [illegible]72-5543

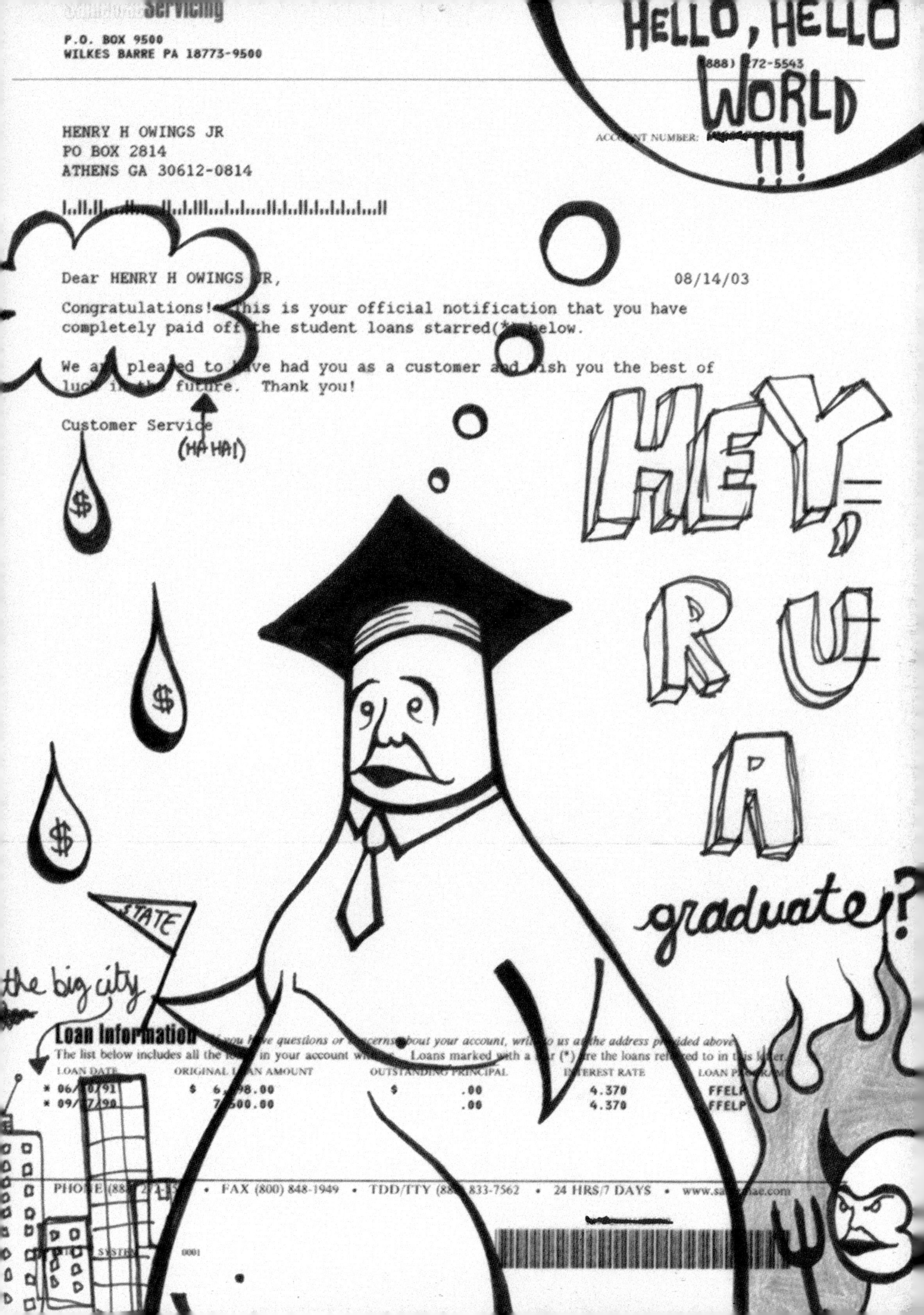

HENRY H OWINGS JR
PO BOX 2814
ATHENS GA 30612-0814

ACCOUNT NUMBER: [redacted]

Dear HENRY H OWINGS JR, 08/14/03

Congratulations! This is your official notification that you have completely paid off the student loans starred(*) below.

We are pleased to have had you as a customer and wish you the best of luck in the future. Thank you!

Customer Service

Loan Information If you have questions or concerns about your account, write to us at the address provided above.
The list below includes all the loans in your account with [illegible]. Loans marked with a star (*) are the loans referred to in this letter.

	LOAN DATE	ORIGINAL LOAN AMOUNT	OUTSTANDING PRINCIPAL	INTEREST RATE	LOAN PROGRAM
*	06/[illegible]0/91	$ 6,[illegible]98.00	$ .00	4.370	FFELP
*	09/[illegible]7/90	7,[illegible]500.00	.00	4.370	FFELP

PHONE (888) [illegible] • FAX (800) 848-1949 • TDD/TTY (888) [illegible]833-7562 • 24 HRS/7 DAYS • www.sa[illegible]ae.com

[illegible] SYSTEM [illegible] 0001

The pre-bankrupting of America's best and brightest, the young men and women who attend private colleges and public universities, is one of our nation's enduring, quiet scandals. Momentarily breaking the silence was a January 28 New York Times profile of young adults who, because of their student loans, are forced to choose jobs solely based on pay. Margot Miles, a legal secretary who borrowed $25,000 to attend UPenn, wants to go to law school but "just can't imagine taking out any more loans." Anisa Brophy, an aspiring cartoonist, ran up a $70,000 tab attending Wilson College in Pennsylvania. Even Connie Chavez, whose $10,000 student loan Hofstra bill doesn't seem so bad, "has virtually given up on her dream of going to business school."

These kids will not take low-paying jobs teaching in the inner cities. They won't join the Peace Corps. If they find themselves with a few extra hours here and there, they won't volunteer at a homeless shelter—they'll take a second job. When young people defer their dreams, when options vanish, America loses.

Average tuition and fees at a private college or university is $18,000 and rising at twice the inflation rate. Meanwhile, what students call "real" financial aid—grants and scholarships, not loans—keeps falling. The result is twofold. The Rand Corporation estimates that 6 million Americans will be "priced out of the system" over the next two decades. And for those who bite the bullet, more students than ever (46 percent in 1990, 70 percent in 2000) end up taking out college loans.

The U.S. college industry churns out about a million newly minted graduates every year. On average, they owe $27,600 to creditors they can't shake even by declaring bankruptcy. Depending on the type of loan, a typical 21-year-old faces a minimum monthly payment of from $350 to $420 for the next ten years. Anisa Brophy, the would-be cartoonist, is in for at least $880 a month. If debtors have trouble paying, they can apply for a temporary deferment, but the interest keeps piling on.

Why do people borrow so much at such an early age? The College Board claims that college grads earn $1 million more during their lifetimes than those with high-school degrees. And most half-decent jobs—positions in corporate offices, not just professional occupations like law and medicine—require that you have a college degree just to be considered.

You may be thinking: tough bananas. This is America. If you're stupid enough to borrow more dough than the average Joe pays for a house to listen to men with bad beards expound on Proust, it's your own overeducated fault that you're stuck with the bills. So what if 17-year-olds don't know jack about loan indentures, future salaries, or what they want to do for a living?

But that's horse manure.

As more and more employers require college degrees, more and more people will seek them. During the age of advancing globalization, national leaders say, Americans need more education to compete. Moreover, student loans are big business. Citibank's Student Loan Marketing Association, which holds outstanding student loans totaling $21 billion, recently announced that it turned a profit of $176 million last year, a 30 percent increase over 2001.

Student loan debt has become even more burdensome as the US enters its third consecutive year of recession. Fifty-nine percent of degreed job-seekers have been looking for work for at least three months, some for as long as a year. "Job-seekers frustrated by last year's tough market have low expectations about this year's job market," says Michael Caggiano of the TrueCareers jobs board.

If and when they find a job, the pay isn't all that great. The National Association of Colleges and Employers says that average starting salaries for the Class of 2002 range from $27,000 for political science majors to $51,000 for computer programmers. Around $35,000 is the national norm.

After taxes, that works out to about $2,000 a month—the rent on a tiny apartment in a borderline neighborhood in New York or San Francisco. When a fifth of your paycheck goes to student loans, it's hard to afford a car, much less purchase a first home. Economists looking for explanations for declining sales of big-ticket items might start here.

College tuition is free or nominal in most industrialized, and many Third World, countries. The United States' insistence that students assume huge debts to pay for their college education is unusual enough that the Chinese government included it in its 2001 report of American human rights violations.

Until the US joins the civilized world, our big-spending government can make things easier on twentysomething graduates by abolishing the student loan industry.

Eliminating the debt racket wouldn't be difficult. Calling off the invasion of Iraq, for instance, would save an estimated $200 billion—that's six years of fiscally emancipated youth right there. Eliminating last year's $1.5 trillion tax cut—money that would have gone to rich people who won't miss it—would pay off everyone's student loans for the next 50 years.

At age 39, I'm just $400 away from paying off my last student loan. Nonetheless, I could use the break.

©Ted Rall

HUNKLET PRESENTS:

OVERRATED
BOOK

PART TWO

OVERRATED:
THE MUSICAL

THE MOST OVERRATED INDIE/UNDERGROUND/ART FILMMAKERS OF ALL TIME!

by Sam McAbee • illustration by Eryc Simmerer

Anyone who is 29 (or so) and wants to be seen as ahead of the pack, informed, with-it, and of course, cool, has seen "Stranger Than Paradise," "8 1/2," "Weekend," "El Topo," and "Geek Maggot Bingo" (okay, maybe not that one). They've seen Hal Hartley movies, and they've maybe even seen a bootleg tape of Warhol's "Sleep." But did you know that many of these filmmakers who define hip in the realm of hipster film are grossly and hilariously overrated? Yes, it's true, much like musicians, college sports players and anal sex with a prostitute, indie filmmakers can be shockingly overrated! Also, the more arty and self-absorbed the filmmaker, the more profoundly overrated they become, so you can bet mother fucking Jean-Luc's ass is on here somewhere!

So let's get to the list. You may disagree, and you may even get mad at me. But please try to remember as you read this, I *am* right, and deep down, whether you know it or not, you did see Peter Greenaway's "The Cook, The Thief, His Wife and Her Lover," and you know fucking well I am right.

GUY MADDIN

Since when does making silent film parody that looks like it was produced by "Saturday Night Live" make you an underground film hero? Why do respectable film critics give this guy the fucking time of day? "Heart of the World" was like being hit over the head with this guy's film school ego, all jelly-filled, polished film symbolism. What a pompous, self-important jerk-off. "Careful" made me want to beat his "influenced" ass. And let's not even go down that "Twilight of the Ice Nymphs" road. He seems to think he is making these authentic tributes to cinema's early days, but all he is doing is making ADD renditions of Carl Theodor Dreyer films via Godard's near plotless influence (thanks again, Frog). Go fuck your couch, you Canadian!

ANDY WARHOL

Warhol couldn't direct his way out of a paper bag. Have you ever watched "Chelsea Girls?" No, I don't mean have you heard of it, have you ever actually *watched* it, all the way through, from beginning to end? If you said yes, maybe you should know that Drano tastes great in beer. I once went to a screening of "Flesh For Frankenstein" and they ran a Warhol "short" before the movie that was longer than the feature. It was the Warhol film "Beauty #2." It was the most painful movie experience of my entire life, and I saw "Arthur 2: On The Rocks" in the fucking theatre! I defy you to speak positively about a Warhol-directed film without spewing diarrhea from your mouth.

KENNETH ANGER

Everyone, put this book down for a second and ask yourself, "Do I really like Kenneth Anger movies?"

Hey, welcome back. Now that we are all on the same page here, let's try and figure out why this queeny, wannabe transgressive phony ever got to be the Grandfather of the Underground. "Scorpio Rising" is more gay than "Crusin'," and it's about as skillfully put together as a late-'60s Ed Wood movie (without any of the charm). "Lucifer Rising" feels about as insightful as Otto Preminger's "Skidoo," and Anger's association with people like Mick Jagger and Manson family members only makes him a name-dropping fake, not dangerous or brilliant. You just know guys like Dennis Hopper and Anton LaVey used to snap him in the ass with a towel or something. He gets credit for helping create many of the styles we might see on MTV today. Gee, thanks a lot, cocksucker!

JEAN-LUC GODARD

Yeah, yeah, "Breathless" was so influential that some say it's the most influential movie of all time. But just because something is an influence does not mean it is a good influence in any way. Think William S. Burroughs as a father figure, think the dude in the hoody standing by that chain link fence over there, think Michael Jackson as a sex therapist, think "Breathless" as an influence to future filmmakers everywhere. Godard was really the first filmmaker to use the movies to show how much he knew about the movies. He spent more time making reference to other films than he did making a movie. He turned most of his film narratives into self-referential brags and created an iconography out of surface disguised as invention (Tarantino is like Godard with his guard down). He was the first filmmaker to fit that mold of never living a life that wasn't spent watching movies. His films were fueled by other films, not his experiences, and with the coming of Godard went the days of real life moviemakers like John Ford, Samuel Fuller, Orson Welles, Howard Hawks, and Robert Aldrich. He made one great film, "Weekend," a truly brilliant melding of all of his mishmash of ideas, societal upheaval, a hatred of classism, materialism, and Americanism, yet there is a strong love, albeit satirical at times, for American film, fashion, and music. So call him a genius, but don't forget to call him hypocritical and derivative when you're done. Every other movie he made, including "Breathless," can be dissected on a napkin and will make you feel like you are locked in a room with a 19-year old stoner who just watched "Shock Corridor" for the first time. Watch Robert Bresson instead, please!

HAL HARTLEY

I really don't have too much to say about Hal Hartley except he has neither made a good movie, nor can he write real dialogue. He is one of those people who *almost* makes good movies, but once you get about an hour in, you notice that it pretty much sucks. He makes me feel let down and deflated. All he can do is frame people pleasingly, hire a good cinematographer to save his own blundering ass, and furthermore, he writes an ending about as well as Stephen King. I used to co-own a video store, and we had a "respected American directors" section. Hal Hartley was not in it. People wearing untucked dress shirts would always ask me why he was not in that section, and I would reply "Because we don't respect him, his movies are over here with the Mike Leigh and Atom Egoyan stuff."

JIM JARMUSCH

He is more concerned with indie cool points than having a point. Makes visual carbon copies of Eastern European art films, but replaces the heavy, weighted symbolism and meaning about oppression and resistance with deadpan Honeymooners humor (and lately he has been injecting a kind of Seinfield quality to his work). Has one truly great film, "Dead Man," and that's the only one he didn't have final cut on! "Night On Earth" was like a really bad collection of Italian soap opera episodes with ugly actors. "Stranger Than Paradise" is about as poignant as "Cinderfella" done by Wim Wenders, and the only cool thing about it is the original Sonic Youth drummer guy being in it. I do like "Down By Law" and "Mystery Train" to some degree, but neither film puts him above creative independent film-makers like Alex Cox or William Klein, who get zero credit in the states.

NICK ZEDD

Imagine Richard Kern after a hor-rific motorcycle accident. Now imagine him high on heroin and wearing leather pants. At this moment, you are envisioning Nick Zedd. Throw in a skanky Pabst-drinking bar whore cutting herself with a razor blade in front of a blue screen flashing Six Flags-like video effects, and you are imagining almost any Nick Zedd movie you can think of. Yet, this guy is looked at as some kind of mysterious, con-frontational and angry filmmaker who carries the weight of the New York underground film scene on his shoulders. People need to under-stand that filmmakers like Nick Zedd stomped on the shoulders of the New York underground film scene, and turned it into one big fucking joke, a parade of death metal shock tactics (they do it bet-ter in Tampa—and not on film—in their goddamned apartments!), neutered anti-porno eroticism, and uninformed meathead politics that add up to directionless, moronic masturbation. But he does dye his hair all kinda crazy colors, dude! Keepin' it real!

MAN RAY

The guy is consid-ered a pillar of the experimental film community, but he only made seven movies while Stan Brakhage made over 300. Fuck Man Ray, and his American Dada ass. Go throw a whipped cream pie, or roll around in your shit or something.

PETER GREENAWAY

My absolute most hated filmmaker of *all time*. Name any movie he's made, and I will start to wretch. I want to run this fucking stuffy prick over with my car...fourteen times. Never, and I mean never, has there been a more insulting, vapid, bor-ing, laughable filmmaker (or artist, author, musician, mime, anyfuck-ingthing!). His films represent the absolute worst elements in art film. Take Cocteau, give him a big hard-on for over-analyzing Shakespeare along with the visual flair of the "Flashdance" set designer, and you've got Peter Greenaway's sorry ass. Every movie he has ever made is a steaming pile of exploitative bullshit. I have met film snobs who deem this guy one of the few true artists in *cinema*, and I've told each and every one of them "You're lucky I don't throw a pot of boiling coffee in your fucking face!" It's because of this guy I feel sick whenever I see an orange or blue color jell shining over a man's penis. And to think I used to get so much out of that!

The 10 Most Overrated Film Genres

1. Anything and everything by those abortion peddlers at Troma.
2. Movies with transvestites.
3. Movies with goths.
4. Canadian art films.
5. Porno that is more or less just a bunch of college guys in sports jerseys gang-banging a 98 pound crack whore.
6. Greg Araki movies.
7. Downhill-comic-careers-resurrect-ed-by-magical-fat-suit movies.
8. Hip, late 20's/early 30's movies that exude a snide self-aware-ness, but fall flat of reaching any kind of real hip culture. Think *High Fidelity*, which is nothing more than a movie made for Dave Matthews Band/Radiohead fans who keep stacks of photos of themselves wearing dumb hats in Mexican bars.
9. Non-David Lynch David Lynch movies.
10. Experimental films that *no one* would ever want to sit through even if they were related to the filmmaker. Think Maya Deren. It's like having my dick abnormally swell up inside a shampoo bottle. Bad stuff. I'd rather spend some time in Rick James's basement.

SAM MCABEE
ILLUSTRATION BY RICH TOMMASO

THE OVER & UNDERRATED CROSSWORD

by Ryan Stacy

The grid, with handwritten entry at 71-Across: **CABLEGUY**

ACROSS

1 Actress Mia of *Legend, Ferris Bueller's Day Off.* Most underrated example of a woman succeeding in Hollywood without breasts.

5 Comedienne Joy. Original practitioner of the Lady Lame style of comedy cited in *Chunklet #18*. Probable inspiration for the "Coffee Talk" SNL skits. Most underrated reason to be thankful the comedy "boom" of the late '80's is over.

10 Mentally competent homey.

15 "40 ____ and a Mule." Spike Lee's production company. Most underrated example of the fact that people who name things associated with themselves after historical minutiae are assholes.

16 Most underrated pretentious word to use in place of "regarding."

17 With "air quotation marks," most underrated way to refer to something as being fashionable.

19 Bobby Dooley portrayer. The Damon Che Fitzgerald of prank calls. Most underrated reason to hate "Crossballs."

21 Haven't released a good album since *Millions Now Living...* Most underrated example of the rock truth that once a band that used to sound like it was doing a lot of drugs sounds like it's doing no drugs at all, it's time to stop listening.

23 Most overrated way to say "each."

24 "My other wife got _____ I got me a new one!"

25 Lewis and Belafonte.

27 Most overrated acronym for an Indian financial center.

28 Michael Eisner or Lee Iacocca. Most overrated character in Robert Loggia's arsenal of one character.

29 Principal of virtue.

30 Most overrated killer of Cain.

31 Underrated hair metal band whose members looked collectively more cretinous than Metallica, and whose singer later changed his ways to front his own contemporary/Christian/country band. Sample lyric: "We are United Nations/Under the flag of rock and roll!/We are United Nations/Together we stand...to take control!"

32 The _____, Poison bassist Bobby and his kin.

34 Paris Hilton and whomever.

36 Most overrated word signifying fear or vexation amongst foppish dandies.

37 Most overrated flakes.

38 "He _____ not only because ye hath sullied His Rock's good name, but also because ye, Eddie Vedder, hath invented that dumb, fake-emotional voice, which record executives shall decree the only voice which shall be heard on radio for these next 25 years."

40 Most underrated film rating.

42 _____ Schwartz. Most overrated store of which I have no idea what they sell inside.

43 Most overrated record by The Jesus Lizard on Touch & Go.

45 Most overrated all-pervading, infinitely elastic, massless medium formerly postulated as the medium of propagation of electromagnetic waves.

46 Most underrated synonym for crazy people used by actors like Tom Sizemore.

49 "They did their ____, you know." Most overused indie-word. It can be argued that except in rare circumstances, the use (or non-use) of this word makes a person indie or non-indie, accordingly.

51 Most underrated *Karate Kid* installment, featuring Mike Barnes, a.k.a. the bad boy of tournament karate.

52 Most overrated, now illegal, former staple of stupid British aristocratic silliness.

54 "Still Life with Old Shoe" surrealist Joan. As opposed to Still Life with Old Shoe Jones, the town drunk.

57 Most underrated shitty type of person to be sleeping next to.

59 Most overrated place for Napoleonic exile.

60 Most overrated word used to start a stupid, mock performance of a Vanilla Ice song that ceased being funny the second time it was done 15 years ago.

61 Most overrated words to put between "happy" and "pig in shit."

62 Most underrated falsely identified time signature. Cited by kids at shows who aren't smart enough to just enjoy the show, but instead let us know that not only do they not know what they are talking about, they don't know that what they are talking about does not exist.

64 Bush or Kerry.

65 Most underrated Roscoe P. Coltrane hazard.

67 Most overrated alternative word for "primo."

68 Most underrated rock drummer brothers.

70 Most overrated alternative word for package.

71 Most underrated stoner job.

73 Most underrated masculine German article.

74 Most overrated derivative of My Bloody Valentine and precursor of Mogwai.

76 Most overrated profession of a Patrick Swayze film character.

77 Most overrated article of clothing that signifies retardedness.

79 Most overrated Scotland follower.

80 Most underrated butt follower.

81 Country singer Kenny. Most underrated reminder that country music fans like their music like they like their men: tan, buffed and stupid.

83 _____ Rico, most underrated reason to respect statehood.

87 _____, do solemnly swear to look metrosexual with Barbie when we are on the scene, so we can achieve self-actualization.

89 Most overrated bar responsibilities.

90 Shitty barbeque side that no one truly likes.

92 Most underrated female organ to men, and the inverse.

93 Most underrated follower of "the Todd."

94 Karen _____ is a legend of women's professional pool.

95 Most overrated film of all time.

In one boringly incoherent, yet loud, statement, all you ever needed to know about anime is answered. It's retarded.

97 Underrated fraudulent ministry. Laid the groundwork for Dollar, Hinn and Tilton.

98 Dot follower.

99 Tulip negotiating technique.

101 Overrated place to keep goods.

102 Abbreviation for another name for a lawyer.

103 Miraculous delivery alternative.

105 Most overrated stoner job.

108 Most underrated object of unfair *Chunklet* ridicule by association. "Australasia" creators band name listed in Dreamo vs. Emo challenge even though their music and name aren't in line with the gayness of emo. Even if they were just thrown in

to be, like, a decoy, that shit's still fucked up.

109 One of the only bands that can ever claim having one of the most underrated and overrated albums of all time. *Tweez* is strange, ominous, playful, ridiculous, and is sung praises by this crossword's author. *Spiderland* is retarded, melodramatic, loud-softy, Julia Robertsy, and is praised by Steve Albini. Which goes to show you that history always sides with the asshole people have heard of.

110 _____ are losers and...

111 Mark territory... anew.

112 "Right here from the _____, motherfucker."

113 "I loved her because she _____ me young."

DOWN

1 Thee _____d Canaries. Most underrated alternative band name hidden on the *Life Like Homes* LP sleeve.

2 Most underrated way to say "each."

3 Belief system cut short.

4 Equally foxy.

5 El _____. Most underrated way to refer to Burt Reynolds' character The Bandit in a language other than English.

6 Play directive.

7 Orgasmo, e.g.

8 _____ DiFranco is a hit with lesbians.

9 Abbreviated methods of travel.

10 What 57 across diidd to be so fucking annoying.

11 _____ Lavigne doesn't get the credit she deserves for being retarded.

12 Multiple dumb Mike Myers overused negating catchphrases.

13 Most overrated (if not appropriately refined) lead singer quality.

14 Conakry is its overrated capital.

15 Seem to be.

17 "Only fucking idiots call _____. It's referred to as a candy stick. Dipshit."

18 "_____ mein scheisse!" Overrated directive to Cartman's mother from the South Park movie.

20 Most overrated nickname for a school encompassing grades 1-12.

22 Most underrated serpentine fish.

23 Most overrated Rye Coalition influence.

26 Most overrated adorable loser/Viking.

29 Most overrated way to say "stop up," a few hundred years ago.

31 Released the album *To Rock Or Not To Be* only a few years ago. Consistently gave a half-assed Swiss interpretation of whatever music was already

popular in the arena rock realm in real rock countries. Overrated to talk about, underrated to listen to.

33 "In the relay race it was the final _____ I decided I would run like I'd never run before. Not just for my team...but for the Lapps!"

35 Most underrated pretentious word for "job."

36 Most overrated beginning class in French partying.

37 Most overrated composer cited by rock guitarists hoping to be taken seriously.

39 Most overrated words associated with Mr. Miyagi.

41 Most underrated way to play drums.

42 "I can't _____ a goddamned thing! What makes you think I can start with your faggot ass?!"

44 Third most underrated way to say "okay" in a way that is trying to be funny, but never is.

46 Most overrated way to play drums.

47 Most overrated count on which to hike a football.

48 Most overrated middle-tier vodka.

50 Second most overrated term used as a substitute for "zany" in 80's screwball comedies.

52 Most underrated British way to say "leaves quickly."

53 Most overrated Lee Ving bodily fluid.

54 _____ Wilson. Most overrated late 90's straight-to-video leading man.

55 Most overrated Newton, besides Juice.

56 Most overrated half-German, half-Sioux, misunderstood fictional American vigilante P.O.W.

58 Most overrated thing to do to the day.

59 Work unit.

63 Most overrated wading birds.

66 Most underrated word to use in place of "package."

67 Most overrated goofy British way to say "old."

69 (…) Most overrated acclaimed parody of a TV genre, that was actually just bad TV itself.

70 Most overrated prefix used to insinuate a lack of deserved value.

72 Most underrated word used in hotel/restaurant names to attract nouveau riche patrons.

73 Fails to live.

75 Jamaica predecessor, in song.

77 Most underrated response to the question, "What's your favorite band, dude?"

78 Most overrated euphemism for ordering.

81 Most overrated cigarette purchasing quantity.

82 *From _____ to Jerkov, My Story.* Underrated, yet-to-be-actualized, possible autobiography of Branson, Missouri's most unfortunate adopted son.

84 "The _____." Most underrated reason to never trust anyone from Seattle, WA or Decatur, GA's opinion on music.

85 Most overrated misspelling of "titties."

86 Members follower.

87 "_____ all the fuckin' time, man, that's why I'm so crazy!"

88 Most underrated type of household party.

89 #1 pain in the ass.

91 Most underrated band of serious assholes cited way too many times as some kind of musical godfathers. Read any interview of theirs and you'll essentially be told that you are wrong for listening to any music other than theirs, except for the shitty bands that copy them, of course.

93 Most overrated component of thatched dwellings.

94 Most overrated smart way to say "aroundabouts."

96 Stroke more.

99 "Get _____, motherfucker. Let's rock this bitch!"

100 Mr. Lover's friend from "tha hood."

101 Small incision.

102 Time, maybe.

104 Most overrated geographically-specific term for Mauritius, in French.

106 Rapper Eric Wright, familiarly, in Mexico.

107 "____ blue?" The hip-hop way to ask in a letter why someone is depressed.

SOLUTION

THE MOST OVERRATED CITIES TO PLAY IN AMERICA!

A study of why you should've toured Europe instead of wasting your time driving the never-ending brick roads in the states

by Brian Teasley • artwork by Eryc Simmerer

LOS ANGELES, CA

Over-inflated guest lists, know-it-all sound and crew guys that got job placement at the venue via their Full Sail degree. If a celebrity comes out, forget about your show because it will become all about them. Like Sofia Coppola gives a shit about your band anyway.

SEATTLE, WA

No all-ages shows. Ex-Sub Pop band (probably Love Battery) will be thrilled to help load your shit. No really, they will. Nothing like the false hope of a town built on a scene that never existed.

SAN DIEGO, CA

You might as well just play an in-store in Ensenada, but at least if you're there, the meth is good and cheap (thanks, Tijuana!). Too bad hipsters here couldn't take a cue from local upstart visionaries, Heaven's Gate.

LAS VEGAS, NV

If anyone shows up, it'll be tourists or hardcore meatheads. Might as well take all the tour money and hit the slots, because no one here's going to open their wallet for a t-shirt. Blow off the gig! Go see Cook E. Jar perform instead.

SALT LAKE CITY, UT

It's like one giant Mormon Disneyland without any rides. Maybe you'll actually have a chance to have a crowd if you've had a song on a hot snowboarding video. Play here for masochistic purposes only.

HOUSTON, TX

George Bush's backyard has got to be the biggest shithole per capita in the country. Have fun loading up the stairs at nearly every club here as if the humidity and redneck threat weren't enough by themselves. Maybe one day Houston clubs will discover air conditioning, but there again maybe one day terrorists will take out this metropolitan-sized ass sore.

ATLANTA, GA

If you play the first half of the week, you might as well be in fucking Peoria or some shit, because Atlanta acts like it was stuck in the middle of Hazzard County. You will not find a greater collection of has-beens and burnt-out major label dropees running the show in a city of this size.

NEW YORK, NY

Impossible parking, high ticket prices, early shows, No room to store cases, and unrelentingly hostile attitudes. Your sound guy was runner-up to play guitar in L.A. Guns and he's not happy about mixing your shitty band. You will move there to get signed, but stay for the heroin addiction.

WASHINGTON, DC

Is there really a scene here? I suppose it's only made of people who only support their own bands. These days, worrying about the DC barometer is like worrying about the Portuguese military.

GAINESVILLE, FL

The city that's a solid decade behind the third wave of punk rock. When I think "Gainesville," I think DIY — Dick in Yogurt.

NEW ORLEANS, LA

No valid small venues whatsoever. People's taste is rather tainted by all that gay ass voodoo shit, and there are hardly any decent local bands to play with. Enjoy the view of the interstate while you wait for the door guy from the Mermaid Lounge to show up to let you inside.

DALLAS, TX

Two words: Deep Ellum. The security here is corn-fed, tattooed and ready to beat your monkey ass. Don't tell them how to do shit neither because they've been around the world with The Toadies or the Reverend.

NASHVILLE, TN

Even though only 15 people will be at your show, 12 of them will be drunk sorority girls from Vandy. During the day, enjoy looking at amazing vintage gear that you could never afford. If ending up strung-out and homeless is your plate of grits, feel free to try and make it as a session musician here.

DETROIT, MI

If you're doing anything slightly original or cool, you know the kids in this town will soon copy it and market it far better than you ever dreamed. Don't worry about getting your shit stolen in this real-life post-apocalyptic nightmare because it's a rite of passage here. Eminem's doo-doo has more architectural flair than downtown Detroit.

CHAPEL HILL, NC

While this may not the be the best show of your tour, there will be no shortage of over-priced burritos to choose from on Franklin Street. Oh yeah, Merge doesn't want to put out your record. Which part of "no unsolicited material" don't you choir boys understand?

MEMPHIS, TN

Too bad they don't make rock club Viagra because Memphis clubs keep it up about as long as a high school kid getting his first hand job. A city where you play a different place every time and always to nobody. Long may rock'n'roll stay dead. Only true assholes wear Sun Studios t-shirts.

1000 UNRELATED OVERRATED *Things*

Daring rescue mission: Jessica Lynch
Paranormal experience: Past-life regression
New Age alternative medicine: Intestinal massage
Fashion trend: Low-cut waist gypsy belts
Brady: Marsha
Diet food: Celery sticks
Party: Costume
Teen year: 16
Space campaign: Apollo
Cowboy: Kevin Costner
Firework: Sparkler
War: World War II
Wax museum: Madam Tussaud's
Institute of higher learning: Harvard
Religious cult: Scientology
Game show host: Pat Sajak
Murderer: Charles Manson
Patriotic disaster: Challenger explosion
Porn title: *Saving Ryan's Privates*
End to civilization: *(tie)* Fire and ice
Air conditioner setting: 72º F
Tom Hanks movie: *Forrest Gump*
Statue: Statue of Liberty
Breakfast table item: Aunt Jemima maple syrup
Plastic surgery: Collagen lip injections
The Price Is Right game: The one with the mountain climber
Vegetable: Sweet corn niblets
Form of canine discipline: Hitting nose with newspaper
Symbol of the '60s: Peace sign
Punctuation symbol: Comma
Gag item: Alfred E. Neuman $3 bill
Jane Fonda reference: *(tie)* Fuckin' Vietnam and *Barbarella*
'90s sitcom: *Seinfeld*
Medieval form of protection: Moat
March: Million Man

Cast member on *Gilligan's Island*: Gilligan
Decadent purchase: Jukebox in the bathroom
Football commentator: John Madden

Cheese: **Chevre**

Import: All the tea in China
Pickup truck: Dodge Ram
Giant moth: Mothra
Zipper: YKK
Yogurt: Go-Gurt
Condiment: Ketchup
European sport: Soccer
Internal organ: Cloaca
Dead clown: Emmett Kelly
Mime: Marcel Marceau
Form of aerial transportation: Blimp
Prison gag: Dropping the soap in the shower
Monty Python gag: The Holy Hand Grenade
Bogus law: "Do not remove this tag"
Cartoon-like spokesperson: Kool Aid's "Oh yeah!" pitcher
Talk-show sidekick: Ed McMahon
Lazy Saturday afternoon activity: Cuddling in a hammock
Caliber: .38
Trench: Marianas
Page number: 3
All-female porn concept: Women in prison
Wordplay on "History": *Kisstory*
Mud flap: Keep on Truckin'
Yearbook title: The Carousel
***Simpsons* character:** Bart
No-wave band: Television
Pillsbury character: The Doughboy
Chappy's Deli slogan: "Just one bite will set you free"
Drug magazine: *High Times*

Thing for a parent to be proud of: Honor student
Bum sign: "I'm not gonna lie to you, I just want a beer"
Planet of the Apes movie: *Escape From The...*
Form of humiliation: Peeing in your pants
Edgy prank: Videotaping strangers in the toilet
Watering hole pastime: Sexual harassment
Chronicle Books release: *Worst-Case Scenario Survival Guide*
Revolutions per minute: 33 1/3
20th century decor: '60s Tiki/lounge
Grooming activity: Filing your fingernails
Late-night drinking activity: Vomiting in a friend's car
Chevy Chase movie: *National Lampoon's Vacation*
Children's television host: Mister Rogers
Article in this book: The overrated record survey
Fashion designer: Christian Dior
Indie director: Vincent Gallo
Frozen Mexican treat: Choco-Taco
Trip: Moses leading his people out of Egypt
Gay reality television show: *Queer Eye for the Straight Guy*
Ronco product: Ginsu knife
Dead porn star: John Holmes
Death in their own vomit: Jimi Hendrix
Smoothie: Mr. Mongo at Planet Smoothie
Movie villain: Hannibal Lechter

Moustache: **Hitler**

Secret queer person: David Hyde Pierce

Action hero: Jean-Claude Van Damme

Comic book character: Harvey Pekar

Ancient structure: Pyramids of Giza

Song on Bob Seger's *Like A Rock* album: "Like A Rock"

Visible element in your stool: *(tie)* Corn and peanuts

Legendary baseball teasm: The 1969 Mets

Character on *Kids in the Hall*: The "I'm Crushing Your Head" guy

Sonic Youth associate: Lydia Lunch

Sexual preference: Hetero

Christmas gift-giving technique: The Secret Santa game

Piece of chicken: Breast

Living porn star: Ron Jeremy

Contemporary artist: Jeff Koons

John Hughes movie: *The Breakfast Club*

Cult movie: *Rocky Horror Picture Show*

Spice: Paprika

Spice Girl: Posh

Picnic food: Deviled eggs

Club drug: GHB

Mixer: Orange juice

Guitar String: E

Protection from a stalker tactic: Restraining order

Member of Fugazi: Ian MacKaye

Hipster store: Urban Outfitters

Goth fetish: Drinking blood

Cannibal: Jeffrey Dahmer

Rock club: CBGB

Place to ejaculate: Tits

Political scandal: Watergate

Breakfast cereal: Frosted Mini-Wheats

Silent film star: Rudolph Valentino

Hideously deformed person: John Merrick

Source of band names: Any movie reference

Contemporary slang word: Blog

High-end alcoholic beverage: Cristal

1960s racial protest: March on Selma, Alabama

Sex symbol: Pamela Anderson

Lame-ass rockabilly haircut: The pomp

Time: Quittin' time

Solstice: Summer

Irish icon: Leprechaun

Continent: Europe

Film festival: Cannes

BBC Channel: 1

Homonym: Whole/Hole

Froofy chick drink: Sex On The Beach

Key-chain do-dad: Rabbit's foot

Freeze-dried pet: Sea monkey

Jihad: Salman Rushdie

Breed of dog: Jack Russell terrier

Druid structure: Stonehenge

Halo of Flies single: Rubber Room

Hot Hollywood actor: Orlando Bloom

Contemporary artist: Matthew Barney

Use of sesame seeds: Hamburger buns

Early '90s poster artist: Coop

Fantagraphics cartoonist: Chris Ware

Dead poet: Jack Kerouac

Mohawk: Mr. T

Novelty pet: Chia

Circus: Ringling Brothers

Vanilla flavor: French

Sugar substitute: Equal

F-stop: 5

Emotion: Melancholy

Reptile: Amphetamine

Igneous rock: Granite

American landmark: Mount Rushmore

Flip Wilson character: Geraldine

Jewish symbol: Star of David

Rose: Yellow Rose of Texas

Animal actor: Spuds McKenzie

Letterpress shop: Hatch Show Print

Regional video format: NTSC

Music format: Compact disc

Speaker manufacturer: Bose

Macromedia program: Dreamweaver

Big Mac ingredient: Special Sauce

Talk show host: Oprah

Serial killer: Ed Gein

Children's book: *Goodnight Moon*

Ethnic food: Chinese Sweet-n-Sour

Time zone: Eastern

Herb for animals: Catnip

Animal narcotic: Ketamine

Twins: Barbie

Vitamin: K

Diet craze: Atkins

Flavor of Jell-o: Orange

Gypsy shtick: Palm reading

Chapter in the Bible: Genesis

World religion: Christianity

Third World ethnic food: Taramosalata

Marilyn Monroe movie: *Some Like It Hot*

Art movement: Abstract Post-War Expressionism

Urban Outfitters purchase: The butterfly chair

Part of Rocket From The Crypt: The horn section

New Zealander: Peter Jackson

Homophobe: Fred Durst

Reason not to finish a Dutch Baby at the Original Pancake House: Getting sick

Plastic surgery chin implant: Reese Witherspoon

Euphemism for a bong: Water pipe

'90s-era SNL cast member: Rob Schneider

European currency: Swedish kronor

Vanity endeavor for hip-hop artists: Designing their own sneakers

Power broker: Donald Trump

Kid Michael Jackson fucked in the butt: Macaulay Culkin

"Smells Like Teen Spirit" rip-off: The 'jam' in the beginning scene of '90s comedy flick *PCU*

Term for feminists: Wymyn

Body piercing: Belly button

Dorm room poster: "Enter At Your Own Risk"

Term for a female dog: Bitch

Magician: David Blaine

McKenzie: Mackenzie Phillips

Bicentennial: America's Spirit of '76

Vegetarian "excuse": Meat Is Murder

Toupee: David Spade's

Abbreviation: abbr.

Unused space in a U-Haul truck: Grandma's Attic

Blooper reel: **Fat chick slipping on ice**

Booze: **"The Blood of Christ" wine**

Mr. Show sketch: **"Titannica"**

Chunklet's *list of 1000 Unrelated Overrated Things*

Marriage compromise: (tie) Hyphenation of bride's surname and divorce

Reason not to hug your grandmother: She smells like old, used diapers

Year in James Brown's career: 1969

Hostage: Patty Hearst

Atari 2600 video cartridge: Asteroids

Thomas Pynchon book: *The Crying of Lot 49*

Cigarette: Camel Lights

Afro styling: High fade

Beatle: Paul McCartney

Street name: Main

Season of *Buffy*: Second

Breakdance move: The Windmill

Elvis Costello song: "Pump It Up"

Sports announcer: Studs Terkel

Ceiling fan speed: High

Hipster perfume: Toga

Razor: Mach Three

Male sexual fantasy: Threesome

Element of spaghetti westerns: Tumbleweed

Breakfast cereal cartoon character: Cap'n Crunch

Annoying backyard pool dive: The Cannonball

Latino gang fashion: Having the top button buttoned on a short-sleeve button-down shirt

Circus sideshow attraction: Siamese twins

Member of Thin Lizzy: Phil Lynott

Postponement: "I haven't found myself yet."

Rumor-that's-really-not-a-rumor about George Clinton: He smokes crack

Foreign exchange student: That one dude from Kenya

Courtney Love conspiracy theory: That she actually has talent

Slang term for being fired: Shitcanned

Form of electrocution: Sticking your finger in the socket

Gene Hackman movie: *The French Connection*

Comparison analogy: Apples to oranges

'60s graphic icon: Peace symbol

Yard chore: Raking the leaves

"Director's Cut" ending: *Blade Runner*

Remake of a foreign film: *Vanilla Sky*

Use of cardboard: Spending hours constructing a table out of three iMac boxes

Pancakes at IHOP: Polynesian

Recording studio tool: Computer

Soft drink ploy: Clear anything

Sense: Taste

Finger: Index

Season: Summer

Opiate: Heroin

Chocolate: Truffle

Hippie pet: The ferret

Plague: Bubonic

Party favor: Kazoo

Diaper: Plastic

Horror author: Dean Koontz

Hour in primetime: 8 to 9 p.m.

Thing to reenact: The U.S. Civil War

Bait-and-switch: The "mystery" box

Ex-Spiegel model: Matthew Barney

Rock band manager: Peter Grant

Stain on Andrew WK's T-shirt: Shit brown smudge in left pectoral zone

Pro Tools plug-in: Aphex Big Bottom Pro

Term for marijuana: Kind bud (a.k.a. "KB")

Mideastern conflict: Israel vs. Palestine

Member of Tenacious D: Jack Black

Long-standing songwriter: Randy Newman

George Carlin skit: "The Seven Dirty Words You Can't Say on Television"

Flashback: The one right before you die

Method of suicide: Autoerotic asphyxiation

Word that starts with the letter "N": The "N-word"

Mid-life hairstyle: The comb-over

Cell phone service: Virgin mobile

Women exploitation restaurant: Hooters

Issue of *Chunklet*: #15, The Asshole Issue

Gerry Anderson marionette show: *Thunderbirds*

Explorer: Columbus

Sexually transmitted disease: HIV

Single malt whiskey: Jack Daniels

1960s cult television show: The Prisoner

Late '90s garage rock band: Electric Frankenstein

Member of Public Enemy: Chuck D

Ad campaign: The ineffectual truth.com anti-smoking ads

Hollywood movie practice: Making sequels

Slang for a motorcycle: Crotch Rocket

Name for a gay couple's pet: Jazz

Pet name for a frat boy: (3-way tie) Guinness, Bud and Hoss

Tropical fruit: Mango

Fictional item that dogs chase: Chuck wagon

Howard Stern sidekick: Stuttering John

Cast member of *21 Jump Street*: Richard Grieco

"Friendly" nickname from a shop teacher who can't remember your name: Boss

Blooper overdub: "Boing!"

Angus Young stage get-up that's not the schoolboy one: Zorro outfit

Pre-Butthole Surfers Butthole Surfers band name: Dick Gas Five

Perversion: Peeping Tom

Type of brassiere: Wonder Bra

Form of ice: Crushed

Space on *Hollywood Squares*: The center square to block

State beneath the Mason-Dixon line: Florida

Surprise: Flamingo-a-Friend in your front lawn

Herb: Ginseng

Suffix: -est

Mythical hybrid: Griffin

Succulent cactus: Yucca

Arcane ritual: Marriage

Secret society: Freemasons

Adhesive: Crazy Glue

Fictitious mixed drink: Roofie colada

Human pain: Childbirth

Muppet: Miss Piggy

Ground cover: Shore juniper
Dead lesbian poet: Sappho
Beneficial insect: Ladybug
"How to": *Our Bodies, Our Selves*
Dessert: Crème brûlée
Table manner: Saying "please"
Item in Grandma's Attic: Her love letters
Brand of pancake mix: Bisquick
Constellation visible in night-time sky: Orion
Indicator of future success: Test scores
Trendy parking lot etiquette: Reserved spaces for expectant mothers
Abuse of personal freedom: Acting like a jerk
Fast food moniker: "Biggie"
Waffle House hashbrown tier in the Scattered, Smothered, etc. line-up: "Chunked"
Planned resort community: Seaside
Way of death: In your sleep
Brand of ice cream: Ben & Jerry's
Missing person: Amelia Earhart
Nazi believed to have fled to South America: Goebbels
Nobel Prize winner: Pearl S. Buck
Expression when saying goodbye: "Take it easy"
Dead lesbian hostess: Gertrude Stein
Delivery service: United States Postal Service
NASCAR number: 3
Local news feature: Kid stuck down a well
Rapper: 50 Cent
Man: Dr. Phil
Sitarist: Ravi Shankar
'70s AOR artist: Steely Dan
Drunk-at-a-bar pastime: Watching women fight
Required high school reading assignment: *The Great Gatsby*
Sex toy: Ben Wa balls
Marlon Brando movie: *The Godfather*
In-city ethnic locale: Chinatown
Saturday morning cartoon: 6 a.m. farm report

Washed up 4-letter 1980s rock band: Styx
Hollywood "yukster": Andy Dick
Hope/Crosby "Road" movie: *The Road to Hong Kong*
Dairy Queen menu item: Blizzard
First lady: Jackie Kennedy
Smell in a pillow: Fart
Jugs: Carmen Electra
Penis: Tommy Lee
Contest: Project Greenlight
Autopsy: Orson Welles'
Reason to exercise: *(tie)* Staying thin and preventing cancer
Novel based on the premise that God will help you through female puberty: "Are You There, God? It's Me, Margaret"
Hors d'oeuvre: Crudités
Shoe collection: Imelda Marcos
African country: Kenya
Campbell's soup: Chicken Noodle
New York crime family: Gambino
British form of transit: Double-decker bus
Childhood prank: Taking a dump in somebody's shoes
Happy Days cast member: Scott Baio
Method of departing New York City: Holland Tunnel
Book on Taoism: *Tao Te Ching*
Feature of quantity: Quality
Feature of quality: Quantity
Nazi war criminal: Hermann Göring
Lame-o Atlanta scene created as an excuse to do coke, get shitty tattoos, play cowbilly and spin David Allan Coe records: The Redneck Underground
Donna to feel up: Donna C
Energy drink: *(tie)* Rush! and Pimp Juice
Symptom of urinary tract infection: Visible amount of blood in urine
Member of the Taliban: John Walker Lindh
Accidental break-dancer: Michael J. Fox

Drummer: Dave Grohl

Mexican artist: Frida Kahlo

Tiresome filler part of weekly shit rags: "News of the Weird"-type bullshit
Children's character who is a dog: Clifford
Boohoo tale of harsh working conditions: *The Jungle* by Upton Sinclair
Reason for not having sex: "Not tonight, I'm bleeding"
Gateway conspiracy book: *Future* by Alvin Toffle
Christmas record: *Boogie Woogie Christmas* by Brian Setzer
Excuse for death: *(tie)* Natural causes and old age
Non-fictional racehorse name: Seabiscuit
Butt of blue-collar jokes: A Hooters waitress
Hanna-Barbera sidekick: Morocco Mole *(Secret Squirrel)*
Reason to get a divorce: Abusive husband
Time to get an abortion: First trimester
Portion of the procedure of getting a gun: The background check
Member of Simon and Garfunkel: Paul Simon
Tennessee Williams play: *Cat On a Hot Tin Roof*
Russian violinist: Jascha Heifetz
Hotel perk: The continental breakfast
Religious hat: The Pope's miter
Part of being a Muslim: The pilgrimages
Lens to use in a rap video: Fish eye
Food group not to eat: Meat
Foot fashion: Not wearing socks
Beat-era boy molester: Allen Ginsberg
Way for a celebrity to have a child: Adopt them from a poor Asian country
Word used to describe what someone does with cancer: Battle
Term used to describe increasing security: "Beef up"
Thing to recycle: Aluminum cans
Baseball-loving nation: Cuba
Way to present yourself in a *Spin* contributor photo: Flattering

Book on the shelf of a 30-plus losing-touch Americana-listening-sap: Woody Guthrie's *Bound for Glory*

Female star of a Russ Meyer film: Tura Satana

Vietnam War-era physical tragedy agent or ailment with a name containing a color and which is used to name punk bands: (tie) Agent Orange and Gangrene

Show that you once videotaped religiously: *The X-Files*

Word that comes up in describing early Bowie: Androgynous

Atomic disaster: Chernobyl

Part of Southern Confederate flag-waving culture: (tie) Ignorance and Stupidity

Art form: Performance art

Easy-ass target for a terrorist to attack: An embassy in their country of origin

Dead reggae artist: Peter Tosh

Street in New Orleans: Bourbon

Way to convey someone going on and on about something: Da, da, da, dum

Rockstar behavior: (tie) Shooting heroin and killing yourself

Profession after you failed at what you really wanted to do: Teach college

Place to dump a dead body in Atlanta: Chattahoochee River

Body adornment for a 40-plus-year-old guy in the music business to have: Single earring in the left ear

Death mourned by gay men: Princess Di

Film to make old people feel that the fact that they can't fuck any more and will soon die ain't really that bad: (tie) *Cocoon* and *On Golden Pond*

Piano movie: *Shine*

Fashion magazine: *Flaunt*

Food group: Dairy and eggs

Cleaning tool: The Swiffer

Foucaultian acolyte: Naomi Wolf

Nefertiti revisionist: Camille Paglia

Gap between teeth: Lauren Hutton

National music scene: New Zealand

Sax player: Clarence Clemons

Way to die in Bangladesh: Cyclone

Tired L.A. music couple dynasty: Aimee Mann/Michael Penn

Genre term used to describe records that Irwin Chusid likes: Esoterica

Part of Barbara Streisand's body to have your crotch rubbed by: Nose

Logo using a guitar neck as part of the image: Africa with a guitar neck design used for Live Aid

Way for British pussies to take out their frustration for the lack of ever having a decent meal: Football riots

Term used to rationalize genocide: Manifest Destiny

Failed attempt at morality control: Prohibition

Pre-1960 way for a white woman to divert attention from some stupid fucked-up thing she did: Lie and claim a young black man raped her

Way to get 99X to play your record: Have (more) drugs and hookers sent to Jay Harren's office

Description for your ass-ugly, nerdy, retro-looking girlfriend: "Classic beauty"

Thing to try to teach your retarded child: Bible verses

Type of music to play as a sports radio show bumper: Surf

Member of Love and Rockets: Daniel Ash

Drum playing grip: Matched

Thing pre-pubescent Jewish boys regularly beat off to: Norman Rockwell *Saturday Evening Post* prints

Anorexic: (tie) Karen Carpenter and Gandhi

Trailer park family activity: (three-way tie) Sex abuse, physical abuse and saying grace before dinner

Facial movement made by Lynyrd Skynyrd members before crashing in Mississippi: Opening their eyes really wide

Chess champion: Bobby Fischer

Way for a girl band to divert attention from their obvious lack of talent: Being pretty

Week in New York: Fashion week

Extracurricular hobby for famous poets: Alcoholism

Blue Blockers glasses wearer: Jeff Lynne

Space dog: Laika

Contradiction imposed by consumerism and revolution: Having an S22 t-shirt with Ernesto "Che" Guevara on it

Free speech student leader: Mario Savio

Ritual that Satanists are too pussy to really do: Sacrificing babies

San Francisco promoter: Bill Graham

Kennedy assassination: JFK

Hippie activity: (tie) Not bathing and face painting

Robyn Hitchcock song: "Balloon Man"

Metaphorical war/survival hobby for sexually repressed men with IQs under 100: Deer hunting

Metaphorical war/survival hobby for sexually repressed men with IQs between 100 and 105: Paintball

Television programming for married men to secretly fag out to: Professional wrestling

Unfathomably profitable capitalization on fatal student shootings: (tie) Michael Moore's *Bowling For Columbine* and Buffalo Springfield's 'Ohio'

Produce boycotted on large scale by the influence of César Chavez: Lettuce

Temple used as a backdrop in action movies: Angkor Wat

American cult: The Mormons

Singer of all time: Frank Sinatra

Gospel singer: Mahalia Jackson

Subtext that is merely a bi-product of war: The Olympics

Underground militant flag logo: Symbionese Liberation Army cobra

Defection: Mikhail Baryshnikov

Hallucination: **Talking animals**

Pollution: **Air**

Celebratory maneuver for neckless college thugs and braindead assistant coaches to do after a big victory: Pour Gatorade on the head coach

AIDS victim: Liberace

Technique Americans use to get a tight grip on the title of being the fattest nation in the world: Eating fast food

Way to waste the money your parents spent on your college education: Start a rock band

Area of New York to show the haphazard, played-out, uninspired shit stains you call art: Soho

Classical guitar virtuoso: Andres Segovia

Place to write your memoirs: Prison

Beatles' album artwork: *Sgt. Peppers Lonely Hearts Club Band*

Manfred Mann song: "The Mighty Quinn"

Music documentary: *(tie)* D. A. Pennebaker's *Don't Look Back* and David Maysles' *Gimme Shelter*

'70s cult film: *Harold and Maude*

All-girl punk band that's really not an all-girl punk band: X-Ray Spex

School to get a design degree: Parsons

Clown: *(tie)* Bozo and Shakes

College football coach: "Bear" Bryant

Post-adolescent diarist: Anne Frank

Performance artist: Karen Finley

Figurative artist feminist: Kiki Smith

Zephyr: Hindenburg

19th Century confectioner: Little Debbie

Midwestern murderess: Lizzie Borden

Metaphysical Oscar quack: Shirley MacLaine

Flash-in-the-pan TV clairvoyant: Miss Cleo

Sentence used in a movie pitch session to a major Hollywood executive: "It practically writes itself"

Memorial in Washington, DC: Vietnam Veterans Memorial

Silent Western film star: Tom Mix

***Chunklet* column that is no longer part of the magazine (thank God):** "Noser Knows"

Dario Argento film: *Suspiria*

Italian prog soundtrack band: Goblin

City that John Waters champions: Baltimore

Poet: *(four-way tie)* William Blake, Rainer Maria Rilke, Sylvia Plath and John Keats

***Zaireeka* listening party sub-theme:** Botox injection

Song of all-time: "Cheeseburger In Paradise" by Jimmy Buffett

Fat-assed black TV talk show host: Star Jones

Writing invention in the last 25 years: The EraserMate

Microphone sound: Rush Limbaugh "Golden" E.I.B.

Synth of the last ten years: The Nord Lean

Sax solo: President Bill Clinton on Arsenio Hall

Kangaroo performance: *(tie)* The cgi'ed one in *Kangaroo Jack* and Ice-T in *Tank Girl*

Group of the psychedelic era: The Moody Blues

Item at Andy Baker's home studio: Manley Vox Box pre-amp

Edible yougurt add-on: Sprinkles

Race of the last 5,000 years: Caucasian

Race of the last 20 years: Black

Performance art piece: Sleeping

Cereal: Frosted Mini Wheats

Thing to eat on a video shoot: an everything bagel

Show on NPR: This American Life

Thing about Thurston Moore: *(tie)* Being in Sonic Youth and collecting records

Television prank show: *Punk'd*

Celebrity soon to be Alice Cooper's golfing partner: Marilyn Manson

Film that tricks you into believing that Anton Newcombe has a shred of credibility: *Dig*

Dead black man: Tupac Shakur

Self-improvement: Losing weight

Additive:
MSG

Future activity for terrorists: Killing/torturing celebrities of the Tiger Woods caliber

Hygiene product that doesn't keep you from smelling like farts and beer: Tom's of Maine deodorant

Placebo shaped like a pitcher full of water: Brita

Way to be smooth in front of the ladies: Not puking

Word that you think makes you sound socially critical: Ironic

Buffet item: Jell-O

Football player: Michael Vick

Hollywood darling/nimrod: Ashton Kutcher

Movie candy: Good 'n' Plenty

Reading material: *Sports Illustrated*

Televised information providers: Weathermen

Record store on the whole fucking planet: Princeton Record Exchange, Princeton, NJ

Music industry trend: Slutty-whore pop singers

Expression of vanity: Camera phones

John Ritter performance: Every time he fell down before the time he fell down and died

Publicity: Testifying to the genius of the recently deceased

Effort to seem authentic: Hating Los Angeles

Opportunity of a lifetime: Roadie gigs

National pastime: Baseball

Insult to intelligence: "Safety" scissors

Metrosexual possession: Health insurance

Use of "Metrosexual": Every time it's used

Excuse for legalizing marijuana: Cancer treatments

God-given gift: Being able to handle your drugs/drinking

Technological advancement: Touch-tone dialing

First date: 9-11

Object of hatred: Cops

Restaurant: 7-11

Disguise for pure evil: 311

Excuse for mediocrity: Homage

Fascist dictator: Mussolini

Magician: David Blaine

Record liner note author:
David Fricke

Drink: Vanilla anything

New trend: Casual sex

Gift bag ingredient: Condoms

Fixation: *(tie)* Sex and Money

Facial hairstyles: The Grizzly Adams (aka The Will Oldham)

Perfection: *AdBusters*

Dictator: *Vice*

Insult: "I heard you play on a softball team"

Methods of transportation: Monster trucks

Place to visit while in New York: Bowlmore Lanes

Facial hair pattern: Frat goatee

Highly anticipated event: The next act of terrorism

Quasi political fanzine: *Punk Planet*

Made-up language: The secret elf-speak of Sigur Rós

Childhood diagnosis: A.D.D.

Convenient ethnic scapegoat: White men

Erogenous zone of a woman: Boobies

Erogenous zone of a man: Sense of humor

Liberal slogan: "Selected, not elected"

"Fish-in-a-Barrel" topics for comedians to use, which are considered irreverent elements of quips used by everyday people at the water cooler: *(five-way tie)* Jesus, Catholicism, Republicans, Satan and Smokin' Crack

Conservative slogans: *(tie)* "Osama, Yo Mama" and "Don't Blame Me, I Voted for Bush"

Unnecessary cause of death: Emphysema

Way to make people think you're interesting: Cite clinical depression

People to worship: Politicians

Art form: Virtuosity on any instrument

Destination of ex-pat Southerners: New York City

Genre to be obsessed with: Ska

Celebrity to be obsessed with and endlessly imitate: Elvis Presley

Indie rock fashion statement: Cheap Velcro shoes

Movie and subsequent sequels: *Matrix, Matrix Reloaded* and *Matrix Revolutions*

Physical attribute: Being tall

Schtick: *(tie)* Orchestrated controversy, and relentless sarcasm

Album you can't escape from on classic rock radio: Pink Floyd's *Dark Side of The Moon*

Pastime the public goes ape shit over: Sports

Use of a car: Daydreaming

Thing on television: Backup dancers

TV chef: *(tie)* Mario Batali and Emeril Lagasse

Beverage: Micro-brewed beer

Cuisine: New American

Holiday: New Year's Eve

Publicist: Nasty Little Man

Novelist: Don DeLillo

Sexual position: 69

Radio personality: Ira Glass

Starlet: Scarlett Johansson

Condiment: Salsa

Drug: Cocaine

Darrin: Dick Sargent

Larry: Hagman

Dick: See hand

Fabric: Denim

Death: Princess Di

Obituary: JFK

Bodily function: *(tie)* Shitting and orgasm

Western European country: Belgium

Chicago Cub: Sammy Sosa

Cartoon character: Hello Kitty

Instant orange drink mix: Tang

Condiment: Astroglide

Lifesaver: Butter rum

Synonym for pancake: Flapjack

Constellation: Orion

Invasion: British

Electrical current: Direct

Cartoon locale: Jellystone Park

Cartoon guest stars: Harlem Globetrotters

Cloud: Cirrus

Puzzle: Jigsaw

Manifestation of self-deprecation: Shame

Commandment: Coveting thy neighbor's wife

Charity: March of Dimes

Genetic defect: Down Syndrome

Underoo: Batman

Women's hair restraint: Scrunchee

Hope for the future: Children

Futile effort:
Resisting MySpace

Post-Warsaw Pact-era Czechoslovakian leader: Václav Havel

Man-made lake: Mead

Wagon: Radio Flyer

Tag: Freeze

Letter of the alphabet: C

Piece of living room furniture: Entertainment center

Euphamism for an entertainment center: "The Holodeck"

Tooth: Bicuspid

River: Colorado

Excuse: "I forgot"

Canadian: Paul Schaffer

Air filter: AC/Delco

Pseudo-shocking term for confusion: Clusterfuck

Symbol of male homosexuality: A lisp

Symbol of female homosexuality: Amy Ray

Ironic statement of this century: Moustache

Co-billing on a split 7": David Cross on the *Chunklet*-released David Cross/Les Savy Fav split single

Gyllenhaal: Maggie

False accusation for musicians: Child pornography

Redux of pointlessly competitive high school yearbook activity: Friendster

Celestial event of the last 59,619 years: Mars being closer to Earth than it's been in 59,619 years

Selective serotonin reuptake inhibitor: Paxil

Premeditated quirk: Pronouncing "schedule" like "shed-jool"

Book series people usually read because "it's much better than you'd expect": *Harry Potter*

Guitar activity: Playing guitar

Currency: Money

Ass-to-mouth scene: Scene 3 from *Weapons Of Ass Destruction*

Form of "comedy": Complaining about George W. Bush

Reason to live: The love of another human being

Sexual practice: The Dirty Sanchez

Ice cream: The marble slab kind

Musical genre: Alt.country

Confusing genre:
Twee pop

Spam: EXTEND YOUR ROCK_HARD MORTGAGE RATxz.*&_jgjo./.'_uwejhsxe

Expensive food: Monkfish liver

Long Gone John claim: "I haven't even heard 'Elephant'"

Assasinated U.S. president: Kennedy

Waste of so-called soul cleansing: Fasting

Sex aid: *(tie)* Ice cubes, candles, penis and vagina

Pseudo-hip goodbye gesture: "The Slide"

Weather condition: Hot

Religion: Buddhism

Vehicle: The SUV

Young Turk author: Jonathan Safran "I-got-$500,000-for-my-senior-thesis" Foer

Way to spend the hours of 9 a.m. to 5 p.m. on weekdays: *(tie)* Work and sleep

Grrrl: Kathleen Hanna

Element: Fire

Black rapper: Puffy

Sport: Skiing

Flash-in-the-pan fashion accessory: Foam-mesh trucker baseball cap with semi-ironic logo

Rating: Underrated

Toe: Pinkie

Ex-girlfriend: Julie

Font: Helvetica

Grievance: Taxes

Fear: Death

Dog: Labrador retriever

Record label: Matador

Sense: Smell

Smell: *(tie)* Rose and toast

Non-naturally occurring material: Polyurethane

Alternative-to-corporeal existence: Death

National comedian: Colin Quinn

International comedian: Eddie Izzard

Reason for an indie kid to grow a beard: Grandaddy

Political band: Super Furry Animals

Band who believes they're a political band: Radiohead

Recording engineer: Steve Albini

Penis: Jon Langford

White rapper: Bubba Sparxx

Decade: 1980s

Blind band: Blind Boys of Alabama

Non-profit religion: Atheism

Rock singer: Robert Plant

Thing to write a joke about: How women are different from men

Group to write a racial joke about: Mexicans

Reason to read *Chunklet*: Because Elyse on *America's Next Top Model* was reading a copy during an episode

Reason to become a comedian: Because you make your girlfriend and/or mother laugh

Reason to be an asshole: You're jealous of others

Ironic piece of wardrobe: 80s rock T-shirt

Pimp: Bishop Don Magic Juan

Holiday: Christmas

Profession-slash-profession: Musician-slash-Actor

Profitable religion: Judaism

Filmmaker: Wes Anderson

Condescending fat fuck: Michael Moore

Suffix: -ica

Necessity: Cell phone

Pants: Free Levis at SXSW

Fools: College grads

Form of reading: Books

Mimes: Insane Clown Posse

Penis privilege: Aim

Area code: 212

Celebrity appliance: The George Foreman grill

Part of pornography: The money shot

Common surgery: Wisdom teeth removal

Vacation spot: Cancun, Mexico

Adjective: Awesome

Bar-B-Que menu item: Ribs

Gen-X food: Ramen noodles

Cum rag/toilet paper: *NME*

Sexual stimulus: *Chunklet*

Life-giving gas: Oxygen

Kitschy interest: Mexican wrestling

Pyramid scheme: Christianity

Hair fad: The irony mullet

Waste of record buying money: *(tie)* Colored vinyl and multiple covers

Type of lesbian sex: None

Graven image: The Alabama courthouse Ten Commandments monument

Semi-annual chain restaurant special: Tony Roma's Endless Slab

Complaint: Gas prices

Hairpiece: Morrissey

Prefix: Post-

Penile implant: The bendable Gumby-style insert

Journalist excuse: Saying "alleged" or "reportedly"

Dis: Saying *Goo* was Sonic Youth's worst album

Praise: Anything referencing Nirvana

Rock "journalist": Sia Michael of *Spin*

Sexual fantasy: Threesomes

White irony rapper: Cex

Avenue for people with zero knowledge to make money on something rare: eBay

Mid-'90s, alt-rock feeling: Jaded

Cause: Fair trade Starbucks coffee bullshit

Laziness: Going with the drum machine

Country that purports to be mystical but is actually one giant bar/tourist trap: Ireland

Famous inventor of a device that's not even used anymore: Eli Whitney

City that's so dirty and expensive it's hard to imagine anyone wanting to live there: New York

Band position: Singer

Cause: Curing Cancer

Big, space-consuming home furnishing that everyone loves but are actually a pain in the ass to take care of: Plants

Religious leader who served only a month before dying but had his name swiped: John Paul I

Place to have sex if you don't mind getting seaweed in your ass: The beach

Illegal sport: Cockfighting

Drug to kick: Crack cocaine

Legal sport: Snowboarding

Food that takes too long to get to your table and requires a loan to pay for: Anything "gourmet"

Legendary pop artist who stole all his ideas from Bazooka gum wrappers: Roy Liechtenstein

Chunklet's *list of 1000 Unrelated Overrated Things*

Marauding force of the Early Christian era, not nearly as good as the Visigoths: The Ostrogoths

Gift idea that's worse than no gift at all: (three-way tie) An acre of the Antarctic, the Moon or a whole star

Indie label of the '90s that had precious few good bands: Simple Machines

Cartoon character: Jaded Robot

Director: Stanley Kubrick

Law: Smoking bans

Martyr: Joan of Arc

Guitarist: Jimi Hendrix

Indie-snob claim: "The Yeah Yeah Yeahs are totally ripping off Glass Candy"

New verb: TiVo'd

Magic trick: ProTools

Misinformation: Heavier vinyl means deeper grooves

Waste of space: (tie) One-sided vinyl and etched b-sides

Book: (tie) The Bible and On The Road

Rock musician of all time: Frank Zappa

Rock anthem: "Satisfaction"

Person who played on a Bowie record: Steve Ray

Plague of Jehovah: Locust

Noisy dude band: The Locust

Jazz musician: John Coltrane

Rock club: CBGB

Drum machine: Roland 808

Afro: ?uestlove

Sex act: Blowjob

Hunger blight: Ethiopia

Bloody windshield: Princess Diana's

Recording studio: Sunset Sound Factory

AIDS epidemic: South Africa

Piece of lawn equipment: Yard jockey

Enviro-friendly transportation: Walking

Attempt at genocide: The Holocaust

Civil rights leader: Martin Luther King, Jr.

Contemporary pop artist: Shepard Fairey

Potential serial rapist/Sports commentator: John Madden

Place to freak out with a rifle: High school

Amount of pot to buy: Quarter bag

Sexual abuse: (tie) Child and rape

Person who has his nipples pierced: Dave Navarro

Power Puff Girl: Buttercup

Delay pedal: Line 6 DL4 Delay Modeler

MTV DJ of all time: Iann Robinson

Prison tattoo received for killing a man: A tear underneath the eye

Dance party: Tigwas

City in Texas: Austin

Incense: Rain

Hat: Beret

Vibrator: The Rabbit

Technology: The Internet

Designer color: Celery

Area in Brooklyn: Williamsburg

New male cosmetic trait: Hairless chest

Ethnicity: Black, formerly caucasian, soon to be hispanic (also describes Michael Jackson)

Soy product: Tofutti

Cooler brand: Igloo

Christian racket: Christmas

Music festival: South by Southwest

On-line activity: Friendster

Styx song: "Come Sail Away"

Way to kill bugs: Stepping on them

Activity while on-line: Jerkin' it

Beat-off publication: Victoria's Secret catalogue

Way to describe a burrito: "As big as your head"

Uncomfortable moment in your life: Mom catches you masturbating to a porn mag

Rock suicide/murder: Kurt Cobain

Frozen dairy treat: Fudgesicle

Female musician: Norah Jones

Alcoholic beverage: Beer

Lunch snack: Lunchables

American president: (tie) Ronald Reagan and Franklin D. Roosevelt

Primary color: Red

Supermodel: Tyra Banks

Brand of beer: Budweiser

Semiprecious stone: Turquoise

Degenerative disease: Lupus

Norse god: Odin

Temp job: File clerk

Viking: Erik the Red

Color of snot: Clear

Piercing: Belly button

Oil: 10W30

Road sign: Stop

Hot button topic: Religion

Snack cake: Twinkie

Libation: **Beer**

Waste of money: **Cocaine**

Wedding accessory: White rice

Reason to get hitched: "For the kids"

Muffin: Lemon poppy seed

Designer appliqué: Daisies

Indian food: Saag Paneer

Asian-American dressmaker: Vera Wang

Eskimo word for snow: Aput

Outdated aerobic workout: Jazzercise

Synonym for "bald": Chrome-dome

Macy's elf Christmas humor story: David Sedaris's

Actor-turned-activist: Alec Baldwin

A.A. Milne character: Tigger

Nature photographer: Ansel Adams

***Three's Company* star:** Chrissy

Ex-pat: Ernest Hemingway

Radio show: "A Prairie Home Companion"

Artificial fruit flavor: Cherry

Poster artist: Frank Kozik

Pilgrimage destination: Mecca

Refrigerator item: Baking soda

Jell-o product: Tapioca

Horse by-product: Glue

Constitutional amendment: The sixth — right to due process of law

Branch of government: Executive

Surgical enhancement: Breast enlargement

Geometric structure: Pyramid

Kitchen item made of plastic: Saran Wrap

Prime number: 47

Crustacean: Lobster

Required Shakespeare reading assignment: *Romeo & Juliet*

Problem in denture commercials: (tie) Corn on the cob and fennel seed

African tourist trap: King Tut's Tomb

Microsoft program: PowerPoint

Architectural style: Bauhaus

Non-American revolution: The French Revolution

Teenage Mutant Ninja Turtle: Michelangelo

Office supply: Post-it note

Pop star: Hillary Duff

Vietnam War movie: *Platoon*

Chunklet's *list of 1000 Unrelated Overrated Things*

Method to get around a cemetery: Golf cart

Syndicated newspaper column: Dear Abby

Character actor: Charles Durning

Burt Reynolds movie filmed in Atlanta: *Sharky's Machine*

Nationality for organized crime: Italian

Trench coat manufacturer: London Fog

Beef alternative: Buffalo

Contemporary black comedian: Dave Chapelle

Clint Eastwood quote: "Make my day!"

Suffragist: Susan B. Anthony

Ass kisser: That guy in accounting

New York City tourist attraction: Statue of Liberty

State in the Union: California

Religious affiliation of comedy writers: Judaism

Pencil lead: Number two

Type of people: Old

Non-Cirrus cloud formation: Nimbus

Children's toy: Tickle Me Elmo

Berry: Snozberry

SUV: Pontiac Aztek

Color of poo: Green

Reindeer: Blitzen

80s puzzle: Rubik's Cube

Hot sauce: Texas Pete

Sexual harassment case: Anita Hill vs. Clarence Thomas

Nose-picking finger: Index

Way to get cancer: Second-hand smoke

Subtle smile: Mona Lisa

School House Rocks cartoon: "Conjunction Junction"

Non-sequitur to "Damn, yo' cat stank!": "Quit lookin'!"

Company expense account: Petty cash

Sperm donor: David Crosby

Misspelling: Affect vs. effect

Neil Young album: *Harvest*

Way to take a shit: Sitting down

Kool-Aid flavor: Purplesaurus Rex

Sidekick: Robin

Voltage: 110

N-word: Not

Way to extract information from a spy: Truth serum

Place to hit a pirate with a dart: Wooden peg leg

Martial Art school: Ninjitsu

Way to take down an attacker: Rackin' 'em in the balls

Rite of passage: Teenage sex

Traffic violation: Speeding

School lunchroom diversion: Spitballs

Thing to say while having an orgasm: (three-way tie) "Mommy!?," "Oh, shit!" and "Dude!"

Figure on the Wall of Respect (on 5th Avenue in Birmingham, Alabama): Person playing hide 'n' go seek behind a tree

Member of Talking Heads: Jerry Harrison

Seafaring people: Polynesian

Band from Buffalo, New York: The Goo Goo Dolls

Humanitarian: Mother Theresa

Part of making money: Not having the time to spend it

Scene in *Red Dawn*: (tie) C. Thomas Howell drinking blood and some dude pissing in the radiator

Part of being American: "Bein' free, motherfucker!"

Technique for staying warm: Wearing clothes

Way to kill random people in a crowd: Pipe bomb

Thing to do during a riot: Throw rocks at cops

Item in The Grit Cookbook: Grit-style tofu

Item sold on eBay: One-penny CDs

Cartoon style that couldn't make the Family Circus cut: Pretentious *New Yorker* magazine doodles

Reason to be burnt at the stake: Being a witch

Form of accidental death: Bear attack

Historical figure who believed that rain follows military battle: Plutarch

Type of school bus: Short

Handicap: Quadriplegism

Star Wars hero: Han Solo

Sleeping position: Fetal

Dr. Who doctor: Tom Baker

70s bikini poster: Farrah Fawcett

Salad dressing: Ranch

City inside another city: Decatur, Georgia

Studio: 54

White bread: Wonder

Hippie fuck scent: Patchouli

Dwarf: Grumpy

Degree for hippies to get: Massage therapy

Fart law: "He who smelt it, dealt it"

Weather scam: Rainmaking potions

Cartoon character billionaire: Richie Rich

Band named after a David Cronenberg movie: *The Brood*

Subliminal imagery: "Sex" in the ice cubes

NBC television show: *Friends*

Government ban on free speech: The "Don't Call" telemarketing list

Monty Python movie prop: The Holy Hand Grenade

Form of propulsion: Steam engine

President of France: Charles de Gaulle

Visual element in show flyers: Skulls

Fire tragedy: (tie) House burning down and full-body third degree burns

Restaurant motif: *Star Wars* theme

Star Wars tragedy: Restaurant motif

Catholic church name: St. Joseph's

Hollywoodiscalling.com celebrity: Brian "Kato" Kaelin

Post-makeup Kiss song: "Lick It Up"

Ancient cult: Minoan Snake Cult

On-screen death: Bambi's mother

Beauty mark: Mole à la Cindy Crawford

Single-celled organism: Amoeba

Direction: North by northeast

Urban hairstyle on a white person: Corn rows

After-school special: *Angel Dusting*

Writing implement: Sharpie (all except the silver metallic one)

Horror novelist: Dean Koontz

Quaker: (tie) The man on the oatmeal box and Richard Nixon

Clover: 4-leafed clover

Transport system: Black holes

Science-fiction creature: Sandworms

True cannibal story: Donner Pass

Objectionist: Ayn Rand

Cartwright: Little Joe

M&M color: Blue

Black Flag song: "Slip It In"

Spice: Paprika

MICHAEL ANTHONY IS A PUPPET BITCH WITH A BAD MULLET

a.k.a. The 50 cool and not so cool things for a bass player to do

by Curt Wells (bass player) • illustration by Aye Jay Morano

50 NOT-SO-COOL THINGS

1. One word: Peavey.
2. Even considering owning a 5 string bass.
3. Wanking on a fretless bass.
4. Chaining more than one distortion box.
5. Envelope filters.
6. Any amp with less than 100 watts.
7. Wearing your bass too high like your some '80s British new wave Euro-fag guy.
8. Raving on and on about how great the dead guy from Metallica was.
9. Anything stereo.
10. Using the term "work" to describe your music.
11. Becoming a bass player because you suck as a lead guitarist.
12. Holding your bass vertically during a crescendo.
13. Putting one foot on the monitor.
14. Subscribing to *Bass Player Magazine*.
15. Using words like 'warmth' and 'punch.'
16. Using a graphic EQ.
17. Complaining about chicks going for the lead singer instead of you.
18. Being Michael Anthony.
19. Playing with power tools.
20. The ol 'cigarette in the headstock' bit.
21. Knowing more than two Primus riffs.
22. Actually playing Primus riffs in front of people.
23. New age jazz.
24. Fusion jazz.
25. Any jazz that uses an electric bass period.
26. Considering going to the GIT (Guitar Institute of Technology).
27. Iceman, Explorer or Flying V basses.
28. Anything MIDI.
29. Solos.
30. Asking the singer to make sure he announces your name during that breakdown so you can solo.
31. Getting behind the lead guitarist while he's soloing and making that 'whoa yeah!' face.
32. Anything Ibanez.
33. String lubricant.
34. Going shirtless.
35. Being overly influenced by anybody.
36. The Chapman Stick.
37. Spend more than $12 on a strap.
38. Being a movie star, and playing bass for a lousy band like Dogstar.
39. 8 string basses.
40. Being in a top 40 band and act like your musical input is relevant to anything.
41. Going to court to gain the rights to your band's name after everyone else has quit.
42. Filling a Jack Daniels bottle with iced tea and taking on a 'I may be the bass player, but I party harder than anyone else in this band' persona.
43. Telling jokes on stage.
44. Studying scales.
45. I can't believe I got up to 45 without mentioning slap'n'pop funk music. Playing slap'n'pop funk music.
46. Anything with a zebra pattern.
47. Acting like you can tell the difference between different exotic wood necks.
48. Bringing your girlfriend to the recording session, and bitching about things in front of her so she is on your side in the 'they don't appreciate me' moments of frustration.
49. Having a nickname in parenthesis between your first and last name.
50. Existing.

50 SEMI-COOL THINGS

1. Making a pawn shop bass into a fretless by removing the fret wire.
2. Using the thickest four strings of a five string pack and tuning down to B.
3. Stealing strings from a band with a string endorsement.
4. Steve Harris.
5. A distortion pedal before the envelope filter.
6. Quoting Derek Smalls.
7. Steinberger, baby, Steinberger!
8. Putting both feet on the monitor.
9. Having a sandwich on your amp for the times where the lead guitarist is taking too long to tune.
10. Playing with non-powered tools.
11. Power chords.
12. Duct tape on everything.
13. That time John Entwhistle played skeet with his gold records in *The Kids Are Alright*.
14. Quitting the Rolling Stones.
15. Being in a rockabilly band and not having any tattoos or acting like a total jackass.
16. Being polite.
17. Heckling at a in-store seminar that features the bass player from Bon Jovi.
18. The Hamer 12-string Bass!
19. Outliving everybody in your band.
20. The new 'bottle rocket in the headstock' bit.
21. Voting for Phil Collins in a 'Drummer of the Year' poll to screw things up.
22. Pink fur covered combo amps.
23. Writing to *Bass Player Magazine* thanking them for that insightful article on Michael Anthony.
24. Becoming a better record producer than everybody else in your band.
25. Telling drummer jokes on stage.
26. Being overtly homosexual.
27. One word: Lemmy.
28. Knowing who James Jamerson and Carol Kaye were.
29. Playing a Travis Bean bass.
30. Poking your headstock into a bandmate's ass when least expected.
31. Facing your amp the entire show.
32. Using a 10 foot coiled cable and standing 9 feet from your amp.
33. Not using any stomp boxes.
34. Going pants-less.
35. Being taller than the guitarist.
36. Playing so hard that you break the strings before they really need changing.
37. Being a girl.
38. Staying sober for a least a little while.
39. Laughing at a Trace Elliot owner that refers to his amp as a 'rig.'
40. Asking a Trace Elliot owner how much he spent on his 'rig,' and then laughing even harder.
41. Bathing.
42. Trying to avoid writing punk rock operas or working for Perry Farrell.
43. Quitting Magnapop.
44. Being a more successful solo artist than your bandmates, and carrying on even after your sister gets busted for drugs.
45. Listening to what the drummer is playing, for chrissake.
46. Sneaking a dead 9-volt into the lead guitarist's wireless unit just before the big show.
47. Carrying your own gear.
48. Showing up at the next practice with a banjo, and excitedly telling bandmates "I decided to move the sound in a new direction."
49. Chalking up indie cred points by writing articles for *Chunklet*.
50. Playing the bass line from 'Groove Is In The Heart' at every opportunity.

OVERRATED ACTORS!

The top 20 good movies that were nearly ruined by one person

by Patrick Gough • collage by Mark Wasserman

KING KONG

The 1977 remake featured Charles Grodin as the oil-thirsty baddy, a hirsute Jeff Bridges as his paleontologist foil, a really cool ape, and a good story, in what could've been an awesome film if it weren't for **Jessica Lange** horribly stinking up the joint in her role as the object of Kong's desire. Somehow over the years, Lange learned enough about acting to work her way up to an Academy award, but you'd never know it from her debut, in which she does enough unconvincing fainting and interspecies flirting to effectively destroy the flick.

PULP FICTION

It's regarded as a groundbreaking film, and in many ways it is innovative and entertaining, but **Quentin Tarantino** nearly renders his own movie unlikable with his ill-advised portrayal of the character who is upset because his hit men friends brought a dead body to his house. Tarantino's amphetamine-induced, N-bomb-dropping, over-agitated, over-the-top performance is a loud thunk in an otherwise snazzy picture.

CASINO

At three hours or so, this film is about an hour too long, especially since the final third veers from the story about mobsters in Vegas to focus on **Sharon Stone**'s coked-up, jewelry-hoarding hustler. It's enjoyably standard Scorsese fare until Stone dominates the final scenes with her (pardon the pun) overblown antics. Critics at the time called her portrayal gutsy and realistic, worthy of the Oscar she received. But it's really the most obvious bit of evidence yet that the Academy is completely full of shit.

BRIDGET JONES'S DIARY

What's the big deal? A mediocre script and mediocre enthusiasm from perennial Brit-studs Hugh Grant and Colin Firth should be accompanied by a mediocre leading lady. But apparently they couldn't find a suitably chubby English actress to dredge this flick from the doldrums; they had to get an American—the marginally talented **Rene Zellweger**—and stuff her with Chips Ahoy until she looked like any other hag from the Home Counties. It just doesn't work.

12 MONKEYS

One of Terry Gilliam's finest works is helped by a decent script, good special effects, and an appropriately confused/desperate performance by Bruce Willis. But how did **Brad Pitt** earn a Best Supporting Actor nod for his slap-happy, scene-hogging, indulgent turn as a mentally ill rich-boy terrorist? Pitt's not even slightly grasping the role with the excessive shouting, face-making, and loony-tune antics that would fit in better with a Mel Brooks send-up or Saturday Night Live skit than in this otherwise passably macabre sci-fi thriller. While we're at it, let's thank Brad for nearly ruining *Snatch* and *The Devil's Own*, too.

FROM HELL

This sufficiently spooky treatment of the Jack the Ripper legend features a reputable cast, including Johnny Depp, Ian Holm, Robbie Coltrane, and, um, **Heather Graham**. She's fine in films where she doesn't have many lines, like *Boogie Nights* and *Goldmember*, so this movie should serve as a memo to Hollywood execs to not cast her in anything that requires speaking at all—much less in a fake Cockney accent. Depp's accent is fine—why can't she get it together? Because she's crap.

ROUNDERS

Speaking of bad accents, **John Malkovich** does the worst Russian accent ever, even worse than that corny uncle of yours who likes to imitate Boris from Rocky & Bullwinkle. Matt Damon and Ed Norton are great, and the story is suspenseful, but Malkovich's Oreo-twisting card shark saps his scenes of their energy. Come to think of it, Malkovich is overrated in general; he overdoes it in everything: *The Killing Fields, Dangerous Liaisons*, you name it. He just hogs the frame and oozes sleaze. You could say that he can't be that bad; after all, he was a good enough sport to portray himself in *Being John Malkovich*. But he's probably an arrogant shit in real life who just loved the idea of a whole movie being named after him.

STAR WARS: THE PHANTOM MENACE

God, where to begin with the mistakes George Lucas made in bringing Episodes I and II to the screen? But is there a person in the world over the age of nine who thought that the shuffling, "yes, massa!" character **Jar Jar Binks** was a good idea? If one person (or digitized entity) *had* to be on this list, it's him.

JURASSIC PARK

What could've been a fun, mindless Saturday matinee of watching dinosaurs romp around an island eating people was pretty much dampened by **Jeff Goldblum**, who smirks his way ironically through the whole thing. Now irony is good, and so is Jeff Goldblum sometimes, but even without all the bogus chaos theory his character spews, his far-too-self-aware portrayal of the eccentric scientist is just too weird and out of synch with the movie.

DOGMA

The weakest of Kevin Smith's efforts ends with an icing-on-the-turd cameo by **Alanis Morissette** as God. What, George Burns wasn't available? Though regarded as a "singer" and not really an "actor" (big clue there, Kevin), it's hard to resist the chance to give a jackboot to the ribs of this limp affair. Time to retire Jay and Silent Bob, too.

FIGHT CLUB

Okay, Brad Pitt is fine in this one, but why is **Helena Bonham Carter** slumming in this picture? She's a great actor, but will forever be associated with prissy Merchant/Ivory films, and is therefore ineffective as the degenerate self-help groupie she plays. Meat Loaf's man-boobs were more compelling in the picture.

GODFATHER III

This film might have found some apologists on the strength of the first two installments, but the blatant nepotism that led to **Sophia Coppola's** appearance in the movie is what's legendary. Every time she opens her mouth on screen, you just want to put your face in your hands and cry.

MUCH ADO ABOUT NOTHING

Another decent Kenneth Branagh adaptation features nice scenes of Tuscany, Emma Thompson wearing too much bronzer, and—hold onto your hats—**Keanu Reeves**. If you've never seen this fiasco, consider yourself fortunate, and rest assured that this buffoon is every bit as incompetent at reading Shakespeare as you'd imagine. Michael Keaton is no bargain either as the Constable, but at least his part is *supposed* to be comic relief.

THE ROYAL TENENBAUMS

Kind of like in *Fight Club*, **Gwyneth Paltrow** is woefully miscast as the moody, 9-fingered playwright sister. She's inoffensive in the movie, but that's not good enough in a film in which all the other performances of the ensemble cast are so great that it's easy to forget Paltrow is in the lineup.

PHILADELPHIA

He's one of Hollywood's nice guys, and a bit of a sacred cow to critics. And it's not very politically correct to pooh-pooh films whose subject matter pertains to homosexuality or AIDS. But you know what? Screw all that, because **Tom Hanks'** performance as the dying lawyer in this film is totally unremarkable. It's just the theme of the movie and the lemming-like social "consciousness" of Hollywood ribbon-wearers that garnered Hanks the Oscar. And the choice of Hanks for the role is offensive to begin with, because the movie-going audience knows Hanks is straight, so he was safe for producers to go with. But what if they'd gotten a real-life, *flaming* gay guy to do the role? Would audiences have reacted the same way had Harvey Fierstein been the star? Absolutely no fucking way.

MAN IN THE IRON MASK

Could've been okay if you're into Gabriel Byrne, lard-ass frog Gérard Depardieu, or swishy musketeer-type stuff. But double smack-downs go to **Leonardo Di Caprio** for his whiny turn as both King Louis XIV and his beleaguered twin. As the first movie he made after the mega-bore *Titanic*, Di Caprio was bound to get tons of screen time, but it's for exactly that reason that this movie bombed so badly. His screeching petulance and slithering "who's the mack?" over-confidence must've been a huge irritation to all the other seasoned actors on the set.

GHOSTBUSTERS

It was a fun movie growing up, and would have been even more fun were it not for killjoy love interest **Sigourney Weaver**. Yeah, she's supposed to be the straight man opposite Bill Murray, but Harold Ramis did that role perfectly fine, and Weaver's tight-lipped bitchy persona was more suited to the role she had opposite Melanie Griffith in *Working Girl* than to light-hearted fare with giant marshmallow men and ectoplasm.

BATMAN & ROBIN

George Clooney is gritting his teeth throughout the film like he can't believe he got hornswoggled into this dud. It's easy to have this image of him going out on a bender, waking up the next day, reading *Variety* through bloodshot eyes, and realizing to his horror that he must've been completely wasted when he signed the contract. This kind of thing must happen all the time in Hollywood. Admittedly, Tim Burton's first two *Batmans* with Michael Keaton were fun, but Clooney knows he's totally wrong for the title role, and doesn't even try to salvage it.

GLORY

In spite of what became an impressive Broadway and film career, in 1990, when *Glory* was released, **Matthew Broderick** was still too one-dimensional to carry the burden of playing the white leader of an all-black Civil War regiment. And there is more to it than only being four years removed from Ferris Bueller: It's that the supporting cast of Morgan Freeman, Denzel Washington, and others acted circles around him. Broderick didn't have the appropriate facial hair, much less the bravado, to convince audiences that he was something other than the smirking wiseass he'd been typecast as up to that point. True, the colonel he plays was only supposed to be 23, and therefore green and insecure. But there had to be someone more convincingly heroic to play that part—maybe his lieutenant Cary Elwes?

FIFTH ELEMENT

Kind of a fancifully underrated movie with its Jean-Paul Gauthier-designed costumes, cheeky post-modern randomness, and good use of loudmouth Chris Tucker. But the picture stalls out whenever brainless eye-candy **Milla Jovovich** is on the screen. And *Joan of Arc* was doomed anyway, but she took what could've been a respectable biography and turned it into a farce. Director Luc Besson should have been publicly flogged at the premiers of both of these movies for continuing to give this flatlining ex-model paychecks and an excuse to appear on talk shows. *[The fact that Besson was putting it in her is no excuse either. —ed.]*

Q: Which is the overrated one?

THE MOST OVER-RATED RECORDS IN ROCK

an OVERRATED INTRODUCTION to the most OVERRATED RECORDS in rock

intro by Brian Teasley • collage by Andrew Quinn • illustrations by Aye Jay Morano and Matt Loomis

We could never have imagined that we would be commissioned by the RIAA to come up with a definitive list of the most overrated records of all time. We never expected that the highest-ranking officials of an industry that had always made us feel like outsiders would honor us with such faith and recognition.

Our being given not only a hefty bag of dimes, but also official recognition, to do what we have always done (while losing tons of money) is unfathomable. What were once half-thought-out drunken ramblings will now rest in the archives of academia. The thought of future generations of music historians studying our text as a Bible of definitive judgements is utterly astounding. We are now officially the James Lipton of the rock critic world; for this, dear reader, benefactor, or admirer, we thank you.

Any effort to define exactly what makes a record overrated brings to mind Justice Potter Stewart's much denounced "I know it when I see it" definition of pornography. Nonetheless, it is doubtless true that love or hate for a certain piece of music results from combination of reason and emotion; thus, indeed, "I know it when I hear it." It could be called an obvious abstract. When a record (or song) reaches the point of universal acceptance from both popular and critical circles, it stands to reason that the stench of mass marketing would be blatantly fucking obvious to anyone with a sense of discernment. Sure, logic dictates that everyone will declare different boundaries according to their individual tastes, but, while most people just have their fingers up their own asses, we truly have our finger on the pulse of what

the top 20

as written by the Chunklet staff

#1

THE BEATLES
Sgt. Pepper's Lonely Hearts Club Band

No, it was *not* the best Beatles album… not by a long shot. One of the cornerstones of The Beatles' popularity was that they were not ashamed to admit that they smoked, drank, (and later on used drugs—just check "Cold Turkey" for that) or came from Liverpool and had funny Northern accents. John Lennon once said that they wanted to let kids know it was okay to talk like they did, and they didn't have to alter their accents or selves to meet society's needs. So what we have here is the Beatles pretending to be another band, and assembling a set of less-than-great songs. (It is also the one album in the Beatles catalogue that now sounds dated, overproduced, and doesn't transcend the notion of sounding strictly of a particular era.) "Fixing A Hole" and "When I'm 64" are easily the best songs on the album, the former for the endless debate about the potential heroin reference (still an active argument today about songs—just read up on "There She Goes" by The La's, also from Liverpool), and the latter because it was actually written about 1961 and even performed by the Fab Four a cappella at The Cavern Club whenever their equipment would break down. It also could have fit, with a different arrangement, comfortably on either *Rubber Soul* or even *The White Album*. (And, actually, the songs that have aged best and proven to be worth the hype from these sessions didn't even make the cut for the album: "Strawberry Fields Forever," "Penny Lane," and "Only A Northern Song.") So what is the hoopla over this particular record? Perhaps the "sensation" that it caused when it was released? In retrospect, had Brian Wilson come out of his acid/paranoia haze to finish *Smile* and release its brilliance to the public before the turn of the century, we maybe would have been playing by a different set of rules here 35 years later. (The most eye-opening observation about *Sgt. Pepper* I've ever heard came from Tim Morse, former drummer for Anal Cunt: "Man, *Sgt. Pepper* was just The Beatles trying to outdo *Pet Sounds* and failing.")

NICK BLAKEY

is great—or, at least, what isn't. C'mon, when your dorky ex-frat boy/sorority girl co-worker is talking about the aesthetic virtues of Slint in the break room, you know it's time to bust out the Merzbox.

The tree in the unpopulated forest makes a sound when it falls; I know because I was there with an All-Access Pass. Truly great records always have a measure of timelessness, but let us not forget that a record's context plays a monumental role in determining whether it is celebrated, and whether it becomes overrated.

Crudely put, overrated records are a lot like high school pussy, or, more precisely, like the one slutty cheerleader who is about a year and a half ahead of the adolescent fuck-curve. You know… there's much locker room excitement over the ease of getting laid from a post-pubescent pushover, but the more people that hit that shit, the more ragged-out and possibly disease-ridden it becomes. Rarely does the excitement of knocking boots beneath the bleachers persist after the aforementioned arm candy pops a bun out of the oven in eleventh grade. Records are much the same way. Once you see some all-too-willing Senior Editor of a mainstream rock magazine wax anecdotal on VH1 about Marvin Gaye's "What's Going On," it's hard to listen to the music without thinking of couples dancing in their socks at a loft party like they were in a fucking deleted scene on the *Ghost* DVD.

The most annoying companion to "overratedness" is the epidemic of "Greatest Records of All Time" lists. These lists, like Rolling Stone's Top 500 Albums and VH1's Top 100 Albums, merely serve to codify the canon of supposedly great albums. One of the many comical aspects of these inventories of "Great Records for Dummies" is the phenomenon of joe-dumb-ass rock journalists, who haven't any significant knowledge of jazz, soul, hip-hop or other non-rock genres, fulfilling quotas with all the white-bread subtlety of a music critic's affirmative action board. Why else does completely obvious shit like Miles Davis's missionary position smooth jazz bargain blowout *Kind of Blue* end up on a list that is otherwise dominated by rock music? Oh, it was a spontaneous reaction to the frenzy of modern be-bop? So are the majority of my morning bowel movements.

We all know how these stupid fucking things go by now. The Beatles take half of the top ten. *London Calling* and *Pet Sounds* are situated toward the top.

Exile in Guyville makes it in because some Brooklyn fucko journalist thinks he may get to meet Liz Phair at the next SXSW. No one knows shit about hip-hop, so they throw in De La Soul's *Three Feet High and Rising*—Christ, why don't they just go ahead and put Urban Dance Squad in there?

Rolling Stone's December 2003 "Special Collector's Issue" of the 500 Greatest Records of All Time places The White Stripes' *Elephant* (less than a year old at the time of the list's publication) at #390, far ahead of Gram Parsons's *Grievous Angel* (#429), Eno's *Here Come the Warm Jets* (#436), and Big Star's *#1 Record*, which is ironically #438. Pavement's *Slanted and Enchanted*, which is certainly an influential record in certain circles, is at #134, while the Velvet Underground's *White Light/White Heat* is at #292. That's like some idiot mall kid hearing the MC5 and saying, "Cool, they sound like the Foo Fighters."

The assholes who compiled the Rolling Stone list were so goddamned diplomatic that they included two Def Leppard albums: one with a two-armed Rick Allen (#384 *Pyromania*), and one with a one-armed Rick Allen (#472 *Hysteria*). Boo-hoo, he lost his fucking arm and now has to electronically trigger the snare with his left foot. Fuck if I'd blow my ass on a record whose top single was "Pour Some Sugar On Me." What about the paraplegic guy who played the guitar with his feet for the Pope? How come he's not in there? He hammers-on with his toenails, for Christ's sake!

Yet fear not, ye true of heart. In what is otherwise an Armageddon of trailer taste, we are here for you, the jaded asshole that is reading our magazine in the store—you cheap, unsupportive fuck! Thank God for *Chunklet*, or, better yet, have him thank us. We have finally built a fortress that is impenetrable to diplomacy. There is no sanctuary for ham-fisted zealots within these pages. Maybe we can't take you all to the Promised Land, but at least we can show you where it ain't. Yet another list, you might say; but it's our list this time. We're sick of your hippie-era *Cream* magazine bullshit. It's time to reanalyze everything, and, don't worry, we know just the people for the job... that's us, you knob-twiddler! You just keep transcribing Lester Bangs's elementary school reports, and we'll all be fine without you. The RIAA believes in us. So should you.

#2
THE BEACH BOYS
Pet Sounds

The harmonies are stellar. The arrangements are inventive. And there are some kooky instruments being played—wild! But how did this album become the touchstone for hipster cool? I can't remember the name of any of the songs, or even hum a single melody from this "concept album." Well, maybe "Wouldn't It Be Nice," but give me some of those surf tunes with the *real* rock'n'roll in 'em. With this faux legitimacy, all of a sudden people who didn't know anything about music could sound educated by saying stuff like, "Oh, the harmonies on 'Wouldn't It Be Nice' are so rich and multi-layered." Really? The best line I heard about it was when the 4-CD *Pet Sounds Sessions* came out—like this 30-minute, masturbatory, Beatles-beating exercise deserves 320 minutes of anyone's time—and I was waiting outside a Stereolab show and heard one hipster exclaim, "Man, have you checked out the stereo version of *Pet Sounds* on that?" (Fool, it's always been in stereo! Typical feel-like-you-know-about-music-from-liking-*Pet Sounds*-syndrome.) To which the other indie rocker replied, "Yeah, but dude, have you heard the *mono* version?!" Dude! Mono! That's so sixties! Here's the basic equation, in my mind: The Beatles make *Rubber Soul*, Brian Wilson makes *Pet Sounds* to retaliate. Then the Beatles make *Revolver*, the best album ever, and Brian Wilson goes crazy. 'Nuff said. There's your indie prophet, crying alone in his room. Also, Brian Wilson sings the entire record a quarter-step off-key, and *no one seems to care! What the hell?* They wrote some good melodies, but it sounds like he gulped a quart of whole milk right before they went into the studio.

ALEXANDER STIMMEL & JULIANNE SHEPARD

#3
THE ROLLING STONES
Exile On Main Street

I hear endlessly and infinitely how great this Stones record is. There would be no Come, Royal Trux, or later period Primal Scream without *Exile*, but like *Sgt. Pepper's*, this notion has been beaten so far into and through the ground that now lesser trumped albums such as *Goat's Head Soup* and *Tattoo You* come off as more satisfying because not everyone and their local critic have jumped all over it. Has it struck anyone as superficial and ironic that the very English Rolling Stones made their great tribute to Southern American blues... in a mansion in the south of France? Brian Jones was the blues nut, you freaks, and he was two years dead and gone by the time they started recording this (not to mention that their big return to the blues album, *Sticky Fingers,* was the first one recorded after Jones's departure). There is no arguing that *Exile* is a great record, and there are some bona fide Stones classics on here—"Happy," "I Just Wanna See His Face," "Tumblin' Dice," "Shine A Light," and "Ventilator Blues" among them. But so many people's notions of the Stones begin and end here, without them ever having checked out the other aforementioned albums plus *Some*

Girls and the UK versions of *Aftermath* and *Out of Our Heads*, and this is why *Exile* made this list. For some, the Stones don't even exist before *Let it Bleed*, and that is just plain sick (though not as sick as paying scalpers over $1000 for tickets to the upcoming 40th Anniversary Tour). With five great songs and 13 yawners, this album is so overrated that both Pussy Galore and Liz Phair covered it. Fuck you, Mick and Keith. Die! It's because of you guys that rock 'n' roll social security won't be around for younger musicians like Jon Spencer.

JOE GARDEN, CHRIS MCGARVEY & NICK BLAKEY

#4

DAVID BOWIE
Ziggy Stardust & the Spiders from Mars

Because everything from *Stationtostation* through *Scary Monsters* is so fucking incredible and still does not get the kind of recognition *Ziggy* gets. Because *Ziggy* is a sugar-coated version of what he would later do better on *Aladdin Sane* (and nothing on *Ziggy*, barring perhaps "Suffragette City," matches the sheer anger and vile acidity of such tracks as "Cracked Actor"). Because the hair really doesn't work. Because his later persona, "The Thin White Duke," was much cooler and far scarier. Because in retrospect the central band unit Bowie used from 1976-81 of Carlos Alomar, George Murray, and Dennis Davies with guest lead guitarists like Robert Fripp and Adrian Belew far outshines in interest *The Spiders From Mars* fair and square, all due respect to the late Mick Ronson aside. Because Bowie didn't make a bad album until *Never Let Me Down* (*Young Americans* notwithstanding), and even that turd far outshines *Black Tie White Noise*.

NICK BLAKEY

#5

R.E.M.
Murmur

R.E.M. may one day actually be able to give the Beatles a run for their money as most overrated band ever—that is, unless they insist on continuing with their current Genesis-like incarnation where there are more studio musicians in the room than actual members of the band whenever they record or tour. I can keenly remember the first time I heard *Murmur*, R.E.M.'s debut LP in the mid-80s. It was sort of like a breath of fresh air, what with the jangly guitars and the mumbled, understated singing. Who knew then that they'd become as massively annoying as they have, or that that record would sound so horrible all these years later? And it really does sound horrible. It sounds poorly recorded, muddled, and pretentious as hell. Wasn't punk supposed to wipe out arty rock music? And Michael Stipe manages to be even more obnoxious and unnecessary than Mick Jagger. What an accomplishment. Bill Berry seems a very smart man these days. A horrid influence on a generation of shitty college "rock" dolts.

JOE SELBY & JULIANNE SHEPARD

THE 6THS
Wasp's Nest

Here's a novel idea. Let me get a bunch of my hipper-than-thou rock friends to guest sing my crappy songs with dorky instrumentation that some might find "charming" or "clever." Hell, I'll even guest sing one, and I wrote them, which will make it even funnier. Then I'll push my nerd glasses up, and pretend to cover "Crazy Rhythms" by the Feelies. However, most people don't get past track two before they eject the disc for its final destination as the third coaster on the other end of the couch...

JIM RAYMOND

AC/DC
Entire discography

Years ago, while discussing the band's last studio album, *Stiff Upper Lip*, Angus Young spoke to the accusation that AC/DC has made the same album 13 times. "That's a lie!" he protested, "we've made the same album 14 times!" That, people, is bald-faced fucking lie! If those too-cool-for-their-own-country Aussies made the same album 14 times, the rest of their catalog might live up to *Back in Black*. The truth is, while they've recycled rhythm figures and chord progressions too many times to count, the problem is much worse: aside from the whole of *Back in Black* and the odd gem, AC/DC can't write a song to save their miserable hides.

RANDY HARWARD

RYAN ADAMS
Gold

His albums are just as good as any other albums from the whiny, self-indulgent singer/songwriter genre. However, to compare him to Bob Dylan (as many critics do) is to trivialize the accomplishments of a cultural zeitgeist. The only thing Ryan Adams has in common with Dylan is an acoustic guitar. Sure, Dylan had his share of "love songs," but Dylan also wrote songs describing the struggles of the poor working class, as well as documenting the civil rights struggle. So, while "It Boy" Ryan Adams traipses blithely through the streets of New York lamenting a lost love—but professing his love for the Big Apple—Bob Dylan has us know that New York isn't so kind to those without a pretty face and a record contract:
"Well, it's up in the morning trying to find a job to work
Sit down in one place till your feet begin to hurt
If you got a lot of money, you can make yourself merry
If you don't have a nickel, it's the Staten Island Ferry"
— From "Hard Times in New York Town"

NEIL EBER
Rock And Roll

I don't know of one straight male that likes to listen to this pretty party-guitar Romeo. I don't care that he was in Whiskeytown. If anything, that just makes him more of a dick. Hey asshole, thanks for continuing to exploit the alt-country movement! Cowboys that cite the Sex Pistols and Black Flag as their influences, and play shit that sounds like fucking Buck Owens?! If I were from New York, I'd hate him even more for building up his already massive ego with a 9-11 tribute right off the bat. Shut your mouth, dipshit, and just give them the money.

DAG LUTHER GOOCH

AEROSMITH
Toys in the Attic

Compared to their later records, *Toys in the Attic* is a masterpiece. It's also their first record that sounded like something more than a lame Zeppelin rip-off. But one thing that is totally annoying about this album is the campy and overt sexual innuendoes that sound like a horny kid in junior high wrote them. Let me just whip out my ten-inch... record, that is. Indeed. "Uncle Salty,"

"Adam's Apple," "Walk This Way." That backstage boogie sure sets my ass on fire—like a cup of coffee washing down a hot sausage Po-Boy and a side of jalapeno poppers.

DAG LUTHER GOOCH

AIR
Moon Safari
I make television commercials for a living. Every time a client comes in and can't decide what music to put onto their commercial, they go through this exhausting explanation of what it should sound like. I then usually duck out in the middle and dredge up this record. They fall for it every time. It takes about 10 minutes to recreate an exact replica of every song on this record for any car, soap, beer or toilet paper spot that will ever come up. Worth listening to? Why not? Worth fawning over? No more than any needle drop music library.

DAG LUTHER GOOCH

The Virgin Suicides
This is probably the most appallingly unsuitable place to confess that I have killed someone, but presently I can't think of an apropos place—so here it is: my confession in wide-scale publication. When I was eight, my entire family gathered at Aunt Sarah's for our routine Easter dinner. She had just had a beautiful baby, who she and my Uncle named Ashley, some six weeks prior. After a day of eating marshmallow-filled peeps and hiding/finding eggs colored by the magic of Paas, everyone began to wind down and the baby was put to bed in the early evening. While the rest of the family was sitting around at the dining room table, I covertly sneaked into the baby's room and played with all the "little kid" toys. I began to spin her Winnie the Pooh mobile around to see how fast Tigger, Eeyore, and crew could go. The baby was startled by the noise whirling loudly over her tiny head in a wobbly counter-clockwise

direction. She began to scream like a cat whose tail had caught fire, and I was sure I was going to get in big trouble for even being in the baby's room in the first place. In the folly and sense-lessness of youth, I quickly put a pillow over her face and held it down until she stopped crying. She soon stopped kicking with her feet in their little footies, which were trying to desperately move the force of my much stronger arms. Like a Christian or someone who has fled a hit-and-run scene, I left the room and assumed all would be okay. That became the worst night of my life, or truth be known, my Aunt's and Uncle's—I was rather unaffected by the whole incident. Baby Ashley was soon found dead by my hysterically crying Aunt, and it was all blamed on crib death. I, the one who had inadvertently taken a life, went home and played Chopper Command on my Atari. I was never grounded or punished or found out in the least. I was never even questioned about the incident. No one has ever known otherwise. In absolute honesty, I have never admitted this to anyone. I suppose now I have. Thank you for letting me divulge this dark secret without judgment. Oh, about this Air soundtrack to the *Virgin Suicides*: nothing more than diet *Meddle*-era Pink Floyd served on a Lunchable cracker and shoved up a crib-dead baby's pussy. Hey, I know it's bad timing, but are you going to eat the cheese block in your Lunchable pack?

BRIAN TEASLEY

ALICE IN CHAINS
Dirt
When I was in the Navy this guy I shared a barracks room with would have "buds" over and they'd listen to this god-awful album and talk about how "dark" Layne Staley was while they played Everquest on separate computers. Grown men

who discuss the quality of the looting on imaginary islands in role-playing games seem like the appropriate demographic. I mean, somebody had to claim the crown once held by Dio.

BEN HELLMANN

AND YOU WILL KNOW US BY THE TRAIL OF DEAD
Madonna
I remember listening to this and thinking, oh, it's another one of those "noise is my beautiful self discovery" bands. I must have made a face like I had smelled microwaved shit when someone chimed in, "Dude, those guys totally go crazy and break their guitars on stage and stuff." These ass-wipes should have smashed their guitars in the studio while recording.

BOB SCHRINER

ANTIOCH ARROW
Gems of Masochism
Oooh, somebody want to play dress-up like Gene Loves Jezebel dry humping Adam and the Ants? Guess who it is? A bunch of fake hardcore goth-goobs from San Diego, Antioch Arrow—named after a fabled ancient Indian arrowhead jewel that was deemed to have great mystic powers bestowed on it by Chief Still Bull. Sound like some Jim Morrison bullshit? Well yeah, so does this band. How taxing is it on you to tour around the country playing house parties in the mid '90s while wearing paisley shirts and china doll makeup? Just ask Aaron Montaigne, who's cold kickin' it in Iraq and probably putting those industrial strength garbage bag twist ties around the wrist of some Iraqi family.
Lessons to be learned: A. There is no piano in punk rock (Don't fucking tell me a single note played over and over and mixed super

low is really having a piano and don't pull out some stupid no wave anomaly act, you putz!). B. No one is impressed if you can count to five or seven as opposed to four. C. Even pretentious mid '90s goth punk can spawn shit that's worse than itself (see the daunting influx of shitty goth/hardcore hybrids at an all ages club near you). If you like watching the *Lost Boys* while suffering from food poisoning by undercooked Mongolian Beef, then Antioch Arrow has some doom jams for the soundtrack.

BRIAN TEASLEY

ANTONY AND THE JOHNSONS
I Am A Bird Now
In 2003, I skipped my high school graduation to see Lou Reed on the *Raven* tour. I got in for free and went in with pretty low expectations. The ads in the paper promised an evening of "POE-try", so I assumed that I was going to be treated to a bunch of boring bullshit from Lou's most recent record. Nothing could have prepared me for the horror I was about to witness.
Lou opened with "Sweet Jane," and everything seemed to be okay. Lou was rather low-energy, but it wasn't terrible. I assumed that seeing Lou Reed was going to be okay. How wrong I was. Towards the end of the song, each member of Lou's band took a turn shouting "Sweet Jane!" The last person to chime in with his version was a pudgy, balding man with a ponytail who was awkwardly writhing around at the back of the stage. He let out a hideous "SUUUHHH-WEEE-HHHEEE-HEEEEET JANE!" that sounded like a cross between Morrisey, Kermit The Frog and a cat who was in the process of being neutered. Lou introduced him as "Antony." Antony

#6
THE EAGLES
Hotel California

Possibly the most putrid band ever to soil the airwaves. The absolute embodiment of what is shallow, showy, and just plain shitty about southern California. What made them think that if they put 15 people onstage it would distract us from the fact that none of them had any talent? Don Henley is enough to make any living thing hack up, but throw Glenn Frye, Joe Walsh, and that guy with the hair like Crystal Gayle's grandmother into the mix, and you've got Grade A crap. Wouldn't piss down their throats if their guts were on fire.

DAVE BATTERMAN

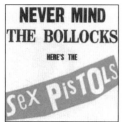

#7
THE SEX PISTOLS
Never Mind The Bollocks, Here's...

Any one of their contemporaries was ten times better than they were. I'm not saying the record was bad, but it was no Ramones, or Clash, or "Neat, Neat, Neat," or "Suspect Device," or "In the City," etc. Yet, it received by far the most acclaim. This is because of business and socio-political influence. Rock critics, being too dumb to be real intellectuals but too square to be real rockers, pay oh-so-much attention to that kind of irrelevant shit. More than anything else, the Pistols were a moment, with the Bill Grundy broadcast the Black Generation's makeshift version of Elvis on *Sullivan*. Those of us who weren't there can't really relate, especially because, based on the recordings alone, they were a sloppy mod/pub-rock band with designer shirts and mildly antisocial lyrics. By the time I heard *Bollocks*, for instance, I was a precocious 15-year-old who'd already been exposed to the Ramones, Wire, Black Flag, and the Dead Kennedys. In comparison, the Pistols were a big "So what?" Not the first, and certainly not the best. I try to listen to it again once every few years, and each time it sounds as dated as Canned Heat. The only thing this ever *really* did was give the Brits a reason to think they invented punk rock. Of the other first wave UK bands, the Clash and the Buzzcocks had better songs and bigger hooks, the Damned had triple the intensity, Wire had a clue and some dignity, and the Stranglers had...uh, sweet keyboards and a bass player that could play circles around Vicious, Matlock, and Jones combined. Everyone goes on about the guitar bombast as if it hadn't been done just as loud, with more conviction, and with tons more attitude by the Stooges, MC5, and many others years before, and by Motörhead, AC/DC, et al. concurrently. I've never owned a copy of this LP and never will. Never mind the marketing machine.

UNKNOWN CONTRIBUTOR , MIKE APPELSTEIN & KEVIN TROWEL

(fuck anybody with a one word name) proceeded to ruin the show for me. At times, his singing was so obnoxious that he had my friends and I laughing uproariously. At other points, he ruined some of Lou's best material. Lou got my hopes up by introducing a song as "the first song from the third Velvet Underground record" only to be subjected to Antony performing an excruciating "Candy Says." Antony also ruined "Perfect Day" by vocally masturbating all over my favorite lyric: "You made me forget myself/I thought I was someone else, someone good." Funny, I never had you confused with anything close to good!

The pain of seeing that Antony jerk stuck with me for a long time. A few months after graduating from high school, I started dating a friend of mine. She thought Antony was just as funny as I did, which is a stellar example of how great she was. A friend of hers had also seen Lou on the Raven tour, and he had a similar reaction to Antony. That pony-tailed asshole became a reoccurring joke to us. My girlfriend realized that he had a solo career, and found an MP3 of one of his songs, a God-awful lament with the completely retarted title "I Fell In Love With A Dead Boy." The song was Antony, with a small string section and tinkly piano accompanying him, singing a song about his dead lover. This song was notable for containing the lyrics "I fell in love with a dead boy, oh what a beautiful boy!/I ask him, are you a boy or a girl?/Are you a boy or a girl?" It was also notable for being really fucking awful. Jump ahead a year. The girlfriend is now an ex-girlfriend, and she's not speaking to me anymore, I've moved to a city I hate and I'm working at a soul sucking, oh-so-hip record store. Antony's full length "I Am A Bird Now" is released, and garners the type of hype not seen since the invention of penicillin.

I'm miserable, and I'm forced to listen to it constantly. Magazines and friends I usually trust are comparing Antony to Nina Simone (I wonder if most of these people have actually *heard* Nina Simone), Klaus Nomi and any other weirdo who attempted to sing a ballad. That jackass even managed to win the Mercury Prize, which would outrage me if I thought that the opinions of the English mattered in the least.

Beyond the awful voice, the ridiculous appearance (he's even worse now that he's taken to wearing a series of hideous wigs) and unjustified hype, *I Am A Bird Now* mainly sucks because it's a collection of self-obsessed songs about love that have no connection to real life, and a total lack of restraint or subtlety. I'm not kidding when I say that I take the success of Antony and the Johnsons as a personal affront to everything I hold dear in this world.

ABRAHAM SCOTT

APHEX TWIN
Selected Ambient Works Vol. 2

Anything "innovative" he did with software, Coil was doing *without* software ten years earlier. He just had the assistance of a major label, music videos and tons of money from his commercial work.

JON WHITNEY

THE APPLES (IN STEREO)
Fun Trick Noisemaker

This record sounds like it was made in a toilet by a bunch of hicks who studied under The Shaggs. Even when audible in the mix, Robert Schneider's voice is so over-processed and his lyrics so incomprehensible that it sounds like a mongoloid boy-choir. They probably thought that using a gong in a song was "avant-garde," and using the old satellite broadcast at the beginning of the album was "retro" or "hip" or "not absolutely fucking retarded." It is truly incredible that Schneider could help produce someone else's record with amazing results (see Neutral Milk Hotel) and yet release such an obvious piece of shit.

LOGAN KEESE

ARAB ON RADAR
Queen Hygiene II/Rough Day at the Orifice

When will bands ever realize how quotidian and pointless it is to scream about incest, molestation, and general expletive dementia in such a way that no one will ever understand what the fuck they're saying? Sure tub-a-lub fan boys will download the lyrics, but that's just pandering to the Fantasy Con portion of the audience. Due to journalists' general lack of critical balls you've probably only read about what a great noise they made, perhaps described as something like an "unholy racket." Arab on Radar's music itself did evolve somewhat over the years, especially between the two albums *Queen Hygiene II/Rough Day at the Orifice* as one CD on Three One G, but only in the way the smell of your farts changes with your diet over the years. There was one summer in particular that I ate a shit-load of Captain D's and I swear you could almost taste those bottom-feeding, deep-fried fish cracklins in the air when I let one loose. The point is that I was the only one who could enjoy the fine aroma of my classical gas. I smelled tasty, battered and dipped, orangish fish of unknown origins; everyone else merely smelled the inside of my winding, loop-to-loop-filled colon coaster. After seeing Arab on Radar perform over the years, they definitely seem like a band that enjoys taking in the harsher aromatic flavors of their own farts.

Lucky for them, each new year there's a fresh harvest of lonely collegiate New England spazzbos who appreciate the aesthetic of just freaking out rather than making any true artistic statement. If running all your shit through turbo rat pedals and singing about hermaphrodites who can suck themselves is your idea of music, then crank this shit up and watch the girls leave the room. In fact, find me a girl who likes Arab on Radar and I'll stick the broad side of a rake up my ass. This is music for sad, pathetic college white boys who will soon be complaining about their IT jobs. Long live the death of Arab on Radar.

BRIAN TEASLEY

anything
Recipe is as follows:
Take:
-1 copy of Captain Beefheart & The Magic Band's *Lick My Decals Off, Baby* running at 78 RPM
-1 copy of any Albert Ayler album
-1 copy of Kraftwerk's *Trans Europe Express* running at 45 RPM
-1 copy of *How To Succeed In Business Without Really Trying*
-2 cats fucking
-1 Cuban sandwich
Put into blender. Blend until chunky. Result: Harry Pussy
Now:
-Remove Cuban sandwich
-Remove Kraftwerk
-Remove *How To Succeed In Business Without Really Trying*
-Slow Captain Beefheart down to 45 RPM
Now add:
-1 copy each of *Hardcore Devo 1* and *2*
-1 copy of Dale Carnegie's *How To Win Friends & Influence People*
-1 copy of P.T. Barnum's "There's Sucker Born Every Minute"
-1 copy of any album by The Osmonds
-Junk food of your choice
-2 more cats fucking
Put into La Machine. Blend until smooth.
Result: Arab On Radar
AOR worked much better as the Providence sector of

TEENAGE BLUES MEN

I guess this sort of thing will go on until the end of time. I'm not gonna name any names, but you can easily insert your favorite into any slot in this long line of bulk-copied, pentatonic-worshippin' teenage blues man jack-offs. You know the proverbial drill...just like it's your dad's foot kicking you in the ass for fucking up his porn collection at about the same age as most of these chicken-fuckers start their white bread careers: the son of some influential white blues/jam band guitarist rides in on those beer and bullshit-soaked coattails, beefing up his initially flaccid portfolio by playing with all the greats (i.e. old black blues men who are still alive and wanting for some good publicity and a few extra dollars back from what some record company fucked them out of back in the day). Then, these kids are *in*. Every other white-as-polar-caps fucker twice their age and still milking the blues cash cow says that they are *the shit*. The *new* shit. Shit like they haven't smelled since Mumbo Jumbo Mint Julep Johnson perfected his grease-finger 12-bar devil stroke in 19whatfuckingever. If you're any kind of musician who knows that this blues thing has been beaten into the goddamn ground to the pathetic point where it's well past ever having *any* sort of innovation *ever* again, then you know just how completely laughable this is. But, such is life. Bring on the vast, white armies of teenage blues men. Keep those hilariously lazy licks a-comin', you foul music industry, you. Your blind and groping market of morons has settled for just this sort of mediocre, pandering, insulting, overwrought garbage-made-out-of-garbage.

JEFF MCLEOD

#8

WEEZER
Pinkerton

Awful Pixies/Pavement rip-off ironic rock band puts out pretty good record for what they seemed to be capable of, critics give it props for not sucking, fans reject it, record tanks. Seems like a pretty sad story...until the fairy tale ending. Nearing end of decade, record is called one of the "best albums of the '90s" by virtually everyone. Now it's an "overlooked classic." This is the same logic as finding a dollar in the toilet and upping its value because you didn't notice it when you accidentally ate it. Here's the big question: now that Weezer fans all agree that *Pinkerton* was by far and away their best album, why has it still not sold as many as the rest of them? And why is this record that is one of the "Best of the Nineties" not selling as well as any other '90s classic? Because it's a predigested dollar with shit all over it.

DAG LUTHER GOOCH

#9

JANE'S ADDICTION
Nothing's Shocking

Jane's Addiction grew from the dying glam-metal scene in late '80s Los Angeles like a psychedelic mushroom from a cow turd, and they're routinely credited with bridging the music of that era with the seemingly unstoppable flood of "alternative" acts that followed. Both of these facts tell you all you really need to know about the band. Rising above the likes of L.A. Guns, Love/Hate, and Bang Tango is an accomplishment, on par with taking the gold medal at the Special Olympics. And as bridges go, theirs is about as impressive as the one that connects Dubuque, Iowa, with East Dubuque, Illinois. Neither direction takes you anywhere you really want to be. Sure, *Nothing's Shocking* kicks off with the über-kick-ass "Ocean Size." And *Ritual* has a few moments that suggest what Zeppelin might have sounded like if its members had been drug-addled Angeleno low-lifes with artsy pretensions rather than drug-addled, Brit low-lifes with the same. But *Nothing's Shocking* also guaranteed us that we'll all be listening to Zima-drunk sorority cows bleating "Jane Says" for the rest of our natural lives. Ritual prominently featured "Been Caught Stealing," foreshadowing the vapidity Perry Farrell would continue to subject us to (e.g., Porno for Pyros' "Pets," etc.) as long as *Rolling Stone* continues to retroactively anoint him an "important" artist. Looking back now, it certainly isn't "shocking" to see the Gap ads Dave Navarro would soon be featured in and the neo-hippie drum circles that Stephen Perkins would end up leading. And when you see the part of the recent rockumentary, *Some Kind of Monster*, where bassist Eric Avery tries out for the well-past-its-prime Metallica—and loses out to the third-generation Suicidal Tendencies (and first-generation Infectious Grooves) bassist Robert Trujillo—you just cringe.

CHRIS ISELI

FBLA than they ever did as a band. Believe me, they even had Op Pop Pop Records and most of Germany fooled, too. Kudos goes to AOR, however, for having been booked to play at The Middle East in Cambridge, MA on 9/11/01. This is not an urban legend; this is the truth. And the band didn't cancel the show; the club did.

NICK BLAKEY

AT THE DRIVE-IN
This Station Is Non-Operational

The degree to which a band is overrated can usually be determined by the bloatedness of the bigger stars who name-check said band. Usually, it's in bigger stars' futile hope of re-establishing some sort of credibility as they themselves fade into irrelevance. In At the Drive-In's case, that bigger star was none other than Bono—circa *Pop*, no less. Then for a moment, it seemed as though ATDI was going to salvage some dignity and respect when they broke up shortly thereafter. But three of the band members resurfaced in Sparta, about whose music the best and worst that can be said while it's playing is, "Well, there's music playing." The other two guys went on to form the Mars Volta, a tribute to '70s prog-rock that, over the course of just two albums, has managed to create an "experience" roughly equivalent to listening to the entire recorded output of Santana and Yes (including the Rick Wakeman solo records) while an erectile-dysfunctional Geddy Lee feebly tries to assault you with his flaccid dick. To be fair, they did give us some advance warning. For every "Pattern Against User" and "Pickpocket" in ATDI's back catalogue, there's an "Enfilade" or a "Chanbara" that prefigure the concept-album pretensions and noodly, faux-Latin groove-flogging they'd later expand upon at absurdly great length and to stultifying effect. But at the time, as

they came screaming out of El Paso like their gigantic afros were on fire, lighting up a punk-rock scene that seemed in danger of going completely stagnant, they seemed like such a breath of fresh air that I guess it's not entirely our fault that we missed the distinct whiff of rancid bongwater that followed close behind.

CHRIS ISELI

BAD COMPANY
Bad Company

Should have been named *Bad Record*. The band used Led Zeppelin's formula of blues-based power chords and a capable lead singer to complete this collection of junk. *Bad Company* is heavy metal for 10-year-olds. There is nothing intelligent or compelling about it.

MICHAEL RYAN

THE BAND
post-Music From Big Pink

In retrospect, Robbie (sorry, Jaime) Robertson has turned out to be just an average (if that) songwriter (especially after the release of that wretched '80s solo album), and not the utter sub-Dylan genius he was first made out to be (while the late Richard Manuel, in retrospect, has turned out to be pretty great). Much of their post-*MFBP* work poorly rehashes earlier greatness, with the power and fury in their role as Dylan's backing group (especially on *Royal Albert Hall* in 1966 and *The Basement Tapes* of 1967) sadly lacking. Since then, The Band have exhibited their capabilities in rock 'n' roll debauchery with the suicide death (while on tour) of Richard Manuel, the bloated and disgusting OD death of Rick Danko (not to mention that alleged *Last Waltz* outtake in which Danko's nose is apparently drenched in coke backstage at Winterland), the horrid loss of any audible cohesion in the voice of Robbie Robertson, Garth Hudson's producing The Call, and the entire acting career of Levon Helm. (As an aside, when The Band's entire catalogue was recently re-mastered and re-issued by Capitol, a reviewer at the *Boston Phoenix* called *MFBP* and their eponymous second album "the two greatest records of the 20th Century." He (and his editor, too, for that matter) got the name of the first album wrong as *Music For the Big Pink*. Fucking figures.

NICK BLAKEY

BAUHAUS
The Sky's Gone Out
Peter Murphy never seemed funnier than on this album. He was trying so hard to be scary, God bless his black, little heart. He was so thirsty, he just had to chop that baby up and drink its blood. I was in Kinko's a few years ago, and there was this silly goth fellow who had this album playing while everyone was making copies—mostly sorority girls. When the part came when Mr. Murphy says he eats barbed wire in the morning, all the kids looked at each other and laughed. I've never seen a goth rocker look more like he was going to cry in my life.

DAG LUTHER GOOCH

THE BEASTIE BOYS
Ill Communication
Throughout the 20th century, upper-middle class white kids, desperate to be "cool," have co-opted black styles in both music and fashion. The Beasties are no different, just Amos & Andy with a New York patois. What I don't get is why Generation X hipsters love the Beasties, but loathe Kid Rock. It's the same shit—mixing rap with arena/classic rock—but Kid Rock doesn't take himself nearly as seriously.

MATT THOMPSON

Check Your Head
I liked the Beastie Boys a lot better when they were hard-drinking New Yorkers who rapped about gay-bashing and sluts who get drunk and

fuck everyone at the party. Two words: Fuck Tibet.

SETH LOSIER

BEAT HAPPENING
Crashing Through box set
How in the world this mediocre attempt at slow death by three tea room ninnies managed to make it into the pages of Mr. Ultra Blowhard Himself Michael Azerrad's "Our Bland Could Be Your Strife" remains beyond comprehension (I mean, how in the hell did they get picked over The Melvins?) So they based their entire career on the already way overrated and over-referenced Shaggs...well, whoop-dee fuckin' do, that's like *so* original, man. They are single handedly responsible for spwaning the entire "it-doesn't-matter-if-you-can-play-but-you're-up-there-doing-it" Olympia thing that is now one of the primary reasons so many former l.u.g.'s and hipsters now vote Republican. And Calvin Johnson's continued sheer awfulness has done more for the anti-gay sentiment than Anita Bryant's wettest dreams. Blech.

NICK BLAKEY

THE BEATLES
Abbey Road
It was the overblown production and excess of *Sgt. Pepper* that eventually drove The Beatles to make the group therapy session known as *Get Back* (which was later scrapped, reassembled, and eventually released as the even more overproduced *Let It Be*) so that the band could, as Lennon stated (paraphrased), "show people... this is what we are like with our trousers off" (though by this point folks already knew from *Two Virgins* what Lennon looked like sans trousers). The absolute misery of the *Get Back* sessions (which caused George Harrison to quit for a week at one point) drove the group in the opposite direction from making another well-pro-

duced and assembled album. It was this feeling that gave us *Abbey Road*, perhaps the slickest record the group ever did. Dominated by McCartney to the point where this could be the first Wings album, there is some true grit (Lennon's "I Want You," "Come Together" and "Polythene Pam") that is washed out by cuteness (McCartney's "Her Majesty," "Maxwell's Silver Hammer" Ringo's "Octopus's Garden") and schmaltz (Harrison's "Something," McCartney's "Golden Slumbers/Carry That Weight"). Plus the damn thing is just sooo slick. Sure, it's good, but it's nothing compared to the landmarks achieved on *Rubber Soul*, *Revolver*, or even *The White Album*, all of which always seem to get left out of the same sentence as *Sgt. Pepper* and *Abbey Road*.

NICK BLAKEY

BECK
Mellow Gold
The year: 1994. The crime: white-boy rapping. The white boy: Beck Hansen. This record had just enough distance between its release and your nostalgic yearning to relive summer camp (where you secretly listened to *Paul's Boutique* and *2 Live Crew* when the counselors weren't around) to hit the top ten in the U.S. The sound of this record cleared the snort trail for those dysfunctional crackheads The Butthole Surfers to have a hit with the Smash Mouth-ish XFM jam "Pepper"—a crime in and of itself. Multi-platinum *Mellow Gold* is an unmistakable piece of all-things-disposable early '90s indifference that wears thinner than repeated listens to the commentary track on Richard Linklater's *Slacker* DVD. Still, as pathetic as Beck's fossil supreme of white hipster hip-hop is, I'd

much rather listen to it than the leaf blower-sounding lo-fi stream of pissing consciousness acoustic toilet bowls (that's almost as bad as something Beck would write) of *Stereopathetic Soul Manure* (Flipside) or *One Foot In the Grave* (K). The bumper sticker art gallery clichéd kitsch contained within *Mellow Gold* constantly splats like bugs on a windshield, and an entire forced listen serves as one of the most distinct reminders that genre walls are often in place for good reason. I recently saw Beck play a greatest hits-type set, and I think even the most loyal of his old-school fans realized that a skinny white guy saying shit like "cut it" or "break it down" into a microphone is like eating ten year old chicken out of that guy Buckethead's empty skull.

BRIAN TEASLEY

Odelay
You're a loser? Well, you sound like a guy who's getting plenty of pussy to me. *Odelay* cements Beck's role as the Ben Affleck of the indie scene. Too Hollywood to ever really fit in, but good looking enough to command attention. Dust Brothers aside, the "Two Turntables and a Microphone" song only inspires me to ironically break dance on your pampered nuts, dude.

BEN ARNOLD

BELLE AND SEBASTIAN
The Boy With The Arab Strap
Here are the facts: they have 20 members, which is 4 times as many as the Stones, and they are five times as bad, maybe more. (I told this to their "singer" Stuart Murdock when I saw him dancing at a club in Boston.) And for the first few years they were a band, they refused to be photographed; I remember their press photos were of goats and various other barnyard animals. If these

#10
BIG BROTHER & THE HOLDING COMPANY
Cheap Thrills

Janis had a voice, but she also made a lot of bad choices. It's hard to understand how someone can be so emotive in their vocal delivery when backed by a group of "musicians" who sound like they've rehearsed together four times at the most. Even my dad, a champion of this album when it was released, admitted ten years ago that this "classic" simply does not hold up to the test of time, nor does it add to the Joplin legacy.

ROCK ACTION

#11
THE CLASH
London Calling

No, this is not because of the title song's usage in those fucking Jaguar commercials (although it puts them in the same company as Sting, which is probably what really killed Joe Strummer). I've nearly been killed for saying this, and avoided at least three knife fights, but flat out, *London Calling* ain't a hair as good or as ballsy as *Sandinista!* hands down. If you have the ability to get through the six sides of *Sandinista!,* and not see the brilliant chances The Clash took on that record (not to mention the pounds and pounds of dope they must have smoked), *London Calling* comes off as the band's weak and blatantly commercial attempt at *Sgt. Pepper.* Want more proof that The Clash were punk's true Beatles? Here's a breakdown:

a) The Clash: *The Clash* (debut) = The Beatles: *The Decca Audition Tapes* (bootleg), *Live At The Star Club, Hamburg 1962!*, *Please Please Me, With The Beatles, A Hard Day's Night, Live At The Hollywood Bowl 1964* (bootleg). John Lennon: *Plastic Ono Band.*
b) The Clash: *Give 'Em Enough Rope* = The Beatles: *Beatles For Sale, Help!, Rubber Soul, Revolver.*
c) The Clash: *London Calling* = The Beatles: *Sgt. Pepper's Lonely Hearts Club Band.* Paul McCartney: *Band On The Run.*
d) The Clash: *Sandinista!* = The Beatles: *The Beatles* (*White Album*), *Magical Mystery Tour, Carnival Of Light* (bootleg). George Harrison: *All Things Must Pass.*
e) The Clash: *Combat Rock* = The Beatles: *Get Back* (bootleg), *Abbey Road.* John Lennon: *Some Time In New York City.*
f) The Clash: *Cut The Crap* = The Beatles: *Let It Be.* Paul McCartney: *Pipes Of Peace.* Ringo Starr = anything excepting *Ringo.*

NICK BLAKEY

#12
NICK DRAKE
Pink Moon

To say any Nick Drake record is overrated is a stretch, considering he was never really held in high regard until long after he was cold and dead. However, if any album of his is overhyped, it's this 11-song, 25-minute snore-fest. It's just him in a room with an acoustic guitar. Drake himself was quoted as saying that he just had no more to record.

DAVIS REA

---

two reasons are not enough, they have just put out a soundtrack album. Their last efforts were basically soundtracks for large girls to lose their virginity to.

JUSTIN FITTERMAN

BEN FOLDS FIVE
Whatever and Ever Amen

Some skinny shit-kicker from North Carolina teaches himself to play piano and sing out of his nose. Antics (and albums) ensue. This particular record has aged about as well as his already dashingly good looks.

LOGAN KEESE

BEVIS FROND
Son of Walter

This record actually has a few great moments. It's just all too unfortunate that Nick Saloman couldn't have stacked that 5 to 7 seconds right at the top of the album and spared us from the following fifty minutes of wanky, sub-psychedelic, one-man swamp-sludge jams. For God's sake, man, get the band back together.

BRIAN TEASLEY

BIG BLACK
Atomizer

You can't really be that "scary" with a drum machine, no matter how much you rip off Whitehouse.

JULIANNE SHEPARD

BIG STAR
#1 Record

Does anyone else find it interesting that this album, put out a year after Badfinger's *Straight Up,* is hailed as an achievement of epic proportions by rock stars everywhere, most of them from England? What the fuck is that all about? This would be like Americans picking up a Radiohead record and considering it a milestone, despite its obvious regurgitation of *Doolittle.* Oh wait. We did that. Fuck me running.

DAG LUTHER GOOCH

Third/Sister Lovers

What kind of asshole drives somebody out of their own band and then puts out what

---

essentially amounted to a solo record under the same band name? Alex Chilton. That guy has an ego so big that the English can't even top it. No wonder they love him so much. He's a bigger dick than Andy Partridge, Julian Cope, and Morrissey combined. Every time a British person covers something obscure, it comes off this fucking disc. Five times out of ten, it's "Holocaust." Eight times out of ten, it sounds like shit. Ten times out of ten, we get the fucking point: your record collection is smaller than your penis. Also, we don't want to hear your version of "September Gurls" either.

DAG LUTHER GOOCH

BJÖRK
Medulla

Amazingly, when a Japanese human beatbox, an Inuit throat singer, an Icelandic choir, Rahzel from the Roots, Mike Patton, and Björk lock themselves in a studio to trade pithy, breathy verses about womanhood, it comes out sounding remarkably like a donkey being raped by a Clydesdale.

J. BOWERS

BLACK CROWES
Southern Harmony and Musical Companion

Sensitive yahoos. That's rich. If the brothers weren't such skinny, weak twats, they probably would've offed each other while making this piece of shit. After the rumor they were racists got blown out of proportion, this must have been their defense. Funny, it's just that much closer to a Skynyrd record.

DAG LUTHER GOOCH

BLACK DICE
Creature Comforts

This record just proves that white people will eventually destroy our planet. Black Dice is the Battlefield Earth of "experimental" music, and hearing them is the scrotum seepage of listening experiences.

BRIAN TEASLEY

BLACK FLAG
Damaged
Referred to by Black Flag purists as the "where it all went wrong" album, *Damaged* marked the first appearance of Henry Garfield in the band. Who is Henry Garfield, you ask? Oh, you may know him as Henry Rollins—the muscle-bound, meat-head Ted Nugent of punk rock who appears in Apple PowerBook ads and is ready for hire any time VH1 needs a new talking head to make jokes about Bobby and Whitney's marriage. Seriously, Greg Ginn even hates this guy—even though without him, he'd be a lot less rich.
BRIAN MCMANUS

THE BLASTERS
American Music
Note to everyone with a vintage car and monkey dip in their hair: Rockabilly after 1959 is like fucking your little old grandma after they have removed her feeding tube some two days prior. C'mon, Jethro, the flowers around this grave have long been dead. Put down the coffin-shaped upright bass and pump my fucking gas!
BRIAN TEASLEY

BLIND FAITH
Blind Faith
It's not just because he dated Sheryl Crow and he never shaves... Clapton fucked up. Specifically, his musical sin was his integral hand in legitimizing (and popularizing) honky psych blues. The people who really "felt" what Clapton et al. were "saying" back then also "dug" paisley bellbottoms. The pot/acid-fueled "revolution" obviously did lead to the oft quoted "derangement of the senses," or at least those of sight and hearing.
P.S. I totally "felt" the prepubescent topless girl on the cover; too bad "The Man" had to add one more heartache to your long, sad, hard life by banning it. That's what happens when you've got the

"Psychedelicpastyfacedbig fatroyaltycheck-Blues".
PABLO A. ROCKAFUCKER

BLONDIE
Parallel Lines
The term "punk" stopped meaning anything when it came out of this fashion princess's mouth. What could be less punk than "Heart of Glass" going #1 on the disco charts? I saw a lot of interpretations of punk back in the late '70s and early '80s: the TV and film punk (i.e., all punks wear mohawks), the suburban heavy metal/new wave hybrid (i.e., safety pins + studs = punk), hardcore, ska, skate punk, surf punk, cow punk, etc.; but dance punk never made any sense to me. Who are they rebelling against exactly? The authority that prevents sunglasses from being worn on the dance floor? The Anti-Doo-Wop League? Thank you so very much, Debbie, for the future punk legends who would follow in your footsteps: Corey Hart, Corey Haim, Corey Feldman and Molly Ringwald.
DAG LUTHER GOOCH

BLUE CHEER
Vincebus Eruptum
I know...I know, you overly-researched-irony-mustache-havin' pussy dribble: the name of this album is an LSD term. But I have long appropriated it for my own uses. You see, sometimes, especially after wearing tight underwear during inclement weather, the head of my penis will retreat back into the flaccid, nerf-like skin of my dick shaft like a small, scared turtle in a meteor storm. Yet, after just a wee-bit of coaxing by the thumb and index finger of my right hand, the mouthpiece of my skin flute will pop back out like a hide-and-go-seek-playing Cedric the Entertainer to say, "Wazzup My Niggaz?" And just what do I call this process you ask? Well, what better phrase to describe it than *Vincebus Eruptum*! Oh shit, I fucked this all up. I for-

GRINDCORE
Heavy metal is about extremes. In grindcore, metal reached the last level of extremity. It's the most brutal, the most grotesque and often the fastest—which makes it insufferably masturbatory, not to mention cartoonish. Most of these bands don't believe half of what they write about: they're just trying to trump their peers. The guitarists risk carpal tunnel syndrome as they engage in a pecker contest to see who can play fastest, leaving any melody utterly indiscernible. The vocalists do likewise, trying to write the most disgusting—yet, we're supposed to believe, socially relevant—lyrics, then shred their larynxes barking the fucking things. What's left is double Y-chromosome rock for 98-pound nerds who simply aspire to antisocial behavior.
RANDY HARWARD

#13

LED ZEPPELIN
Led Zeppelin IV

They literally sold "Rock And Roll" to a fucking Cadillac commercial. Maybe Jimmy and Bob wanted to get an early start on paying back their debts to Lucifer. Maybe they just like General Motors. Who the fuck knows? Because they can't possibly need the money. No one's surprised when Sting shills his world music diarrhea to Jaguar because his douchebag credentials were firmly established a long time ago. But why, oh why sweet Satan, did the two remaining members of Zeppelin forsake us this way? I suggest that upon reaching hell, they be forced to listen to *Coverdale/Page* for eternity.

BEN ARNOLD

#14

PINK FLOYD
The Wall

First, we all hated grade school and our parents, we all did a lot of drugs, and (thanks to "Behind the Music") we all know too well the price of fame. Now, a lot of records have assumed that it would be fun to listen to some guy talk about these issues, but only *The Wall* is bold enough to assume that it would be fun to listen to *Roger Waters* whine about these issues. The album is one man's temper tantrum stretched out for more than an hour, and is obviously the creation of someone who has started to believe his own hype. Anyone who claims to identify with *The Wall* is either impossibly self-absorbed or is seriously padding his resumé of life experiences. Second, a comparison with the band's earlier work (and I speak not of the equally overrated Syd Barrett tripe) shows clearly that the band was falling apart during *The Wall*. It just wasn't a team effort. David Gilmour was pulling a Paul McCartney-style puss out (as evidenced by his lackluster writing contributions) and Waters had been engulfed by his resentment of, well, everything. Listen to any interview with the band, and they'll all say that they hate to listen to this album. Anyone who thinks of *The Wall* as superior to Floyd's other work is essentially just a Roger Waters fan, and would do much better with the largely unheard of (for a reason) *The Final Cut*, which is pretty much a Waters solo effort plus some tolerable singing and maybe one or two Gilmour mid-life crisis rock tracks. Ask me ten years ago if this album was worthy of its praise, and I would wholeheartedly say "Yes." With age comes wisdom; I guess I'm still as stoned as I was ten years ago, so we can't suggest that I've merely sobered up. A recent revisit to this perennial favorite gave me listener fatigue. Is that Michael Kamen I hear conducting? This thing's got more filler than most rap albums I've heard lately! How much cocaine did Bob Ezrin do to stay up for all the overdubs? What's Bob Ezrin doing producing Floyd anyway? Who's got enough balls to tell Roger Waters that *Animals* was Floyd's last certified classic?

ROCK ACTION & SILAS DAMERON

---

got to first tell you that I call my dick Vincebus.

BRIAN TEASLEY

BLUR
Blur

Damon Albarn discovered a new path to success in America. Just write an uncharacteristically shallow song with a catch phrase (woo hoo) similar to some popular hip hop song out at the time (woot). Then, pad the album with songs that wouldn't make the b-sides catalog of Oasis. The result is the longest, most expensive single in history, with numerous bad b-sides. It's no wonder you see five copies of this one in every used CD store. "Chinese Bombs" indeed…bombs pretty much in every country.

JIM RAYMOND

THE BREEDERS
Last Splash

The Breeders were the Pixies' Foo Fighters. Sideperson switches to guitar and starts watered-down pop version of original. Some will argue that they had existed before the Pixies, but who knows this to be absolutely true other than some fact sniffing website hound who believes every piece of shit he sees in print? What we *do* know is that The Breeders were a consolation prize. They were a house pet in a divorce settlement. If you try to sell this to a used CD store, they won't buy it. They already have fifty of them that they are trying to find homes for.

DAG LUTHER GOOCH

BRIGHT EYES
Lifted or the Story Is in the Soil, Keep Your Ear to the Ground

A. Don't name your album two different things.
B. Do you see the six little white things at the top of your guitar? Those are tuners. It's been 15 years of making music for you now; you can try turning one.
C. Singing on your new album about how you hate

---

your new-found fame while releasing four videos for MTV is, if nothing else, in bad taste.

DAVIS REA

BROKEN SOCIAL SCENE
You Forgot It In People

Let me cut to the fucking chase here: Why a group of black hip-hop artists from Atlanta would be so distraught with the present industry dominance of indie rock that they would disguise themselves as a scrappy collective of Toronto scenesters who make abstract Pro Tools rock that is so unconditionally adventurous it doesn't even stray from clichéd melodies is well beyond me. Without a doubt, this is a new low in the ever-growing Afronazation of all things "indie." I know…I know, indie rock has practically been owning the Billboard charts for a while now, and it looks like the trend is about to become a veritable spewing geyser of unmeasured selling potential.

And yeah, it's no secret that indie bands as wide-ranging as Red Eyed Legends, Ladybug Transistor, Oneida, Midlake, Silkworm, Wolf Eyes, Minus the Bear, and the Chromatics are all able to retire with their booming royalties from the last couple years, but just because being humble, awkward and just simply put, "all things white" is so goddamn in right now, doesn't mean people should sell out their roots. I mean, I don't necessarily agree with the recent crop of black bands performing in "whiteface," but the ironic thrift store clothes and inaudible stage banter just seems hackneyed at best. Don't we all know that black people look better in baggy clothes and just plain goofy in hip vintage clothing store threads? Sure, sure white people got the goods, and I know Caucasians know art-school-reject lyrical abstractions like no one else, but 50 Cent recently citing Air Miami and New Radiant Storm King as major influences is just complete affectation and nothing more.

As much as anyone else with a partially sincere interest in political correctness, I indeed want cultural barriers to be broken, and I think it's fabulous that inner city blacks are so interested in the indie rock dialect and think that it's ironically fashionable to be understated, overly self-aware, and super quiet in movie theaters. Ever since KRS-One begged Michael Stipe to let him rap on R.E.M's *Out of Time*, MC's have been doing double-back flips (made possible by an overabundant amount of fast twitch muscle fiber) to link themselves with musicians free of the constraints of dark pigment. Black people always follow the footsteps of the white man's beat and then popularize it in a way that's palatable for all races. Nothing new there.

Let us just be honest with ourselves. This goes all the way back to the days of slavery. While the slaves would pick cotton all day under the blistering Southern sun, the plantation masters were busy inside sharpening their chops, and creating unrivaled riffage that the black man would soon childishly attempt to imitate, accidentally creating what has been imprecisely labeled by rock historians as "the blues." Maybe in a few hundred years, African-Americans will close the gap on what seems like an almost impossibly effortless gift for rhythm and melody possessed by every blonde-hair, blue-eyed child, seemingly from birth.

Ask yourself this: Why is it that light-skinned blacks are always way better musicians than darker ones? Duh...as the saying goes, "Get some of that White, make your music tight."

People should genuinely know the origins of this new Afro-centric obsession with everything from twee-pop to straight edge hardcore, especially since the BET weekly playlist is now over-run with Black artist making pale imitations of music that comes from the raw, desperate ghetto of college radio—the frenetic frontline for the beat of the street.

I realize I've spent almost zero airtime on the actual music of Broken Social Scene and have used this review as a platform to deal with the phenomenon surrounding black artist pretending to be white—what anthropologists call the "Great White Out," but I feel it's important to let the black youth of America, and Broken Social Scene for that matter, know that you can be cool even if you're black. Of course, it's okay to dream of being the first black president in the "White" House," but that's just not realistic. Is it...a black President? C'mon, that's almost as crazy as thinking a black man will one day walk on the moon. We all must admit that Michael Jordan made a better basketball player than he would have a NASCAR driver or hockey player, but truly something you people have to be proud is the fact you have a lot of great ball-sport-oriented athletes, and I don't want to take away from that. I do wholeheartedly encourage young African-Americans to develop their own culture and slang, and not to worry about what the latest trends in Lawrence, Chapel Hill, Portland or Athens are going to be. Kids killing each other over horn-rimmed glasses is just plain nihilistic and stupid. This is my message to black people: quit killing yourselves and start being yourselves.

BRIAN TEASLEY

JEFF BUCKLEY
Grace
Funny how this wasn't as universally acclaimed until

RIOT GRRRL

Gee, that was nice, wasn't it? Like it wasn't bad enough being a teenage punk boy in *Daytona Beach* in 1991. On top of that, I had to endure bullshit revolutionary posturing from every chick who got her information about music from fucking *Sassy* magazine just because I wanted to get *laid*—like all young Americans. The female version of mook rock. Suburban white angst split up like middle school gym classes with the boys on one team and the girls on the other. You'll find more liberation in Christina Aguilera's nose ring than you'll find in anything Kathleen Hanna says.

BEN HELLMANN

#15

CREAM
Goodbye

Side one has 17 minutes of live material (two songs), and side two has four studio outtakes. And that, folks, was good enough to take an album to #2 on the charts in the spring of '69. Surprising, until you remember that this is the same American public that had just elected Nixon.

MICHAEL FALOON

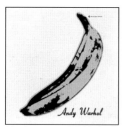

#16

VELVET UNDERGROUND
The Velvet Underground & Nico

It is nowhere near as satisfying or as heartfelt as *The Velvet Underground* (third album) and doesn't even come close to being as utterly frightening or mind-fucking as *White Light/White Heat*. And while Nico's spotlight songs are very pretty, a handful of her vocal turns do not make up for the avant-ego silliness of "European Son" (never minding the Delmore Schwartz dedication). Also, even well into 1969 (and Nico and John Cale's departure), the Velvets could still rip the living shit out of such numbers as "Run Run Run" and "I'm Waiting For The Man" and far outdo their tepid album versions (despite what Byron Colely may have you believe). This *is* a great and barrier-breaking album, but unfortunately most schmucks don't get past Nico, the banana, and the Warhol autograph to venture further into the oceans this seminal band parted.

NICK BLAKEY

#17

PATTI SMITH
Horses

Groundbreaking? Hardly. It was marketed to elitist music critics who thought that, because a woman could possibly sing punk rock (and "possibly sing" is as generous as I'll be), it was some sort of earth-shattering event. Also one in a long line proving "poet" does not equal rockstar/musician/singer (see: Jims Carroll and Morrison, Jewel and my girlfriend in high school). As far as talentless loudmouths of that era go, I much prefer Jayne County. At least she had the sense to tie beer cans to her wig. Patti Smith is like a crummy author whose books never sell. Bullied her way into legendary status by prancing around stage yelling "nigger." One day, some "critic" notices they've never sold and suddenly the author is viewed in a whole new light. Single-handedly has created untold numbers of self-absorbed, driven, outspoken, and "artistic" young women (and men, too, shut up) with little or (more often) nothing to say simply by riding a scene to critical success. No one born after 1980 even gives a shit who she is.

JOHN DAVIDSON, MICHAEL RYAN & PABLO A. ROCKAFUCKER

after Buckley's death. I hold this album directly accountable as a springboard for the careers of Dashboard Confessional, John Mayer and Ryan Adams.

AARON LEFKOVE

BUILT TO SPILL
Perfect From Now On

Twee's answer to Dream Theater, this bloated rumination on white male insecurity tolled "This is our music!" bells for spoiled college kids nationwide, all paralyzed by the can't-get-laid/are-these-my-real-friends? conundrum. Watching thousands of them wince along to all eight of Doug Martsch's seven-minute, self-pitying beer shits is as close as I've come to experiencing scat porn. Four chords, two ideas, three hundred tracks.

CHRIS OTT

THE BUTTHOLE SURFERS
post-Touch and Go output

If it isn't the saddest sub-Dead Milkmen shit to come out in ages, I don't know what is. The most precipitous slide into utter irrelevance since Van Halen hired Sammy, and about as random a candidate for one-hit wonderdom as Chumbawumba.

BEN HELLMANN

BUZZCOCKS
Singles Going Steady

I'm putting my foot down. If your flagship record is a best-of, greatest hits, or singles collection like this one is, then it is fair to say that you are overrated. Because you don't even have a single album that stands alone, and the one you do have in its place took eight fucking records to make. If, as in the Buzzcocks' case, you re-release singles collections under different names (why did we need *Operator's Manual* or *Lest We Forget*?), you are proving just how many records of filler you have floating around out there. The only people that

have proper Buzzcocks records are diehard Buzzcocks fans and used record stores.

DAG LUTHER GOOCH

CALEXICO
The Black Light

If Giant Sand is Cinnamon Crispas, then Calexico is a melted Choco-Taco. *Spoke*, their debut, was a genuinely touching work. Full of quiet, inspired subtlety only two appalingly talented, long-time friends could make that while having no great expectations. Unfortunately, the album's small but ever-growing praise soon pushed Calexico closer to setting up shop in their own theater in Branson, Missouri. Their live show soon turned into what only *The Black Light* could be a blueprint for: a rocket-ship made of Adobe that only the Dutch could appreciate. Maybe a mariachi band playing "La Cucaracha" while singing (in English) shallow tales of scorpions and ghost towns sounds like true desert romanticism if you're from Eindhoven, but it just reminds me of that two-part "Brady Bunch" episode where they go to the Grand Canyon and get locked up by Thurston Howell III playing a senile old timer who thinks the Bunch is trying to get at his gold. Come to think of it, *The Black Light* is kind of the alt-country opera version of *City Slickers II: The Legend of Curly's Gold*. No, at least that would be funny.

BRIAN TEASLEY

CAP'N JAZZ
Analphabetapolothology

I've often said that I will never like a band with a Kinsella brother in it and this, the most listenable of the Cap'n Jazz, Joan of Arc, Owls, etc. family is about as interesting as, say, a colostomy bag: you want to see what's inside, but afterwards you wish you would have left well enough alone.

AARON LEFKOVE

CAPTAIN BEEFHEART
Trout Mask Replica

Maybe, had I bought this in '70 or so when it came out, I'd be saying how great it is, but in this century it sucks. I'll give 'em points for the song titles—if I ever start a zine I'm sure I'd use something like "Hobo Chang Ba" or "Pachuco Cadaver"—but as something to listen to? Nah.

MICHAEL SEGHINI

THE CARS
The Cars

Let's all stand up and give a big "Thanks, Dick!" to odd-ball Ric Ocasek! SAAAA-LUTE, Ric! You made new wave the waviest! You made it okay for hot chicks to date ugly dorks who wear designer clothes and cleaning products in their hair. You stole the sound of the Modern Lovers and made it into classic rock radio fodder! You're a genius! Except for one thing: the chick on the cover of *The Cars*. How come we didn't get to see her naked until *Candy-O*?

DAG LUTHER GOOCH

JOHNNY CASH
American Recordings Vol. I-IV

A producer of rap metal pap trying desperately to obtain some credibility meets a waning, lost without a map, blown-voiced, former country star who fits the bill for a the hipster makeover? And what's the common denominator between these two men, you ask? Oh, they're both bad-ass outlaws trying to live the way they know the good Lord wants 'em to. A pitch for a sitcom entitled "Ross and Buck?" Unfortunately, no. This is the real-life story of Rick Rubin and Johnny Cash that began in the '90s before Rick Rubin had run the American record label into the hot asphalt ground of Sunset Blvd.

From 1993 to the present, Rubin paraded Cash through four albums (soon to be joined by a posthumous fifth) that many jour-nalists have taken to be the final link for a brilliant, troubled artist who was fortunately allowed the opportunity to bring his unfathomable stature to a rightful and dignified completion. What these records really are, however, is nothing more than the slow, progressively fading blip on an EKG machine put on tape and sold for profit.

Don't get me wrong; the man is a well-studied hero of mine and a near mythical figure in every sense. I suppose Ronald Reagan is similarly revered by some golf-obsessed, right-wing talk show host nut jobs, but I wonder if they would have enjoyed it if Nancy had rolled his old bones out so "The Alzheimer's could do the talkin'." And, yes, truly would I have loved to hear what *Bedtime-for-Bonzo-on-PCP* shit the big RR would have spewed out of his fluttering, dehydrated lips, but I have a good deal more respect for Mr. Cash than I do for Captain Trickle Down Economics.

I ask you, what could be more exploitative than convincing a doddering old man in his 70's that it would be a good idea to cover Soundgarden and Nine Inch Nails? The video for the Trent Reznor-penned "Hurt" is, without doubt, one of the saddest and most exploitative things I've ever seen, but we unapologetically live in a country where the last thing people want to do is honestly address death, and applaud haphazard substandard creative work from our aging legends.

Luckily for Christopher Reeve, he escaped (well, besides the terrible and pandering *Rear Window* remake) such unflattering retreading, because another year or so could have brought on the tasteless C.G.I.ing of him flying across the screen sans wheelchair to save a still-inebriated, weatherworn Margot Kidder. The only decent way to immortalize our icons is to honor the life and not rape the corpse. Let the Man in Black rest in peace; God knows he deserves it.

BRIAN TEASLEY

NICK CAVE AND THE BAD SEEDS
The Boatman's Call

I love Nick Cave, think he's a genius, would buy his next ten albums even if the clerk at the record store cut off one of my fingers every time I bought one, but *The Boatman's Call* stank up the joint—his weakest lyrics ever, dull melodies, totally uninspired playing. Everybody talks about how "refreshing" this "change of pace" is. "New directions." Spare me. When I want piano ballads I'll write 'em myself.

JOHN DARNIELLE

CHEAP TRICK
Live At Budokan

A record so pressed that there are enough for all 6 billion+ world inhabitants to own one and *never* be able to get rid of it. The only way to pawn this thing off is by having a child, just to create hands that do not already own this mediocre, yet ubiquitous, slab.

JEF HOSKINS

THE CHEMICAL BROTHERS
Exit Planet Dust

When this record came out, every dickhead with a mustache and VD simultaneously shit and came in their pants. This is proof that anyone with a sampler can make a record that will make asshole critics love you. Anyone who fucks either one of these uglies would have to be high enough not to be able to tell how incredibly hideous and deformed they are. I blame these fucks for the very existence of bands like Linkin Park.

LOGAN KEESE

BILLY CHILDISH
Brimful of Hate

Remember back in the early nineties when a new Billy Childish single came out every week? Remember that feeling when you realized that most of them were just crappy cover versions? How much better is it to realize that The Hives got all slobbered over for ripping off a guy who made a career of ripping off other people? After last call, with the PA shut off by the sound guy, I saw Thee Headcoats finish their set with a stomping and clapping a cappella number. That was among the most wonderful live music experiences of my life, but it only barely excuses *Brimful of Hate*.

BEN HELLMANN

CIBO MATTO
Viva La Woman

Homely + Japanese girly + mid-'90s NYC obsession with kitsch + shitty sounding samples + songs about food + the sound of babies on LSD dying in a microwave = Cibo Matto. Warner Brothers sure knew how to pick them way back in the '90s. If that A&R agent still has a job, I'm glad the music industry is fucked.

BRIAN TEASLEY

ERIC CLAPTON
Slowhand

There is no shortage of Clapton critics out there, which calls into question his inclusion in a book of over-rated records. But until the annual worldwide sale of Clapton-related records falls into the single digits (we should allow for Yardbirds newcomers), there's still work to do. On *Slowhand*, it sounds like Clapton had a raging hangover throughout the making of the album and the prime directive was to avoid aggravating Sir Eric's perpetual headache by playing anything too loud or too fast. The album opens with "Cocaine" and "Wonderful

#18
BRUCE SPRINGSTEEN
Born To Run

Bruce Springsteen has long been heralded as a voice of the working class, but the Boss's 1975 "master-piece" is everything the proletariat ain't—overblown, lifeless, and drenched in stilted poetics. The comparisons to Orbison, Spector, and Dylan are unwarranted. Like a Phil Spector nightmare colliding full-on into seventies' no-nothingness.

WILLIAM TYLER

#19
BOB DYLAN
The Freewheelin' Bob Dylan

Is there any more proof someone is overrated than when their songs are continually covered and performed better by other artists? Pick any song off this record and I'll pick you out the cover that sounds ten times better. Dylan also refers to himself in the third-person in two different song titles. That's just weird.

DAVIS REA

#20
FRANK ZAPPA
Anything/Everything He Put Out (Especially What You Call "The Good Stuff")

"Definition of rock journalism: People who can't write, doing interviews with people who can't think, in order to prepare articles for people who can't read."
This Frank Zappa attributed quote is often cited by musicians who deem themselves clever enough to be above rock journalism, usually due to the copious amounts of pussy they're receiving on the road. Pussy settles it, right? "Let's see…you have both pre- and post-show threesomes in motherfuckin' Salt Lake, Mr.-Living-With-Your-Mom fanzine editor!"
Well, there would probably be more than a single sperm's worth of validity to this statement if it hadn't have come from the dude who made the gayest, polka dotted, odd time signature "dude" rock of all-time. Zappa, thankfully now made of ashes, never apologized to all the musicians who he made dance stupidly and act "wacky" on stage. Too bad Zappa's real intent wasn't to make noodle-prone musicians like Terry Bozzio act like complete fucking idiots. If he had done so purposely, Zappa may have indeed been a genius, because unarguably, he definitely hit a novelty rock home run in making his musicians appear as if they had just come in last in the Jazz Competition of the Special Olympics for Senior Retarded Citizens. The real truth is that our aforementioned, sinewy, greasy Jew 'froed, SG-playing dick-whistler was as serious as he wanted to appear not to be.
Zap for Prez? Put down the gravity bong and strangle yourself with the rubber band which now binds your hair in a ponytail, you useless, sedentary, High Times-subscribing ass-licker! Long live the death of Frank Zappa, and may Dweezil and Moon Unit soon have theirs!
"Definition of Frank Zappa: Douche-bag filled with Berkeley School of Music Dropout Jiz."

BRIAN TEASLEY

Tonight," and there are no two better songs to epitomize the self-serving, lazy excesses of '70s classic rock. The gist of the lyrics is, "I'm really, really wasted. Sure, baby, you look great, just drive me home and have breakfast ready in the morning. And don't talk so much, my head's killing me. I am rock star! You serve me, remember! Did I mention how wasted I am?"

MICHAEL FALOON

CLINIC
Walking With Thee

Oh good! This song has a melodica! This one too! And this one! Awesome! Oooh! And this one! Also this one! How could anyone get tired of this?

BEN JOHNSON

COACHWHIPS
Bangers vs. Fuckers

Sonny Boy Williamson once said that the Yardbirds wanted to play the blues so badly, that that's how they played it—badly! The odd thing about this statement in relation to the Coachwhips is that they sound exactly like a crystal meth-fueled Eric Clapton, Jeff Beck, and Jimmy Page furiously fucking Sonny Boy Williams in his prostate cancer. I suppose many of you will think that's a good thing.

BRIAN TEASLEY

LEONARD COHEN

Were that many people on drugs in the '70's? It has always baffled me how this guy got passed off as America's precious pop poet laureate by writing sappy, overly sentimental songs like "Suzanne," "So Long, Marianne," or "I'm Your Man"—the "-an" rhyme scheme being his favorite, apparently.

RON BELL

COLDPLAY
A Rush of Blood to the Head

Remember the '89-'91 hey-day of oil spill disasters? Between the Exxon Valdez partying in Alaska's Prince

William Sound and Saddam Hussein's troops dumping hundreds of millions of crude oil into the Persian Gulf, these few years were truly the golden era—black gold that is…Texas tea! Thousands of pristine shorelines were turned into apocalyptic-looking sludge and countless millions of defenseless wildlife perished. Nightly news became inundated with images of oil-soaked birds and fish. Okay, here's where you have to leap with me just a tiny bit—what's weird is, if you replace those birds or fish with my dick and then put it up on a Jumbotron at my twenty-year high school reunion in front of my own children, then you could begin to take the entrance exam in understanding how much I hate Gwyneth Paltrow's fake-ass British accent.

BRIAN TEASLEY

ELVIS COSTELLO
My Aim Is True

Elvis Costello is one of my all-time favorite songwriters. I love the majority of his catalogue, and I'm one of the few souls who will dare to defend *Mighty Like A Rose* and *North*. Despite my fanaticism, there are two records of his that I just can't stand. One is the universally abhorred *Goodbye, Cruel World*. The other is *My Aim Is True*. Elvis readily admits that he was still struggling to escape from the shadows of The Band, Little Feat and Randy Newman—and it shows. The record is filled with bad puns in the place of clever wordplay that would become Elvis' trademark. The backing band, Clover (a band normally fronted by Huey Lewis, some pedigree!) provide limp-dick country rock for a set of unsure songs. "No Dancing," "Blame It On Cain" and "Less Than Zero" are all great songs, but they lacked true power until they were rearranged by the Attractions. "Welcome To The Working Week" and "The Angels Want To Wear My Red

Shoes" are mediocre at best, and I'd be blown away if anybody could explain how "I'm Not Angry," "Pay It Back" and "Sneaky Feelings" are good songs. My Aim Is True isn't a terrible record, but it's certainly overrated and showed little signs of the incredible run of records to come. The Elvis Costello of *Armed Forces*, *This Year's Model* and *Get Happy* was a furious madman known for getting wildly drunk, womanizing and making inflammatory remarks. I can hardly see the Elvis of My Aim Is True doing anything more than wearing a lampshade on his head and passing out after a few too many Peppermint Schnapps.

ABRAHAM SCOTT

JOHN COUGAR
American Fool

While "Jack and Diane" and "Hurts So Good" don't sound half-bad after several cans of domestic light beer, the rest of this album is unbearably patronizing and samey. "Cougar," as Mellencamp was then known, tries so hard to be the blue-collar everyman, you'd think he'd slob the gearshift of a primer-gray Chevy just to prove it.

RANDY HARWARD

COUNTING CROWS
August And Everything After

When this record came out, everyone said, "Wow, it sounds so much like Van Morrison." To which these douchebags replied, "Oh yeah, we're huge Van Morrison fans. Guess it shows, huh?" Well, buy me another drink because I'm not wasted enough to swallow that shit. I got your number, Adam "Jew-fro" Duritz. When Toad the Wet Sprocket came along and introduced R.E.M-lite to the world, you flipped out. You said, "Hey Crows, let's go back and listen to all that obscure shit R.E.M claims to be really huge fans of, like Big Star and Television." You know, do a little more homework

than Toad. Then what happened? You put out a perfect replica of *Out Of Time*. And not a minute too soon. You got your foot in the door right before Hootie did.

DAG LUTHER GOOCH

Pollack on Pollack!

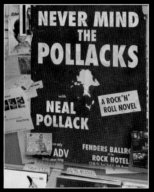

NEAL POLLACK
Never Mind The Pollacks

Chunklet asked me to talk about why my book, *Never Mind The Pollacks,* is overrated, but that's going to be hard for me because I think the book is being rated about where it deserves to be rated. People like it, are amused by it, find it a little overlong, think the songs are dumb, the satire biting, and the characters a little thin. They get the joke that it's supposed to resemble a short, dumb, loud rock album. I'm not being praised as the best young novelist of my generation, and my name isn't being mentioned along with anyone named Jonathan. My position in the culture (toward the middle bottom) is exactly what it should be.

Also, my album is certainly not overrated, though I'm a little stunned at some of the *CMJ* reports, particularly the station in Jacksonville that is charting us at #2, above every single album in the country except for the new Ween. Well, I guess it is a little overrated. Some kid wrote me and said it was one of the greatest albums "of all time." You make your independent judgment. Some reviewer called it "an enjoyable novelty, if nothing else." Again, you make the call.

Where I *am* overrated, however, is as a political pundit. I can't believe people read my website and find interesting my hackneyed observations about the Bush administration's stupid military adventures and assaults on civil liberties. I mean, yes, the site can be funny sometimes, but anyone who considers me any kind of a political pundit lives in a world of sad delusion. Michael Moore, Al Franken—now *those* are serious political figures. Me, I'm just a suburban housedad ranting at the TV. Remember that the next time you want me to be the grand marshal of your May Day parade.

Eh, who gives a shit?

NEAL POLLACK

CROOKED FINGERS
Crooked Fingers

I also think that making fun of effeminate gay men

and/or rednecks is easy. Sure it's fun and we all do it, but...come on.

You know, there's nothing more beautiful than a song about shit, scum, rape, vomit, sodomy, vaginal dis-

charge, physical deformity, animal abuse, mental illness, rotting, drowning, lung disease or manic depression. This record has them all. If Springsteen's *Nebraska* was a sawed-off shot gun in your lap, Crooked Fingers' first record is explicit directions on how to kill yourself with it.

DAG LUTHER GOOCH

THE CULT
Love

There are lots of records about which you can say, "Man, that shit all sounds the same." But there are an elite few about which you can actually say, "Man, all of this shit *is* the same": *Java Jive* by the Ink Spots, Rage Against the Machine's debut, *You'd Prefer an Astronaut* by Hum. But *Love* by the Cult is the mother of all one-song albums. The chord structure of every single song is exactly the same and, to make it more obvious, the bassist plays the same three notes—and only those notes—on every single song, picked out like a trip hammer. Why does everybody say this shit sounds like Led Zeppelin? It sounds like Big Country revising the Cure.

DAG LUTHER GOOCH

THE CURE
Wish

Supposedly, it was the third album of the Cure's second great trilogy (*Seventeen Seconds, Faith,* and *Pornography* being the first). But where *Kiss Me, Kiss Me, Kiss Me* showed truly wild mood swings, and *Disintegration* showed depth rarely seen, *Wish* really just glosses over the top with a couple of hit singles and songs that are long for the sake of being long.

JIM RAYMOND

MILES DAVIS
Sketches of Spain

Okay, I like Miles a lot, but I do hold him responsible for all of those lanky, white, technically-proficient-but-utterly-soulless Berklee College of Music turd monkeys, because this is the album they buy. If they really wanted to be more like Miles, they'd score some coke on the way home.

AMANDA NICHOLS

DEAD BOYS
Young, Loud and Snotty

Stiv started with so much promise, but the ghost of Iggy haunted him until the day he died. It's sad to see someone trying so hard to get past his influences and failing. An unforgivably bad second record didn't help much either.

RUSS FORSTER

DEAD KENNEDYS
Bedtime For Democracy

As if already putting out 8 billion other albums of self absorbed poetry slam politics set to amphetamined surf crap (as sung by a tuneless frog imitator with Parkinsons) weren't enough, in 1986, the Dead Kennedys managed to release *Bedtime for Democracy*, an album of the same sans whatever it was that tricked us into liking them in the first place.

PABLO A. ROCKAFUCKER

THE DECEMBERISTS
Her Majesty The Decemberists

I will never understand the connection people make between this band and Neutral Milk Hotel. Sure, both bands employ a vast array of instruments and replicate a sort of vaudevillian sound, but they are two different beasts entirely. If anything, The Decemberists are simply Neutral Milk Hotel light—very, very light. Jeff Magnum was at his best when the images he evoked in his lyrics became the most harrowing. This, combined with his powerful, dark, acoustic arrangements, formed some of the '90s most original and captivating music. Kind of the brilliant dark side of the Elephant Six collective. The Decemberists are simply too light, airy and even optimistic to be comparable to Neutral Milk Hotel. But that's not why they're overrated. They're overrated because they're more caught up in replicating an era than in forging their own identity. At points, like the sparse, affecting "Red Right Ankle," all the cogs in the machinery of The Decemberists clicks. But when songwriter/vocalist Colin Meloy gets his words too tied up in the imagery of yester-century with lyrics like "Billy Liar's got his hands in his pockets/Staring over at his neighbor's, knickers down/He's got his knickers down," it all becomes a bit ughh-worthy. Their sound is fine, but the lyrics need to catch up with the 21st century. Reading Dickens is boring enough, having to listen to it is downright unbearable.

DRYW KELTZ

DEF LEPPARD
Pyromania

Many claim *Pyromania* is Def Leppard's finest moment—perhaps the greatest record to come out of the early-'80s pop-metal crossover years. The only explanation I can think of for otherwise intelligent people's impassioned defense of the album is that, as children of the '80s, they first heard *Pyromania* when they were too young to really be responsible for their taste. And with the help of the highly-selective memory that seems to power both nostalgia and classic-rock radio, they only seem to recall how rocking songs like "Photograph," "Rock of Ages," and "Foolin'" seemed to their still-forming, borderline-retarded pre-teen brains. As I was once one of those children myself, I will grant that those songs still stimulate the vestigial remains of whatever pleasure center they acted on in the first place—and with irony as my armor, I will turn every single one of them up when it comes on the radio and sing it loud. But let's be honest here. Beyond those tracks (and maybe "Too Late for Love") this record's pretty much a wasteland. For example, try to remember what "Billy's Got a Gun" or "Comin' Under Fire" sound like. And try to conceive of the reserves of irony it would take to claim with a straight face that "Die Hard the Hunter" (sample lyrics: "You don't know how to change from bad to good/You brought the war to your neighborhood") is a legitimate song. It's somewhat akin to imagining the reserves of alcohol one would have to consume to claim present-day Kirstie Alley as a legitimate sexual fantasy. As for *Pyromania*'s place in the pantheon of Def Lep records, keep in mind that what came before was a bunch of ham-handed retreads of AC/DC riffs and what came after was a bunch of one-armed, synth-drum-powered soft-rock hits like "Animal," "Hysteria," and "Love Bites." And as for its place at the top of the early '80s pop-metal crossover heap, if you're the king of a hill whose other denizens include Dokken's *Breaking the Chains*, Triumph's *Allied Forces* and the Yngwie Malmsteen-Ron Keel vehicle Steeler, I don't think you're going to have to worry too much about anyone making a play for that crown.

CHRIS ISELI

THE DELTA 72
000

Actually, the band wasn't that bad, but Gregg "The Foreman" Foremann (as he referred to himself) is a colossal douchebag who—through talking behind backs, dope shooting and date rape—managed to alienate any club/band/person who tried to befriend the group. When he refers to his band as "going through our *Exile* period," you wonder what happened to all the shitty electronic music that he made in college before seeing The Make*Up and stealing their shtick. Just ask Ian.

BEN BLACKWELL

THE DICTATORS

These guys just don't do it, and just because they're a bunch of aging toughs plus a nerd in good clothing from New York, it doesn't make me want to respect them anymore than, say, the current Stranglers line-up. These guys are the same ones who used to kick your faggoty little Wire-listening ass up and down the high school hallway while laughing at your hair, glasses, and clothing the whole way through. And now they want you to bend down and kiss their asses as they manage to crank out second-rate Blue Oyster Cult riffs and ultra-macho poses? Fuck that shit. "Burn Baby Burn" is killer, as is "All I Need Is A Kiss," but the lack of any sort of swish factor makes them next door neighbors to those fraternity assholes who, while bombed on Piels, gang-raped your little sister on a pool table last year.

NICK BLAKEY

THE DISMEMBERMENT PLAN
Emergency & I

If I wanted to hear white funk, I'd take KC and the Sunshine Band over this group of suburbanites. Eager to cite weirder musical references than anyone else, the closest these "more clever than thou" pansies will ever get to the raw emotions of Sly and the Family Stone is when they get the shit kicked out of them in Harlem to the beat of "Don't Call Me Nigger, Whitey." Can't you just picture it? The Dismemberment Plan pull up to the Apollo Theater, random sports team t-shirts/dirty jeans/mop top haircuts intact, *Shaft* soundtrack in one hand and Swiz singles in the other, trying to unite the races like condescending televangelists. If they had any talent at all (which they don't), it'd all be beat out of 'em along with their brains and guts.

TIMOTHY DEN

DJ ALBUMS
all of them
...Except two, which do not need to be mentioned because they were hyped enough already. DJ albums are the ska of emo. I would rather be addicted to TV in a world where the only shows are called *ConAir* and *Seven* than to be forced to have ears during another phase of pretentious, vapid DJ culture. Actually, that's not true. I could not handle seeing another second of either *ConAir* or *Seven*, so bring on the DJs! (Maybe I should die.)

PATRICK HUGHES

DJ SHADOW
Endtroducing...
I read the advance reviews—fawning, ubiquitous (in NYC, at least), overripe to the extreme—and thought, my, oh my, this electronica thing certainly has a lot of potential (I'll mention Tricky again here, with a nod to that rad Lee Perry jungle record). Maybe I'll go buy this DJ Shadow thingy. I don't have the vocabulary to describe my shock when I threw this thing on. When I listened to this, all my self doubt vanished instantly. I realized the rock press were a fraudulent bunch of sheep that can't make up their own minds about anything.

I mean this literally: this one record changed my life (along with the groundwork laid by hosannas for *Odelay*). I knew I could do anything, nobody would ever care, and I'd be a better human being for it.

FAT BOBBY

DJ SPOOKY
Subliminal Minded
Hyped as this profound DJ/artist ("post-modern poet") to the point where I indulged in supporting him for a bit, assuming that it was all an ironic attempt to signal the end of DJ culture. Then, he got in that tiff with Crosby (or some other crack-addled fat guy with a mustache, bad whiteheads and millions of bastard children) in the *Village Voice*. So, I vote for DJ Spooky for leading me on. He hurt my feelings by being serious and sucking at the same time. Apparently, he also majored in French. Double-suck on you, Spooky!

PATRICK HUGHES

THE DOORS
Entire catalog
Idiotic keyboards, musicians who can't play, and drunken faux shamanism? Where do I sign? The fact that these elements have led to rock godhood, a biopic, and countless rotations on classic rock radio should embarrass everybody. "Dude, he pulled his cock out in public!" So do countless drunken frat boys, and you don't see them on the cover of *Mojo*. Lowest Point: "Touch Me;" but, to be fair, there are many.

PAPA CRAZEE

Jim Morrison, a poet? Fuck me in the asshole with a ten-inch, serrated, aluminum spoon. The cat was a decent lyricist at best, but mostly a drunken, tripped-out casualty from an era when only one person whose full name was James could ever be considered a genius. Not even mentioning that lousy garage band (in the most un-hip sense

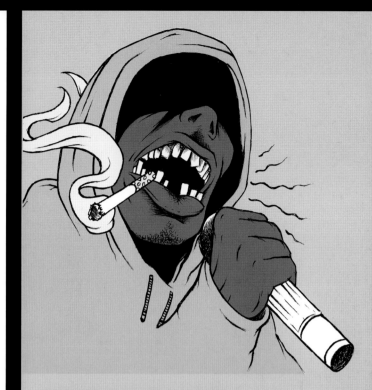

UNDERGROUND BRITISH HIP-HOP
'Ello, Guvna! Whot's oll this abou? Yeu fink yor 'ard? Blimey, that's impossible, it is. 'Ow can yeu be 'ard if yeu ain't got guns, then? Yeu ain't been 'ard since bloody India. That little bloke with his diapah, sittin' round not doin' nuffin', was enough to stop the 'ole Bri'ish army! If yeu fink yor as 'ard as eese blokes across 'a pond, yor bleedin' steupid, mate. Whot's 'at? Yeu been stabbed? Yeu daft git, 'at bloke 50 Cent's been shot more times 'en yeu been stabbed. And ee's a be'ah MC, too. Bloody wankah.

And yeu! Prancin' about! Yeu coll yeself The Streets? Whot streets izzat, exactly? Piccadilly? Yeu bloody poof. Git offa staige!

And oll the rest a yeu! Ain't nobody 'ere cares about yor "garage" meusic. It's bloody boorin', it is. In fact, we've 'ad it wiff the lot a yeu. Leave the rappin' to us yanks, fank yeu. Daon't embarrass yeself wiff 'ip-'op like ye did wiff de blues.

BEN JOHNSON

DANCE ROCK
Didn't rock once do epic battle with disco? Weren't there on-air record smashings back in the day when radio was still semi-relevant? Didn't pot-bellied coke-snorters get rich by manufacturing lines of merchandise carrying the slogan "Disco Sucks"? Didn't rock win? And shouldn't somebody tell Ok Go, Junior Senior, !!! and the Electric Six?

BENN RAY

of the term) that tried to back him up, only to fail miserably in some pretentious excuse for improvisation. They couldn't even find a fucking bass player that would dare to embarrass himself behind "The Lizard King." The Doors might be genius to a twelve-year-old kid that just found out that he has testicles, but groundbreaking classic rock? Please, if you disagree, then take the time to lick the no-man's land between my asshole and my scrotum.

ANTHONY MELITA

DR. DRE
The Chronic
You can just buy a real George Clinton record, and you'll have more money left over for pot. No, wait! Bad idea. Pot smokers generally make lame, boring music, and this is a prime example.

JEFF SMITH

DR. JOHN
Gris-Gris
People who aren't from New Orleans eat this Dr. John shit up like pancakes. They can't get enough of it. Those of us that have to be around it all of the time hate you people. Quit egging this fat fuck on. What is it about this particular album that you like? You just pulled it out of thin air, didn't you? Anything would have done, really. How about *In the Right Place*? You like that album, too? Really? Let me guess, you showed your tits to get those beads, didn't you? You are God's gift to French Quarter drunks: a slutty tourist.

DAG LUTHER GOOCH

DREAM SYNDICATE
The Days Of Wine And Roses
A reminder that neo-conservative Atlanta rock critics weren't getting any pussy in the 80's either.

EMERSON DAMERON

DROPKICK MURPHYS
Do Or Die
Jesus shitballs. In '97 here in loverly New England every skinhead I knew was all jazzed about these guys, and, like, overnight they get comparatively huge for that scene and now ugly fat high school boys whose parents won't let them shop at Hot Topic can wear plaid shirts and have their own little closeted homo-erotic fantasy land of brotherhood and brawling. And the goddamn Boston Hibernophilia thing drives me absolutely bonkers. Makes me ashamed to drink sometimes.

BEN HELLMANN

STEVE EARLE
Anything From The '90s
I prefer "New Hot Country" to this dude's boring, been-there-done-that demeanor and blues rock masquerading as rebel country (even if the critics disagree). He should shitcan the outlaw pretense and just join Social Distortion already.

PAPA CRAZEE

EMINEM
Slim Shady
2 Live Crew was nastier. NWA and Public Enemy had more to say. MC Paul Barman is funnier. The Beastie Boys are smarter. L.L.'s still got more muscle. Triple Six is more ghetto with-it, and even Kid Rock (picking up where Aerosmith and Run DMC left off) is more innovative. What is it about this poster boy for boilerplate shock-rock that makes critics ejaculate? I'd rather listen to Rod Stewart giving Elton John phone sex, while wearing Whitney Houston's flayed skin like an Armani suit, than suffer through this disc one more time.

CHRIS DAVIS

BRIAN ENO
Ambients 1-4 & Music For Films
Yawn. Yawn. You know the rock records are really, really good, even though that one had Phil Collins on it. Yawn.

CHRIS MCGARVEY

ERASE ERRATA
At Crystal Palace
Rule number one: if someone from Sonic Youth produces a record or goes on for fifty pages about it in some shit magazine interview it's automatically overrated garbage. Rule number two: if only the freaky hardcore fans claim it to be your best, it's garbage.

ERIN O'NEAL

ROKY ERICKSON
All That May Do My Rhyme
I'll say one thing for Roky: the dude is old-school-fucking-crazy. After the mental institution stay and digesting enough psychedelic drugs that he actually became poisonous to the touch, Roky's brain was completely fried by the time the '80s rolled around. So much so that working with The Butthole Surfer's Paul Leary seemed like a cool idea and failing to even complete some of the lyrics was only a minor setback.

DAVIS REA

FACES
A Nod is as Good as a Wink
Being sloppy, drunk, and handsome in that snaggle-tooth British working-class sort of way never worked quite as well as it did for these wankstains. Anyone with Rod Stewart/Ron Wood hair: please pull the pin out with your teeth and then place the grenade in your underwear. Hopefully, if it doesn't kill you, then at least it will blow your dick off, thus not allowing you to spread your diseased seed to future generations. C'mon, you fucking hair club for boys—the buck...err, rooster stops here!

BRIAN TEASLEY

THE FALL
This Nation's Saving Grace
Weren't Mark E. Smith's rants and Brix Smith's twanging guitar supposed to predict both The Pixies and Pavement? Or were they a more accessible version and I just had to be their maaaaan? I've noticed lately that *This Nation's Saving Grace* is popping up on best album of the 80's lists. Hey fools, you ever hear *Thriller*?

ANTONIO DEPIETRO

FAUST
Faust
If Faust prided itself on a wealth of ideas, then they were spent rather at the expense of Jews. Okay, let's deal with the obvious first, which is the link between band members' ancestry and the Nazi party. At least three members are merely two generations away from prominent Nazi party leaders and politicians, and original member Arnulf Meifer is the beloved grandson of none other than the ruthless SS and Gestapo commander, Heinrich Himmler. Of course, it is their prodigious use of Third Reich imagery that makes their music what could only be termed as "hate art." If scientists and musicians were given a task to spew forth the most vile of contempt for the Jewish race, then Faust would have been created—and it was. The blood of Auschwitz lies deep within the grooves of their debut LP, which boasts an x-ray (Nazi scientists had looked into using radiation to torture those left in the Warsaw ghetto) of an iron-like Hitler fist. It is widely known that the torturous cut-and-paste mixture of sound Faust created was said by the band itself to be Muzik Gaskammer—or gas chamber music. In fact, it was leaked (unfortunate pun) to Virgin Records (who would put out the dreaded *Faust IV*) that the band actually intended to have a jacket which would unleash Buntkreuz, a mixture of a lethal phosgene-type gas and an irritant that could

penetrate even army-issued gas-masks. Thankfully, the whole gas-releasing sleeve only went down as a legend; but, without a doubt, the lethal mix of power, fear, and cruelty of the SS was carried into the 1970s by the recordings of Faust. It is unfortunate that the fruit of such a poisoned tree has, over the last 10 years, been devoured by a crop of American bands who, in fairness, duplicate the genre fairly well. More unfortunate still is the fact that the British have done wretchedly poor imitations of the genre—one that should have ended with the Nuremberg Trials. Such attempts that are still going strong in the U.K. only beckon the image of Paddington the Bear attempting to build a V-1 rocket out of string, a rubber band, pigeon feathers, and a single onion bhaji. Let us now and forever end the idea of racial cleansing in our hearts, minds, and music. The world needs peace and solace from the acts (and sounds) of genocide.

BRIAN TEASLEY

FIERY FURNACES
Blueberry Boat

Jesus Christ, are people just not interested in buying used records anymore? That's the only reason I can think of for the popularity of bands like this. I don't listen to new punk rock, and I'm certainly not going to buy new interpretations of early Psychic TV. I am a dinosaur, I acknowledge this, but can we get past this post-rock nonsense already? How the hell is re-contextualizing the music we heard in doctors' offices in any way interesting?

BEN HELLMANN

FLAMING LIPS
Zaireeka

Aside from the novelty of this release (four discs that must be played at the same time), the only reason people give *Zaireeka* so much credit is because most people who own it have only

heard it once. For the amount of trouble it takes to get four CD players in the room along with four friends sober enough to hit the play button at the same time *Zaireeka* better fucking be *Pet Sounds*, and it ain't.

BENN RAY
The Soft Bulletin
Proof that anyone can make a *great* album using Pro Tools software.

JIM RAYMOND

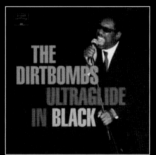

Dirtbomb on Dirtbomb!

THE DIRTBOMBS
Ultraglide in Black
Anyone can cherry pick from the soul greats Curtis, Smokey and Marvin and make a great record, but there's nothing on this album that elevates The Dirtbombs over bar band status. Sounds like the whole thing was recorded in one take and that Mick Collins, after 15-plus years on the music scene, still has yet to buy a tuner. The faux-live tracks make imagining a Lou Reed bowel movement actually sound appetizing. The only reason this album got any attention is because it was released relatively close to *White Blood Cells* and all the dumbshit music writers were playing the revisionist historian game giving credit to the Gories, vis-à-vis Mick Collins and The Dirtbombs.

BEN BLACKWELL, DRUMMER

Yoshimi Battles The Pink Robots
Proof that anyone can make a *mediocre* album using Pro Tools software.

JIM RAYMOND

FRANZ FERDINAND
Franz Ferdinand
Every year, rock's (supposed) Next Big Thing is trotted out and foisted upon the listening/buying public to critical acclaim and commercial success—often times before even a single note from these misbegotten dog-and-pony shows can assault one's ears. The formula has become cloying, pre-

dictable, trite, obvious and comedic: every-fuckin' year, unsuspecting music listeners/buyers are subjected to overrated acts like The Postal Service, Coldplay, The White Stripes, The Strokes, Interpol, and the countless other bands who preceded them. These are bands whose spectacle, theatrics, image, and hip-thrusting stimulation far outweighs their marginal musical output. This year is no different. Enter Franz Ferdinand—a group of pea coat-bedecked Scottish lads whose angular ruckus sounds like a quartet of pseudo-intellectual, thrift store enthusiasts licking the shit out of the asses of Wire, XTC and Gang of Four. Named after Hitler's dad's golf-buddy's enemy or something, Franz Ferdinand is the hottest, most innovative and groundbreaking band since last year's hottest, most innovative and groundbreaking band. Yes, they are that good! It's only a matter of time before Franz Ferdinand will be

everywhere at once: dance clubs, magazine covers, television commercials, post cards, t-shirts, those little 1" pins, billboards, your girlfriend's pants, etc. Franz Ferdinand's obnoxiously bland CD cover will grace end-caps at record stores like Tower, Virgin and your local record shop with that cute guy who has slept with everyone. Look for this cheeky bunch to mug it up in every mainstream magazine's Hot List/Sheet/Spot, cashing in on their scruffy Scottish-ness. Their hit song ("Take It Out," "Let's Get Take-Out," "Take The Rough-Housing Outside" or whatever the fuck it's called) will be in every $3 club in every dive bar in every town in America. If Franz Ferdinand were a good band, they would have taken the time to tour and gradually built up a fan base through word-of-mouth recognition. But, like most of these overrated bands, the Clear Channel hype-machine has kicked-in full swing, thus making Franz Ferdinand this year's "It" band by decree of fast-track marketing. And it seems as if tasteless Americans are perfectly willing to comply (especially those fashionably shallow gals that just love being up-to-the-minute on dudes with foreign accents that are in bands). Any hipster worth his weight in Sauconys will already have Franz Ferdinand's entire album on their iPod, nestled between Modest Mouse and The Stills. Indeed, who can't get enough of songs whose narrative drive deals with nubile librarians, ether binges, or experimental gay lust? Yes, appealing to the seemingly edgy, yet conventionally fey, university art student trump card rears its ugly, beaten-to-death head once again! A&R suits from every hole on Earth have nipped at this band's heels in a bid to cash in and cash out Franz

HIP HOP FOR WHITES

I'm sure we'd all fuck Fergie eight ways to sundown (as if she hasn't been already, repeatedly), but she and Aesop Rock can rap about robots and enlightenment until the mad cows come home and this shit will still be overrated. Kanye can convince Midwestern jocks to wear pink and this shit will still be overrated. Kids can wear backpacks and cocked hats to shows, steadily nodding their bearded heads to off kilter beats, and this shit will still be overrated. Know why? Because "intelligent hip hop" is (and always will be) an oxymoron.

BRIAN MCMANUS

POST PUNK

Had Gang of Four only known what their influence would have been, they would've dropped their balls in toaster ovens, thrown them into a tub filled with blood and set their taints on fire rather than add angles to disco music and dress it in skinny ties. They're good guys. I honestly think they would've done that for humanity.

BRIAN MCMANUS

Ferdinand's marketability to these Suburban Outfitted dupes. You will soon bow before Franz Ferdinand's dance club sensibilities—like it or not. The only bright spot in all of this is that Franz Ferdinand's hype will subside when they release their sophomore effort in the year following. Both rock snobs (you know, those people who hate all of those bands that you like) and those British music tabloids that just absolutely loved Franz Ferdinand's first slab-o-crap will both rate this band as shit (actually, those fickle British rags will have probably railed on Franz Ferdinand by the time this book is published). By that time, people who still own Franz Ferdinand's first album will all be using the same excuse these people always do when the topic of why they actually still own an out-of-date album comes up: "C'mon. Some of these songs are still pretty good." Not that this really matters too much. Next year, these same schmucks will be singing the praises of a new accessibly crappy band that's even more mediocre and overrated than Franz Ferdinand. It happens every year.

TONY P. KING

FREE
Fire and Water

When I was at the 2004 British Music Hall of Fame awards, I witnessed Paul Rogers having his roadies put gaffer tape marks where his mic stand was suppose to land when he—more predictably than visible peanuts and corn in your shit—threw it in the air at the end of "All Right Now." Such scripted showmanship is just the sort of cornball professionalism that slaughtered everything that was loose and impulsive about late '60s rock. Just throw the goddamn thing and let it land in the fucking orchestra pit or something, you later-Bad-Company-forming faggot! Oh, how little we've learned

in 35 years since this sort of Vietnam-back-turning mega-rock was in all of its carefree glory. Even on the most cocaine-fueled nights, Free's feel-good, summer-time-jammin' boogie blues couldn't knock the skin off rice pudding.

BRIAN TEASLEY

FUGAZI
13 Songs

Although they improved with later albums, every song on this sounds the same, and that one song is utterly boring, utterly unsexy, and utterly devoid of any humor, wit, and real intelligence. This record will not stand the test of time. It has spawned a thousand even worse bands. In fifty years, people will look back and ask, "Were these people incapable of having fun in their lives?"

THOMAS DAVIES

PETER GABRIEL
So

So? What? So...So...S-s-s-s-spit it out, bitch! And just admit, the reason you have "so" many musicians propping up this record is because it's the only way to cover up the fact every song on it sounds like filler material from your better records? "So," ever notice there are enough musicians on this record to have one band playing the songs, and another band just for the reverb. "So," why do you need eight fucking drummers again? "So," why do you think you needed Kate Bush for backing vocals? Answers, motherfucker! The way I see it, if I have to listen to your tunes while I'm rolling around with the older chicks, I at least deserve to know what your excuse is.

DAG LUTHER GOOCH

GANG GANG DANCE
Gang Gang Dance

This half-assed medieval-midi schlock sounds like a pissing contest by a bunch of fat, drunken goth girls who like to think they are witches...until   they're crushed in a car wreck and find out the hard way that they have no real power. Most annoying is how the drummer plays the same accents that fall heavily on the first half of the phrase on every goddamn song. Ladies and Gypsies, please stop making these horrible audio incantations and go back to the Falafel-making industry. Baby is hungry!

BRIAN TEASLEY

GANG OF FOUR
Entertainment!

I love this record. If I could, I would get a chip implanted in my brain that makes me perpetually feel the way I did when I first heard it. That said, this record is not the Rosetta Stone that will help one trace the roots of any trend. Even the bands that say they're influenced by Gang Of Four are probably thinking about the *idea* of them rather than the actual music. Side one has good songs bookended by better songs. Side two has weak songs bookended by less weak songs.

BEN HELLMANN

GORILLAZ
Gorillaz, G-Sides, Spacemonkeyz Vs. Gorillaz, Demon Days

Talk about drawing blood from a stone! 2001's *Gorillaz* was, like all "all-star" projects, a classic case of too many cooks in the kitchen. Most of the participants were marginally talented, but the sum of the parts added up to an unsatisfying whole. The best thing about the record was Tank Girl creator Jaime Hewliett's packaging. If I thought that was reason enough to buy an album, I would own a CD by Mindless Self Indulgence, and I would in turn be a terrible person. *Gorillaz* should have been a forgettable one-off. Instead, it became some type of inescapable cultural phenomena. Kids at my high school would sing the chorus from "Clint Eastwood" in the halls, and adult hipsters actually believed that the Gorillaz were "cool!" I could

hardly believe my eyes when I saw the release of *G Sides* (ugh) a crass rip-off that had a scant nine songs. I was even more stunned when a fucking DUB REMIX RECORD hit the racks. I couldn't imagine anything more useless. I was proven wrong when *Demon Days* was released. The first record's production seemed like a bunch of leftover beats from *Deltron 3030*. Demon Days managed to be even more dull, enlisting the 'talents' of producer DJ Dangermouse - a guy who was primarily known for popularizing "mash-ups." In a more perfect world, the entire Gorillaz catalogue would be rotting in the bargain bin with *Chipmunk Punk* and *The Adventures Of MC Skat Cat and the Stray Mob*.

ABRAHAM SCOTT

GRANDADDY
The Sophtware Slump

This album proves that if you go "dit-ditditdit-diddly-diddly" with some sort of computery noise in the background of a bunch of dumb songs about drunk robots, then you'll have an album that everybody loves. But be careful! If you take away the "dit-ditditdit-diddlydiddly" everybody will know you're a jackass. So for God's sake, stick to the diddlies. Jackass.

BEN JOHNSON

GRATEFUL DEAD
American Beauty

If I was forced—at gunpoint—to choose between listening to any Grateful Dead album or lick my Uncle Milton's taint, I would choose *American Beauty*. But I imagine that the entire time I was listening to it, I would be thinking, "A taint is just skin, and after all, he is my uncle." By the time it got to "Brokedown Palace," my uncle would be pulling his pants down because that's what it would take to make me keep listening to the rest of the record.

DAG LUTHER GOOCH

GREASE
Motion Picture Soundtrack

They sure got some mileage out of this bullshit Fonzie musical. Boy howdy, it's a late '70s re-enactment of life in the sock-hoppin' late '50s! Have you ever noticed that nothing on this record sounds like it was from the '50s? Or the '70s, for that matter? How many doo-wop bands do you remember had 60 people in them? I guess you could argue that it's in a soundtrack class of its own. To which I would reply, "Fuck you. It sounds like a school play," and then slap the shit out of you. Now, grow up, give your yearbook back to your mom, and wake up to the fact that Olivia is wearing diapers.

DAG LUTHER GOOCH

GREEN DAY
Kerplunk!

Wow, even more great riffs, fellas! Hey, speaking of which, what songs did you get them from?

BRIAN TEASLEY

GUIDED BY VOICES
Bee Thousand

When hearing the second decent song on this record, you realize that you would have had time to do your taxes, fold some laundry, and maybe cook dinner since you heard the first one. Robert Pollard probably has one of those refrigerator magnets that says, "I know I ain't junk cuz' God don't let people drink two cases of beer in a day and have a home studio."

BOB SCHRINER

Alien Lanes

I remember when this record was released and I thought to myself, "Oh, wow, another 30 or so tracks of worthless aural bed-pissing." When I gave it a listen I had found out that I was wrong about this record. You see, I figured that there would be four songs that made me think of a full grown man scrunched

into a little elf suit doing his best home-recorded Paul McCartney going off on Michael Stipe. As it turned out there were only three of those songs on the record, leaving much more time for that "classic" Robert Pollard style hissing, noise, annoying guitar repetitions and muttering vocals. I always thought that the state of Ohio would have better standards than this.

BOB SCHRINER

THE GUN CLUB
Fire of Love

What do get when you add a tragic band member death and fistfuls of hard drugs to the paradigm popularized by the Stray Cats? Well, you can see where this is going, my little 12-bar blues hipster. Again, it seems white people wish more than anything to be slaves and play bastardized, snotty suburban versions of field spirituals originally spawned by the blistering North Mississippi sun. Mostly they do this so as not to actually have to learn to play their instruments very well. I just don't remember a whole lot of sharecropping in LA, but history isn't one of my strong suits, and what better human travesty to have a fetish for than slavery? Nonetheless, sped-up, narrative-steeped Marty Robbins-inspired tales set against poorly recorded X wannabe-isms are now perfectly suited to be in rotation at Urban Outfitters across greater Metropolitan United States. Every time you hear some wretched, ear-splitting, bassless record you can blame The Gun Club or, at least the Blondie Fan Club of which Jeffrey Lee Pierce was the a one-time president. Of course, we all are aware that the Blues Hammer band in *Ghost World* was based on The Gun Club, and that has only further made them into the pathetic legends that they are. God, please forgive the white race for we know not what we do.

BRIAN TEASLEY

GUNS N' ROSES
Appetite for Destruction

Even the name of this band is so cliché that I had trouble taking them seriously when I first heard about them. I actually kind of liked that "Welcome to the Jungle" song (though it felt like a New York Dolls rip-off) when Z-Rock (the syndicated "real rock" radio station of the late-80's) used to play it, but when I heard the other "hits" I realized that these guys really rocked about as hard as Bon Jovi on a bad hair day. They tried to use some racist statements in a song or two to prove that they were "bad ass," but it came off as "dumb ass." The proof of the pudding is the god-awful ballads they started performing to clinch the female demographic. Come to think of it, didn't Kiss do the same thing?

RUSS FORSTER

HANOI ROCKS
Anything/Everything They Put Out

I've never understood why hipster DJs cum out of their tight, toddler-like assholes over Hanoi Rocks. Those limp-riffed hairspray terrorists couldn't have found a decent glam metal hook if it was in a worm that was in one of their own feet. Seriously, Spread Eagle, or maybe Vain, could have thrashed these guys like the little, two hour pre-show primping bitches that they were. Michael Monroe and his preening girlish cohorts now actually make, equally irrelevant, but more current, wannabe aurora borealis-rockers, the Backyard Babies, look like they rock as much as, say, a Bullet Boys cover band—something Hanoi Rocks couldn't have done, even on their best night (which was probably in Tokyo in '83). Jesus, for all that raping and pillaging the Vikings did, Scandos of the modern age rock it like your grandmother's pussy after it's just been stuck full of a local anesthetic.

The Hanoi Rock Cockers simply were just untalented queens who may, at a time, have gotten a lot of pussy, but unfortunately, for their unwanted children, they probably wasted the little in the undeserved record advances they received on lavender-colored neckerchiefs, not sound 401k plans. Put forthrightly in their place, they should now merely be remembered as a third world Poison without any vision. Falling (failing) somewhere betwixt the oily ass-crack of late period, Revenge-era T.S.O.L and anything Kip Winger has done post-Winger, the Hanoi Rocks should have invested in some halfway-to-memorable vocal melodies instead of costume store ruffled shirts and handcuffs for their belt loops. Please remember this rock lesson: Finland (plus) Dudes wearing blue zebra-print shit (plus) Isle of Wight ham-fisted drummer (plus) egregiously worn lipstick (plus) a complete lack of talent, has always (=) totally gay.

Stop spending way too much money for their jokey-ass Japanese picture discs on eBay (a.k.a. the hipster equalizer for those who can't go find shit for themselves). Of course, what choice did Scandinavian glam boot lickers who were mostly known for their cover of Creedence's "Up Around The Bend" have but to achieve success with gullible, taste-less Asians. It's such a lucky thing (for him) that a drunk-driving Vince Neil killed Razzle, because the death he would have gotten at my hands if he had kept up that shitarded, weak-ass, sub par New York Doll-ish drumming would have been far worse.

My only regret now is not being at the crash site in '85 to put my asshole up against his cold dead lips.

BRIAN TEASLEY

HAPPY MONDAYS
everything post-Bummed

While Bummed remains the single greatest record ever made by white people freebasing heroin and cocaine (and is also the last notable production job of the late, great Martin Hannett, who did the record purely to fund his drug addiction), the Happy Mondays must have sold their abilities along with their souls to their dealers immediately following its release.

Despite 24 Hour Party People's claims, New Order were the actual kings of Factory Records, while the Mondays were merely their mindless sycophants. Shaun Ryder's tendency to be about as coherent as a stoned Finn with a stutter certainly has its charms (especially when you're high), but his endless repeats of "you're twisting my melon, man" on their cover of "Step On" doubtlessly does not refer to his wallet or his tits. Anyhow, most of the people who bought their records got rid of them when they gave up E and raves for jobs or death.

NICK BLAKEY

PJ HARVEY
Dry

There was a local AM station that did this show once a week where they played new releases and let the public call in with their opinion. They played a track off this CD and I called up as Calvin in my finest Down Syndrome voice. The DJ announced my name and the city I was calling from, then asked what I thought of the song. My response was, "uhhhh, da witch lady scares me..." Calvin was cut off before anything else could be said, but really I think that says it all.

BOB SCHRINER

HAWKWIND
Hall Of The Mountain Grill

I'm still pissed that this band turned Lemmy (from Motorhead) so far down in the mix that you could barely hear him and then ended up kicking him out anyway. There is something in me that just despises humorless hippies, even "cool" British Stonehenge/Pagan/Sci-Fi loving ones. And they've crossed the line between jamming and wanking one too many times for my taste. At least the Krautrockers knew enough to keep it minimal so they could never be accused of musical masturbation—a lesson lost on these drug-addled Limeys.

RUSS FORSTER

JIMI HENDRIX

Sure, he did the squealy anthem and did acid and, like Stevie Ray Vaughan, was a great guitar player. Unlike Stevie, though, he managed some worthy tunes. That's not to say that most of his music isn't way overrated. Did I mention he was black and played the guitar backwards?

MIKE ELLIOTT

THE HIVES
Veni Vidi Vicious

C'mon, Sweden, the fucking Proclaimers were not a riddle. Even if they were, you didn't need to come up with an answer. The Hives were a lot cooler when they just played instrumental music while your animated bass player went around eating power-up mushrooms with his brother Luigi trying so save the princess from the evil Koopa. What's with those corny names anyway? Hey, Dan Destroyer, that must look awesome on a credit card when you're at J.C. Penney buying five Kentucky gentleman neckties and matching coats.

BOB SCHRINER

HOLE
Live Through This
Worst album Kurt Cobain ever wrote.

JIM RAYMOND

Celebrity Skin
Worst album Billy Corgan ever wrote (and that's saying something).

JIM RAYMOND

HONOR ROLE
Rictus
This band's debut (*The Pretty Song*) and their singles were amazing, but this record spawned a million math-rock imitators and I wish it hadn't. I'll take their debut over this any day.

TIM HINELY

HÜSKER DÜ
Zen Arcade
Does anyone who has listened to this whole album still consider it a classic? It feels, like, two hours long, with the last hour being that lame psychedelic jam song. If I ever have to listen to it again, I'll blow my brains out like the character in this album's "story."

ED PARKER

IGGY & THE STOOGES
Fun House
Let me explain this: *Fun House* is a great record. I own it and love it. It's only overrated because it's an obvious slide from their first record, and so many people seem to say that *Fun House* is the best Stooges album.

ROB CARMICHAEL

INTERPOL
Turn On The Bright Lights
A friend of mine recently asked the musical question: "Are Interpol The Knack of the 21st century?" Sure enough, the release of their new album confirms this. Sadly though, they have indeed attempted to mimic (badly) the shirts-and-ties look of The Knack, Interpol's reliance on their Williamsburg hipster attitudes (see also Radio 4) and clueless haircuts (note to Carlos the bass player: you are not

Phil Oakey) let them come across as if they think none of us will notice a dime store suit when we see one. The even sadder part here is that Interpol actually do have talent. On much of it, while "PDA" is not nearly as subversive or maddenly catchy as "My Sharona," Paul Banks does at least have as good/as interesting a voice as Doug Fieger. However, had Interpol spent a little more time actually studying Joy Division's methodology (read: doing away with publicity photos—therefore making the music faceless so that no one can see your cheap attempts at ironic fashion...resulting in 15-year-old girls not forgetting about you the minute they notice your bad complexions, smug-ass grins and creepy drummer who would look more at home behind bars than behind a drum kit) rather than aping them, The Chameleons and The Kitchens of Distinction—as if positively no one had ever heard the music of those bands ever before (see also Radio 4, TV On The Radio, !!!)—might have had a bit more credibility with the cynical fucks. Despite the suffocating cries of "well, at least they're ripping off those bands and not certain others" (the "certain others" never, of course, specified) from former hipsters—now divorced and well into their thirties still trying to look 23 and very with it—this is nothing but an enormous crock of shit. So again we come back to the Interpol/Knack connection: both are actual solid and real bands who can sing in tune, but borrow a little too much from elsewhere, hoping that folks might merely be tickled rather than pissed. However, the Knack nuked themselves when folks came to the realization that what drove them to purchase *Get The Knack* was not drummer Bruce Gary's eerie resemblance to Erik

...but is it art?

The Ten Most Overrated Album Covers

THE BEATLES
The Beatles
Called "The White Album" because of its lack of cover art, the color isn't even white. It's more like the off-white color of the walls in those pre-fabricated houses they make in factories. If this cover was a snack food, it'd be an unsalted potato chip.

BIG BROTHER AND THE HOLDING COMPANY
Cheap Thrills
Famed underground illustrator Robert Crumb set the mold for the whole "If the Music Is Lame, Get a Hip Alterna-Artist for the Cover" record company strategy. No matter how good the cover is, never pick up a record with cover art by Dan Clowes, Charles Burns, Peter Bagge, Los Bros Hernandez, Coop, etc. for the music.

DURAN DURAN
Rio
Thanks, Nagel, for a whole fucking decade's worth of lame "fashion illustration" that somehow passed as legitimate design work.

Estrada, but rather the LP cover's near cloning of *Meet the Beatles* (and both records were on Capitol too, y'know). Sorry to remind you that the emperor is not wearing any clothes, but when was the last time you compared the front of *Turn On the Bright Lights* with the cover of the "Transmission" 12"?

NICK BLAKEY

JACKIE BRENSTON & HIS DELTA CATS
Rocket 88

People who give a shit say it's the first real rock 'n' roll record, which is really gross and sad. It's not like one day the wind shifted slightly and Alan Freed was all like, "Hey man, you feel that? Something's changed. Things are gonna be a lot different from now on." Apparently, the first time you hear this, you will be so overpowered by its primitive rockin' action that fireworks will shoot out your ass.

BEN HELLMANN

MICHAEL JACKSON
Thriller

Okay, the guy could dance, and employing the vocal talents of Vincent Price was a genius move, but the grooves are wafer thin, and the sound is generally weak. Since the world is peopled with tasteless denizens of hotel bars with names like Ziggy's and Fantasy Station, it's pretty obvious that this album would have been a hit, even without the innovative videos. It just wouldn't have been the monster it was without them. *Thriller* pales in comparison to the genuinely great *Off the Wall*, but as we have all noticed, Jackson gets paler and paler with each new release. At some point, he may actually become Art Garfunkel.

CHRIS DAVIS

MUMIA ABU JAMAL
175 Progress Drive

If I were Jello Biafra and had bothered to put this out, the least I would have expected was a fuckin' tour to promote it. Is it any wonder that Mumia is not so prolific these days?

PETE WILKINS

JANDEK
Somebody In The Snow

Side two, track three ("Remind You") seems a little too Jandek-by-numbers, thus ruining what would have been the perfect back catalog.

PETE WILKINS

JANE'S ADDICTION
Ritual de lo Habitual

During the making of *Ritual*, none of the band members could stand each other enough to record at the same time. Yet they found time to shit out a Grateful Dead cover for a tribute disc. But I always thought of Perry as a shitty Jim Morrison. Jimbo did massive amounts of LSD and penned "The End" and Perry shoots a bunch of heroin and gives us "Three Days". What is it about California that subjects us to overblown, self-indulgent crap? Thanks to *Ritual*, A&R guys just started handing out blank checks at methadone clinics to anyone with a drug habit and a stupid hat. I remember being impressed with this album when it came out, but then again, I was 12. The recipe is basically a shitty Guns N' Roses plus the Doors. Differences: Dave Navarro is no Slash, Guns N' Roses never used steel drums, and Izzy Stradlin wrote songs for only one of them. And I don't even want to start on Perry Farrell. What is it about Los Angeles and guys who get high and think they're poets? Don't believe the hype as the innovation is gone, the songs are boring and the

only thing remotely racy about it is the cover, and they covered that up anyway. This is a foreshadow of the tedious mediocrity that would be Porno For Pyros.

PAPA CRAZEE, RYAN JONES & BRIAN O'NEILL

JAPANTHER
Leather Wings

Dear people who like this band: Why do you insist on wearing your t-shirts inside out? Is it an anti-commerce thing? I saw Japanther play in San Francisco and there were eight people who all had their t-shirts outside in so you couldn't read whatever text was originally printed on the t-shirts. Why not just buy blank t-shirts? They come in all different colors and they're cheap as shit. I would bet my life some of these kids spent $30 for a "vintage" Van Halen or Police tour shirt only to then flip the outside inward. I just don't fucking get it. Will someone please write to our post office box and explain this shit to me? I'm not blaming Japanther per se, but it does seem that something about them embodies this printed t-shirt inside-out movement, but alas, all plebeians have their lords to rule over them, and I'm not entirely letting them off the hook either.

Maybe Japanther should only print on the outer panels of their cd inserts so their fans can turn them inside out. I mean people do actually buy them, so that's anti-corporate right there. They could even print some blurred, faint, reversed image on the inner panels so it would reference this hip reversed t-shirt thing. I probably will receive zero gratitude for this idea, but there again I would most likely just get a thank you note that was blank except for the faint trace of OUY KNAHT, and signed from someone or another from the NYLKOORB FO STOGGAF RETSPIH FO NOITAICOSSA. Oh well, I'll just go on wear-

ing T-shirts the way God intended me to wear them. How and where I wear my underwear is how I express my true individualism.

BRIAN TEASLEY

JAWBREAKER
Bivouac

If I wanted to hear the Descendents, I would put on *Milo Goes To College*. I don't want to hear the Descendents, though, so I won't put on either *Milo* or *Bivouac* albums.

ED PARKER

JAY-Z
The Blueprint 2: The Gift and The Curse

These songs are from Jay-Z's "I could fart on a mic and get five stars from *Rolling Stone*" phase. It was later followed by his "See? I actually farted on a mic and got five stars from *Rolling Stone*" phase, which started shortly after this album's release.

BEN JOHNSON

JEFFERSON AIRPLANE
Surrealistic Pillow

This album ruined psychedelia before Janis Joplin got the chance. It sounds like the soundtrack to an anti-drug propaganda film they used to show in physical education class. No wonder there was a riot at Altamont.

DAG LUTHER GOOCH

THE JESUS AND MARY CHAIN
Psychocandy

When I was 15, this was the shit. Now that I'm 34, it's just shit. Actually, if you've ever heard *Barbed Wire Kisses*, you know what this record would have sounded like without all the feedback dumped on top: a really weak Beach Boys doo-wop. Here's what's really funny to me, though. Love and Rockets surfaced around the same time, and sounded really electronic, slick, and programmed. Jesus and Mary Chain just sounded like a pile of shit thrown off a cliff. By the time Love and Rockets put out their self-titled album and Jesus and Mary Chain put out *Automatic*, Jesus and Mary Chain sounded like Love and Rockets, who in turn sounded like Jesus and Mary Chain.

DAG LUTHER GOOCH

Barbed Wire Kisses

I would say that this collection of B-sides sounds like having a root canal drilled into you via your asshole, but the dynamic dildo known as the Reid brothers would probably actually get off on that description. What they truly sound like is an absolutely tuneless version of the Velvet Underground and the Beach Boys run through a few Ibanez Tube Screamers. Oh shit, I shouldn't forget the other mainstay of their sound—the unimaginative drum machine bits that couldn't be programmed past a four bar loop churning away beneath all that pube-infested dryer lint. When your only contribution is redoing familiar melodies through pedals your little ole Scottish mum bought for you, then, yes indeed, you are entering your music career via your own asshole. Beyond a doubt, the Jesus and Mary Chain is the worst live band I have ever seen—and I'll have it be known that I've seen New Order on three separate occasions.

BRIAN TEASLEY

JIMMY EAT WORLD
Clarity

A 45-minute document of what it's like to put on a striped thrift-store sweater, smoke a lot of weed, whine about the fact that your garage band isn't making it, and crush on that sweet Lisa Loeb-looking girl in your Astronomy class who comes over to your room and watches Adult Swim with you until...fuck, you just can't take it anymore, so one night you end up at the soccer field taking shrooms and maybe even making out or something, but the spring semester's ending, and she lives in Pennsylvania, but you're from New Jersey, and

neither of you has a car. Silly emo fucks.

J. BOWERS

JOAN OF ARC
The Gap

Never grew on me, and I felt like the biggest "scenester" trying to find depth in such a ridiculous record. The worst part—and the reason I'm writing this—is that everyone loves it. A local promoter kept them in his playlist for weeks and wrote stunning reviews for every track, including the first one, which made me hate the CD when I first bought it and when I tried to listen to it for the 15th time. The first track is obviously a fair warning that this is a retarded Kinsella project. It repeats a sampled synthesizer and the famous Kinsella voice over and over in no rhythmic order. It just sounds like your CD player is screwed up. I even took out the CD at first and kept looking to see if it was scratched. And just because he played the trumpet in fifth grade doesn't mean he should toot that shit every single record he's on (all 300 of them). I do like every Joan of Arc CD, minus this one, and I do like the Kinsella boys—I love them, in fact—but *The Gap* has to go. The insert is an atrocity, and it's tough to keep inside when opening the CD (it always slips out). The art's okay, but that sucks even more because you love that simple Jade Tree style, and then it fucks with your mind. Also, why is there breaking glass? Unique? Or suppressed insanity? It sounds like an Eminem sound, like one of those backup noises after he spits out a witty and disturbing line. This record is overrated to the highest degree. Joan of Arc kicks ass; *The Gap* doesn't.

DAVID CHO

BILLY JOEL
The Stranger

If you ever want to have your own distant youth to come

FLEETWOOD MAC
Rumours

Who wants to go to the Renaissance Fair? What, you mean the blonde chick really thinks she's a witch? Couldn't tell from this cover. No sir!

LED ZEPPELIN
Houses of the Holy

Hipgnosis' naked children climbing on rocks in an alien landscape perfectly conveys the geekiness inherent in any Led Zeppelin album. Also, if this design were released today, Hipgnosis would be under a child pornography investigation as soon as the record hit shelves. Finally, an album for everyone! Pedophiles, fantasy geeks and arena cock rockers.

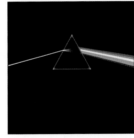

PINK FLOYD
Dark Side of the Moon

Hipgnosis' cover design is as much a testament of how drug-soaked the '70s were as is the success of this album. "Dude, cue it up and play it along to the Wizard of Oz." Fuck you. The rainbow through the prism would be considered a sign of gay-core today.

THE ROLLING STONES
Sticky Fingers

Andy Warhol's original design, with the pull-down zipper in its up position, damaged the vinyl. Finally, the problem was resolved by pulling down the zipper. The vinyl was still damaged, but at least it was only damaged where the label was located, not on one of the album's tracks. Oh, and the cock behind those tight-pants? It's rumored that isn't even Mick Jagger's, but a member of Warhol's Factory.

SPAZZCORE

Really, how many albums of this shit do we need? The only kids listening to this are wasting attempts at gaining some attention, trying to trick their 70-hour workweek neglectful parents into thinking they're doing coke. Dudes, sticking a gasoline-coated toothpick in your dickhole would achieve the same results and be way less painful.

BRIAN MCMANUS

NO WAVE

The audio equivalent of a Jackson Pollock painting, No Wave architect Weasel Walter knew that some folks feel so intellectually intimidated by New Yorkers pretending to be world-weary that he could cram this ass cake down the throats of Ulysses-reading, non-prescription glasses-wearing dillholes without them ever even gagging.

BRIAN MCMANUS

back and slap you in the head like a frying pan, whip this bitch out and drop the needle (FYI: if you have this on CD, you are a schmuck). When this album comes on, my mind drifts back to the good old days of bullies, time-out room leper crushes, shitting in my pants in class, and my parents' divorce. Why? Fuck if I know. Maybe it's because somebody kept putting it on the airwaves, and I used to listen to the radio to forget about my problems. How fucking stupid of me. How come this doesn't happen when I hear Joe Jackson? I think it may have something to do with the shelf life of sentimentality. Whatever the reason, listening to *The Stranger* is like watching a VHS tape of my first crap.

DAG LUTHER GOOCH

ELTON JOHN
Honky Chateau
Want a perfectly good reason why this album is a scam? Here's three:
1. "Honky Cat." Fuck you, you British twats! What the fuck do you know about rednecks? City people don't say shit like, "Get back, Honky Cat," to rednecks. They say, "Boys, please take that boar outside if you want to have sex with it. Our customers are not interested in your little game."
2. "I Think I'm Going To Kill Myself." Total lie. Neither Elton John nor Bernie Taupin ever thought they were going to kill themselves. Even worse, they never did kill themselves.
3. "Rocket Man (I Think It's Going To Be A Long, Long Time)." This is a new concept: lonely, depressed astronaut stuck out in space wonders if he'll ever return home. Congrats, fags. You rewrote "Space Oddity!" Why? Well, maybe Bernie Taupin assumed Elton liked David Bowie because they're both gay. Us straights do that all the time.

DAG LUTHER GOOCH

Goodbye Yellow Brick Road
I'm convinced he had the Princess Di Death re-recording conspiracy of "Candle in the Wind" way back in '73 when this piano-driven glory hole was originally recorded. What did that sell…like 80 million copies? And even gay dudes think Elton is a homo. Well, I suppose we have at least learned this: We all like our Beethoven impersonators fat.

BRIAN TEASLEY

Captain Fantastic and the Brown Dirt Cowboy
There's a million things wrong with this album. For starters, the cover looks like Mardi Gras vomit. The name of the album sounds like a redneck slur against gays (why not call it *Princess Moustache and the Sperm-Burping Blowbuddy*?). It's mostly filler, with roughly seven out of 10 songs not making the cut; that's a fairly shitty ratio for a record in *Rolling Stone*'s Top 100. But what really sucks about this one is having Elton John call you "Sugar Bear." Elton, you're gay. We all understand. We're all for your rainbow-waving happiness, but calling me "Sugar Bear" is damn close to grabbing my ass at a bar. It makes me feel violated. Violated by Captain Fantastic and the Brown Dirt Cowboy. On a side note, you may also note that this album title isn't the first time Elton has given homophobes grist for the mill. May I submit: "Benny and the Jets," "Rocketman," "Ballad Of The Boy In The Red Shoes," "Billy and the Kids," "Cage the Songbird," "Don't Let The Sun Go Down On Me," "Cockboy Dinky Does the Ass-Pirate Shuffle"? Does it really surprise anybody that Elton is the only outed homosexual that likes Eminem? What does that tell you? That he's a masochist who enjoys being fag-rolled by Bernie Taupin.

DAG LUTHER GOOCH

ROBERT JOHNSON
The Complete Recordings

Ol' Bob Johnson, the original Satanic rockstar. He traded the Lord of the Underworld his soul in exchange for superhuman guitar skills. What kind of piece-of-shit deal is that? Think about it. This guy became famous posthumously. No one gave a flying fuck about him while he was alive, selling his broke-ass soul to the devil! He may have been better than your average asshole in a juke joint, but what did it matter? Compare his story with what happens when white people sell their souls to the devil. Jimmy Page is still kicking, and he fucked some groupie with a mud-shark! Even the most average metal bands these days are flying to Amsterdam, fucking porn stars, and getting high beyond belief, all thanks to sweet Satan—and most of them will live long enough for the reunion tour to come around.

DAG LUTHER GOOCH

JON SPENCER BLUES EXPLOSION
Orange

He and the twin fuckwits in his band wore out their welcome even before Weird Al Yankovic directed one of their videos. The Blues Explosion were clowns without the face paint.

PATRICK GOUGH

JOY DIVISION
Unknown Pleasures

There are a couple of ways to take this album. On the one hand, some non-band members got a lot of press for their contributions to the album, which is rare. Peter Saville's cover art and Martin Hannett's production are rightfully praised. But on the other hand, the music is like *Fantasy Island*: you have a wonderful wish in mind, but in the end, you only get a well-learned lesson in its place. The music itself is deep and unnerving; the background samples are woven perfectly into continu-

ally intertwining songs. Then, Ian Curtis comes in. Sad-ass Ian bitching about growing up in Manchester and how he can't keep a relationship together. He drags the entire record right down the shitter. I wish he would have done us all a favor and removed himself from the picture. Oh, wait, he did. Now, if only we could get the rest of the band to play. Then my wonderful *Fantasy Island* wish just might come true.

DAVIS REA

THE KINKS
Arthur (Or the Decline and Fall of the British Empire)

Black people have Fubu, white people have The Kinks. It's for us by us. *Arthur* is hailed as an overlooked gem, but come on, folks, it's a fucking concept album written by a guy who should have gone into sociology, not rock. Oh, but what about those biting insights Ray Davies makes about hum-drum life in post-war England! Zzzzzzz. I don't know what could be less compelling. Maybe a Tori Amos album about her pussy? Thanks to England's version of Bruce Springsteen, the Kinks went on to inspire such acts as Huey Lewis and the News and Elf Power.

BEN ARNOLD

KISS
Destroyer

The first couple of things we got from Quentin Tarantino were *Reservoir Dogs* and *True Romance* (he wrote the script). They were a couple of genre films with little substance of their own that stole shamelessly from far better writers and directors. But they succeeded because they were light, fun, free of pretensions and enjoyably over-the-top in ways that made us forget that we'd seen it all before. Same goes for Kiss's eponymous debut and its follow-ups, *Hotter than Hell* and *Dressed to Kill*. But then Tarantino gave us *Pulp*

The Ten Most Overrated Album Covers (continued)

ROXY MUSIC
Country Life

Bryan Ferry and Eric Boman came up with this cover, based on the concept that hot chicks sell records. Which they do. So do good songs, but whatever. Looking at the women on the cover today, if they were selling $5 blowjobs on the corner, you'd walk by with the sawbuck still in your pocket.

THE SEX PISTOLS
Never Mind the Bollocks

Designer James Reid had to improvise with the cover design since the Pistols were considered by EMI as too ugly to put on the record cover. His solution? Well, some say it democratized art and design. What it really did is provide an excuse for lazy, sloppy "art" that continues to pass as "punk" design today, and befoul light posts and telephone poles everywhere in the form of flyers.

BRUCE SPRINGSTEEN
Born To Run

Eric Meola's photograph pretty much sums up the "Springsteen Experience." The cover says it all: "Looks like someone's gonna get an ass-fucking by 'The Boss.' Looks like it's the black guy."

BENN RAY

Fiction. Despite a few undeniable show stopping scenes, the film buckled under the weight of the kind of excess that comes with an unlimited production budget and the kind of self-importance that comes with widespread popular adulation and grudging critical acceptance. You can talk all you want about the brilliance of the twist contest at Jack Rabbit Slim's, the gimp sequence, or any of Sam Jackson's "Ezekiel 25:17" spiels, but somewhere along the line, you're going to have to acknowledge the god-awfulness of the "dead-nigger-storage" scene, in which Tarantino injects himself into the proceedings to utterly mortifying effect. For the similarly bloated *Destroyer*, Kiss enlisted the aid of Pink Floyd(!) producer Bob Ezrin and dropped a handful of grade-A classic cuts ("Detroit Rock City," "Shout It Out Loud," "God of Thunder"). But you can't mention those songs without also mounting a sheepish defense of "Great Expectations," a toilet-clogging steamer that inexplicably and inexcusably attempts to corpse-rape Beethoven's "Pathetique" sonata by playing it on electric guitars and pairing it with lyrics that render Spinal Tap-style parody completely superfluous (sample lyric: "You watch me playing guitar/And you feel what my fingers can do/And you wish you were the one I was doing it to"). And every time a friend of yours named Beth gets married and the wedding band launches into the maudlin, piano-ballad mediocrity of the same name, you have this flatulent slab to thank.

CHRIS ISELI

Alive!

How's a big, wet fart from a bunch of right-wing drag queens aping rock and roll sound to you? Good? Well then, slap on this piece of shit and enjoy. Because *Alive!* is the premiere 50% carny, 50% dumb machismo blend of dog feces that '80s hair metal was spawned from. As if Peter Criss' impossibly limp-dick drum sound didn't clue you in, this is shameless camp without an ounce of backbeat, all treble and flash meant only to inspire 13-year-olds to buy the overpriced merchandise. How apropos the lead track is called "Deuce," because that's what you get on your turntable: a fucking log.

BEN ARNOLD

KORN

Every damn album they've done

Not only should they be shot for helping jumpstart the whole rap/nü-metal genre, but the music mags and other media sources that have sung the praises of Korn over the years should be shot, too. Musically, they didn't really break any new ground, certainly not enough to justify the media hype. What they did was take what bands like Anthrax and other thrash-type metal bands had been doing for years, added some rap-type lyrics, packaged it up, and shoved it down the throat of white, teenage suburban America. The tough-guy attitude coupled with the jock-posing (the whole Adidas thing) proved to be a siren song for every stupid, insecure high school male in America.

DAVE STEINER

Cross on Cross!

DAVID CROSS
Shut Up You Fucking Baby!

Well, for starters it's longer than it needs to be, which is called "self-indulgence." People seem to feel that just because you make fun of the President or The Pope or someone or something in authority that you've got huge balls, when actually it's just the lack of other comedians doing so that makes you look ballsy by proxy. Then, if your humorous observations (I won't call them "jokes," that way it comes off as more intellectual) have any effect whatsoever, then people might be inclined to give you more credit than you deserve.

DAVID CROSS

KRAFTWERK
Autobahn

What's so fucking fun fun fun about four German guys who have more or less given us techno? Rotten Kraut fuckers.

CHRIS MCGARVEY

Trans Europe Express

Everyone says this album started everything; hip hop, electronica, disco, blah blah blah. It's little but Philip Glass snobby indulgent horseshit to me. "Bleep bloop beep beep?" Fuck that. If I want to pay respect to those who "lead the way," it's not going to be the group that invented cold, disinfected, mind-numbingly repetitive calculator farts. Plus, Trans Am were better when their Satriani licks outweighed their Komputer Scheiße. Ich bin ein playerhater.

NEIL MAHONEY

BEN KWELLER
Sha Sha

I know it's been said about this album before, but it's worth saying again. Ben, Weezer did this ten years before you did, and they did it better. If only Joe Butcher were still writing your songs for you. Go away, little dude.

LOGAN KEESE

THE LA'S
The La's

You know this album because some shitty band covered "There She Goes." Lead lad Lee Mavers wanted to sound like an early-'60s skiffle group or something, so he hates this album. Smart man.

ED PARKER

LAMBCHOP
Nixon

Ever wonder what it sounds like when a bunch of Nashville alt-country hacks try to make a Mercury Rev record? Well, have your thirst for failure quenched once and for all. If the lesser members of the Cowboy Junkies and the Swans were dying on some old Confederate submarine, you could probably at least feel sympathy for their plight—but Lambchop did this shit on purpose to represent themselves. On top of that, they asked people to buy it. Even with a hefty ad campaign, Americans had sense enough to leave it dying in the new release rack—but our English allies were duped into the audio equivalent of what was being presented as fish'n'chips...but in reality was your own shit. Great cover art. No, seriously. It's a great record to look at, but unless you wished the mellow acoustic jams of later period Fishbone could only sound whiter and less authentic. Leave this in the shrinkwrap.

BRIAN TEASLEY

LEADBELLY
Alabama Bound

This sorry bastard might have had a real overrated record if he could have stayed out of jail long enough. Instead, we get compilations like this one. Sure, it's cute, and there are even assholes like Moby that might "sample" it. But seriously, Leadbelly's music was irrelevant compared to his legend. He was a great storyteller, a bad-ass street fighter, a cunning escape artist, and a proficient ass-kisser. However, if you believe he wrote (not stole) anywhere near a third of the 500 songs he is purported to have played over the course of his life in and out of jail, you are as stupid as the two guys Leadbelly claimed pardoned him from prison after writing them both the same shitty song.

DAG LUTHER GOOCH

LED ZEPPELIN
Led Zeppelin

Pretentious, wanky, and the band didn't even write some of the songs that they took credit for (e.g., "Dazed and Confused"). Bonham is the only redeeming part of the record, and he is still playing way below his ability. How many times does Plant screech out "baby, baby, baby..." on the fucker? The grandfathers of stadium cock rock at their worst. Have you ever heard a band suck the soul out of the blues as much as Zeppelin does? It isn't bad when they're laying down the less bluesy rock, but they shouldn't have messed with the blues, at least until *IV* with "When The Levee Breaks." Why is this album constantly on critics' "greatest albums" list?

JAMES BRUBAKER

JOHN LENNON & YOKO ONO
Double Fantasy

John spent five years raising his son only to emerge with a comeback album that sounds like something a father would make. Makes you wish for one last "lost weekend," so that he'd get drunk and clock producer Jack Douglas for adding that extra layer of varnish to the mix. Daddy, come home!! (Notice how I completely avoided the Yoko factor.)

ROCK ACTION

TED LEO / PHARMACISTS
The Tyranny Of Distance

It's hard to imagine someone who uses the word "ne'er" in a lyric as something other than a failed English Lit major.

BENN RAY

LES SAVY FAV
Inches

We had this cool concept to release a 7" on nine different labels over the course of seven years and then put them together to form an album that still sucks. Right now, we're tooling around with a concept album where we make an album which doesn't suck. It's tentatively titled *The Cat and the Cobra Reissue* and it'll probably come out sometime in 2018.

BEN JOHNSON

THE LIBERTINES
The Libertines

Okay, so I saw the Libertines play at Reading a few years ago, and Jesus H. Ripoff, am I wrong in saying they are nothing but a more sloppy Strokes with a less talented version of the Fishbone drummer hanging on for dear life? And The Libertines ripping off the Strokes is like fecal incontinence ripping off erectile dysfunction. Seeing those guys try to pull it off live was like watching two oil-covered homosexual penguins play their last game of grab-ass. By the way, fuck Kate Moss! I've seen her suck more spew at the Columbia than a street

HIPPIE ROCK

There are many notable exceptions that I could list here, but those with common sense and taste will know what I'm talking about. In Britain at this time, more bands seemed to be exploring new ground. True "psychedelia" (I hate to even use that term, but...) seemed to be an exploration of a new musical form, as evidenced by AMM, early Pink Floyd, the Soft Machine, etc. American bands, however, decided that all they needed was to steal some old blues songs, put different lyrics to them, make sure the audience was so blown that they couldn't feel their own hands anymore, and that was it. The Grateful Dead, Janis Joplin, Jefferson Airplane—admittedly, they might have had a song or two where they experimented, but always it led back to the worst kind of musical chicanery—white-people blues. As a matter of fact, it makes a lot of sense that these bands were making big money re-recording Motown hits or old blues songs and taking money out of the hands of the original black artists who crafted them. That sums up the greatest fallacy behind these bands, repeated over and over by Jurassic hippies and sympathetic documentary makers: that they changed the world through their music. Does anybody think that a bunch of dirty, over-drugged idiots, dancing around with flowers and fucking each other really stopped the Vietnam war? Wake up and smell the word "unprofitable"! Nobody cares about their old "peace" stories. We should round up the remaining members of these bands and slaughter them like cattle.

DAVE BATTERMAN

cleaner slurping up used condoms in Brixton. She's a skinny, frog-faced star-fucker who sells panties for a living. Just because someone fucks Kate Moss doesn't mean their music is worth a sewer rat's dick. In 2005, is it really a surprise that she sucks rock star cock like a vampire bat on fresh raccoon roadkill? C'mon, ya'll—get involved. Let's kill that fucking limp-wristed Libertines wilted-dick ego slut. Or at least help him kill himself! He wouldn't know a hook if it was stuck in one of his track marks. Here's how it should work: A. Write a few greats songs. B. Become a heroin addict after you have some songwriting credibility and success. Get in front of the music before you get "Behind the Music," asshole. I promise I will have a big party with clowns and exotic pets when he is dead, and anyone who has donated money is invited. I am only asking $25 a month until he is dead—as in forever—as in every stupid hipster whore that gave him a cumless blow job while crying her fucking mascara off. That's it, $25. Price of a cup of coffee a day—Sally Struthers-type shit right? People that survive heroin are pussies. Do it right, you fucking wee-dicked hipster cock-drip. I'm tired of this cry-for-help bullshit. Also, don't send me some gay joke about how much you hate that band. You're probably one of those stupid-ass Anglophile girls who DJs Britpop night at some warehouse district rat's nest. Have you had a trip to the U.K. that was more than just spending a weekend in London? It's a fucking shit-hole, and even British people will tell you so. If you want to romanticize England, think more of a sad, uniform-wearing store clerk who puts on shitty punk rock shows at a pub once a month, and spends their girl-friend's bartending (that's her second job by the way) money on Simpson's action figures. Send me serious donation offers only. I don't want to bond with you. I want this guy to be dead. The end.

BRIAN TEASLEY

LIGHTNING BOLT
Wonderful Rainbow
Free jazz bubblegum for urban art school kids with ADD. I swear that Lightning Bolt will become (if they haven't reached this point already) the music disaffected, already divorced post-punks well into their 30's and 40's buy and "listen" to to prove to the women they are courting to be stepmother figures to their children that they've still "got it" and are still "with it" when in reality they are secretly crying into their Michelob Ultra's while blasting Joel R.L. Phelps and The Sea & Cake. And sure, Lightning Bolt's music is dynamic, but then so is a root canal. Chalk yet another one up to the Grand Ringmaster of Load Records, Ben McCosker.

NICK BLAKEY

LIVE
Throwing Copper
I can picture these guys in high school, sitting around watching U2 videos (it's easy because they really did start playing together in their high school band class, not to mention, they all still look like they're in high school):
"We could do this way better."
"Totally. We could be way preachier than Bono."
"And if we add some kind of funk element...whoa, watch out."
"Let's call our first album *Mental Jewelry*. Show everybody how small minded our materialistic culture is."
"Let's get that Hare Krishna guy, Ed, from the airport, to sing that shit!"
Here's how I picture them working on *Throwing Copper*:
"Ed, you are seriously taking away from my image with that weird Hare Krishna dancing you keep doing, and for crying out loud, put some fucking clothes on."
"Chad, my son. Why are you given to such hostility? Consider young Patrick."
"Patrick? What do you mean? That guy wears sunglasses onstage, so he doesn't have to look at you anymore."
"Chad, you are so angry. Why can't you see that I am here to edify us all? We must throw off our golden cloaks and leather pants. We are all naked in the eyes of God."
"Chad, make him stop."
"Ed! Put your fucking clothes back on! Don't—shit!—again with the fucking glitter!"
"We are throwing not gold, but copper! Not gold! Look at the dust! Because the color confounds us, we worship it!"
"Oh shit. MTV just walked in. Chad, quick! Throw a sheet over him!"
"Hi, guys!"
"Tabitha!"
"What's under the sheet?"
"Nothing!!! Soooo, what's up?"
"Is that Ed under there?"
"....throwing copper...we are all...just...covered in dust. Dust in the wind, all we are is..."
"Yeah, let's just leave him alone. He's working on the lyrics for our new record, *Dust In The Wind*."
"Is that a reference to Kansas?"
"Umm, no. Ha-ha...um...Chad was just joking. The album is called *Throwing Copper*."
"Great! Can't wait to hear it. I'm a huge fan. So, will you stick a pencil up my ass?"

DAG LUTHER GOOCH

LOVE
Forever Changes
Arthur Lee wasn't a genius; he just did too much acid and wrote songs with incomprehensible titles and half-baked psych music. Why didn't this album lose all credibility when Lee went to jail?

ED PARKER

LOVE AND ROCKETS
Seventh Dream of Teenage Heaven
Boy, these guys sure showed New Order how to ditch a lead singer. Or rather, they sure showed Peter Murphy how much he was ripping-off Ian Curtis. No, wait. They sure showed Jesus and Mary Chain how to sell records without any songs on them. Not to mention, this fucking record sure got a lot of airplay considering how much of a turd it was. I've never heard something sound more pre-recorded that was actually played by real people.

DAG LUTHER GOOCH

LOW
Things We Lost In The Fire
Steve Albini recording married Mormons with a Codeine fetish singing about having their first baby. Sign my non-caffeine drinking ass up! Top seller on the BYU campus Student Union store, and sounds great while laying nude on your childhood NFL sheets trying to suck your own cock. Turn that baby up, bitch!

BRIAN TEASLEY

LORETTA LYNN
Van Lear Rose
I absolutely adore the idea of Jack White getting all down and dirty in some ancient *Coal Miner's Daughter* pussy! Strangely enough, working with White was just the way the public wanted to have Lynn's old bone bag rolled out on MTV2. The record itself is a boggy, reverby mishmash of alt.country revisionism and overly borrowed yesteryear songwriting conventions. Here's the great thing though: supposedly on a few nights where Meg White got hit by the cocaine truck, Loretta (roughly the same-size in red and white) filled in on drums and no one

noticed or was any worse for it. I guess I just never thought having sex with your grandmother could be so popular. You know, I say that, but when my own grandma would take her dentures out it would make for some of the softest, most delicate blow jobs I've ever had.

BRIAN TEASLEY

LYNYRD SKYNYRD
Pronounced Leh-Nerd Skin-Nerd
Recipients of the "drunk bastard" award for writing, recording and performing that concert "joke" staple, "Free Bird." Can you imagine how blissful classic rock radio would be without having to hear "Sweet Home Alabama" after every Neil Young song?

AMANDA NICHOLS

MAGNETIC FIELDS
69 Love Songs
This record is so fucking smug and self-diddling that I can't believe it's not English. Everyone kept hailing this as a pop wonder...what the fuck is going on here? I know Merge Records can't bribe everyone. Could it be that I am the only person that thinks that the vocals sound like an autistic impersonation of Jonathan Richman? And musically, I fail to see what is even remotely "pop" about any of these songs. Each track makes me think that a different programmed demo song is backing up the singer from a keyboard that's on sale at Radio Shack. Some things you listen to and want to like, but it just won't take. I listen to this and try to hate it more, but it's just good enough to loathe.

BOB SCHRINER

THE MAKE*UP
If Nation Of Ulysses were the Beatles, then the Make*Up were Wings. Ian Svenonius and co. had become everything they used to ridicule in the songs of their previous band. Of course, the hipster

crowd didn't mind. Hell, they put out records on K and Dischord, so the *Punk Planet* subscribership had no choice but to like their bland genre pastiche. Thankfully, they broke up last year. Perhaps that ass-beating they got from the Murder City Devils knocked some sense into them.

JAMES SEIZURE

THE MAKERS
Strangest Parade
The Makers forego garage rock (a bit too early) for a stab at glam rock revivalism. This bloated, pretentious concept album (has there ever been a concept album that wasn't bloated and pretentious?) sounds every bit as sleazy as an '80s era LA hair metal band covered in crusty herpes.

BENN RAY

MAN...OR ASTRO-MAN?
Experiment Zero
Bleep-Blop-Bloop-Ding-Dong-Bleep... and then some surf music played in a weird tuning, played at an annoyingly speedy velocity. Genius? Yeah, maybe in the same way that a wheelchair-bound Special Olympian who, thanks to extreme wind conditions, makes a three point shot is genius. *Experiment Zero* was the beginning of these dorks' way over-associating themselves with Steve Albini, and the recording of the record truly sounds hi-fi in that same plunking, delayed-room mic sort of way that most of Albini's recordings do. Big deal. The record was mastered properly and sounds okay. Congrat-u-fuckin'-lations.
Sorry, I'm not staying on track here, but they sample a fucking Big Track toy, for dick's sake! How far did the cock of Geek Chic have to be shoved down our throats in the mid-'90s? I think my esophagus is still bleeding just from the endless onslaught of these dweebs' countless, disposable releases that have matured about as well as that early

The Most Overrated Metal Albums Ever
by Brian Posehn

This was hard to do, because—even though I coul not be a bigger metalhead—I know that among musi snobs like Henry (BONER!) and his buddies, likin metal is like telling Trekkies you prefer Space 1999 To some readers, my record collection might appea silly. Some might think I have the music taste of a fit teen year-old boy; they wouldn't be wrong. And yo wouldn't be wrong if you thought my favorite CD would look at home in the pick-up truck of crank addicted roofer in Fresno. This assignment (favor) wa really tough. What makes a bad metal record? Is it a bad? Is the stuff I cherish really not great? Do Th Scorpions kinda suck? Is Iron Maiden as corny as Three's Company episode fucked by a turd with cor in it? I can say that about Maiden, because I fuckin love Maiden. If one of you said that about Maiden, I' beat you like you made fun of my retarded cousin. Bu this isn't about what I like, it's about what I don't like

THE DARKNESS
Permission to Land
The second coming o Queen? Not really, more like the second coming of Rox Gang. More hype than Andrew Who? K. I knew the sucked before I heard them because my "college-rock-fag" friends recommended them to me as a band "I would like" and "kinda metal." They don't know what I really listen to. They've only heard bad metal and never went any deeper.
There should be no "kinda metal" only "not metal at all" or "totally metal" or "Deicide." They're so *metal* they have their own category. I hope by the time you read this the Darkness is dropped by their label. Death to false metal.

80s diet supplement unfortunately named Ayds. Now, I can admit that the guitar work is nimble and the drumming rather solid, but the music is fuckin' gayer than a film festival in the Castro district. After this record, the Astro-nerds messed with everything from new wave and Krautrock to spacey psychedelic wankfest yielding, if not interesting, at least less predictable, results than surf music played by Sonic Youth and promoted by Devo for a generation of lame, nostalgia-obsessed hipsters who would eventually make *Napoleon Dynamite* a smash hit at the box office.

Oh yeah, did I mention they're from space?

BRIAN TEASLEY

BOB MARLEY
Legend

I'm so glad you're dead, Bob Marley. Because, seriously, even you wouldn't be able to stomach how much this disc gets played everyday in every goddamned country around this world. Hey mon, I and I think *Legend* is the soundtrack to the Ikea-ing of our planet. Go to Mexico City, it's "Buffalo Soldier!" Go to Prague, it's "No woman, no cry...No! Woman! No! Cry! (fade out to crowd noise)" Go to fucking Ulaan Baatur, it's "Oy-yoi-yoi! Oy-yoi-yoi! Oy-yoi-yoi-yoi-yoi-YOI!" To every dude playing "Redemption Song" right now in some hostel somewhere, stop. Those German girls that you got drunk with last night don't even like black people.

BEN ARNOLD

THE MARS VOLTA
Deloused in the Comatorium

Since when did Santana become cool among the hipster elite? Is it some sort of ironic statement or are

people for real? It was somewhere between the breakup of At The Drive In and the release of this record where the noodling of Phish and The Grateful Dead replaced the drone of bands like Modest Mouse and Red House Painters—and I'd almost prefer to hearing The Dead over this. Frat boys looking to be down will tell you this album is "some profound shit, dude."

AARON LEFKOVE

JOHN MAYER
Room for Squares

James Taylor (post-heroin, post-shock treatment, post-Carly Simon and most definitely post-*Two Lane Blacktop*) sodomizing Michael Franks in the day lounge of Hell: music for divorcee's who have given up on Shania Twain and Ricky Martin. At the very most, John Mayer finally answers that ever-plodding and wondrous musical question: "What is the sound of utter, total and complete destitution?" Plus, he is absolute living proof that the Berklee College of Music is really the U.S. National Headquarters of Al Qaeda.

NICK BLAKEY

CURTIS MAYFIELD
Superfly

The best thing about this album was the kick-ass gatefold. Other than that, every song is drenched in so much of Mayfield's token falsetto floating obnoxiously over the mix that the instrumentation becomes a Cliffs Note. This guy is so in love with his fucking kicked-in-the-balls tone, you begin to wonder if he isn't his own pusher—packing more and more Columbian marching powder into his burning nostrils as he slides the knob marked "vocal" up and up.

BRIAN MCMANUS

MC5
Entire discography

Name one song besides "Kick Out The Jams." MC5 are the rare case of a band whose reputation outlasts their music, what with all the White Panther bullshit it was blanketed in. The current alterna-staples mimicking MC5 (Jet, etc.) are reason enough to despise these Jew-fro wearing, hand-clapping douchebags for ever existing. Fuck you and your Levi's-sponsored reunion tour, Wayne Kramer.

BRIAN MCMANUS

PAUL AND LINDA MCCARTNEY
Ram

This record sounds like winding up a box for forty-five minutes and right when it's supposed to pop—you get raped by a sweaty, amped-up, recently worked-out Carrot Top shoving a ram's horn up your ass.

BRIAN TEASLEY

MELVINS
Houdini

"Wow, major label money! Corporate morons at Atlantic! We're not changing shit. You signed the Melvins, so you're going to take King Buzzo up the ass, motherscratcher! Yeah, watch what subversive fucked-up riffage we'll give you, Atlantic."

This record is bone-crushing, but only in the way that staring at roadkill can't ruin your hard-on. Actually, if Cobain hadn't felt so bad for making the FM pap-pile of *Nevermind*, *Houdini* would have never happened. Trying to "stay credible," Cobain both produced a large part of the album and even "rocked" on one song.

Many Melvins records are too scatterbrained to approach as being as intense as Sabbath—and an obvious sign that they were in trouble was their inability to play Kiss songs better than Kiss. *Houdini*, however, is cohesive in the same way that a long turd refuses to break against the

cold wall of toilet water. I think if this record is remembered at all in five years it will be thought of as the sonic equivalent of a Coop "Devil Lesbian Chicks" poster being sold at an art gallery for $450.

BRIAN TEASLEY

MERCURY REV
Deserter's Songs

The sort of records that your grandparents might buy you for your birthday, because you're into "different music" and this is what the record store employee recommended.

PETE WILKINS

METALLICA
Master of Puppets

Do you remember when everybody came together and decided that *Master of Puppets* was the one album they could all agree on? The world was in harmony that day. I remember everyone holding hands: fans of punk rock, fans of heavy metal, and listeners to whatever the fuck came on the radio. Everyone in 9th through 11th grade held up their *Master of Puppets* tape and smiled to the heavens. The bully and the bullied laid together in the shade of the smoking tree by the teachers' lounge. Bread was broken in the lunchroom, the yeast was huffed, and visions were had. That was a great day. The following day, I found the guy who made that tape for everyone but me, and I asked him to make me a copy. He offered me a Megadeth tape instead, and said it was way fucking better. Later, it was turned into an MTV jingle. I eventually bought *Master of Puppets*. But I still think it would have been way better if I had gotten it for free. Almost as good as Megadeth...for free.

DAG LUTHER GOOCH

The Black Album

Here's the album where many longtime fans started to understand how devastating Cliff Burton's death really was. Burton was the cornerstone of Metallica, and, with him out of the picture, it left the band's direction squarely on the shoulders of Hetfield and Ulrich. How much money did it take to get that perfect snare sound, guitar tone, or compressed vocals, thanks to über-producer Bob Rock? With this album, they went from a land-breaking metal unit to a land-locked one.

ROCK ACTION
St. Anger
Metallica's supposed "return to form." Yeah, right. While I'll admit that jettisoning the sour, slightly flat, unintonated guitar solos was probably a good idea (and this highly-overrated guitarist—who should have been in Cliff Burton's bunk on the day of the wreck that brought the band to a literal screeching musical halt—shall remain nameless), that alone does not make a great record—and certainly doesn't herald anything near this hyped-up return. There may be 10-15 seconds on *St. Anger* where the band touches on things resembling good riffs—but they're quickly snatched back to badly-produced, hacked-together attempts at modern metal punctuated by what is quite possibly the worst excuse for a snare drum sound ever recorded. I won't even get into the vocals—except to say that when I first heard them, I said out loud: "Is this a fucking joke?"

JEFF MCLEOD

THE METERS
Anthology: Funkify Your Life
I think the problem here begins with twisting the word funk into verb form (not that it's that much better when used as a noun, adjective or adverb). No band has had more of an influence on white bread college Bonnaroovians than the Meters. If their goal was to connect with rich, Caucasian, collegiate yippies who like to play for hours

with absolutely no purpose, then man, did they hit the nail on the head…of their own dicks. With New Orleans having been underwater for weeks, we can only hope that as many of their master tapes as possible were completely destroyed.

BRIAN TEASLEY

MIGHTY MIGHTY BOSSTONES
Let's Face It
What is funny is that someone actually thought this was a good idea. Let's go find a singer from the Tom Waits School of Glass Gargling, team him up with guys just rejected from the local Specials cover band tryouts, then add a guy that doesn't do anything but dance badly. Then, let's add some punk rock to the ska sound and create ska-core. Then, we'll write lyrics about our hometown (Boston) and wear plaid.
They would have gotten away with it if it weren't for those meddlin' kids…er, I mean, if it weren't for one big mistake on their part. Selling out? No, it's not the eventual dashing of plaid or wanting greater fame on their part…it was the fact they had a trombone player. Everybody knows real rock bands don't have trombone players.

JIM RAYMOND

STEVE MILLER BAND
Greatest Hits
Apparently, this piece of crap has sold about 10 million copies. What this tells me is that there are a lot of idiots in America. Miller's music is bland and devoid of emotion. Whoever gave Steve Miller a guitar should be forced to live in a cell with Dr. Kevorkian.

MICHAEL RYAN

MINISTRY
The Land Of Rape & Honey
I don't even know where to begin with this poor excuse for a "band." "Alain Jourgensen" lied about everything, including his

The Most Overrated Metal Albums Ever (continued)

SPINAL TAP
Funny movie, but those songs were never funny. I'm sorry, you're wrong if you disagree. NEVER FUCKING FUNNY. AND NOT METAL. "Take Off" by Bob and Doug McKenzie and Geddy Lee is funnier. Scatterbrain is way funnier. What? You've never heard Scatterbrain? Pull your head out of your pussy.

BON JOVI
Slippery When Wet
Not METAL at all, but people lump it in with metal. Those people should go swim in a pile of dicks. Sold like 20 million copies, but I think that's because all the fat girls who loved Jovi would eat their albums and have to go buy new ones.

DEF LEPPARD
Hysteria
This and the Darkness are tied for the easiest entries to come up with. This band is a sore subject for me. No one has ever turned on me so hard. It's like if your stepdad bought you a puppy and eight years later fucked your full grown dog in front of you. To death. That's how I feel *every* time I hear "Pour Some Sugar On Me." I loved this band when I was a freshman. Their early shit holds up. I really, really love (with no irony at all) *On Through The Night, High and Dry* and four songs on *Pyromania*. Not "Photograph," though, that track was a sign of the suckiness to come. Anyway, everybody loved this album and it stinks. They should have stopped when the guy whose job requires two arms only had one arm. That was sign from God for them to pack it in early.

METALLICA
The Black Album
I like some songs on some of these records (except for the first four albums I listed). Metallica's Black Album is only here because it's so massive and it's not their best album. Not even their third best album. This actually should be number ten, if I was going in order…because compared to *Hysteria* I love this album.

lineage (c'mon, that British accent is so *fake*, an infant could see through it), and rips off everyone from Howard Jones to Big Black to Nine Inch Nails along the way. He was a loser junkie scumbag to boot. Probably his best work is represented by the advertising jingles he wrote for local Chicago businesses that still play on late-night TV from time to time.

RUSS FORSTER

MINOR THREAT
Out Of Step
First of all, this record sounds like shit. Did these dorks record this in an empty dumpster? My new Blink 182 album was recorded in a house and it sounds, like, a billion times as good. And what's with the no sex, no booze, no smoking? Hey, guys: Rock and Roll called, and they said the Sex Pistols are better than you. What these guys know about punk I could fit in my Von Dutch plastic mesh hat. "Make do with what you have? Take what you can get?" *Hello?* Make up your minds already. I swear, bro. Those short haircuts must have cut off the oxygen supply to their brains....grow some dreads already, and fucking dye that shit!!! Punk rock is about getting fucked up, banging ugly chicks, and wearing plaid pants with a studded leather jacket. Period. Sell that self-reliance sobriety crap to Tony Robbins.

PAUL POISON

MISFITS
Earth A.D.
Midget lives in mother's basement in Lodi and collects Japanese robot toys. Bad Elvis-esque vocals atop paint-by-numbers punk rock. Scary graphics entice comic book readers worldwide into a collectable fren-

zy. Misfits records are the audio equivalent of Cabbage Patch dolls. Plus, going from their best record, *Walk Among Us*, how could the band release this metal-infested piece of garbage? Glenn must've really needed the money.

JIM HAYES & TIM HINELY

Mogwai on Mogwai!

MOGWAI
Young Team
Of all the records revered in the dubiously titled post-rock genre, Mogwai's debut album is surely one of the poorest. Their so-called ambition seems to consist of playing the same two chord sequence over and over whilst very occasionally putting on their distortion pedals ad nauseam. Far from being forward thinking, as it is occasionally touted as, this record is a clumsy mix of what Nirvana and Smashing Pumpkins had been doing much earlier but with the oh-so-ingenious touch of not bothering to do any singing. Check out the desperate attempts at artiness with the two piano songs (plus pointless noises in the background...see, Eno! Look, we're smart too!). It has also inspired some of the worst bands to ever grace the planet. Buy Rodan, God Machine, Slint, Codeine and forget that this sorry shower of crap's parents ever let them buy guitars. I hear that four of them went to Catholic school. Pricks.

STUART BRAITHWAITE, GUITAR

MISSION OF BURMA
The "Inexplicable" Reunion
Yeah, yeah, so MOB has proven itself to be the greatest living post-punk band ever, but all the same, Peter Prescott still works as a fucking record store clerk (have you no shame, music fans?). The "inexplicable" reunion has inevitably turned into the "infinite" reunion with shows now piling up on top of each other like collectors onto a promo

copy of *Signals, Calls & Marches*, and a new album (*OnOffOn*) on Matador (the press bio of which makes no mention of Matador's previous [and now out of print] Prescott outfit Kustomized; that's history for you). Of course, the new album is quite good, but it's a non-strange bedfellow to, say, the reunited Crispy Ambulance's new album.

However, the cold hard fact remains: what made Burma so cool in the first place was that they were never going to reunite, and this fan at least has walked away from the whole experience with a bigger appreciation of Volcano Suns if anything. It also used to be that not a season went by when you didn't read or hear something in the Boston press about MOB, but now it's every fucking

week. Hey, good for them, they deserve it, but doesn't anyone remember The Titanics? The Zulus? The Girls? The reunion has proven that even post-punk can have its own version of the dreaded Tom Waits fanatic, but even Burma will tell you that Boston rock was not built on the back of Roger, Clint, Peter and Martin (now being subbed for by Bob Weston). Do yourself a favor: buy a Burma record and then go start your own band.

NICK BLAKEY

JONI MITCHELL
Blue
Look, I know it's been a while since you got some action. It can be really lonely sometimes, man. We all get lonely and listen to really crappy music in order to get laid. In high school, you had *Blue* for the hippie chicks, *Back in Black* for the metal sluts, and the Cocteau Twins' *Treasure* for the wavers. But there is simply no reason to subject yourself to this album now. Any tail this record assists you in getting is either way too old or way too foul. All you're doing listening to this Sesame Street, glee club crap is reminiscing about the tail you got at summer camp. Look around you, big guy. Hippie chicks do not age well and the young ones don't even know who the fuck Joni Mitchell is.

DAG LUTHER GOOCH

MOBY
Play
If you are into jingles, you probably own and love this record. You also love trailers for Hollywood vehicles for Leo DiCaprio and Gwyneth Paltrow. You also fuck to Enigma on repeat. You eat lots of Otis Spunkmeyer bran muffins. You hate Eminem. You drive a Honda, and have a Sony stereo. You are a number. Welcome to the fold. I love you. Your hair is very soft. Let me rub your feet, and read to you from *USA Today*

while we watch FOX News. I really love modern art, don't you?

DAG LUTHER GOOCH

MODERN LOVERS
Modern Lovers
Blow your nose, motherfucker. Clear your throat. Take some cold medicine. Take a sick day. I don't want to catch what you have, bitch, so close your mouth and stop breathing all over me.

DAG LUTHER GOOCH

MODEST MOUSE
The Moon and Antarctica
First complaint: Isaac Brock's voice. It's whiny, annoying, and frankly, pretty crappy. When the voice is coupled with typical Modest Mouse lyrical content, it leads me to believe that Mr. Brock is in need of some serious testosterone treatment. Their music has some potential—lo-fi, a little shimmery, and a touch psychedelic. The problem is that there are a butt-ton of bands out there with the same credentials. Do these bands get the press, the rave reviews? Of course not. Lisp rock made by some drunk kid from the Pacific Northwest. Probably molested as a child. Try speech therapy, kid.

SETH LOSIER & DAVE STEINER

THE MONKS
Black Monk Time
I think I'm just pissed about this because I just read their whole book and it was boring. People think this is so insane. It *would* be if the Monks (a) did drugs, and (b) came up with the concept themselves. They did neither. They were American idiots with a svengali from a German ad agency. Of course, Germans are weird. Is that a surprise?

PAPA CRAZEE

THE MOONEY SUZUKI
Electric Sweat
The Mooney Suzuki were doing the garage rock revival long before the garage rock

revival became profitable. So, lucky for them, they were able to get swept up by a nice, cushy major label once the pendulum of music trends swung in their direction. Unfortunately, their sound comes across as more "shtick" than sick. This group of copycats would make an excellent bar band for a '60s biker flick because that's exactly what their music, style, and performance play out as—acting.

DRYW KELTZ

VAN MORRISON
Astral Weeks
Jehovah's Witness smokes pot and listens to light jazz. Bullshit music for sandal-wearing crypto-fascists. His elder statesman status confuses me, but most likely confuses himself. Oh please, just one more strum and one more poetic line!

JIM HAYES

MORRISSEY
You Are The Quarry
This is the worst case of The Emperor's New Clothes since *Yankee Hotel Foxtrot*—and I didn't even listen to that. Somehow, I'm sure Wilco's terminally-ill sad-dick watershed record is better than *You Are The Quarry*, which undeniably sucks. Just because everything on the radio sucks doesn't mean the stuff not on the radio is any good. Sorry, we are shooting for higher than "not terrible" nowadays. This is being heralded as his comeback record, but the problem lies in where he's coming back from. LA? Fuck that! I want boring, sad, gay British Morrissey back. I don't want to read about him in *Rolling Stone* eating Thanksgiving dinner with Pamela Anderson for PETA. Just because she's vegetarian doesn't mean she's cool, asshole. Back to the album in question. Boring songs and crappy production don't make for great comebacks, Morrissey. And what the

MOTÖRHEAD
I know I'm gonna catch shit for taking down the Ramones of metal…which I mean in the negative way. I barely like the Ramones either. To my ears, they're both kinda samey. That's all I've got. I like that one song. You know the one.

VAN HALEN
1984
One of their biggest selling albums and it too has only one good song. I'm not telling which. Go ahead and guess which song I like, but just know that for any wrong answer I will pay Patton Oswalt to head-butt your nards or vajay.

RAGE AGAINST THE MACHINE
Every record
I love Tom Morello, but I can't listen to too much of this band. The singer drives me crazy. As redundant as something that's redundant. I know that was weak, but I'm not getting paid for this and my wife just made me a sandwich. I want to eat it. But, she said I have to finish this first.

DEEP PURPLE
Machine Head
Considered by many burn-outs and journalists to be a classic metal album, it is mostly gay (like Andy Dick). "Highway Star" is actually pretty cool and fast compared to their other bullshit. Do I even have to go into how boring "Smoke On the Water" is? It's as boring as the sophomoric humor and bad high school paper music review writing I've subjected you to. Anyway, this album sucks and "Space Truckin'" is one of the worst rock songs ever, in my opinion. I know bands like Maiden and douchebags like Yngwie Malmsteen consider Blackmore God, but next to other heavy bands of the time (Sabbath and Zep) it just seems kinda balls-free. And I like balls with my metal. Some might say I like balls while I listen to my metal.

I only have nine and guess what… I don't give a shit. That's how fucking METAL I am.

BRIAN POSEHN

fuck is up with that swooshing noise at the end of "Irish Blood"? Can't blame producer Jerry Finn who has been quoted as saying, "That is all Morrissey." Which leads me to go back to my original thought that Morrissey is: A. Completely crazy, B. Totally gay and C. In need of some serious deep-dickin'.

TOBY HALBROOKS

THE MURDER CITY DEVILS
Empty Bottles, Broken Hearts
Never have I been so convinced that a bunch of so-called hard-asses were fakin' the funk. This band looks like they got average grades in their posing lessons from Social Distortion. The sound of their records is much worse than the idea of the switchblade on the cover. The basic formula for this band is as follows: find the worst Big Black song, copy it, add five or six more minutes, pepper it with some "spooky" keyboards, change the vocals to that of a man bitch, then multiply by three full lengths. Oh, I almost forgot, this mix will not come out right if you're lacking a retro belt buckle. Bon Appetit!

BOB SCHRINER

In Name and Blood
This hunk of shit really teaches you that music is a lot about how you stand around posing for cool photographs, maybe smoking while you're at it. If this record were to be described in a newspaper headline it might read like, "Local dipshits discover Big Black, miss point, look great."

BOB SCHRINER

MY BLOODY VALENTINE
Loveless
You hate to think of Axl Rose and Kevin Shields in the same mental breath, but let's face it: the two most anticipated albums of the '90s (and, now, the new millennium) were and are *Chinese Democracy* and whatever the follow-up to

Loveless will be. And we all know that neither of one of 'em will ever happen; but we continue to anticipate and sit on the edge of our seats and wait with bated breath. The Red Sox winning the World Series last year just made things worse (or better, I suppose): If that can happen, then *anything* can happen! In fact, let's just hope that both records will be released on the same day, the day that the goddamn Cubs win it all! Gas prices will fall. It will be a perfect 65 degrees and sunny with a light breeze. And everyone will get time-and-a-half for hanging out in the park eating gelato. It's gonna rule.

I'm not a betting man, but if I had to put odds on which of the two records would be finished first, I'd say it's about even. I tend to think that Axl is never going to get his follow-up done because he's way too busy snorting and drinking to get his increasingly fatter ass into the studio. The recent tour was certainly a hopeful sign for G'n'R fans, but then again, both the band and the new songs sucked, Buckethead or not. If nothing else, the tour generated enough cash to keep ol' Axl in piles of whatever for another few years. When he runs out of that money, do you think he'll do yet another tour, or finally release *Chinese Democracy*?

Kevin Shields, the mastermind behind My Bloody Valentine, succeeded in creating a seminal and absolutely gorgeous guitar album, the likes of which will probably never be heard again. *Loveless* was released in 1990, before the advent of ProTools and all. Lord knows how Shields got the sounds he did out of guitars, what combination of pedals and amps he used to wrench these sheets of extraterrestrial static out of six strings, but he did it. If you listen to the rumors (which you do, admit it), he's been holed up in some studio with a razor

blade and some tape, painstakingly splicing the next record together. The dude's a perfectionist. Can he ever construct the record that he hears in his mind? Has he driven himself mad like a latter-day Brian Wilson? Is he pissed off at Sonic Youth for crankin' 'em out? Ask him if you see him.

MICHAEL FALOON

NEUROSIS
Times of Grace
The toughest article of clothing I own is my long-sleeve Neurosis t-shirt. Wearing it is like being a Mason—doors open wide for members. Seriously. There is no faster way to get weird looks at work (not that I have any problem with that), no faster way to get people to move one seat down on the train, and most importantly, no faster way to get into the Model without I.D. The guys at the door see the shirt, give a slight nod, then open the door for me. Tough dudes inside smile slightly as their eyes do the t-shirt check and stop squarely on my chest. The drunken throngs part silently, as I walk past the line for the graffiti-scrawled men's room. Membership has its privileges.

Not that anyone actually listens to Neurosis or anything. I mean, sure, you go through record collections, and occasionally find a Neurosis album. Usually it's *Enemy of the Sun*, the record that's considered to be their seminal album—even though, again, no one ever actually listens to it. The thing is the band's material is so unyielding in its howling ferocity that it's hard to sit through more than a few songs at a time. It's absolutely punishing stuff—the heaviest music I own. The t-shirts and hoodies the band's fans wear are like badges of honor, testa-

ments to the fact that the wearer has made it through a few songs, anyways. I have a Swans shirt that serves a similar purpose but less often—it's my heavy Fagen shirt.

There's a companion disc to *Times of Grace* simply titled *Grace* which you can play at the same time as *Times of Grace* to be punished even further. Can you imagine? I think if you listen to both records at the same time, you should get a chevron on the sleeve of your Neurosis tee, so that everyone knows how badass you are. Again, it's like being a Mason—if you get to the second-to-last level, you get to be a Shriner and drive around in a little car at a parade. I'm not sure what the last level of Neurosis Masonry is, but I'm trying hard to find out, because the last level is when they teach you mind control.

MICHAEL FALOON

NEW ORDER
Substance
It would be a singles collection that everyone would buy to ensconce the band in legend, wouldn't it? Stupid fucking Americans. The albums bookending *Substance*, *Brotherhood* and *Technique* showcase the band's mercurial album genius, a much more telling barometer of the four/threesome's importance to 80's pop music.

HEATH K. HIGNIGHT

THE NEW PORNOGRAPHERS
Mass Romantic
The New Pornographers use hooks like the Czechs use consonants. Perhaps I just have a beef with the term "supergroup," but this release comes off as nine publicists' worth of overhype. The songwriting is so crowded that you get the impression that each person came to the table with a

song idea and the other members added to it to the point of clusterfuck-pop overdose. Maybe that's what it takes to win a Juno , which I envision looking somewhat like the Stanley Cup, but with musical notes on it. That being said, I do enjoy this record a great deal. However, you have to agree this recording touts some so-so tunes painted-up with extra keyboards and pretty girl singing.

ROBERT SCHRINER

NEW YORK DOLLS
Too Much Too Soon

Do you want to know how to become a pop culture reference? First, dress in drag. Second, take as many drugs as you can fit into a syringe, and shoot them into your arm. Third, after no one cares about the first two things, hire producer Shadow Morton to make you a shitty Stooges record. Now, sit back and soak in your undeserving praise.

DAVIS REA

NIRVANA
Bleach

It's time to out everyone who claims that *Bleach* was Nirvana's best album. Let there be no arguments: the songwriting, arrangements, creativity, and (yes) production is much more impressive on later releases. This is simply a good document of a competent Pacific Northwest rock band circa late-80's. Put *Bleach* up against any Mudhoney release around this time and see who wins.

ROCK ACTION

Nevermind

This one's like a fish in a barrel since it's been lauded as everything from the greatest record of the '90s to the album of a generation. Shitty, washed-out production does little to mask songs that just aren't that good. The Beatles meet the Sex Pistols? I've heard it called that, but the

Sex Pistols were harder, wittier, and better pop craftsmen. Cobain wished he could have written songs as good as Ozzy, never mind Lennon/McCartney. Dave Grohl hits the hell out of a drum kit, you can't hear it here. To their credit, their audience esteemed the band more than Nirvana themselves did and they brought a lot of punk heroes to the national consciousness (Meat Puppets, Raincoats, etc.). Still, this record does not hold up to the elevated status the media has thrust upon it. Plus, it's directly responsible for a decade of shitty radio.

PAPA CRAZEE

In Utero

This album proves two things: all great records are accidental, and major labels should never sign bands to multi-record deals. Upon first hearing *In Utero*, I got the impression that these guys just woke up in the studio, and saw that the tape was rolling. The lack of continuity coupled with the lyrical self-deprecation of a millionaire makes this a prime candidate for an outtakes collection.

ROBERT SCHRINER

NO NEW YORK

Besides looking really neat nestled between The Beatles Butcher cover and an eight-track of *Metal Machine Music* in record store display cases, the only value *No New York* has is that it documents early efforts of folks who went on to lead 3/4 of an interesting career, that fraction being shared by Lydia Lunch and James Chance (Mars and DNA are not worth the cost of the shipping slip accompanying returns to Atavistic). Nonetheless, being the record that contains what came before Eight Eyed Spy and that badass version of "Don't Stop 'Til You Get Enough"

does not explain praise of the sort this record gets. For that, it had better fellate me and serve beer once I remove it from the sleeve.

BEN HELLMANN

O BROTHER, WHERE ART THOU
Original Soundtrack

It's nice that roots, folk, and country music are enjoying an upswing in popularity, but it's also a bit annoying for someone who's been a fan for over twenty years to watch the Johnny-Come-Lately's worship this rather so-so compilation. This shit's been around for over 70 years, and you'd do well to go back to the originals.

MATT THOMPSON

OASIS
(What's The Story) Morning Glory

Grating, fourth-rate Beatles tribute band with a penchant for press-grabbing in-brawling. The fact that so many in the British music press still list this as one of the best albums of the '90s helps illuminate everything that's wrong with music from the U.K.

BENN RAY

THE OFFSPRING
Smash

Fans of The Offspring often employ the impressive levels of education obtained by various band members as a means of defending the group's output which makes sense because only the most gifted swimmers in the gene pool could come up with the likes of "Pretty Fly for a White Guy." If fans of The Offspring wish to explore meaningful music created by Ph.D. punks they need look no further than the lyrical crooning of Milo Aukerman and Greg Graffin: two mature punks who haven't let age affect their spirit. This further proves that all Gen Y kids have to do to be "authentically" punk rock is have the right Germs T-shirt.

DRYW KELTZ & AMANDA NICHOLS

THE OLIVIA TREMOR CONTROL
Dusk at Cubist Castle

A prime example of what happens when children don't embrace playing sports (not the Huey Lewis album—but that wouldn't have hurt either): They end up shunned from their surroundings, stuck inside their rooms with nothing but a shitty Tascam cassette 4-track and a bong. The end result is this low-fidelity nightmare. I mean, haven't we come a long way in the realm of sound in the last 40 years? Take a look at ZZ Top, they made several unlistenable records through the '70s but then embraced technology and cranked out the shining gem that is *Eliminator*. Tell me I'm wrong. These boys could do with a little more on the playing field and a little less time in the room with the Thai Stick.

SETH LOSIER

YOKO ONO

Although she is underrated for inadvertently creating a moniker for the most delicious putdown (just ask Tom Arnold, Courtney Love, etc.), she is even more of a menace for her music career. Rating her at all means she's overrated.

JOHN DAVIDSON

OUTKAST
Stankonia

There is a difference between "black people drugs" and "white people drugs." Black people smoke loads of chronic and chill to jazz and soul music. White people ingest ecstacy and go to raves in gigantic pants and wear candy necklaces. This is what happens when one team crosses over to the other side. I'm sorry, Ms. Jackson, this record licks anus.

AARON LEFKOVE

PALACE BROTHERS
There Is No One What Will Take Care of You

Yeah, Will Oldham (the mastermind of all things Palace) looks like an authentic inbred. He also sounds like one...but who cares? If I wanna get "ig'-nant," I'll put on the 2 Live Crew! If one more snobby Williamsburg jerk tells me how "la-di-da" Will Oldham is and how I'm such a loser for not owning any of his records, I'm gonna throw 'em right through the window of Enid's or Galapagos or wherever the fuck those people fraternize in Brooklyn. He might be the bomb, but I'll never know because I used to work at *CMJ*, ground zero for misinformed elitism.

RON HART & ANTONIO DEPIETRO

VAN DYKE PARKS
Song Cycle

Like so many sensitive, stoned men of my generation, I followed my teenage enjoyment of the Beach Boys' *Endless Summer* greatest hits package to the holy grail of *Pet Sounds*. What a mind-blowing album! What a justifiably hyped album. From there, I got caught up in the Cult of Brian, which identified and glorified his psychoses at the expense of all contributions by the rest of the Wilson clan and hateful Mike Love. Brian was sad and in search of his masterpiece. I was sad and in search of his masterpiece. Brian was boyishly good-looking, but prone to pudginess. I was boyishly good-looking, but prone to pudginess. As I dug into the post-crack-up mystique and caught my first whiffs of the legendary *Smile* album, I learned about this Van Dyke Parks character. Sounded cool. Sounded like a guy with good weed. I thought I read that he had something to do with the music for *Jungle Book*, which was A-1 Steak Sauce in my book. Heard about his "brilliant," but poor-selling, *Song Cycle*

THE SINGER/SONGWRITER GENRE

Many otherwise cool critics try to force these whiny troubadours on us. I pick Joni Mitchell and Ani Di Franco just because there seems to be some critical consensus that one *must* appreciate them. Well, I don't. Maybe rock journalists, since they work with words, put too much emphasis on lyrical cleverness. As a listener, I think the "music" part of the equation is more important than the "words" part. *That's why they call it music!* I suppose you could call this genre "poetry with some half-hearted guitar accompaniment," but I still wouldn't like it. These people can't write a catchy tune, and they don't rock.

Now, I give Bob Dylan a little more credit, since he does sometimes rock and can write a catchy tune now and then. However, he deserves a lot of blame for starting the whole genre and causing every boy in America to go through a Dylan phase and write horrible, whiny, sensitive songs. Plus, how does he get away with virulent sexism when someone like Danzig is raked over the coals?

Here are some ways even we cool punk rockers are made to suffer by the insidious influence of singer/songwriters:

1. One acoustic song put on an album to "vary the mood" is one song too many.

2. No matter how many Misfits posters and Weezer T-shirts you own, people think you must like this crap because you're a chick.

3. You never know when one of your favorite artists will go "unplugged" and try to get you to cough up $20 of your hard-earned money for one guy and a guitar. If they've been around for more than 10 years, read the fine print on the flyer, people!

4. While "poetic" or mystical hippie-dippy lyrics are easier to bear when drowned out by music, they are still annoying. If you are not the Flaming Lips, don't try this at home.

P.S.: I'm sorry, I don't know the names of individual albums. Just pick one at random and I'm sure it will do.

ANDREA HERMAN

album and eventually tracked down a copy for what was then the price of buying my own good bag of pot. Before I continue, I should say that I'd already heard bits of *Smile* bootlegs and was unimpressed. I bought *Smiley Smile*, fully knowing that it was the compromise of Brian's brilliant plan for *Smile*, and I agreed with that characterization, likening its "best" songs to something from one of the more "accessible" albums by the Residents (e.g., *Duck Stab, Buster & Glen*). I took home *Song Cycle* with high expectations (excuse the pun), placed the needle down and heard high-pitched whining of "poetic" lyrics over what sounded like canned carnival music. Over the next few months, I listened to that album high on pot, mushrooms, and alcohol, in the morning, at night, etc. Each time, it was more annoying and less musical than the previous listen. Eventually I sold it and used the money to buy the bag of pot I should have bought in the first place. I since concluded that Parks must have been the worst sort of hanger-on for Brian Wilson, offering him some pseudo-intellectual and classically-trained cred while getting a taste of the rock star party life of the Beach Boys. Van Dyke Parks was tried and convicted for crimes against pop at my personal Rock 'n' Roll Nuremberg Trial.

JIM SLADE

PARLIAMENT/FUNKADELIC

Another example of suburban white kids trying to hear something they can dance to without admitting that they want to dance. But this shit just went on and on and on and on and on. They played the same riff for, like, 20 minutes at a time. Sure, it might be nice to hear "Make My Funk the

P-Funk" in the background at a party where you really don't have to pay attention to it. But *God!* It's like having to listen to a ghetto-Phish with better drugs.

TOM BAGBY

GRAM PARSONS

Another rich boy slumming, this time in that most blue collar of music: Country. Thin vocals and tired lyricism can't mask an overall dull sound. Sure, he wrote a few good songs—"Sin City" and "She," to name two—but his worst offense is causing millions of hipsters, particularly in Atlanta, to think country music didn't exist before 1972. Country music, like the blues, demands soul and pain, and no matter how much junk you shoot, you can't buy cool.

MATT THOMPSON

PAVEMENT
Slanted and Enchanted

I don't know how many times the trust fund kids in "Der Clawhammer Gruppe" shirts (that they got for free from the college radio station where they DJ'd from 8-11 on Tuesday mornings for one semester their sophomore year) have tried to get me into this record. But in their estimations, this was the cornerstone album of "Slacker Rock" and was the future of music as we knew it. Then they stopped smoking weed, got jobs, grew up and started listening to classic rock on the radio.

JIM RAYMOND

Crooked Rain, Crooked Rain

Steve Malkmus is the Dave Eggers of rock—a too-clever, solipsistic brat who thrives on encouragement from an audience of pseudo-intellectuals he also struggles to disdain. His message is cute, but life-denying; he wore out his welcome *long* before any-

one noticed. Blame him *and* his legion of shit-eating apologists.

EMERSON DAMERON

PEARL JAM
Ten

Over a decade ago, Cobain blew his fucking brains out. It should have been you, Eddie. You were supposed to be the "troubled" one. Why wasn't it you? Every lousy "alterna-whatever" band in rotation on the big dumb rock stations claim Nirvana as an influence, but that's because they're too stupid to realize the sound they're really aping is Pearl Jam, and this is the album that sent them on their way to mind-numbing, formulaic emoting.

BENN RAY

PEDRO THE LION
Winners Never Quit

And so it was told that when Jesus died on the cross, his soul went into limbo, where the souls of good people who died before Jesus came to take them to heaven. The body of Jesus was lying in the grave for three days. At dawn on Sunday morning, all at once the earth began to tremble and a mighty angel of the Lord came down from heaven and rolled away the stone and sat upon it. Jesus then rose by his own power. His body was beautiful and able to move about suddenly and freely. He appeared to his followers to make them share in the joy of his victory. Yeah, and then that angel blew me and multi-colored pixie dust shot out of my ass! Man, the Christian resurrection fairytale is such utter folkloric bullshit. Can you believe that people (of the modern world) actually think this umpteenth savior cliché (in a line of many where the hero comes back from the dead) really happened? That's like saying, "Aw *naw*, dog—Batman, Wonder Woman, Superman, Aquaman, and the Wonder Twins—all that shit was fake, but Green Lantern? Yeah, Green Lantern was real, and

now I and millions of other people worship him!" Keep *waiting*, assholes. Keep waiting until the day you die.

BRIAN TEASLEY

LEE PERRY
Legalize It

"Some call it marijuana." What? Marijuana? Some people call marijuana "marijuana?" I didn't know that. I thought it was just marijuana. I'm going to go out on the street and ask a dealer for some "marijuana." He'll totally dig my street cred. And then I'll stuff a Rastafarian kitten into a tin can. Because that's what this album sounds like.

BENJAMIN JOHNSON

LIZ PHAIR
Exile in Guyville

You'll be enticed as you look at a picture of Liz with open mouth. You'll be chagrined as you hear the girl-next-door say "fuck" and "blow job." You'll be intrigued as you hold all 12 inches (okay, I never bought the LP, and the CD at 5 inches is a lot more accurate) in your sweaty palms. You'll be *bored to death listening to nothingness*. I wasn't going to get so low as to start quoting lyrics (which in a positive review only reinforces my theory that the more lyrics that are quoted, the suckier the album), but since Liz's claim to fame is that she wants to be your "blow job queen," the people who like this album must have been serviced by Liz either in reality or in their fantasy. If they were pleasured in reality, no problem, that's sufficient to put an album at the top of my list. If it was fantasy, believe me, folks, you could have done a lot better than this. As for ripping off a Stones title, Mick must be proud of Liz's marketing flair.

MICHAEL SEGHINI

PHISH
Any album

So there's a slight chance

Phish may have a decent following in the U.S. They can sell out the local gargantua-plex 30 days in a row, pack it with a different crowd of veggie-eating, Kerouac-reading, THC-inhaling, mushroom-experiencing Nader voters each evening, and satisfy their fans every time with varied set lists and energetic performances. Unfortunately, the band seems incapable of transferring its manic live performance to the studio. Live, the band is able to captivate an audience; experiencing one of their CDs, the listener simply feels captive.

DRYW KELTZ

PINK FLOYD
The Piper At The Gates Of Dawn
The early Syd Barrett-model of Pink Floyd inspires as much moist sentiment from rock hipsters as the later Roger Waters-dominant version draws contempt. But in either incarnation, the band blows. Maybe I just prefer my acid casualties cut with a little more strychnine (e.g., Roky Erickson, Skip Spence), but *The Piper At The Gates of Dawn* is every bit as dreary as everything else in the Pink Floyd catalog. It simply replaces Roger Waters' sophomoric rants and dead-daddy complex with Syd Barrett's infantile and deadly earnest musings on house cats and gnomes. Sure, everyone from Pere Ubu down to The Shins has held archaic, candle-lit, jack-off ceremonies to *Piper*, but that only proves that "influential," "ahead-of-their-time," "cult" records can be sloppy and boring, too. As for Syd's solo career, I'll submit this metaphor: the Wesley Willis of Carnaby Street.

JOHNNY V.

THE POLICE
Outlandos d'Amour
This doesn't happen very often, but with *Outlandos d'Amour*, the Police decided to chance it and managed to get away with it, for the most part. What did they get away with, you ask? Playing down to their audience. *Outlandos* is a far cry from what this band could already do, but in the late '70s, punk and new wave were the only selling styles of music in England. So, Sting and the gang decided to play along with the mainstream, instead of growing balls and just playing the way they wanted to. Instead of trying to build their own sound, they made an album of what they believed people wanted to hear and would sell. There's nothing lamer than that.

DAVIS REA

Synchronicity
Sorority girls will tell you that this is a totally great Police album if you can't get the greatest hits or the soundtrack to "Ally McBeal." If *Synchronicity* is *your* favorite album by The Police, then it is safe to assume your favorite time of year is whatever time of year someone asks, your favorite movie is the only movie you've ever seen, and your favorite personality trait is genital herpes.

NEIL MAHONEY

THE POLYPHONIC SPREE
Together We're Heavy
Remember Tripping Daisy? Me neither, but proper rock journalism etiquette dictates that I mention it, since the maestro behind The Polyphonic Spree "got his chops" in that band. Tripping Daisy broke up in 1999, leaving frontman Tim DeLaughter to nurture his hard-on for Brian Wilson. The theory is to "cram as many people as you can on a record and you have a lush wall of sound that envelops the listener." The reality is that if you put on the record, you have an acceptable cacophony with a handful of pretty good songs. Now, I don't hate The Polyphonic Spree. In fact, I saw them perform where an indoor swimming pool once stood in Brooklyn, and I was impressed by the sheer

The Most Overrated
'90s
Production Techniques & Other Incidental Bullshit That Seemed Cool At The Time

Written (and partially attempted during the '90s) by Brian Teasley & Henry Owings
Artwork by Eryc Simmerer

1. Inclusion of an answering machine message that's fraught with inside jokes and was probably left by a drunk friend.

2. Superfluous use of a Mellotron, usually as an ill-fitting intro to a song.

3. Drum machine beat that mysteriously changes into real drums after the first chorus.

4. Having the sound of a tape machine rewinding at the beginning or end of an album.

5. Backwards guitar solo when there wasn't much attention given to what it would sound like backwards. (Commonly called "Backwards is good enough.")

NEU COCK ROCK

There shouldn't be "neu" anything—especially cock rock. This is coming from someone who doesn't necessarily hate the stuff, even though it's probably the most unintentionally funny music ever made. The problem with "neu" cock rock is that the bands responsible for it are trying to legitimize a guilty pleasure by wearing their spandex and pouts ironically so nobody makes fun of them. The Darkness and Ten Benson don't really wanna rock you and they don't wanna be rocked—but they'll do anything for yuks. But even when a neu cock rock artists is completely sincere, as with Andrew W.K. and his Tony Robbins motivational party rock, it still sucks. Fuck all these guys. Except Supagroup.

RANDY HARWARD

---

visual spectacle. Ten well-lit people in white robes played a menagerie of instruments while ten more similarly clad people, strongly lit from the front and from floodlights placed behind the stained glass windows outside, stood above them to provide a back-up choir. Pretty cool. It made me wish I still took drugs. Close your eyes, though, and again, the cacophony. To be fair, The Polyphonic Spree is the kind of band that I would shit twice over if I were a music reviewer because they were trying something different. There's no end of bullshit* flooding music critics' inboxes, so I can at least appreciate the hype. Different, however, is not synonymous with great. Perfect for VW commercials and mix tapes for pitching woo, though.

JOE GARDEN

PORTISHEAD
Dummy

It's trip-hop. I don't care how hot the lead singer is, trip-hop is still the musical equivalent of mime.

DAVIS REA

ELVIS PRESLEY
The Sun Recordings

In 1954, they say a young Elvis Presley made history when he and his band got together at Sun Studios and basically invented rock n' roll. Really? I thought I liked rock n' roll. In fact, I thought I liked Elvis. These recordings are the sort of mascara-wearing Tin Pan Alley pop that Chuck D warned me about (or was it Flava Flav?) and serve as a prime example of an yet another "actor trying to be a rocker." Trash this CD and go rent *It Happened At The World's Fair*—now on DVD!

ANTONIO DEPIETRO

---

* I swear, if I hear one more half-assed power pop band marketed as "garage," I'm going to lock the members in a room with nothing to eat but their vintage guitars while blaring The Drags' *Dragsploitation Now!* at top volume.

PRETTY GIRLS MAKE GRAVES
The New Romance

Yet another instance of Matador looking at another label's roster and saying: "Need it, need it, got it, need it..." In this case, they needed a Yeah Yeah Yeahs. We, however, don't need the one we already have.

DAG LUTHER GOOCH

PRINCE
Sign 'O' The Times

After all the critical and commercial success of *1999*, *Purple Rain*, and *Around the World in a Day* (not to mention the retroactive raves about *Controversy* and *Dirty Mind*), Prince's megalomaniacal tendencies were significantly peaked. Thus, *Sign 'O' The Times*. This hyper-indulgent, unfocused two-disc wankfest marked the first in what would become a long list of the Purple One's grandiose crapfests, and the beginning of a decline that impossibly reaches lower than the midget himself.

RANDY HARWARD

PUBLIC IMAGE LTD.
Album/Compact Disc/Cassette

Public Image Ltd. was totally on the wane by the time *Album* came out. I love the first three PiL discs, but the live and disco records were unlistenable, and let's face it, not in the *Flowers of Romance* way either. Unlistenable like painfully awful. And don't think for a second that Johnny didn't know it; he was starting to dry up, and needed to do something fast. So, he assembled a crack team of musicians in the studio, including Ginger Baker from Cream (?!) on the skins and Steve Vai on guitar. Those two names alone would have sold records. But leave it to Rotten to pull out another bullshit schtick to fuck up his last chance at legitimacy. *Album* was the record modeled to look like generic products, some high-falutin' attempt to embrace consumerism by circumventing it (or was it the other way around)? Jesus, I can never remember). So, instead of crediting the players, maybe getting people outside of "the scene" to buy some records, and possibly revitalizing the band, Lydon strikes a pose and shoots himself right in the foot. PiL's post-Album output consisted of two tepid, pandering LP's worth of songs begging for airplay on 120 Minutes and a greatest hits album that was a vehicle for a lame quasi-environmental screed with an even lamer video. We won't even mention that techno record.

MIKE FOURNIER

PUSSY GALORE
Groovy Hate Fuck

No, really, I had a snare drum—you could've borrowed it. Grating, abrasive and obnoxious in all the wrong ways. Their best song, never recorded and only played live once, was "Who's Got the Biggest Trust Fund?" I think Cafritz took the cake. The best thing they ever did, covering *Exile on Main Street* in its entirety, was a slow response to Sonic Youth's nigh-genius threat to cover The Beatles' *White Album*.

BEN BLACKWELL

QUEENS OF THE STONE AGE
Songs for the Deaf

This record picks up where Alice in Chains left off...or where Mother Love Bone left off. It's got the annoying fake radio DJ's between many of the tracks, and the songs are so boring and cheesy sounding. I felt embarrassed listening to it. It was not even close to being metal, or punk, or rock 'n' roll at all. The not-so-evil but really gross "Aaahhh's" in the background and the unenthusiastically placed "Yeah's" just add to my frustration with it. And the record cover sux, too. They need to get some *good* songs.

ALICJA TROUT

QUICKSILVER MESSENGER SERVICE
Quicksilver Messenger Service

Good things usually come to those who wait—except in child abuse and extended hippie jams...and this record may just contain both. Recorded while the guy who actually started the band, Dino Valente, was in prison (thanks, guys), it is impossible not to follow the sticky trail of spilt Phish-food ice cream back to the laborious San Francisco scene the Messenger Service helped create while most certainly stoned. Because of this lineage, I now have a 50 percent chance of walking into any random bar and having to either leave or endure some aimless, doobified, Yippie yawn-rock. Why everyone in the QMS couldn't have been put in prison for the crime of indulgence I will never know. Guitarist John Cipollina's main contribution to the canon of rock guitar solo-ing ("Dude, if I'm not back in an hour...then just wait longer!") is in monk patience-testing, which we all know is only a match-strike away from monks burning themselves in protest. Hey, maybe that's what a lot of that was all about. I mean, it did happen in the exact same time period. Anyway, who could blame those simple Buddhists if they just couldn't take all that unnecessary white boy noodling?

BRIAN TEASLEY

RACHEL'S
Handwriting

An incestuous gaggle of self-involved dilettantes, infected with the nautical-imagery plague that turned Louisville and Chicago into the most embarrassing, pseudo-intellectual poseur communes of the '90s. Backed by slow-motion 8mm films and their sit-down namesake cellist, this pretend-classical "collective" was so fucking dirty-white-T-shirt-and-jeans art school you'd have to rip

The Most Overrated '90s Production Techniques & Other Incidental Bullshit That Seemed Cool At The Time (continued)

6. False take...psych!

7. Real out-of-tune vocals, before Cher taught us all to believe in the power of Auto-Tune.

8. Bass through a Rat pedal. Balls out, man.

9. Having way too much hi-hat in the mix. Love that sizzle!

10. Vocals that are mixed way too low or sound like someone talking out of their asshole while wearing body armor.

11. Tight rhythmic stops that seem "extreme" because the guitarist hit the noise gate pedal. Stoppin' on a dime, chief.

12. Enough room sound for a few hundred drum kits.

13. No guitar solos 'cuz that shit's for rock stars.

14. Even better and more ironic than #13 is the perennial, irreverent "sloppy" solo.

15. Vocals-thru-a-telephone sound. Awesome, now I can sound like the 411 operator!

16. Band chatter after the song ends, usually concerning an affirmation that the take was "good enough."

17. One word: Albini.

18. 4-track tape hiss (either intentional or unintentional).

19. Twenty minutes of silence followed by a bonus track (a.k.a. a sub-par song that wasn't even good enough to make it on your "really out there" side project).

20. Ambient disc. Yo, we're more than just a rock band!

21. Interludes (or vignettes of sound) wherein the band plays instruments.

Radio 4 to The Replacements

farts between "movements" to give the place some atmosphere. Heads down, backs to the audience, they never even noticed.

CHRIS OTT

RADIO 4
Gotham!

This is what happens when 1) Urban punters believe they are the only humans on the planet who have ever listened to PiL's *Metal Box*, everything by the Bush Tetras and A Certain Ratio's *To Each,* 2) Dumb kids thinking they are on to something buy all of the crap records out of the import bin, 3) Even dumber consumers make up excuses like "well, at least they're ripping off ACR, PiL and APB and not Real Life and Mr. Mister" and fork out actual cash money for this tripe (Shaw, if you want to go back to your youth, get a face lift and go down a 40), and 4) Actual critics proclaim this shite the second coming of NYC and LA in an attempt to avoid the reality that American music is so far into the shitter that we're gonna need a Herculean-sized industrial plunger to help us get even halfway back on track, and all of these bands are merely the fourth generation of snake oil salesmen making their rounds. In the meantime, where is David Horowitz when you *really* need him? The best quote about Radio 4 comes from Mark Kates, svengali of the reformed Mission of Burma and head of Fenway Recordings: "I'd sign these guys, but they remind me too much of other bands I already like."

NICK BLAKEY

RADIOHEAD
OK Computer

Feeling sorry for yourself has been big business these last 20 years, and was even more so in the fat, prosper-ous '90s. Radiohead were marked to be a one-hit won-der with their debut single, the über-self pity anthem "Creep," until they managed to bitch slap anyone and everyone who might have doubted them with their incredible second album *The Bends* (*still* not given the acknowledgement it fully deserves). Because so many critics missed the boat on that one, they vowed through their embar-rassment not to fail on Thom Yorke and his boys again. They did. *OK Computer* doesn't reach the heights scaled by *The Bends* or the seriously out there and *Metal Machine Music*-like fuck you's of its follow-ups *Kid A* and *Amnesiac*. *OK Computer* seems to be based entirely on the blue-prints laid down by The La's song "Looking Glass" and The Chameleons' album *Strange Times* , and fea-tures a lot of half-baked melody and semi-structures that fall somewhere between pop music and a drunken, spittling nervous breakdown. On that level, perhaps, it is a fine album, but mostly it was embraced by critics trying to cover their asses, and shithead subur-ban kids looking for yet another reason in the grooves to justify their feel-ings of oppression from their parents. Nothing was more satisfying, though, than when Yorke and his crew whipped out the desolation twins of *Kid A* and *Amnesiac* and raised a solid square middle finger into the faces of their fans who merely bobbed their heads along with the sterile beats in the hopes that nobody else would notice that they just didn't get it. But because this was Radiohead, they went along with it (almost identical to the achievement of Nirvana's Kurt Cobain grafting the intro riff of their mega-hit "Smells Like Teen Spirit" onto the beginning of the later should-have-been-huge "Rape Me" taken off their backhand slap of an album *In Utero*). You just *know* that the band laughed all the way to the bank on that one.

NICK BLAKEY

RAGE AGAINST THE MACHINE
Rage Against the Machine

All the guitar people keep blah-blah-blahing about Tom Morello's guitar play-ing. Oh my god, he's scratching on the fret board! Groundbreaking? I think not. It is not a difficult thing to do. Maybe I'm just really jealous, but I think this band has gotten more credit then they deserve. I like them and everything, but it's amusing that they're all political, and seem to have communist leanings, yet are signed to multi-con-glomerate Sony. Makes you think, doesn't it?

JAMES KORBA

RAILROAD JERK
Railroad Jerk

Why do white college dudes want to bang on pots and pans, sing (holler as they would have it be known) through a green bullet mic and play uninspired slide guitar? Because they have never come to terms with the fact that their great-great-grand-diddies owned slaves. That's why. Is Railroad Jerk any better than say Skeleton Key or The Chickasaw Mudpuppies? If you know the answer to that please shove a stick of lit dynamite in your ass and pray there is better music in the afterlife.

BRIAN TEASLEY

THE RAMONES
Rocket To Russia

Ramones and *Leave Home* are always name-checked, but they are not overrated. In fact, I contend that they are underrated, because if they were valued anywhere near what they should be we wouldn't have had all those bands over the years trying (and failing) to make what are essentially newer versions of those albums. *Rocket to Russia* is where The Ramones begin that long slide towards *Pet Semetary* and being the token punk reference in any issue of *Rolling Stone* in the 1980s.

BEN HELLMANN

End Of The Century

It sounded good on paper—a strange pairing of pop-rock lovers with the wall of sound master producer. One can admire them for trying to grow out of the typecasting that had taken place by this point in their career, but (like AC/DC has learned) why fix it if it ain't broke? Overproduced by a Spector who was clearly past his prime, *End Of The Century* isn't as ground-breaking as people were led to believe.

ROCK ACTION

THE RAPTURE
Echoes

If I want to get yelled at in a gay discotheque, I'll go to a gay discotheque wearing chaps that aren't assless.

BEN JOHNSON

THE RASPBERRIES
The Raspberries

Did you get into "alterna-tive" music because even though you actually liked all the pap offered up by dom-inant culture, people *still* wouldn't accept you? Great, because that's why God created power pop—non-threatening and bland enough for every beige chino and lite mayo whitey... yet containing enough "power" chords and "just-shy-of-good" song-writing to give the listener enough hip cred needed to write freelance CD reviews for the local "Indieweekly, Inc." The Raspberries and their ilk were made for music critics (read: closet Bryan Adams fans).

PABLO A. ROCKAFUCKER

RED HOT CHILI PEPPERS
Uplift Mofo Party Plan

What started out as amusing, semi-sexy white boy funk you could turn chicks on with went downhill fast when the jocks at school realized the band was singing about pussy. That, and the fact that Anthony Keidis might have the worst delivery in the world. He might as well be singing "yabba-dabba-doo" most of the time. Don't lie: everybody thought slap-bass was cool for about five minutes.

TOM BAGBY

Blood Sugar Sex Magik

Screamin' Jay Hawkins once put out a record called *Black Music For White People*, and this record is nothing but that. The Peppers were fun when they were wearing socks on their dicks, but Anthony Kiedis' weak attempts at poetry and "depth" are just pathetic.

MATT THOMPSON

LOU REED
Transformer

Lou Reed is so, so cool. So is New York. But you know what is really the coolest? Selling your image to a nifty, little scooter. Lou never lost his head, even when he was giving Honda head.

DAG LUTHER GOOCH

Metal Machine Music

Okay, I've never even heard it, but neither have most of the critics who name-check it. Plus, it set the precedent for self-indulgence disguised as avant-garde (or a "Fuck You" to the record company).

BRETT ESSLER

New York

Lou Reed has fallen for every bullshit guitar store trick in the book and hasn't made a good record since *Take No Prisoners*. Now, he's the Diane Vreeland of poetry rock, or New York's answer to Sting. No mention is ever made of Rachel.

JULIANNE SHEPARD

REFUSED
The Shape Of Punk To Come

Revitalized hardcore my ass! If revitalizing hardcore means mixing in disjointed half-baked politics (isn't that what hardcore is all about anyways?) with some electronic gizmos, then the musical style is in more trouble than was previously thought.

AARON LEFKOVE

RENTALS
Return of the Rentals

Weezer and that dog. were clever enough to make their cutesiness sufferable. Somehow, the Rentals jettisoned the brains, distilled the cute shit and channeled it through a shallow LA sewer. Aren't you guys due for an earthquake? Can you play "The Sweater Song"? Okay, can I at least have some coke, then? You have to understand, Kindercore veterans, it's nothing personal: that fucking "Friends With P" song sent me scurrying back to my Swans records, and I haven't trusted deadpan twee pop since.

EMERSON DAMERON

THE REPLACEMENTS
Let It Be

For a band that never quite managed to make a good record, the 'Mats have harvested buckets of overripe praise over the years. That's why *Let It Be* is a useful template for measuring the band's shortcomings, since it's widely surveyed as their best record. Get rid of the eminently disposable thrash toons, and the shitty cover of an even shittier Kiss song, and *Let It Be* comprises— count 'em—exactly five Paul Westerberg compositions that traffic in the type of maudlin navel-gazing that's closer in spirit to James Taylor than to Johnny Thunders. Of these, two are passable pop songs, one is a lounge piano number that winds up suggesting that perhaps the transgendered actually deserve the derision

THE SIXTIES

Anything written during, about, or in the spirit of the sixties. We need to get over this period of music; it has been overdone so much that I think I am going to have to start killing hippies. But, seriously, there have been equally proficient, sincere, and production-oriented people working in music before and after this period. The sixties were just the inauguration/co-opting of blues and folk into white, mainstream culture.

ERIC VAZQUEZ

R.E.M. to The Rolling Stones

they receive, and the other two are gussied-up acoustic tunes that offer such disingenuous graduation-speech platitudes as "Your age is the hardest age/Everything drags and drags." If scribbling this shit on your biology notebook was the only thing that made high school bearable in 1985, perhaps—like the students of Westerberg High in Heathers—this world was not meant for someone as beautiful as you. Fare thee well, our brave little Eskimo, fare thee well.

JOHNNY V.

Tim
Cameron Crowe once gushingly wrote of the "emotional perfection" of this record. If that had come from the same Cameron Crowe who wrote *Fast Times at Ridgemont High* or directed *Say Anything*—the one who knew a little something about emotional perfection—it might legitimately be considered high praise. Unfortunately, it came from the Crowe who was directing *Singles* at the time, and the other "emotionally perfect" band he mentioned in the same breath was Mother Love Bone. Okay, okay— "Left of the Dial" still makes me nostalgic for the '80s rock-chick girlfriend I never had, and "Bastards of Young" still makes me want to get up from a hungover couch-nap and kick in a stereo speaker. But if there's ever the equivalent of the Nuremberg trials for crimes against rock, Paul Westerberg's going to have a lot to answer for from this period in his career. Turning his back on Bob Stinson and providing a template for the Goo Goo Dolls' entire catalogue will land him in the dock. But it's the novelty twang of "Waitress in the Sky," the faux-boyish mincing of "Kiss Me on the Bus," and the noodle-dicked schmaltz of "Swingin' Party" that'll send him to the gallows. Many Replacements

fans will tell you that if you only own one Mats record, it should be this one. They're right. This one's got all the Hallmark moments you'll need for that mix tape you're making to try to seduce the hot teenage All-American girl-next-door's retarded little sister. Should you fail, you can console yourself by actually listening to *Tim* all the way through. It's guaranteed to make you feel just as stupid and ashamed as if you had sealed the deal.

CHRIS ISELI

R.E.M.
Out Of Time
When *Document* came out I thought that they had to make a shitty album eventually. It's not great, but it's not all that bad. After a few weeks, I gave it away. There wasn't one song on it I really liked. However, R.E.M. must have loved them all, and why not? *Document* got them into the Top 40. They must have done something right. So they put out *Document* again and called it *Green*, only this time there was music for the kids too, and the kids loved it. How could a ten-year old not love "Stand?" As a big thank you to all the kids that bought that album, and broke their cherries to the remaining tracks on *Orange*...excuse me, *Green*, R.E.M. wrote a song just for them: "Shiny Happy People!" Those kids bought the record, and discovered "Losing My Religion," and turned a droning, repetitious song about nothing into a modern hymn. God bless R.E.M. for making it so easy to feel like you are on the cutting edge of modern art.

DAG LUTHER GOOCH

Automatic for the People
How could one album sound so soulless and still have song titles like

"Everybody Hurts?" I guess Michael McDonald does it all the time. He might as well cover that sugary piece-of-shit song. If Andy Kaufman knew his name was on this album, these hippies would pay in pain.

ED PARKER

THE RESIDENTS
Meet The Residents
Not one tangible song on the whole album, just incoherent sludge. The fact that these guys and this record are compared to Beefheart is a shame.

ROB CARMICHAEL

RITES OF SPRING
End on End
Fugazi has been solid for the past decade, and I understand the role that the members' previous bands—and all early punk—played in getting us to where we are now. That said, I found Rites of Spring to be boring and repetitive, and they weren't nearly as innovative as their contemporaries. Even when it's as sincere and well-meaning as Rites of Spring, they never impressed me as much as the jazz-influenced Minutemen, the speed and tightness of Bad Brains, and the blinding fury of Hüsker Dü. 1980s D.C. punk was for the most part, actually pretty lame when compared to what else was going on around the country at that time.

PATRICK GOUGH

RODAN
Rusty
I just do not get it. Why should I care if some group of Louisville art school losers suddenly realize they can play metal while still playing flutes? So what if they went on to greater things? This record is a bad idea, poorly executed. Quiet, loud, quiet, loud...yeah, I get it. I can imagine that if I did not sell my precious vinyl copy (or did I give it away to some art school student in a gasoline attendant's jack-

et?), the record would sound even worse than it did back in '95 or whatever. And don't even get me started on June of '44!

TIM KABARA

THE ROLLING STONES
Black and Blue
I haven't spoken to my friend Steve since he bought this on CD. He says *Black and Blue* (a.k.a. *Where's the Blackface?*) is where the Stones branched out and moved into a new era, but I know he bought it just to fill out his collection. No one wants to hear Mick pretend to be from New Orleans ("Melody") or lead the band through confused stabs at reggae ("Cherry Oh Baby") and funk ("Hey Negrita"). And even Steve will admit that "Memory Hotel," a seven-minute ballad, is painfully misguided. There are times on the album when the rhythm section nearly drags to a halt. Obviously, this was not out of incompetence—Watts and Wyman are usually great— but more likely out of protest. Already known as the worst Stones album, future generations will come to realize that *Black and Blue* is one of the weakest records ever.

MICHAEL FALOON

Some Girls
Mick Jagger, former London School Of Economics student, came to a huge realization in the mid '70s: the Stones could work really hard on an album and make an obscene amount of money, or they could barely try and still make an obscene amount of money, like they did with 1976's *Black and Blue*. The Stones' brand name was held in such high regard at that time, people would buy anything the band did. But Mick's no fool. He knew people might give up on the Stones if they started putting out all-crap albums. So, he and Keith made sure to include one or two good songs on each record—just enough to snag a lot of radio

RAP

As a white kid who grew up in the '80s with a black step dad and a mixed brother, I was unusually racially sensitive growing up. Add to that a family with roots in Utah and Alabama (no shit), and you have the makings of a young, white, Marcus Garvey. As a kid, my first natural inclinations towards music were towards shit like Quiet Riot and Roth-era Van Halen. As that kind of fun, boisterous, party-metal gave way to retarded "meaningful metal" shit like Cinderella, and the even worse "I'll kick your ass with my knee-high, medieval, moccasin boots because I'm 3 years older than you and in the same grade...and even if I were your age I could probably still kill you, faggot, because I've been fist-fighting with my dad since I was 4" shit like Metallica (still the dumbest name for a band in history until someone names their band Jazz'o'Rama), I had no choice but to abandon the metal ship. Looking for something meaningful, and not wanting to be a g(ay)oth kid, I started listening to rap as a desperate attempt to continue enjoying music. It really just turned out to be a slow, painful rape of whatever artistic/intellectual dignity I had from my 12-14 age period.

What's particularly fucked up about this is the fact that the time that I was going through this (about '88-'90) is referred to as "The Golden Age of Rap." A lot of the intentions of what was happening during this time were noble: i.e. showing black people in a realistic light, confronting issues of black existence and racism with strength and unwavering honesty, not being be a pussy to whitey... whatever. But as music, rap follows a very clear historical path (I would have used the word *trajectory* in place of path, but I heard Andy Garcia say *trajectory* once): 1) Shit people can break dance to 2) Shit black people can bitch about white people to 3) Shit people can sell Keebler cookies to 3) Shit black people can fool white kids into buying to make them feel cooler to 4) Shit black dudes can use to score with all the chicks in the world they couldn't score with for years because of racism.

None of the aforementioned things are inherently wrong, but none of them are about music. Everyone has that one friend (or pray to God, acquaintance) who's into old punk for stupid, obvious reasons. "Punk's real. It's not fake. Punk's what it's all about." The only thing that separates punk from rap is that punk never greedily collected on a nation's collective guilty conscience. Otherwise, they're identical: unlistenable, ostentatious, simplistic, dumb or some combination thereof.

And just to be a bigger fucking dickhead (I will not say *hater*), I want to address the fucking faults of this shit at its core. Rap is essentially a set of rules."I will rhyme and shit. I will sample music (which sounds really thin and shitty even if compositionally inspired) and shit. I will act like a really cool guy and shit."Rock at its best and worst has at least been about people's perception of it, which is something punk and its bastard son rap have never been able to say.

RYAN STACY

time, but not so much as to require a whole lot of effort. Paternity suits and drug busts take up a lot of time, after all. *Some Girls* has a good single—"Shattered" b/w "Beast of Burden"—and a load of filler wrapped in a then-controversial (at least to anyone oblivious to punk) record cover. More telling, though, is that even when they seemed to try, the Stones couldn't pull off the old tricks. In 1972, Mick could convince us that he got a good talkin'-to from a preacher man. But by 1978, when he was singing "Faraway Eyes," it was clear that Mick had one foot out the door and was thinking a whole lot more about the South of France than the south side of Chicago.

MICHAEL FALOON

Entire career

The Rolling Stones would be a bit more respectable if they kept pace of dying members on par with the Beatles or even Lynyrd Skynyrd for that fact. Brian Jones was on the right track, but they shoved him out or was that into the pool? Fuck this band and fuck all you denim activists who struggle to keep them relevant. The Rolling Stones have been like musical Silly Putty for the last 40 or so years. They did a disco record to keep current. Way to go bad asses, those lips deflated while Gerry Ford was still a goddamn U.S. Senator.

JOE SELBY

ROYAL TRUX
Twin Infinitives

The glory of '60s garage rock represented righteous indignation, self-reliance, and redemption through passion—to wit, all the things to which Noo Yawk's master and mistress of stylized incompetence are diametrically opposed. Start your own band before you accept anything from these pampered, pretentious

fuckwits. Never trust a junkie, kids. Royal Trux deserves to be left face-down in their own puke.

EMERSON DAMERON

SCISSOR SISTERS
Scissor Sisters

Every three years or so, the Culture Club contingent opens back up and allows a few more feather-boa victims to "play band" over recycled disco beats. Scissor Sisters are today's answer to the question of whether the world will give us a much more remedial Dee-Lite for people who thought Seth Green was *fabulous* in Party Monster. This is music for the *Queer Eye for the Straight Butthole* generation only.

BRIAN TEASLEY

SEBADOH
Bakesale

Every credible musician has that "fuck it, I'm the man, I'm goin' for it" moment as they approach adulthood, sure that they've lived and learned enough to take this little world by storm. They talk to their friends, tell them "I'm not fuckin' around anymore, man, I've got a life to lead," and set out to record their defining statement. And it's a piece of shit like *Bakesale*, every time.

CHRIS OTT

THE SHADOW RING

Sheer proof that one man's puke is another man's diarrhea. I liked these guys much better when they were the three- day hang-over I had after my brother's wedding. This was best exemplified at the last show Harry Pussy ever played in Cambridge (and yes, it's all on tape):
Heckler/punter to Adris Hoyos (drummer of Harry Pussy): "Shadow Ring!"
Adris to Heckler/Punter: "Fuck you!"
And if you own any of their

records you probably also chose future stock options instead of cash payment when you later worked at Kozmo.com.

NICK BLAKEY

TUPAC SHAKUR
All Eyez on Me

Don't know how it went 10-times platinum. Guess there are a lot of mindless thugs looking for a spokesperson. Hey, didn't Tupac start out touring and dancing for Digital Underground? How did he go from humpty dancin' to drive-by criminal assaulting?

ADRIENNE ARAMBULA

SHELLAC
Terraform

Yes, they have Steve Albini and Todd Trainer, but then they also have Bob Weston. Nothing Shellac has done has ever equaled anything Big Black ushered forth or even what Rapeman may have promised. They are, in a word, the emperor's new clothes in the guise of a power trio that contains two of the most respected producers/recorders of the last 15 years (but they manage not to achieve the pleasures of The Sniveling Shits, The Invisible Girls, or even The George Martin Orchestra). So then, as the kids have been known to say, they *must* be good, right? 'Natch, not even close. Yes, "Rambler" is good, and even parts of *At Action Park* indeed, but c'mon, *Terraform*? For non-believers, refer to Greg Chapman's nuclear assault disembowelment in issue #13 of "The Ugly American." I need not say more.

NICK BLAKEY

THE SHINS
Chutes Too Narrow

Sometimes guys will do some seriously limp-wristed shit to get into a girl's knickers. The only redeeming thing about this album is that you can convince some folks that the title is a thinly veiled euphemism for ass-

sex. With song titles like "Kissing the Lipless," the argument writes itself.

BRIAN MCMANUS

MATTHEW SHIPP
Antipop Consortium

I hate free jazz with the loathing of a lover scorned. I've tried to appreciate it. In a live setting, I find it relaxing. When I put on a free jazz record—any free jazz record—I forget it's on. Same deal with backpacker hip-hop. I understand why I'm supposed to like it. I understand its creators are proficient, and probably smarter than the guys in Onyx. But, I'm sorry, it's boring as shit. This DOA collaboration brings the two bloated, over-appreciated genres together, like two wooly buttcheeks every NYCenster can nestle between while I'm downloading the new Cali Agents track, and maybe some Louis Armstrong. I don't care to expand my horizons in that particular direction.

EMERSON DAMERON

SIGUR RÓS
Ágætis Byrjun

Gotta give 'em credit for that idea about letting fans submit their translations of these made up lyrics and using the winners for the official lyrics. I got this great fucking idea: buy an English dictionary and start singing words. I guess in Iceland people don't need words since the only thing you need to say is "I'm cold."

CHRIS MCGARVEY

SILVER APPLES
Silver Apples

"Hey, let's invent an instrument that can do all kinds of amazing shit, and then sing a bunch of lyrics from Jethro Tull B-sides. I think I can even get this thing to sound exactly like that gay flute."

BENJAMIN JOHNSON

GENE SIMMONS
Asshole

Oh, wait...this one's not overrated. *Everyone* knew it

sucked as soon as hit the shelves. If you didn't, one listen to the cover of Prodigy's "Firestarter" (overrated to begin with) and one look at the album cover (featuring notorious lady-killer and heroically ugly Gene lounging with a roomful of naked and scantily-clad women) would have confirmed it.

JEFF MCLEOD

PAUL SIMON
Graceland

Aging whitey rings up a mess of Africans to record himself a colorful record. Africans happily agree, and also offer to dance in whitey's music videos. Everyone is pleased. Whitey then hangs up the phone, pulls out his copy of the Africans' Shaka Zulu record, records it onto a 1/4 tape, and proceeds to sing stuff only the lamest caucasians could possibly care about on top of it. He names the album after the diamond-encrusted home of a fellow whitey who stole gospel from black people, and made a fortune whitening it up. Then he marries cute hippie girl who thinks she's Janis Joplin. What a life. I saw a TV show one time where Paul Simon talked about how he writes and records his songs. Apparently, he has this remote control sampler-programmer sound system that has all manner of crap on it, and he walks around his living room writing canned music by himself in much the same way most people watch the tube. He also pointed out that his friends, Eric Clapton and James Taylor, also "compose" in the same manner. I wonder if he ever thought about the fact that preschoolers do this, too.

DAG LUTHER GOOCH

SIMON & GARFUNKEL
Bridge Over Troubled Water

A commercial folk album whose target audience is 40-year-old Jewish doctors who live on Long Island. Paul Simon looks like he

just rolled out of a fucking duffle bag.

JASON DIEMILIO

RONI SIZE/REPRAZENT
New Forms

I once watched some live footage of Roni Size and his group performing at Montreaux. The drummer was a solid robot behind the kit. The bass player was fluid and funky on the upright bass. Then there were about ten other people behind keyboards or turntables. Lots of times they were smoking weed. I swear I saw one of them playing Solitaire. For a solid hour, I was bored out of my skull, only watching to see if the drummer's arms would indeed fall off. Then I realized they actually had an album of that stuff. And it was two discs. Of *that* stuff...where you *can't* watch the drummer to see if his arms fall off. Then again, maybe they're making it for people who want to smoke weed and play Solitaire at home.

JIM RAYMOND

SLADE
Slayed

Be honest. I know that when you shed yourself of your Williamsburg hipster affectations that you like the Quiet Riot version of "Cum on Feel the Noize" better. Wait...I didn't mean to call you out in front of your friends. Please don't cry, little guy. Just take off the tight thrift store suit and Beatle boots, leave your copy of Saul Bellow's *Seize the Day* on the table of the coffee shop in which you now sit, and start the long drive back to Iowa City. Your parents have kept your room exactly as you left it.

BRIAN TEASLEY

SLAYER
Reign in Blood

Supposedly this record was conceived as a modern rock opera that was written by watching *The Passion of the Christ* with the sound turned down. What it really proves to be is nothing more than

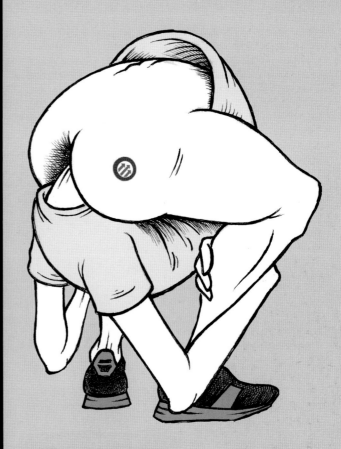

MODERN ROCK CRITICISM

No, I'm not some dude who got a bad review in *Pitchfork* and got all huffy and defensive about it. I don't even play music. If I did, I'm damn sure I wouldn't be all "well if you hate it so much, do something better. Why not be creative instead of trying to tear me down, man?" when I got a bad review. That's the stupidest thing I ever heard. That's like pissing into your own mouth and then getting all upset because the people who call you an idiot for doing it have the good sense not to do it themselves.

No, I'm not talking about "rock criticism is overrated" because critics should "lighten up" and "enjoy the music" more. Fuck that. They should just shut the fuck up about it for two seconds. I'm saying, "Rock critics, eat a dick."

I could be all theoretical about it, but that'd be stooping to their sad level. I could talk about Walter Benjamin and the age of mechanical reproduction. I

loosely played suburban-style Christian emo-core with your predictable soft/loud verse/chorus thing, the "everybody jump" parts, and, of course, the campfire melodies for the ladies. You know this formula like the back of your mom's ass. This is so safe and lily-white it makes my pussy hurt. Couldn't they have—if not let loose a true curveball—at least thrown a splitter by not being yet another copycat version of Trust Company or Thrice? Fellas, give me a hammer, some wood, and a couple of nails, and I'll crucify myself. Now listen, I don't agree with that crazy dude from Kansas who protests AIDS victims' funerals and says that Jesus hates fags, but that doesn't mean I don't think that Jesus doesn't hate pussies.

BRIAN TEASLEY

SLEATER-KINNEY
Entire Discography
Greil Marcus really got off on the fact that he "discovered" (shades of Diana Ross and Michael Jackson here, folks) a couple of "dykes" (ha ha, they pulled an Ani DiFranco on you there, kiddies—only one of them likes to sleep with girls, regardless of what momma Mrs. Tucker may have told you back in 1999) who could "play" and made it out like this sorry excuse for a rock band were the new rock and roll saviors. Bullshit: I think he jerked off on their album covers in the hopes of getting a three-way, and maybe a rim job to boot, in exchange for his glowing hype. He sucks. They barely scratch by. They were, and are, yet another reason to hate Olympia (exceptions being The Melvins, who moved the fuck outta there, and The Gossip, who don't count because they're originally from Arkansas).

NICK BLAKEY

SLINT
Spiderland
A curious point at which something becomes so overrated that it's actually incredibly influential, despite not being very good. I blame it on Chicago. The city.

FAT BOBBY

SLY & THE FAMILY STONE
There's A Riot Goin' On
Five reasons why *There's A Riot Goin' On* isn't as good as its follow-up, *Fresh*:
1. Greil Marcus didn't devote an entire chapter to *Fresh* in *Mystery Train*.
2. The cover of *Riot* doesn't feature Sly in Hong Kong Phooey-mode in full leathers.
3. Doing a quaalude-laced, cadaverous cover of one of your own biggest hits is pretty cool. Doing a quaalude-laced, cadaverous cover of one of Doris Day's biggest hits is infinitely cooler.
4. Everything Sly was trying to articulate on *Riot* was said more succinctly by Swamp Dogg on "I've Never Been To Africa and It's All Your Fault."
5. *Riot* is the sound of everything gone to shit. *Fresh* is the sound of someone desperately trying to convince himself that, with enough coke and cognac, he can turn back time before everything went to said shit. As such, *Fresh* is the sadder, funnier, more doomed, and prophetic record.

JOHNNY V.

SMASHING PUMPKINS
Mellon Collie And The Infinite Sadness
Even the title reeks of pretension, but we already knew how important Corgan thought he was even before this was released. But two hours worth of material goes beyond ego—it becomes a swindle. And Corgan himself should know that most of the albums from the '70s he's trying to build upon (or ape) topped out at 45 minutes, or fewer than 80, for a dou-ble LP. I wish Leslie West would sit on him and work some of that hot air out of Billy's body. No wonder Chamberlin was always smacked out of his mind; he needed something to do while Corgan was adding extra touches to "Zero."

ROCK ACTION

THE SMITHS
Morrissey, that whiny fuck. If there ever was a case where a great, solid rock band was tanked by such a sucky lead singer, it's The Smiths. I've tried so hard to get into these overly romantic Limey crackers time and again, predominantly in order to get in good with some of those tasty Britpop chickens who usually worship at their altar. I've wasted my money on *Meat Is Murder*, *The Queen Is Dead*, and *Louder Than Bombs*, only to sell them back for half the money I ponied up for them. If you're gonna spend $12.88 on sadness, just pick up the Leadbelly anthology. At least he doesn't cry like a woman. Hey Morrissey, in the words of Don Corleone, "You can act like a man!"

RON HART

(SMOG)
Red Apple Falls
This record should be called *I Don't Live With My Mom Anymore* or *A Fat Girl Sucked My Dick Outside That Club*. Jesus, Chan Marshall makes you do some crazy shit.

BRIAN TEASLEY

SMOKING POPES
Born to Quit
Whenever American bands decide to dabble in mixing "their" sound with the Smiths and something else, it usually sounds anything but genuine. Sadly, the other piece in the equation for the Popes was college date rape rockers, The Smithereens. This is not to mention that Crystal Lake, Illinois' finest (now that's real condemna-tion) were one of the gazillion bands from the mid-90s that never figured out how to channel their occasionally lukewarm live energy into anything above freezing cold bath water on record. *Born to Quit* was yet another originally released on an indie record that got (thanks to some Capitol Record's A&R crap slinger who surely retained their job only a few weeks after this album bombed) reissued on a major label as nothing more than a study in pure economic failure. And, truly, it is failure (as a complete motif) into which the Smoking Popes put most of their stock. Nothing in music, better or worse, would be any different if this band had never existed.

BRIAN TEASLEY

SOFT CELL
Non-Stop Erotic Cabaret
Reasons: 1. Marc Almond cannot sing in tune or out of it. 2. It sounds horrible. 3. I'm jealous (we did drag shows together at college with Frank Tover/Fad Gadget). 4. Hardly anybody knows the song "Tainted Love" was written by Marc (T. Rex) Bolan's wife.

HUGO BURNHAM

SONIC YOUTH
Daydream Nation
It was a good concept that somehow lost its way: to bend, spindle, and mutilate rock music and its beloved instruments in a time-worn effort to create a truly new variation on a theme. But too soon they decided not to bury rock music but to praise it. As they became the Kings of College Rock in the late-80's and early-90's, their screwdrivers and hacksaws started to look and sound downright cute and adorable. From street-wise music terrorists to the cuddly darlings of *Sassy* magazine, it was a transfor-mation that I found hard to stomach.

RUSS FORSTER

Everything They've Ever Done

Just a bunch of formalists. It's always been clear that they could have just as easily found another career, or less cynically, a way to express themselves. They're so damn professional it's sickening. Most of my favorite artists are exciting because there's a sense that, if they weren't in a rock band, their lives would be meaningless. There's never been that sense with Sonic Youth. I've heard members of Sonic Youth praise people like Glenn Branca, Joey Ramone, Mark E. Smith and D. Boon. They can appropriate all they want—they'll never have an ounce of the raw inspiration that any of those folks had.

Even one solitary incredible song can justify a career's worth of crap. The first verse of "Black Angel's Death Song" excuses the entierty of "Legendary Hearts," "Ecstacy," and "The Raven." The entierty of "Tuff Gnarl" (my favorite Sonic Youth song) hardly comes close to fixing the damage done by the "In The Fishtank" record.

Plus, Saccharine Trust were *way* better.

ABE SCOTT

SPACEHOG
Resident Alien

You've heard this record, right? It's a bunch of car and beer commercials for the Bowie generation. It's hard to believe that they could outdo Love and Rockets for gentrifying goth rock.

DAG LUTHER GOOCH

SPIRITUALIZED
Ladies and Gentlemen We Are Floating In Space

First off, the title is way too fucking long. Secondly, the two previous albums were actually good and didn't have that much horn overuse. But because Volkswagen used that one song to sell an über car to Americans, all of a sudden it made it into a bunch o'people's top ten lists.

CHRIS MCGARVEY

BRUCE SPRINGSTEEN
Born in the USA

This is not a record I would recommend just simply passing over as goofy '80s nostalgia; it is one I would recommend be stolen from a Wal-Mart and pulverized with homemade explosives, the remains placed in a hollow-point bullet to be shot into the face of The Boss himself.

BRIAN TEASLEY

STEELY DAN
Aja

I always wonder what the 20 year-olds of the Steely Dan generation were doing when they listened to "Deacon Blue" or "Black Cow." Clearly, a great many of them had said "no" to LSD, and said "yes" to heroin and coke. This album must have been their cloak of shame. Every morning before going to work, they must have seen it lying out next to the record player and nearly retched at the memory of the hag they fucked the night before. What's the matter, buddy? You were happier than a pig in shit last night. You don't remember? "It will come back to you." "It's your favorite foreign movie," man. You've got 10 minutes before your shift starts, so put the needle down, get back in there, and rub one out for Donald.

DAG LUTHER GOOCH

STEREOLAB
Emperor Tomato Ketchup

Actually, I could insert any Stereolab album here. Their vast catalog is really only two super-long albums. The first one consists of everything up until *Transient Random Noise Whatever,* where they were ripping off My Bloody Valentine so blatantly that Kevin Shields hired an Accounts Receivable person. The second album

really could. I had to in college. Just like all the other wangdoodlers who write about rock. But I won't. That would be a pathetic waste of everybody's time. Because we all had to talk about that stuff in college and we don't need it thrown in our faces by yet another limpdick cockhandler with a B.A.

Instead I'll say this: "Rock criticism just plain blows." You know how I know? Because some jacknut once wrote that it was really good—I believed him—and actually bought a copy of Kings of Convenience. That's how I know. That guy deserves to be punched in the face by a shit demon over and over again for all eternity. Seriously. Why even write reviews if you're going to tell people that album is good? You might as well tell people that AIDS is good. Not even the Kings of Convenience think they're good. They just play music so they can date rape American girls.

And of course you're right. I should have known better. I should know that anybody who writes anything about rock (or Kings of Convenience, which is some sort of Swedish pencil-dick approximation of '70s AM radio finger-bang garbage rock) is necessarily going to be some kind of gayballs fanboy who secretly wants to be date-raped by the Kings of Convenience, both of them at once like a rotating pig on a spit. I should know that. I do know that, actually. (Just like I know that Kings of Convenience are an easy target. And also that they're old news. I don't care. I'm still angry about it. Plus, didn't that one guy just come out with some sort of faggy techno album? I'll bet a thousand dollars that it sucks harder than a black hole. *Pitchfork* probably gave it an 8.6.)

But the point is: If you're that stupid, why even bother writing it down? What the hell's the point if you're just going to be some sort of mindless drooling retard who pretends to like what everybody else likes starts with "Mars Audiac Whatever," where they ditch the guitar and "create" music that people who hang out at the Standard Hotel in Los Angeles would pretend not to like.

Still, they attract the biggest scenesters from around the world who supposedly know what's new and hip with music. It's the biggest racket going in music today.

JIM RAYMOND

SUFJAN STEVENS
Greetings From Michigan

Not including his work as a member of New England's deeply religious and obnoxiously endearing Danielson Famile collective (or his first "not a noise" record, *Enjoy Your Rabbit*), Sufjan Stevens has recorded three solo albums over the last few years, starting with *A Sun Came*, and followed by *Seven Swans*, and *Greetings From Michigan*. Then *Michigan* was officially released, then *Seven Swans*, and finally, a wider re-release of *A Sun Came*. Having heard *Michigan* recently enough to be sure it is one of the greatest albums of the last few years, I was very excited to check out this, Stevens' previously recorded (although subsequently released) album.

Let me pause here for a moment to say, as a side note, that the backward thinking of the music industry is difficult enough to cope with without the added frustration of having to hear your favorite new artist's entire catalogue come out in reverse order of its being recorded. It's eerie and painful, like turning back time and watching yourself and everyone you know go from being 25 to 15, getting younger and dumber all the way, or witnessing Einstein growing confused by, and eventually forgetting entirely, the theory of relativity. I'm thankful and hopeful that the rest of Stevens' records should be coming out in real, chronological order.

But back to the matter at hand... I have a deep appreciation for the humble, creative reverence that seems to permeate much of Stevens' work to date. The problem with this record in particular is that it seems to land heavily on the more pious side of that delicate balance, noticeably lacking in other areas that actually matter to real, perceptive, tasteful people, leaving only the exposed proselytizing of his evangelical counter-agenda. Don't get me wrong; I don't begrudge a man his faith any more than I would deny him any of his other basic human needs or rights, but if he's going to sing about it all day long, he could at least take a cue from Marvin Gaye and have the courage and decency to make the music interesting enough to keep me from having to give a shit about being preached to. This is not to say that there aren't moments on this album as good as on the albums on either side of it (whichever direction you're counting), but unfortunately the rest of it is a misplaced and awkward torture, like accidentally arriving at a Christian high school social just in time for the slow dance after snorting a six-pack, and finding across the disco ball-lit room the one girl you're interested in staring back at you. You approach her directly with a new-found focus and confidence, only to be reminded to leave room for the Holy Ghost. That's what this record is like: a total fucking boring tease. Yesterday you were listening to *A Sun Came*, and everything was fine. Tomorrow morning you'll wake up, a bit hungover with a bad case of blue balls, listen to *Michigan* or maybe some Iron and Wine, jerk off, and get on with your glorious life. But right now it's nothing but a jangly, acoustic, adolescent, faux-folk, easy-listening purgatory, and no-one's copping a feel anytime soon. So if you're not a Michael W. Smith fan and you only have time in your life for one Sufjan Stevens record, please don't make it this one.

BLAINE VANDERBILT

STING
Dream of the Blue Turtles

Until recently, when he could finally dismount his ego enough to make shadowed jokes to his hairline, Sting was the most egocentric, self-important man in music without a catalogue to back it up. (Now come on here, folks: have you given *Synchronicity* a good, hard, *deep* listen anytime recently?) I don't care what people have told me about seeing The Police in 1978, as most them will tell me in the same breath how fucking great Rush were on the '79 tour. Yes, he wrote "Roxanne," "Invisible Sun," and "Canary In a Coal Mine," but he also spewed out *Dream of the Blue Turtles*, and everything that followed that incredibly awful and auto-fellating album of pap. However, those do not top what remains his crowning achievement: that fucking Jaguar commercial.

NICK BLAKEY

THE STONE ROSES
The Stone Roses

It seems everyone agrees that *Sgt. Pepper's* is the most overrated album of all time, and that makes sense because it is "overly" rated as the best on every list out there. Fair enough. However, I call bullshit. Look at me when I'm talking to you! Bullshit! The Stone Roses define overrated. When this album came out, the Stone Roses were indistinguishable from every other band in the Manchester pillhead scene, like the Happy Mondays and Primal Scream. In fact, they weren't that much better than EMF or Jesus Jones. I'd also like to point out that all of this was 15 fucking years ago! So, now it's pedestrian and outdated. But those English—God bless their ugly shoes—they still insist on putting The Stone Roses at the top of their best album lists time after time. It's unreal. Seriously, look up NME's top 100 records of all time. I got time, bitch. Get up and check it out. Are the Beatles at the top of the list? No?! They were English! What the fuck? Is it *Doolittle*? Almost. Surely it's *Nevermind* or something like that, right? No, my friends, it's The Stone Roses. The fact that the English even remember this album baffles me.

DAG LUTHER GOOCH

THE STROKES
Room on Fire

A sophomore jinx for a bunch of fine young men who all were crowned prom kings as freshmen? Actually, I think this record is rather cinematic. Yeah, it sort of reminds me of mixing *Blair Witch 2: Book of Shadows* with *Look Who's Talking Too* with *From Dusk to Dawn 2: Texas Blood Money* with *Cheech and Chong's Next Movie* with *Day of the Dead 2: Contagium* with *Mortal Combat: Domination* with *Love at Second Bite* with *Garfield 2* with *Highlander: The Journey Continues* with *Big Momma's House 2* with *Critters 2: The Main Course* with *Shiloh 2: Shiloh Season* with *The Chronicles of Riddick 2* with *Caddyshack 2* with *Ice Age 2: Meltdown* with *Kung Fu Hustle 2* with *You Got Served 2* with *The Thomas Crown Affair 2* with *Roadhouse 2: Last Call* with *Pirates of the Caribbean 2: Dead Man's Chest* with *Old School 2* with *King Conan:*

Crown of Iron with House of Dead 2: Dead Aim with Fletch Won with Dungeons and Dragons 2: The Wrath of the Dragon God with Basic Instinct 2: Risk Addiction with Cheaper By the Dozen 2 with The Crow: Wicked Prayer with Slumber Part Massacre II with Missing in Action 2: The Beginning with Spy Kids Two: Island of Lost Dreams with Cats and Dogs 2: Tinkle's Revenge with Speed 2: Cruise Control with I Know What You Did Last Winter with Dorm Daze 2 with Miss Congeniality 2: Armed and Fabulous with Deuce Bigalow: European Gigolo. Okay, for this analogy to be accurate, you would—after such double-taking flavors have properly coagulated into a putridly foul celluloid gumbo—dump all that tasty soup into a rotting Jack-o-Lantern and funnel it (along with a heavy dose of Ipecac to induce vomiting) down the throat of Nigel Godrich with a translucent pink swirly straw. Then you would have Godrich puke it all over one of those giant Cookies and Co. party cookies and have it all deep-fried in pygmy afterbirth only to finally be force-fed into the mouth of Gordon Raphael! Voila! A true masterpiece of redundant regurgitation redundancy. Nothing tastes quite like the second coming of ill-conceived backwash! But to be honest, I still really just like that part where the Strokes' singer goes, "Laaaaaast Nigh-hight-ta." That's some good shit. Can't they just loop that "Laaaaaast Nigh-hight-ta" part over and over? That would be just fucking great.

BRIAN TEASLEY

SUBLIME
Sublime

Proof that death is often wasted on the wrong people. A junkie is as a junkie does, but Brad Nowell was no Kurt Cobain or even Brian Cole. That vomit-inducing, statutory rape-baiting Southern California light-ska-punk

blend is about as exciting as warm Corona Light, and Sublime scraped the bottom of that barrel so thoroughly that they made cohorts Sugar Ray sound like Eric Burdon & the Animals. Saddest fact of all: here in Boston, home of far too many colleges, a Sublime cover band headlined the Paradise and sold out. And you wonder why George W. Bush is president?

NICK BLAKEY

SUICIDE
American Supreme

Being out of touch is not always a bad thing: just ask Englebert Humperdink or Wayne Newton. However, at least those two can hide behind Vegas curtains and fabulous hair. Alan Vega and Martin Rev, however, have no excuse. Possibly the only atrocity Mute Records has ever committed, American Supreme reveals the painfully lost and talent-drained duo still trying to squeeze every last ounce of credibility and hipness they can out of "Ghost Rider." Vega "sings" about things that no one could give two shits about, epileptically shouting D.T.-stained strains of "survivin'" where Rev is still trying to pass off his lack of technological knowledge as "cutting edge." Bullshit. These guys couldn't even make it in the Borscht Belt and should realize that all of the groups they influenced way back in 1977-78 have vastly improved upon and bettered the Suicide approach. Wire learned pretty fucking quickly not to go there with Manscape, but obviously Vega and Rev are very tangled up in their own self-importance. An album so fucking bad it makes the duo's previous awful effort (Why Be Blue?) sound like John Cage. I can guarantee you that almost no one has made it through American Supreme and lived to tell about it.

NICK BLAKEY

because you heard it's good? Why aren't we past that yet? And why should I suffer for assuming that guys like this might actually know what they're talking about? They're all over the place. They seem to be doing it for a reason. They can't be writing glowing reviews of the new Air album (it sucks dick so hard it actually sucks dick) just by accident, can they?

Yes. Oh Jesus, fuck yes, they can be. Because they really are retarded. But you know what? I'm actually ok with it. I know it's bullshit. They know it's bullshit. Even stevens. But I'll tell you what I'm not okay with: these fucking losers who write about music like it's a goddamned academic thing. Like their stupid literary allusions are gonna shed some light about what something might sound like to me. If I wanted to watch you masturbate, I'd lock you in a room full of Thirteenth Floor Elevators (sucks) 45s for 5 seconds. Don't get me wrong, I love music, but it doesn't deserve that treatment. It's supposed to be fun. Rock critics would have you believe that a moon bounce "has few merits other than its proud display of its similarities to a trampoline, an admirable and sincere goal which, sadly, goes unfulfilled here." Fuck that! It's a moon bounce! Shut the fuck up, and bounce, fucker!

If you describe the new Xiu Xiu album as "a slowly erupting sonic lava flow, alternating between warm and hot" not only do I have no fucking idea what the new Xiu Xiu album (sucks) sounds like, I'm condemned to forever hate it without even getting the chance to hear it for myself, because your writing makes me want to puke on my balls. Just say "it's peppy" or something, and save the lava flow bullshit for your blog. You know, "I have no penis." Your blog. There is actually a genre of music right now, we'll call it "Pitchfork Bands," that's defined as "any band that

Sunny Day Real Estate to Tortoise

SUNNY DAY REAL ESTATE
Diary

The problem isn't really Sunny Day Real Estate so much as the countless Mineral/Appleseed Cast-type emo bands who make it their mission to sound exactly like them. I remember when everyone told me I should go listen to this album. Apparently, I don't like myself very much and need to go out, get an ironic tattoo, start shoegazing and start one of 30,000 emo bands that play all ages shows in VFW halls. I don't hang out with those people anymore. Plus, I saw them live once and the guitarist was actually wearing Teva sandals (bad enough) with white socks (even worse) on stage. As if their credibility wasn't strained already.

AMANDA NICHOLS & PATRICK GOUGH

THE SUPREMES
A Bit of Liverpool

The Supremes were never content with being just another Motown act doing the motown thing. So, while Barry Gordy perfected replacing the heart and soul of rhythm and blues, soul, funk and gospel with hack—all major key string sections, studio singers to "sweeten" the sound (enough to give you a sacharrine OD), and constant covers of lesser known groups/artists that sounded like they were arranged by Pat Boone—The Supremes thought ahead! Fearlessly tackying, oops, tackling hits by bands of The British Invasion, they made it okay to listen to "rock'n'roll" when Donnie and Marie were coming over for an unsalted, crustless, non-buttered bread dinner or whatever it is that Mormons eat. Note: also birthed Diana Ross.

PABLO A. ROCKAFUCKER

MATTHEW SWEET
Girlfriend

This didn't hold up too well. The fact that Matt felt the need to put it out five more times didn't help either. Okay, all rock songs are just three chords—the trick is to make them sound more complicated. Dumping a classic rock guitar solo on top don't count, even if you are Richard Lloyd or Robert Quine. I figured out how to play "Girlfriend" in under a minute and I am the world's shittiest guitarist. Ask Henry. Seriously, e-mail him. I suck.

DAG LUTHER GOOCH

T. REX
Electric Warrior

Marc Bolan spent his career snorting booger sugar and writing songs about unicorns and fairies, all the while fancying himself a misunderstood genius of mythical proportions. Yeah, dude, "Bang a Gong" was such a revolution that only scholars like Power Station had the chops to cover it. If life were a musical coin flip, Bolan would be kicking off to the receiving team into the wind—and the ball would be a hunk of turtle shit.

BRIAN MCMANUS

TALKING HEADS
Remain in Light

There has never been a more white band that wanted to be more black than the Talking Heads. This is the album where they finally gave up trying to do it alone, and got authentic black people to help them. They sure put some stank on it. Then Adrian Belew and Brian Eno came in, and cleaned up the stank. That's why they didn't call it *Remain in Dark*.

DAG LUTHER GOOCH

TANGERINE DREAM
Phaedra

I read the dictionary, really, and (not at all surprisingly) when I hit the O's recently, I was greeted with a picture of Tangerine Dream under the entry for "onanistic." I thought masturbation was supposed to be pleasurable, yet they are the aural equivalent of jerking it with low grit sandpaper (slow, long chafing until the intense pain overwhelms and reminds you that it's better to get torture over with quickly). This applies to most prog outfits.

PABLO A. ROCKAFUCKER

JAMES TAYLOR
Sweet Baby James

Ever meet a girl and go over to her house to make out, only to have her pull *Sweet Baby James* off the shelf? How quickly did you stand up, snatch it out of her hands, smash it over your knee, pay her for the damages and drive home? Correct me if I'm wrong, but isn't James Taylor a wife-beating heroin addict? Yeah, yeah, yeah. I know he's recovering. Whatever. Ladies, "you've got a friend"...who will get strung out and beat your ass. Congratulations. That's sweet baby James. Next time I see this record in a girl's collection, I'm going to skip the middleman and clean her clock.

DAG LUTHER GOOCH

TEENAGE FANCLUB
Bandwagonesque

There was a good stretch of six years where if critics caught even a whiff of Big Star you instantly got an A+. As far as I'm concerned, this record started it. How did it happen? Alex Chilton once said that Teenage Fanclub was one of the only newer bands he liked. Want to guess another one? The Posies. So is it that if Alex Chilton tells the press you're good, suddenly it's okay to pretend to be Big Star? Hardly! This is the rock version of a McDonald's Olympics endorsement. I know for a fact that Carly Patterson doesn't eat fast food. In his heart, you know the only thing Alex Chilton liked about the "thank you, friends" shout-outs on this sonic blowjob was that they would ultimately translate into a mess of Big Star reissues.

DAG LUTHER GOOCH

TELEVISON
Marquee Moon

Most of my heroes cite this record as a significant turning point for guitar. Maybe it is, but when I succumbed to the everlasting hype, all I heard was a mostly conventional sounding lite rock record with irritating vocals only an open minded housewife could appreciate and some of the stiffest wanking this side of puberty. Influenced by jazz? Wigga, please! No one actually listens to Television. Why would they? These songs go nowhere forever. From the album cover it is clear these people are Burroughsian-leper-zombies. If they played fast their ectoplasmic-fingers would have torn off, so instead we get the much vaunted 'guitar interplay' and Tom Verlaine crooning about statues and communism. I'd rather *watch* television.

CHRIS HAMRIN & TERRY WHITE

TENACIOUS D
Tenacious D

Am I the only guy that heard this and thought that I got the outtakes CD by mistake? If not, am I the only person that feels like I am hearing the Barenaked Ladies sing about wieners and fucking? This is absolutely the worst fucking thing that anyone could mass produce! People kept telling me I would love this. When I expressed some doubt, I was reassured that it was really, really funny. Finally, I gave it a spin. Not only was I without so much as a grin while hearing it, I wanted to fucking punch everyone who ever recommended that I hear this chubby abortion.

BOB SCHRINER

THEY MIGHT BE GIANTS
Apollo 18

There's an entire generation of collegium glee clubbers that discovered TMBG with this album. Due to the "got there first" syndrome, it gets the unanimous thumbs-up from even the most remotely former fans. Now, to be sure, every album is really fucking annoying on some level…so annoying as to one-up early morning preschool programming. *Lincoln* at least had songs that didn't suck after the joke wasn't funny anymore. *Apollo 13* wasn't even funny. It plays like a bunch of purile, re-written Christmas carols ála "Jingle Bells, Batman smells, Robin laid an egg." You get six undersexed 19-year olds singing "Dinner Bell" in the hallway…you got a fight on your hands. The worst part of *Apollo 18* is the oft-randomized "Fingertips." Over 20 annoying joke songs slapped together that repeat some stupid phrase like "pull on the monkey's nuts and he barfs, he barfs, he barfs!" about ten times in various hackneyed genres. Those Johns are so adorable. So adorable they make me feel like driving to New York just to break all the bones in their hands with a ball peen hammer.

DAG LUTHER GOOCH

THROBBING GRISTLE
Greatest Hits

These guys never really got past being an art/performance/shock/joke band in the most self-indulgent sense, but they managed to get a sizeable group of disciples who treated their silly tirades as some kind of gospel truth. As is too often the case, it's the movement away from humor that ultimately makes the Throbbing Gristle philosophy of "entertainment through pain" trite and dreary. It's not really painful enough, or entertaining enough, in the final analysis.

RUSS FORSTER

TOOL
Undertow

Scary Nine Inch Nails fans refer to the band members in a creepy, familiar way. This band was the stepping stone for people of the Goth persuasion to get from Marilyn Manson to Korn. I hold Tool personally responsible for pointing people in the direction of stupidity— and for white guys with dreadlocks, which is always a sign that something's really fucked up. Fawning fans call everything "genius" (even sub par bootleg records made by a drunk guy three towns away from the show) and feel sorry for people who don't "get it."

AMANDA NICHOLS

TORTOISE
Tortoise

There's an old Italian expression that I think applies well to Tortoise: "All smoke, no meat." While some of their audio explorations are sometimes pleasing to the ear superficially (and, from my standpoint, many of the members' previous bands/projects were terrific), Tortoise's work never moved me, or captured my imagination, or elicited any reaction from me other than total boredom, and certainly never brought me to whatever states of rapture that thousands of zine editors, come-lately-scenesters, and on-the-cusp critics have been claiming for the past six years. I've endured their less-than-enthusiastic live show four times in an attempt to quell my own doubts; each time I left the club with my conviction strengthened that, no matter what others seem to hear, Tortoise's music sounds like substance-free noodling to me. While they seem to be very decent and cordial people, and while their musical skill is undoubtedly formidable, Tortoise have worn the emperor's new clothes for an awfully long time now (at

Modern Rock Criticism (continued)

gets any hype at all." This genre includes: electronic fuckaraounders; any rock band that uses either minimal (read: shitty) or dense (read: more shitty) arrangements; any rock band that doesn't; anything that a black person does, like jazz (news flash: jazz sucks. It died for a reason), soul, hip-hop, or Andre 3000 (sucks) taping some white girl's queefs; reissues of anything "undiscovered"; anybody with a haircut; anybody older than 45.

And you know what? It sucks. The whole genre. *Pitchfork* Bands are overrated. Because *Pitchfork* is overrated. And also: *Chunklet's* overrated. And: I'm overrated. And: So are you. Because: everything's overrated when you take it too seriously. So let's stop writing a bunch of bullshit about stuff that nobody actually cares about and go outside. Ah. Yes. That's better. I think I'll go swimming.

BENJAMIN JOHNSON

Traffic to Violent Femmes

least from my vantage point). With so much genuinely exciting and unusual music in the world waiting to be heard, I don't foresee myself wasting any more time searching for the pseudo-revolutionary, purportedly superior musical properties of a Tortoise album. Call me a heretic, but that's my opinion.

JON RESH

TRAFFIC
John Barleycorn Must Die

Groovy English Folk Music...four words that should have forever remained separate. In *Lost and Found Video Volume 3* (Google it), there is a penis pump instructional video where a guy who looks exactly like Steve Winwood uses his pump to jack-off. After he finishes the job in hand, he uses a special scrub brush to clean his sperm chalice. Okay, here's where it moves beyond coincidence: While he's petting the man-ferret, "Higher Love" is playing on a clock radio in the background...and, if that wasn't enough, the bark of a small dog is heard somewhere off-camera. If you don't believe this, put your e-commerce where your mouth is. Anyway, this penis pump instructional video seems far more culturally important than this 1970 bluesy wank-fest. Traffic's most "seminal" of albums is much more akin to a gallstone than a milestone.

BRIAN TEASLEY

TURBONEGRO
Scandinavian Leather

The big sensation over this band still amazes me. That and the fact that without the singular defense of, "dude, they just fuckin' rock" you'll just be left shrugging your denim-clad shoulders if asked why you bothered sewing that stupid

patch onto your jacket. Strip away the predictable "riffage" and cliched choruses and all you have is a bunch of dopes who can't figure out if they want to be The Dictators or the Heartbreakers for Halloween. Do you think the Swedish would really bite on a Bob Seger record played at 45rpm? Because that seems to be an international courtesy that we have extended to them.

BOB SCHRINER

TUSCADERO

Total tripe that garnered a huge following in DC and elsewhere merely because there were two cute girls in the band. They couldn't play for shit, yet I knew guys who went to see them repeatedly. Doesn't that kind of objectification defeat the purpose of women trying to claim their chunk of the rock stage? You might as well go see Lita Ford or Heart. Granted, it's not Tuscadero's fault that they were cute, but as I said, they couldn't play for shit.

PATRICK GOUGH

TV ON THE RADIO
Desperate Youth, Blood Thirsty Babes

As you read this, there are three white kids sitting in the alley outside of Gabe's Oasis in Iowa City crying because their place in the rock hierarchy has been taken by some black guys from Brooklyn. I always thought rock was for rich, white, suburban kids (see Dischord). I guess I was wrong. Or was I? Two words: Living Colour.

SETH LOSIER

U2
Achtung Baby

Whoa. I could understand the point of *War* and *The Joshua Tree*. They're an exercise in being spoon-fed, the imagery is so obvious.

But *Achtung Baby* is just insipid. What the hell is Bono going on about in these songs, anyway? The only ones that seem to make sense are riddled with annoying mixed metaphors. The rest of them have lyrics that confuse drugs, sex, advertising, and religion so much, they don't say anything at all. U2 should have waited another 4 years to come up with something better to say.

DAG LUTHER GOOCH

UNWOUND
New Plastic Ideas

This record is the mid-to-late-'90s anthem for the secret movement against fun. The name was pretty apt, too, since no one had really taken prolonged dullness to such epic proportions. To think they went on tour to play these songs live in front of people.

BOB SCHRINER

URGE OVERKILL
Saturation

Being a professional poseur was never more en vogue than in 1993 when Urge released this little shit-covered ass gem. Shortly before recording *Saturation* for Geffen, our then favorite cocktail-slurpin', velvet-jacket-wearing pony fuckers had just tried to push it through to re-record "Girl You'll Be A Woman Soon" by Mr. Coming-On-Yeah-Haw himself, Neil Diamond. You see, Quentin Tarantino had wanted to use the version that was on their "parting gift" for Touch and Go, *The Stull* EP, for little film he was putting together called *Pulp Fiction*. Nash Kato and gang wanted to have a new version in which they owned the master, in order to receive all the licensing money (both sync and master). Luckily, Tarantino didn't want to fuck with mediocrity and stuck with the original EP version of the tune.

Anyway, Urge (after *The Supersonic Storybook*) was nothing more than a brash movie trailer for itself; a

promise of fireworks that never go off; the absolute archetype of all things apocryphal. How could a single band take the shittiest elements of The Cars, Alice Cooper, The Romantics, T Rex and The Modern Lovers and churn them into something as unimaginable as, say...Gwar, Utah Saints, Mono Puff, Huggy Bear and Ugly Kid Joe? These stupid lounge enthusiast sellouts got exactly what they deserved for believing in their own myth—one of the best examples of a career-ending album that has ever been created...sometimes known to 7 or 8 people as *Exit the Dragon*. If true justice is to be had in these modern times of uber-revivalism, then this record will never be appreciated in the future by hipsters or even hyper-intelligent super slugs that will soon control the earth.

BRIAN TEASLEY

VAN HALEN
post-David Lee Roth

"Right Here, Right Now" will never sound as cool blasting from your car as anything from *Fair Warning*. Please. Van Halen should never equal maturity.

AMANDA NICHOLS

VELOCITY GIRL
Copacetic

If getting hit in the face by a mild pussy fart is your type of music, then this record's for you. You know, first you have to want it, then you gotta get there at it and way up in the p-zone. Close your eyes, and move in for the slow romantic kill of the tongue. Yeah, you're doing something special, take one for the team, bad boy. Fellate that fish, dawg! Shit...naw, aw naw...what was that faint wisp of air movement? Aw, shit girl, you squirted me with vagi-air. Dang girl, that shit smells like a 20-year old mentholyptus cough drop. Thanks for the queef, Sub Pop.

BRIAN TEASLEY

VERSUS
The Stars Are Insane

This is an album I had to listen to over and over again on someone else's car stereo for several years. Every time I heard it I had to ask, "Why is this good? Explain it to me again, I forgot, and really...it's not self-evident. Is it good because they like can't really speak English or because they play their instruments with their elbows or something like that?" The songs are predictable and simple, thesaurus-assisted lyrics set to three chords written in less than an hour. The best that could be said would be a racist and sexist backhanded compliment: "Boy, those Filipinos and that chick are so cute." Actually, now that I think about it, they aren't even cute.

DAG LUTHER GOOCH

THE VERVE
Urban Hymns

Here's the secret to success in rock: make two stellar, critically acclaimed (yet unpopular) albums—then make the third one a turd. The masses will come running almost as fast as the Rolling Stones' lawyers.

JIM RAYMOND

VIOLENT FEMMES
Violent Femmes

Who would have thought that a single album full of whiny potty talk had the power to release the inner junior high glee club member from three generations of college students? How much research do you think Gordon Gano had to do to tap into the collective psyche of all of these people? At the very least, it must have taken him 5 years of hanging around school bus stops and junior league baseball field bathrooms to perfect his "voice." But it was just research, people! Come on and get your minds out of the gutter! But seriously, it's funny how the Femmes' next record would document how to kill children you've fucked.

DAG LUTHER GOOCH

Mike Patton, Mr. Bungle & The Church of Overcompensation.
A point and half assed counter-point
by Andrew Earles

GENIUS. CLEVER. INTENSE. FUCKED-UP. GROUND-BREAKING. GOOD.

There are artists who seemingly exist for the sole purpose of convincing stupid people that they are, or understand art that is, one or all of the above attributes. Mike Patton is their leader.

For all we knew in 1989, the future would prove harmless and laughable. Wrong. A histrionic proto-wigger in sweat shorts gesticulating opposite a flopping, asphyxiating fish shouldn't have been taken seriously. Somehow he was. Even as strains of the (then) freshly-christened Funk Metal genre churned behind him, it all seemed innocent and silly to those possessing the cognitive power to make a sandwich or execute dry sex. To their miniscule bank of credit, Mike Patton and Faith No More would move away from Funk Metal, but Patton would continue on with another, exponentially horrifying battle cry of the ham-fisted hipsters: Mr. Bungle.

THE WAILERS
Tall Cool One

Credit is due to them for mentoring or inspiring passionate and raw younger Northwest bands, creating an amazing regional scene (and something for Lester Bangs to base a career on writing about in some form or another—thanks!). I fell for the hype, buying a copy of this record for a buttload at a Seattle shop for total record nerds. Imagine my surprise when I put the stylus to the groove only to find a subdued, plodding and quiet (even at top volume) version of teen dance sock-hop rock. I wasn't there to witness these "rebels" in '64, but I'd imagine they served cookies and warm milk to their audiences because this record felt like naptime.

PABLO A. ROCKAFUCKER

WEEN
Chocolate and Cheese

Why is it bands with the least amount of musical talent have to try the largest number of musical styles? Not even from album to album; on this CD alone, these brothers suck at Philadelphia soul, Tejano ballads, psychedelia, circus music and more. Now that they're sticking to the prog rock jam band genre, nobody will care if they ruin that.

ED PARKER

THE WHITE STRIPES
White Blood Cells

She can't drum and lo and behold they ain't related. Is this a variation on that Faye Dunaway slap-a-thon scene in Polanski's *Chinatown* instead substituting that "she's my sister/she's my ex-wife" shit? Fuck that—it ain't hip nor cool, and you ain't even Southern, asshole, so shut the fuck up. The Gossip do this shit better and with a lot more conviction, plus I don't really *care* if the *NME* and most of the UK like The White Stripes because that still don't mean shit on the street back here in the USA. Jealousy, do you say? No, it's just that they don't do anything that makes me really give two shits about anything they say, do, or sing about.

NICK BLAKEY

THE WHO
Tommy, Who Are You & Who's Next

Dudes, let's get a clue. Pete got hung up about his band being considered a joke in the press because they destroyed stuff onstage. So he wrote an opera? With, like, an overture? By *Who's Next*, Keith sounds bloated and struggling. Someone once said to me, "Yeah, but playing along to those synth parts was really challenging." Yeah, if you're fucking blasted on pills and cognac. If you've ever bothered to listen to *Who Are You* straight through (I have many times in a dark past), it's like a bunch of fucking show tunes about writing songs. "Guitar and Pen???!!" Give me "Anyway, Anyhow, Anywhere" any day. Simple, perverse, arty, and juvenile. And *Tommy*? Rock operas are lame enough without adding pinball.

KID MILLIONS & ED PARKER

WILCO
Yankee Hotel Foxtrot

If the Meat Puppets hadn't had the good fortune of being idolized by Kurt Cobain, they still could have made a bunch of money by suing the ever-living shit out of Wilco. Man, did Jeff Tweedy ever steal the warmed-over, rock-inflected country/country-inflected rock sound from these guys. We're talking grand theft here. At least Nirvana admitted it.

MIKE FOURNIER

LUCINDA WILLIAMS

Notoriously difficult to work with (though that comes via Steve Earle, himself a massive prick), Williams's attempt to pass off her lyrics as poetry—while good—is tedious. Listen, sister, Leonard Cohen and Patti Smith could do it, and that's it. Dig?

MATT THOMPSON

STEVIE WONDER
Songs In The Key Of Life

You know how you'll buy a current hip-hop CD and think "Who decided that everybody should make 74-minute albums with one good song on them?" Behold, here's your answer.

BENJAMIN JOHNSON

XTC
Nonesuch

If this album rated at all, it was overrated. This is a bad album by any standards. By XTC—what the fuck? *Mummer* and *Big Express* were crappy enough, but at least they had a few good songs to their credit to make up for jacking off. "Omnibus?" "Holly Up On Poppy?" "Peter Pumpkinhead?" Was this album made for Golden Books? I've started to hate Andy Partridge ever since he got stage fright and had to get a physical to keep a club owner in Louisiana from beating his ass after cancelling a show. By now, I think he should have the teeth slapped out of his mouth. Oh wait, he's from Swindon, the real ones are probably long gone.

DAG LUTHER GOOCH

Drums And Wires

Some things seem fine at the time, but in retrospect, are really stupid (i.e. Color Me Badd). Most pop doesn't age well. Other things were so groundbreaking, fresh and cool that we tend to forget how stupid they were. For instance, the new wave vocal stylings of Andy Partidge. Sing "Real by Reel," "Making Plans for Nigel," or "Ten Feet Tall" in your head for a minute. Good songs, no? Now, go put *Drums And Wires* on. Listening to Colin Moulding try to imitate Andy Partridge is like hanging out with the rat-tail guy on Square Pegs. Put together, they sound like somebody fucking with the pitch control. Every word is warbled into 2 syllables, one going high, the other low. It's nauseating. "Row-ond, row-ond, rownd, lakahela co-tuhhr! Rownd-rownd-rownd-rownd-rownd-rownd-rownd boutimethati sto-ptuhr!!!" Great. I just threw up. Even still, XTC's worst albums (a tie between *Big Express* and *Mummer*) are better than the Stone Roses. It's interesting that, to this day, even the most snooty, record-collecting, rocker know-it-alls in England know nothing about XTC. When Americans dumpster dive in the English trash and pull out something they treasure, what can you call that other than "overrated?"

DAG LUTHER GOOCH

YEAH YEAH YEAHS
Fever To Tell

The only thing this band has going for them is Karen O's willingness to soak herself with beer in public. Unfortunately, you can't see this while listening to these haphazard Oberlin School of Art 4-track throwaways that Interscope released as a record. Maybe it would be better if all the songs were only between 30 seconds and 1 minute; I mean nothing changes after the 30 second point in any song on the whole album. So, go see those beer-soaked boy-titties, but you'll lose less hearing just checking out some good old-fashioned internet porn.

TOBY HALBROOKS

YO LA TENGO
I Can Hear The Heart Beating As One

You know what would make this a fucking great record? If before a single note was played, Ira Kaplan came on the mic and said in the voice of the black maid from *Gone with the Wind*, "Y'all know what? Bonnie Prince Billy's mama has an ass so big that every time she takes a shit, it causes one of them lunar eclipses." Come on, you humorless sap! If this was reissued with just that bit added, you'd fucking be the first in line to buy it.

BRIAN TEASLEY

NEIL YOUNG
Harvest

Does this supposed classic redeem Neil's career and make amends for his shrill, grating voice, heavy-handed lyrics and ugly mutton chop sideburns, or does he whine and tell us not to do drugs a lot? Yep, the second one.

ED PARKER

Broken Arrow

This is Young's final album with genius producer David Briggs (who also did Alice Cooper's *Easy Action* and Royal Trux's major label abomination *Thank You*). Briggs was dying of cancer when he did this record with Young, but it isn't Briggs who sounds like the sick one. Upon his deathbed, Briggs told Young to "get closer to the source." Most of Young's records since have strongly indicated that if shit rolls downhill, then diarrhea

Mike Patton (continued)

Mr. Bungle is the illogical (because there shouldn't be *any*) progression from Frank Zappa's legacy—a soul-eroding blight across the last three and a half decades of music if there ever was one. Just add every single fucking special interest genre to the stew. Why? Because that's "eclectic."

POINT:

Anyway, all Mr. Bungle and Mike Patton apologists cite the same five credentials during the inevitable pro-Bungle tirade inextricably associated with hardcore fans of this overbearing, non-stop, parade of faux-intensity. Here's a point-by-point rebuttal:

1. THE JOHN ZORN CONNECTION.

Nothing elicits a ricochet of negative energy from that guy at your local scenester bar who won't shut up quite like the statement, "John Zorn is pretend jazz." You should try it. It's a hoot. Granted, it's a hoot to me because I have a sense of humor, so results may vary. John Zorn attaches an unfortunate degree of "respect" to whatever he touches, whether it be the run of the mill slummer routine with a Japanese blast-core band, or some NYC crusty spazzcakes, or something as loathsome as Mr. Bungle. I also hear that he has been donning camo trousers for the past two decades, something that precipitated the omnipresent lack of style amongst his disciples. Fake jazz? Nooooooo… he is a jazz musician… calm down. At least he was the last time I cared, which was sometime in the mid-'90s. Oh, and we can thank John Zorn for the popularity/credibility/visibility of people like Buckethead and Vernon Reid.

2. "YOU GOTTA RESPECT WHAT THEY ARE DOING. YOU GOTTA RESPECT THE MUSICIANSHIP."

No, I don't. Watch. I don't. See? It's that easy. Just because somebody didn't garner enough attention from their "parents" or "friends" or "anything but masturbating in their basement to Rush" at some point in life's long journey doesn't mean that I have to sit still while they beat me over the head with "ability." Why are people still hood-winked into believing that instrumental prowess = good? Am I supposed to be impressed by some "wacky" bullshit that jumps around from bossa nova to grindcore to soft rock to polka within one song? Hey, I think I need to be reminded of your "impressive musical palette" every four seconds…yeah that's it…dart those little bug eyes out over the crowd while you do it! Let everyone know how "crazy" and "off-kilter" you are!!

3. "BUT I ALSO LIKE…"

Every single note pooped out by The Butthole Surfers, Primus, The Dillinger Escape Plan, The Secret Chiefs ('natch), Candiria, all of that forgotten bass-poppin' "jazzcore" flushed down the black hole of forgotten irrelevance by Alternative Tentacles and SST, Alice Fucking Donut, assholes that bark about licking the inside of a vacuum cleaner bag against the backdrop of thudding bass or white noise, Bootsauce, Mind Funk, anything with the ultimate red flag of two bass players, maybe some throwaway AmRep testosterone mills, and probably something a little "illbient."

4. POP AND ROCK MUSIC IS TOO CONVENTIONAL AND BORING.

Sure, a gaping amount is. You're "above" pop and rock music. Wait a minute. No. You are not. The blind discrediting of pop and rock music—a practice that many noiseniks seem to swear by, is laughable and indicative of a very serious case of social ineptitude. To address the boys (A gender joke? I don't have time) here: only listening to

Mike Patton (continued)

music that pummels you with its fucked-uppitude, its negativity, its volume, its lack of structure, its hate; its evidence of something lurking in the closet. Why else would you have to be constantly reassured of your masculinity? I'm just sayin', dude.

"I CAN'T ARGUE WITH YOU RIGHT NOW, MY CAT IS CHEWING ON MY DREADS."

Then pull some Tender Vittles out of your cargo shorts. And as a bonus, in lieu of a cyanide capsule, a summary of Mr. Bungle's proper Warners' releases goes like this:

Mr. Bungle (1991) - Unfunny doo doo humor.

Disco Volante (1995) - The mature outing. The "really experimental one." A great example of Cleverness 101.

California (1999) - The irony pop album that is...you guessed correct... "all fucked up."

HALF-ASSED COUNTERPOINT:

And if it's still going so bad that you have to play devil's advocate just to shut one of these fuckers up, you can make the following admissions:

1. If forced by sharp stick to witness a Mike Patton production, I would choose Fantômas. There is a scope to Fantômas that is lacking with Patton's other projects. Plus, Dave Lombardo is the drummer, and Slayer always knew how stupid they were.

2. Mike Patton has a sense of humor. Sometimes it's not a great one, but it's one nonetheless. A good example would be his reissuing of Gregg Turkington's *Great Phone Calls*—the juggernaut of all prank phone call releases.

And that's the Mike Patton/Mr. Bungle spew. If experimental a cappella CDs are your thing and you can't make it through the day without being assaulted by unsubtle, quasi-intellectual, insecure art, then stop reading now, cobweb crotch, and continue blowing pot smoke into your pet's face.

ANDREW EARLES

---

must falleth like rain from heaven.

NICK BLAKEY

Are You Passionate?

To quote my disgusted Young-worshiping former roommate, "Are you serious?" Furthermore, did Mr. Young really need to revisit his deportation-inducing *Hawks & Doves/Trans*-era with that exploitation piece of shit "Let's Roll?" Totally offensive and it begs serious consideration of the fact that Young is only a dye job away from Bruce Springsteen.

NICK BLAKEY

Old Ways

So, you're going to get back at your label by recording the last thing they want: a country album? That's great. Fuck those guys and everything they stand for. However, if you were so pissed, why did you have two of country's greatest singer-songwriters appear on the record? Neil, next time you don't want Geffen to make a dime off you, try not inviting Waylon Jennings and Willie Nelson to sing on the whole thing. You just made them 16 million dollars on a recording you didn't even care about. But it was for the principle, right?

DAVIS REA

Greendale

When this desperate hunk of garbage was titled *Preservation*, it didn't work for the Kinks either, but Ray Davies managed to figure that out way back in 1974. So please, please, could we really stop trying to justify this washed up lunatic who hasn't had a clue since 1992? And why, oh why, would you relegate a guitarist as fine as Crazy Horse's Poncho Sampedro to playing a keyboard that no one, including Poncho himself, can hear? Maybe Young is finally showing the effects of spending way too much time around Stephen Stills.

NICK BLAKEY

YOUNG MARBLE GIANTS
Colossal Youth

Minimalism? Fuck that. Some bands take years to "find space" within their music. These Welsh hillfolk always had it, and consequently bore the shit out of me. The music is so spare there is nothing there and the ice-cold bitch 'singing' doesn't help any. This is what Kurt Cobain was listening to when he shot himself.

CHRIS HAMRIN

ZZ TOP
Tres Hombres

Aside from Billy Gibbons' amazing guitar work, this record is a joke. With songs about hotrods and "chicks," the lyrics read like a 14-year-old's chatroom conversation. This was a top ten record and their gimmick was having long beards, sunglasses, and fuzzy guitars. I mean, is there anything gayer than facial hair, wearing shades inside, and pink fringe?

DAVIS REA

DJ CULTURE

You! Behind the turntables! Dressed like a rock star! You're not. You play music. You don't make music. You are nothing more than an exhibitionistic mix tape-maker. A glorified wedding entertainer. Sure, you look aloof. Distant. But deep in your heart you hide a shame that all DJs share: at some point you've played the "Electric Slide." You tried to convince yourself you did it ironically, but you still went home and scrubbed yourself extra hard in the shower (made-for-tv-movie post-rape-scene style) that night. You have no art even though you think you do. It's easy to get confused when drunken knuckleheads just below your perch start rubbing their asses in each other's crotches...wavin' their arms in the air like they just don't care... and they don't. This is what you give to your people...the middle managers and cubicle jockeys who drive to work in suburban industrial parks. The art school student with a name like Seth who thinks graffiti is a legitimate form of expression (and sadly for him it probably is). The man in the International Male shirt and nice shoes who insists on being called Olivier and smells a little too intensely of designer cologne. These are your people. All of them.

The truth—no matter how much you like to force the phrase "DJ culture"—is that if someone were to remove you, and plug in an iPod, no one would even know you were missing. The dancing happens with you or without you. Not *because* of you. You are the music world's equivalent of the Jumble. That's right, you're not even a crossword puzzle!

So, you can look as confident and cool as you want with the headset pressed up to your ear, acting like you're deep in thought when you already know you're going to follow Led Zeppelin with the Doobies, but you aren't fooling anyone. These people who come do not come for you. They come for the music. Something you don't make—something you merely play—for them.

BENN RAY

WAH! WAH!
WAH! WAH!

OVERRATED ROCK GUITARISTS!

by Gary T. Flom & Ben Davis • illustration by Brian Walsby

These guitar players may be the ones in the band that get the best cooze, but they also are in *Chunklet's* crosshairs. Our esteemed staff of (unknown) guitar players, Ben Davis and Gary Flom have sorted through your list of guitar heroes. After thumbing through stacks of *Guitar Player Magazine* tablature, and reviewing countless hours of archival cassette tapes at our offices, they left us with their findings.

ERIC CLAPTON

Gary Flom: Clapton is God alright, God of the most boring catalog of three decades of watered down rock songs. Hendrix would have never played crap like that.

Ben Davis: To top it off, he cashed in on his son flying out of a window...even though that song makes me cry like a newborn calf.

STEVE VAI

GF: Sure, he can play but it's pretty sad when the highlights of your musical career are hammimg it up in videos while in David Lee Roth's band and dueling (and losing) with Ralph Macchio as the devil in the movie, "Crossroads." And yes, we know he played with Frank Zappa.

BD: Alas...when a soloist hasn't a song. Yet even with fringed spandex pants he meets criteria the aforementioned cheesemonger does not.

JOE SATRIANI

GF: His claim to fame is that he gave guitar lessons to Steve Vai and Kirk Hammett, two other guys who made the list. Any guy who ever wore high-top Reebok aerobic sneakers while playing guitar deserves to make this list on that fact alone.

BD: Truly the Jerry Seinfeld of rock guitar.

KIRK HAMMETT (Metallica)

GF: Everyone knows that Hetfield spoon-fed him all of his parts. Unfortunately, he took a wah pedal lesson from Joe Satriani.

BD: Which one is he? The guy that looks like a roadie for Rev. Horton Heat, or the little delicate musical theatre looking chap? Either way, they've all "matured," right? Everybody else will say everything after *Justice* sucks. I say it all belongs stuck in someone's junior high english notebook. As far as guitar playing: somehow these "pioneers" excel at being totally indistinguishable from one another, no matter how much they change.

STEVIE RAY VAUGHAN

GF: He totally ripped off Hendrix and had he not died in that helicopter crash he'd be playing the chili cook-off circuit.

BD: But his blow intake has taken on sort of an urban legend identity of its own... and for that I respect his memory.

CARLOS SANTANA

GF: After a 25-year songwriting hiatus, he reasserts his claim as a guitar god by pairing up with Matchbox Twenty asshole Rob Thomas.

BD: I'm starting to notice a pattern here. All of these dudes are tokers. Everyone take heed: no matter how relaxed you think you get you will noodle like an idiot if you hit the old jarweed. Even his love of John Coltrane can't redeem the foolishness of Señor Carlos.

RICK NIELSEN (Cheap Trick)

GF: Live, his five-neck guitars and pick throwing are a smoke screen to cover up the fact that he is coasting through the set, not even playing half the time.

BD: Why you need all of those guitars to play third-tier pop rock is beyond me. Take off the fucking hat already.

DAVE NAVARRO (Jane's Addiction)

GF: Was it the mesh t-shirts, black fingernail polish or the Gucci luggage that got him kicked out of the Red Hot Chili Peppers? Another wah-pedal casualty, Dave is virtually interchangeable with Kirk Hammet.

BD: To top it off, he dresses like a member of the VSS. Remember them? Exactly.

OVERRATED DRUMMERS!

Three of Chunklet's nine drummers on staff (that's no joke!) debate rock's renowned pizza delivery escapees

by Jerry Fuchs, Patrick Gough & Brian Teasley • illustration by Brian Walsby

Everyone loves to have a laugh at the drummer's expense. How can you tell a drummer is at your front door? The knock is out of time. What do you call a drummer without a girlfriend? Homeless. Drummers are the Rodney Dangerfields—and sometimes even the Carrot Tops—of the music world. To some degree, drummers are valuable; after all, how strange would your music sound without someone back there laying down the groove? But, in the end, drummers are basically failed guitarists and songwriters, musical dumb blondes relegated to the shadows while the frontmen soak up the glory. And they're allowed no margin for error, either; no one really notices, much less cares, when a vocalist forgets a line or a bassist flubs a note. But drop a beat, and *man,* is there hell to pay! Nothing is a bigger buzzkill at a show, nothing elicits more sour looks, than the moment when the sweaty-palmed drummer loses a stick and has to grope around on the floor for another one. And if there's one person in a band who's unreliable and/or completely out of his mind, it's the drummer. They are to music groups what goal tenders are to hockey and soccer: essential to the game, but a lunatic breed of their own.

And that's why this article was so easy to write. *Chunklet*'s panel of drum experts—Jerry Fuchs (from Brooklyn's Turing Machine), Patrick Gough (formerly of the DC band Pitchblende) and Brian Teasley (who has been in more bands than you've been in churches)—jump on the pigpile of drummer-dissing with its list of completely overrated drummers. The criteria were simple: to make the list, the drummer has to be someone the average music fan knows and, almost by default, thinks is a good drummer. Like, "The chick with the big afro who plays for Lenny Kravitz really wails!" doesn't cut it because 999 out of 1,000 people can't name her. And the one who can is probably a drummer.

CHARLIE WATTS

PG: Don't care if he is 70 years old and played for the Rolling Stones his whole life. Fact is, he blows. Ever notice the irritating pause he does with his right hand on the hi-hat when he's hitting the snare with his left? It's something people do who are just learning how to play. The ubiquitous smirk on his face says, "I can't believe I've made a career out of this."

Jerry Fuchs: Possibly the least expressive drummer in rock and roll. He's put out several "jazz" records with his own ensemble, too. Watts gives Philly Joe a real run for his money... no, he doesn't.

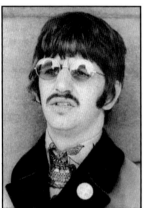

RINGO STARR

PG: That Ringo was overrated has become as big a cliché as has rock critics identification of clichés. That the two biggest bands in rock history had mediocre-at-best drummers goes to show that singer/songwriters can have really long coattails.

JF: The best thing about Ringo's drumming was the array of awesome sounds George Martin got out of his Ludwigs.

PHIL COLLINS

PG: With the deluge of sappy solo pop hits with which this Cabbage Patch-looking limey inundated us in the '80s, it's easy to forget that at one time he was the drummer for prog dinosaurs Genesis. To his credit, Collins recognized how much he sucked at drums and moved to vocals, something at which he sucked slightly less.

JF: Collins's entire progressive rock drumming career was based on a single stroke roll. To the untrained ear, a fast single stroke roll around a drum set consisting of no fewer than eight toms can make any drummer sound like God. Phil knew this and milked it for all it was worth. He is, at best, average rock drummer, and anyone who disagrees probably thinks the album cover of *No Jacket Required* was a good idea.

RICK ALLEN

PG: So he had one arm, big fuckin' deal.

JF: He used to play trad grip* when he had the extra arm, and some think that that alone made him a good drummer. It didn't. (See Charlie Watts)

TOMMY LEE

PG: Lee will be remembered more for his home porn video with Pamela than for anything he did with, er—what were they called?—Mötley Crüe. Mulletheads who say he was a good drummer probably only remember that he had a drum riser that could turn his entire kit upside down during a solo. Whooee.

JF: I don't know about his drumming, but he's awesome at spinning sticks and honking a horn with his dick.

NEIL PEART

PG: We'll get a lot of flak for this, but, frankly, he wasn't all that. Peart's playing was as technically sound as government bonds, no question; it's just that he was kind of passionless and mechanical in his delivery. And he wrote most of Rush's lyrics, which is a definite minus.

JF: Right on. Did he write the lyrics for "The Trees," too? How embarrassing.

DAVE GROHL

PG: Bashed away nicely in Scream, Nirvana, and Queens of the Stone Age (interesting progression, there...), but isn't nearly close to being one of the all-time greats, contrary to what the mainstream rock media has to say.

JF: Dude, Grohl is awesome! Dain Bramage. Don't forget Dain Bramage.

---

* Traditional grip is hard to explain in words, but it's where the hand holds the stick at a kooky angle, parallel to the front of the stage, rather than straight toward the audience. Jazz drummers use it a lot more than rockers; in fact, the only rock drummers you see doing it are those who were jazz-trained or who think they are "musicians" with something to prove.

BUN E. CARLOS

PG: It's easy to like a drummer named "Bun" who looks more like an alcoholic math teacher than a rock star, but, in reality, Cheap Trick could've gotten anyone with a necktie, moustache, comb-over, and two lit cigarettes in his mouth to play for them.

JF: It's true. His entire rep as a good drummer is maintained by the fact that his name is "Bun." How can you not like a guy whose name is Bun?

CHRIS FRANTZ

PG: Everyone clucks about how great Talking Heads were when they went in the direction of funk, but rhythmically they owed more to session percussionists than to anything Frantz did. Watch him during *Stop Making Sense* and you'll see that he very rarely varies from 4/4 time and boring fills.

JF: My God, this is a joke, right? How on earth could this guy end up on anyone's good drummer list?

OMAR HAKIM

PG: You may not know his name, but you've seen him— he's the bespectacled fellow in African garb who's played drums for Bowie, Madonna, Simple Minds, and a thousand fusion bands. A legendarily overrated drummer.

JF: And Sting. Don't forget Sting. Hakim's a hired gun. I'm sure he's got a percussion degree from somewhere we could give a shit about, and I'm certain he can technically show up most drummers. Who cares?

LARS ULRICH

PG: Obnoxious yapper who has spent more time over the past decade flapping his gums about how much Napster ripped him off than actually being an innovative or interesting drummer.

JF: Everyone above age 16 knows this guy is absolute crap as far as drumming goes. I remember friends thinking he was an amazing drummer because he used to be a semi-pro tennis player. I look back in awe at the kind of drum cred Ulrich got in the late '80s at a time when guys like Pete Sandoval of Morbid Angel and Mick Harris of Napalm Death were playing circles around him, as far as metal drumming goes.

CLEM BURKE

PG: We may be stretching it here on the recognition factor (he was in Blondie), but the only thing worse than a drummer who thinks he's cool and makes funny faces when he plays is one who does so while wearing a beard.**

JF: Burke was clearly more interested in having fun and looking good while playing than anything else. He's not a bad drummer; just a little too fashion-conscious. His Keith Moon infatuation might be a little much. When the fuck did he wear a beard?

CARTER BEAUFORD

PG: These frat boy know-nothings who insist that Beauford is the second coming really piss me off. Come on, people: it doesn't take a whole lot of imagination to play drums behind Dave Matthews. Also, a real drummer wouldn't play a show wearing a hockey jersey— you'd get too hot and tangled up inside it. If you were expending any kind of energy, that is.

JF: "Not only do I try to play like Dennis Chambers, but I'm doing everything I possibly can to look like him too."

MAX WEINBERG

Patrick Gough: He's kinda creepy, and Conan O'Brien deserves better than a third-rate Big Bad Voodoo Daddy as his house band.

Brian Teasley: Isn't he playing with the Yeah Yeah Yeahs now? The guy plays jazz like a neanderthal makes love. Stick to the flams on two and four that you unfortunately made so popular on E Street, Max.

**It was the late '70s-early '80s; I'm sure at some point Clem Burke had a beard. But all those mooks in Blondie looked the same to me, so I've probably got him confused with their bassist, Joey Buttafuco.

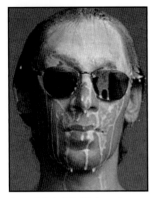

ALEX VAN HALEN

PG: Alex Van Halen and Michael Anthony (he of the Jack Daniels bottle-shaped bass guitar) are the poster boys of overrated rhythm sections. Why was Eddie so eager to scuttle David Lee Roth when clearly it was these two turkeys holding the band back? Either he was blindly loyal to his brother or in complete denial about how crummy Alex was.

BT: Truly Eddie's genetic bitch. "Hot For Teacher" was overdubbed. He didn't play the four kick drums he often had set up. Stole the fast bell shuffle from Toto (Toto!) and then dumbed it down to Twisted Sister levels, and worst of all, even though he was Dutch, the motherfucker looks Asian.

GRANT HART

PG: Hüsker Dü was great, Hart did play astonishingly fast, but it's the same ride/snare/kick/roll thing over and over again—he didn't even have a hi-hat! Not to mention, the weakest tracks on any Hüsker record invariably belonged to him. Imagine how awesome this band would've been if they had a drummer who was musically inventive, but didn't try to write songs.

BT: Anybody listen to a Hüsker Dü record in the last five years? I wish I could believe that it took weeks of studied labor to get drum sounds that shitty, but they just had their finger on the pulse. Singing drummers are generally a horrible idea, but in a punk (?) band and who sound like they have oatmeal in their mouth. Another lesson learned: Drugs make you love high-end. No wonder Bob Mould is deaf.

CARMINE APPICE

PG: Carmine Appice, Kenny Aronoff, and other classic rock clowns who read drum music and shill for percussion manufacturers in drum magazines. They can all stick a metronome up their ass.

BT: The embodiment of drum clinic cock swallowers. Keep hanging out with 12 year old boys who think you're a god and try to actually make some music people will listen to.

MEG WHITE

PG: See Mo Tucker. I'll never understand how White Stripes, which has really sparse arrangements to begin with, managed to get this far when half the duo is just barely hanging on. Not all woman drummers are awful—the ones in Unwound and Sleater-Kinney hold their own—but Meg White isn't even one percent responsible for anything that makes her band sound interesting.

BT: God, she's got a cute smile. I just like her in that red and white and sometimes black. I mean, she has those sagging but youthful breast feeding breasts that seem so comforting. Her wide, beautifully elusive eyes are hypnotic and the slightly weak chin make her seem so approachable. What a gal! What was this article about again?

DOUG SCHARIN

PG: The mercenary who would've been in every indie rock band in the '90s if given the chance, Scharin had a work ethic and commitment to perfection that would've put Neil Peart to shame. But the somewhat overplaying style that he stamped on June of '44, Rex, Codeine, and Him didn't make any of those bands better; in fact, I think he detracted considerably from Codeine's subtlety.

BT: Bald isn't a drum style. Keep dreaming of them Blue Turtles and stay away from the drum set. Hi-hat patterns don't have to change every time the barometric pressure shifts a nano-unit.

ANIMAL

PG: C'mon, everyone knows that Rowlf (the piano-playing dog) was the real talent behind the *Muppet Show*'s pit band.

BT: I bought a puppet version of Animal in second grade. Being a puppet, his puppet mouth opened and I nightly tried to brush his teeth. To this day, the AquaFresh stains fly high. Clearly I was much more worried about his dental hygiene than his drumming. No comment.

BIRDSTUFF

PG: Man or Astroman? should have sold that giant Tesla coil and bought a Roland 808, which I'm sure has a program for playing the same surf-rock beat over and over. At least the drum machine would be less flatulent.

BT: Actually, there's two surf beats, the dum-ba-dum-ba-ba beat and the dum-ba-ba-dum-ba beat, but yeah, he's right. I would rather watch white suburban frustration come out in pure technical aggression that has the visual flair of eight slugs gang-banging a twig. You know, the type of drumming made unpopular in Athens, Georgia in the mid-90's.

NICK MASON

PG: If you didn't think it was possible to make Pink Floyd's music sound even more forced and less natural, I give you Nick Mason. That snoozefest would have been better off not having a drummer at all rather than this lump of flesh back there. And for all his money, Mason's kit sounds on most recordings like a bunch of upside down plastic buckets.

BT: Nick, drop the 7A's and go with some real wood. Your drumming sounds like the world's softest manicure. I'm so glad your bitch ass got fucked on royalties. Roger could smell bullshit when he heard it. Your 7/8 on "Money" sounds like a Special Olympics jazz drummer trying to play on a Dave Brubeck CD.

FRANK BEARD

PG: If you're in a southern-boogie band with two guys who look like rejects from *O Brother Where Art Thou*'s Soggy Bottom Boys, one of whom nearly shot himself to death while pulling a derringer out of his boot in a Houston hotel, you might be a redneck.

BT: Where would modern beer commercial music be without deciding not to use Frank and use a drum machine instead? His influence is still felt today.

MO TUCKER

PG: Aging hipsters who rhapsodize over the understated power and beauty of her drumming with the Velvet Underground should step back, listen to those old records objectively, and realize that shaky, rudimentary pounding doesn't equal some kind of simple gracefulness.

BT: How do you get infinite room for your erratic noodling guitar solo? Get a smacked-out frumpy chick to play the same beat over and over ad infinitum. Brilliant in the way babies crap in their pants, I suppose. The concept, not the drumming, that is. Jesus, it's called Botox, Nancy Reagan. Try some.

AND IN FAIRNESS, DRUMMERS WHO DESERVE THEIR ACCOLADES:

John Bonham set the standard; can't fuck with him. **Keith Moon** was like an octopus, a one-man circus. **Matt Cameron** doesn't get a lot of credit for his contributions to Soundgarden, but his work is brilliantly off-kilter and subtle. On the more obscure side, listen to Bastro to hear the drum clinic **John McEntire** puts on—precise and devastating. **George Hurley** may be the most underrated drummer ever; his distinct style in the Minutemen and fIREHOSE is often overlooked. **Damon Fitzgerald** does things in Don Caballero that are breathtaking, and he manages to fulfill every stereotype about drummers being completely insane. And we kinda went back and forth on **Stewart Copeland**, who did a lot of clever, influential stuff with The Police, but loses points for his pretensions of being a "composer," for that lost cause of a side project he does with Les Claypool, and for being a renowned world-class asshole.

"I'LL BET BEING IN A BAND IS EVERY BIT AS GLAMOROUS AS IT LOOKS!"

"WRONG!"

says a Chunklet writer who's been there

by Patrick Gough • illustrations by Brian Walsby

I know you.

You're a male between, what, 18 and 35? Probably well-educated, but slightly underachieving, kind of nerdy in an ironic-so-it's-okay kinda way, and a huge fan of independent rock music. And if you're like most people in this demographic, it's always been a dream of yours to be *in a band*. Not just any old local band that stinks up basements, and the occasional opening slot at the student union or some dump in the warehouse district, but a *real* band—one that tours and draws crowds, gets interviewed and written about, and inspires people as much as you've been inspired by your punk rock heroes.

Well, gather around, kids, 'cause Uncle Pat's gonna disillusion your ass.

Bluntly put, being in a working band is one of the most overrated experiences a person can have. Sure, there are some advantages if you manage to pull it off. You get to travel a bit, meet new people, be creative, and postpone that vaunted institution known as *reality* for another few years. It all looks so enticing that, surely, it must be a lifestyle worth pursuing, right? Ninety-nine percent of the time, definitely not. In fact, I aim to persuade you that you're better off just going straight to graduate school or getting your career on track and remaining an honest, ordinary music fan with no pretensions of rockstardom.

Here's a breakdown of the whole being-in-a-band thing that should illustrate what a load of rubbish it is. Best wishes.

BOOKING SHOWS

Okay, so let's say you're in a band that's written a set, played a dozen or so local shows, made some connections, and put out a single or—if you're really resourceful—a CD. To get to the next level, you've got to take your act on the road. That's the whole point of this, after all: to get people to listen to your music. An artist doesn't paint something and stick it in a closet, and a chef doesn't cook a meal and stuff it down the sink, so naturally you want an audience for the tunes you've worked so hard to craft, and your records are simply not gonna fly off the shelves by themselves.

The first notion you must dispense with is that it's easy to book a tour. Ask anyone who's done it—it's a colossal pain in the ass. For a start, no one knows who the fuck you are. It's one thing if your band is established, but by the time you've got a bunch of CDs out, someone is probably doing your booking for you anyway. So you've got to start from scratch, calling and e-mailing everyone on God's green earth who you think can help get you a show. The trouble is that promoters and other people who put together shows are at worst scumbags who will screw you over as soon as look at you, or at best flakeoid drug casualties who are good-hearted but thick as a plank of wood. Dealing with them will test your patience to the max, and make you feel like your tour is doomed before you load up the van. Even if you eschew nightclubs in favor of house parties or campus shows, you've still got to deal with college students—and sometimes they're worse than the scumbags and flakeoids, because students are not attempting to do this for a living. For students, putting together shows is a lark to pass the time between exams and their weekly two-hour radio spots. As such, they tend to be completely unreliable and will only humor you as long as you seem to like them. This motley collection of ne'er-do-wells, sprinkled liberally over our vast land, holds the keys to your future in rock. Persevere, cajole, kiss ass, whatever—do what you gotta do, because without them, you and your tour are going nowhere. My advice is to spare yourself the indignity and not interact with these people at all, but if you're still determined, maybe considering the hardships of the road will change your mind.

TRAVELING

Now let's say you've overcome the odds, and somehow cobbled together a several-week tour that takes you to a host of dingy bars and dormitory rec rooms in your region. You and your bandmates chip in to rent or buy some crummy van, pack it up with your gear, kiss your girlfriends goodbye, and roll out. For the first few hours, your mind is flooded with romantic notions of Kerouac, amber waves of grain, and all the brave pioneers who came before you. But after a while it occurs to you that most of the country looks the same: painfully dull. Long stretches of fields and forests are broken up only by the occasional gas station, fast food joint, big box store, or fireworks stand. The faded backs of houses and trailers are stoic reminders of how quotidian much of American life actually is. Truckers look at you with bemusement or homophobic rage, if they notice you at all. After barreling along for hours, you finally arrive, set up, play, pack up, and go somewhere to crash. Then you wake up the next day, and do it again...twenty or thirty times in a row.

The mental aspect of touring is fatiguing enough, but I can't emphasize enough how taxing it can be on the body, as well. Hotels? Forget it. Unless you're independently wealthy, you're staying at someone's house after the show. There may be an available couch or extra bed now and then, but generally you're in a sleeping bag on a hard wooden floor covered with dirt and cat hair. You sweat your ass off in the summer, shiver when it's cold, and usually wake up tired, coughing, and with sore muscles. After the first week, the camaraderie and chattiness in the van is replaced by snoring or staring into space. The worst part is loading in and out over and over. It's a lot different when you play in your hometown once in a while; you only drive a few miles and friends are always around to help carry gear. You think, "Hey, this isn't so bad." But in some distant state, it's only you and your bandmates who are responsible for lugging your shit in and out of venues, sometimes up and down multiple flights of stairs. Even the most hearty of souls wear down from the lack of sleep, repeated heavy lifting, and sweat and grime. Everyone gets sick at some point, and unselfishly passes the bug around. And I haven't even mentioned the food yet. Real bands get catered with deli trays and sandwiches, or maybe fresh pasta. Chances are that you, however, will stop at a taco or burger stand and load up on greasy crap before the show; and instead of juice or milk, you'll probably end up drinking too much beer or soft drinks from the bar. By the second or third week you feel ill and disconnected, disoriented, and maybe even a little homesick, wondering why you bothered doing all this in the first place.

A lot of people start a band to avoid working; ironically, it is some of the hardest work a person can ever do.

PERFORMING

As if the process of spending hours per day staring out the windows of a cramped van weren't dispiriting enough, equally mind-numbing is what happens once you get to your destination: waiting around for several more hours before you play. It's probably too dark to read, so pinball and billiards soothe the pain somewhat. But generally you shuffle about, change strings or drum heads, set up the merch table, and basically… just…wait around. Real bands get a soundcheck so their music will be evenly mixed during the show, and then chat with well-wishers and do interviews for a while before their set. You, on the other hand, will not only *not* get a soundcheck, but the bitter and condescending soundman will resent the fact that you even exist. You will hear nothing in the monitors and there will be no vocals coming out of the PA. After you play your set for ten people (what, you didn't think anyone was going to come out early to see a band they never heard of, did you?), you hastily drag your shambling collection of amps and semi-working guitars off stage so the real band can get up there and proceed to blow you away in front of 200 people. A couple of geeky dudes from the local college/record store kinda dug your set, so they take pity on you and offer you a place to crash. They have several cats.

The next day, you wake up, sore and tired as usual, and drive to the next show. The scumbag/flakeoid/college student tells you upon arrival that the local band on the bill broke up, or the fire marshal temporarily closed the venue, or he simply forgot there was a show tonight and did no promotion whatsoever. So it's cancelled. Undaunted, you decide to drive all night to the next city, sleep in the van, and maybe do some sightseeing the next day. On the way, though, you get a flat tire or the van breaks down, you get pulled over by a cop for speeding, or someone slams his hand in the van door—breaking a finger. Or you get some equipment stolen from your van. Or someone's girlfriend back home finds out she's pregnant. Or someone's mom dies. Or the van rolls over and everyone in the band dies.

You see where I'm going with this. Scores of bad things can go wrong while on tour, and the number of cataclysmic events that can take place is inversely proportional to the popularity of the band. Which means that you—Mister "I want to start a band and go on tour regardless of how retarded and unworkable the idea is"—are destined for not only failure, but abject misery and humiliation.

BEING CREATIVE AND GETTING REVIEWED

If you've defied fate and have come home from tour in one piece, and your band hasn't broken up or had all its shit stolen, congratulations! Now you get to do the most difficult part of all: writing another set of material, and recording a new album. The first one was easy, wasn't it? Everyone worked together and contributed good ideas in a fun, enthusiastic way. But now, the concepts don't flow so readily. You all have improved your chops, but seem to be overthinking and forcing the music to come together. Buoyed by the feeling of success that accompanied the first album or single, you went ahead and booked studio time. But that time is fast approaching and you're nowhere near ready to record; you've only got a bunch of half-baked parts of songs and—Christ!—hardly any lyrics written. Practices are long and tempers are short. You get to the studio—a better one than last time—but feel lost in the array of gadgets and dials you've never seen before. The engineer is a nice enough fellow, but he's running a business, and has no problem with indulging your need to write material in the studio and experiment with different sounds. Eventually, you go way over budget and come away with a tape that sounds nothing like your band. Luckily, an indie label has offered to put the record out, but deep down you don't like it as much as the first one. You're secretly relieved when the label— actually a college dropout who inherited a bunch of money—completely bungles the distribution of the record.

A few publications miraculously get a hold of some copies, and they like the album even less than you do. After the first single or album, which you lovingly financed and released yourself, a few local rags picked up on the buzz generated by some of your friends and acquaintances and wrote some blurbs about it. They weren't at all unfavorable; in fact, they admired your freshness and even compared you to some of your favorite bands. But this time, some reputable publications with rather wide circulations had a listen, and when they weren't totally dismissive, they took the time to lay into your derivative style, your knowledge of dynamics, and even the bogusness of the entire scene in your town. Most people would take the hint and abandon the rock ship; but no, you chalk up the bad reviews to jaded, mean-spirited hacks who can't play music themselves, and are therefore relegated to writing about how much they hate everything. It doesn't matter that critics generally know what they're talking about, and would much rather write a good review on any given day, and it doesn't matter that even you yourself know on some level that what you're doing is just wasting everyone's time. You doggedly press on, taking up shelf space in the pantry of entertainment with your bland, moldy cookies that no one wants to eat.

INSPIRING PEOPLE, GIVING BACK TO THE MUSIC COMMUNITY, BLAH-DEE-BLAH-BLAH

Your family and friends are good people and they don't want to discourage you from following your dreams. But they're not doing you any favors by blowing smoke up your ass about how good your band is. So I'm just gonna give it to you straight:

You have no talent.

Now don't get me wrong. I love a lot of rock music, and am aware that the "do it yourself" ethic is essential to the subculture. A lot of great art—not just music, but graphics, filmmaking, or what have you—started and stayed in the amateur ranks. And I believe that everyone should try to express himself artistically if he thinks it will make him a better person. But the downside of DIY—and this is seldom talked about—is that it opened the floodgates for every swingin' dick with a guitar and 500 bucks to put out a record, and try to get a show at the local rock club. Apparently, it's not good enough for people to recognize their paltry talents and limit their audience to their families and friends. No, they've got to have delusions of grandeur, and believe that they can also achieve fame and fortune, and be an inspiration to others. What a pile of narcissistic shit! It is so rare, so *incredibly rare,* that a musician or group of musicians has the ability to make quality music of lasting value that it's a puzzle that anyone attempts to clamber up on a stage at all. Yet there they are—this non-stop parade of buffoons who continue to annoy us (and embarrass themselves) because someone somewhere said it's okay for them to give it a whirl.

If you're one of those people, let me repeat: being in a working, touring band is extremely hard work, fraught with tension, illness, discomfort, and shady characters. Play music if it makes you happy, but don't get all cocky and assume you can do it for a living, or that you would even want to. The odds are overwhelming that you'll merely make a putz out of yourself, and give it up broke, disappointed, and wishing you'd stayed in the audience to begin with.

The author would like to add that the band he was in during the early '90s was, by many accounts, actually pretty good, but that even then the experience kinda sucked a lot of the time. —ed.

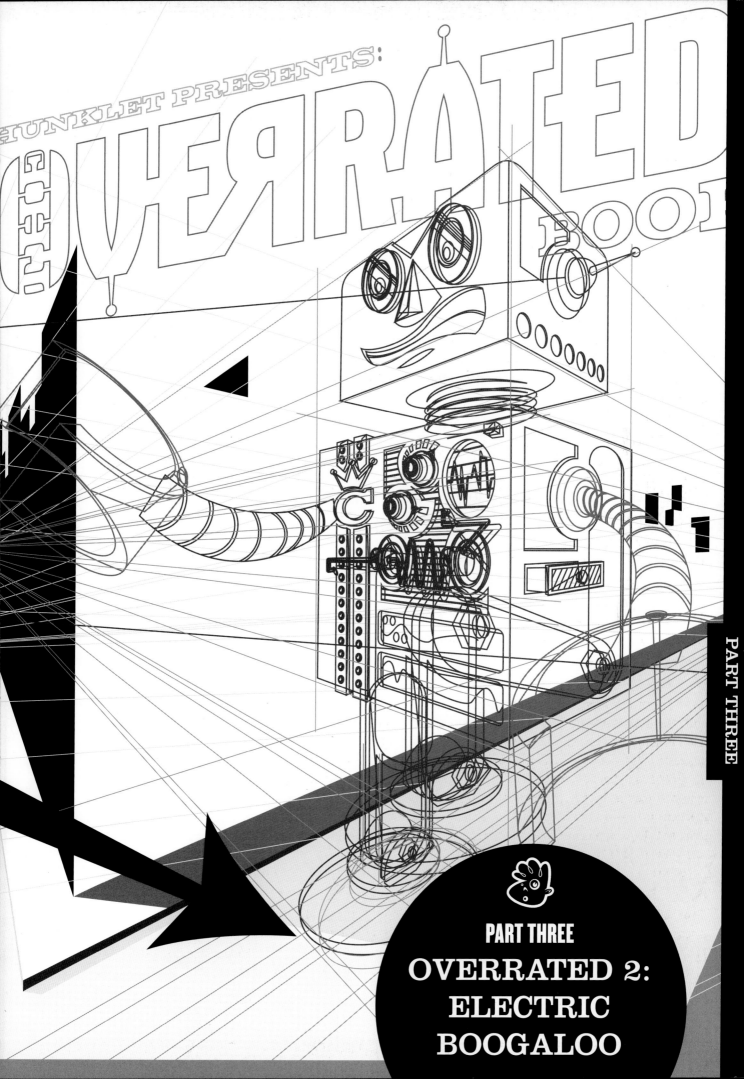

HUNKLET PRESENTS:

OVERRATED BOOI

PART THREE

OVERRATED 2: ELECTRIC BOOGALOO

FUN WHILE GOING VERTICAL

DISCLAIMER: For amusement only!

by Henry H. Owings • illustrations by Jerry Fuchs

After nailing the waitress behind the club and subsequently puking in their dumpster, catching air at a rock show might be one of the final rites of passage for any half-way decent soon-to-be-hipster. Wait, did I say nailing the waitress? I meant, *trying to avoid* nailing the waitress. Sometimes I must sound like I'm whacked out on jungle juice!

Many people, including ourselves here at *Chunklet*, know that the days of great rock front men are as rare as wedding night virgins. The death blow for this dying breed being when David Lee Roth took up his new career as a radio talk show host. Well, we thought we'd document yet more of these classy moves before they are lost forever in the ever disappearing rock world ether.

THE BIG STRETCH

Sure, you might be young. Sure, you might heal well. But what would you think if you hit thirty and you were barely able to walk because you were repeatedly straining your hamstring when you were going to the rock shows of your youth? Yeah, it's not so funny now, is it? So for the love of Jehovah, take a few minutes to get limber. **Entertainment Factor: Hey, man, there's nothing funny about this.**

THE AMP BACK FLIP

Fancy yourself a gymnast? Time to spare on stage? Well, what are you waiting for? Get on top of the nearest amplifier and do what you do best! Go with the bass player's SVT for maximum altitude, then let 'er rip, bro. **Entertainment Factor: 7.8 out of 10**

THE JUDGE'S CORNER

And who could forget the front row peanut gallery? These semi-participatory nabobs keep their sharpies at the ready for rating show activities. Unlike an internet chatroom, at least this way you can pound their asses in the parking lot after the show. **Entertainment Factor (if you're one of them): 9.6 out of 10; (if you're not): 1.4 out of 10**

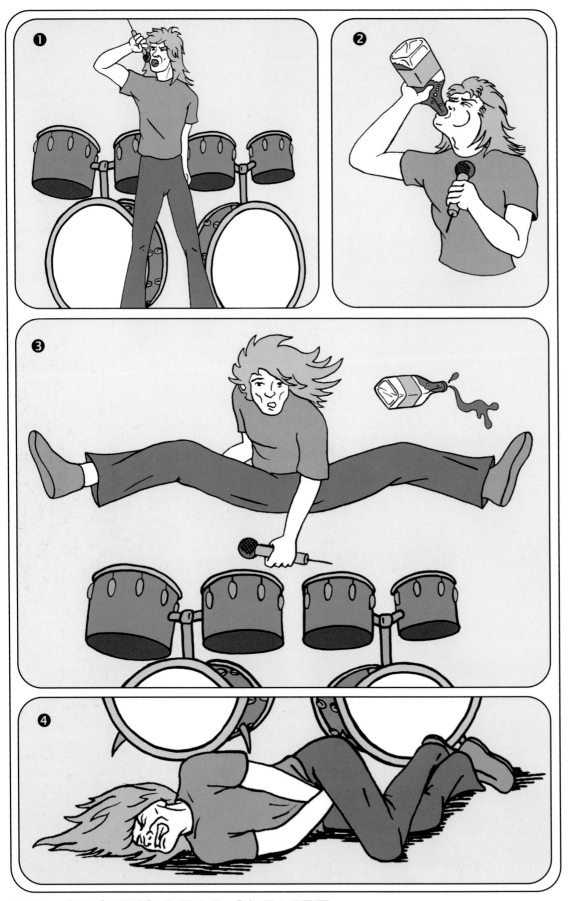

MR. GROIN'S LEAP O' FAITH

A plus-three dexterity move if you dare try it, let alone actually succeed. Prerequisites? Ten years of gymnastic training, a thorough stretching regimen, a kick drum riser, and most vitally, a whole helluva lot of moxie. So what's the difference between passing a kidney stone, and rockin' a stadium full of chicks 'n dicks? Very little, amigo.
Entertainment Factor: 9.3 out of 10

THE 'OL "FAT-GUY-OFF-THE-MONITOR" TRICK

If there is entertainment that out-performs watching a fat guy jump off a stage monitor and crushing a comparative wisp of a human below, well then, I don't think it has yet been invented, galldarnit! Tad Doyle? Half of Poison Idea? Greg Dulli? All of Hey Mercedes bound and duct-taped together? You name it, anybody from the morbidly obese to the most shockingly, er uh, non-obese can hoist their girth around for maximum shock value. Consequently that value-added entertainment is passed along to you, the guy (or gal) that isn't crushed like a grape. Bring it on, slugger! We ain't skeered. P.S. Don't forget to bring a mop for clean-up. **Entertainment Factor: 9.98 out of 10**

Please welcome Rock & Roll's answer to Jeff Foxworthy...

Daniel Terryfeather!

"YOU MAY BE ON THE GUEST LIST IF..."

by Brian Teasley • illustrations by Eryc Simmerer

1. You refer to band members by their first names.
2. You see someone from the band and the first thing you say is, "How was Japan?"
3. You put out an early single by the band before "everybody was into them."
4. You keep checking your cell phone to see if the band is going to call you when they "roll into town."
5. You bring a Pez dispenser for the bass player that you know he doesn't have in his collection.
6. You have brought them a copy of the piece you did on them in the local alt-weekly.
7. Before you left for the gig, you laid out towels out for the band to use if they want to "grab a shower" after the show.
8. You feverishly try to compile your prank-call CD before the band comes over because you've "got to burn them a copy."
9. You arrive at the show with a camera that cost over $85.
10. You're not on the list, but you give the door guy your driver's license to go find a band member, who then comes back and tells the door guy that you're "cool." You get stamped, and get your ID back.
11. The first things you do when you see the band members are to give them hugs, and to take a beer out of their cooler without asking.
12. You have a DVD-R or CD-R to give to the band with meticulous labeling (ex: The New Pornographers/ Wednesday 13 February 2002/12:05AM/Mass Romantic Tour/US Leg)
13. The band thanks you from stage, and you're not part of the venue staff.
14. You throw 4,000 tea bags at the drummer, but he doesn't kill you after the show and, instead, laughs.
15. You keep yelling for the band to play a new song that they supposedly wrote at your house.
16. You get the band drugs.
17. You get the band laid.
18. You don't bitch about one of the band members balling your girlfriend behind the dumpster at the club.

WORK THAT SHAFT!

Twenty three time-worn methods to step up to the mic

by Henry H. Owings with Brian Teasley • illustrations by Terry White

Today's modern microphone-holding techniques are clearly far totally revolutionary when compared with 30-plus years of rock's greats who constantly revamped their approach to this tool that both gave them power and thrust all the attention directly upon them. So, in this, we analyze the good, the bad and the downright silly folks that get up there, night after night, for our occasional amusement and their eternal quest for deification. Oh, the pathos.

Note: Any similarity between the model herein and contributor Brian Teasley is merely coincidental. Oh, and if it looks like he's air guitaring, your eyes are playing tricks on you.

THE "ELVIS" TOUCH

Much like the Lux, this could prove problematic. However, chances are you've got this mic in your road case. Keep it real, bub. Real cheesy, that is.

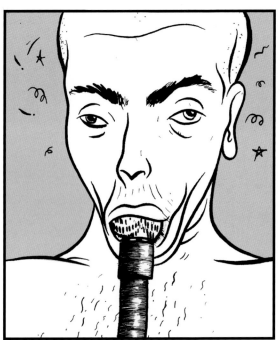

THE LUX

Make sure that mic was thoroughly wiped down by one of your road slaves or this seemingly good idea will lead you right to the emergency room. Momentary lapses of reason shouldn't lead to a series of shots to prevent you from getting a serious case of lockjaw.

THE REVERSE NORMAN

This is best practiced in the garage due to the uneven momentum swings of the mic stand base. One false move in a dark club could result in two things: cracked skulls and lawsuits.

DA 80'S HARDCORE STYLEE

Machismo righteousness never felt so good as during those three or four years when New England thugs could masquerade as punk meatheads.

THE MERRY-GO-ROUND

Getting the crowd to admire your stage twirling will inevitably lead them to think you are above average if not just totally adequate. It's all smoke and mirrors, folks.

THE YOW

Both the best front man of the 90's and the only guy that could take the mic and make it seem like the mysterious fifth member of the band. Righteous!

FEED THE WORLD

If in-ear monitors aren't gay enough, let your trusty index finger steer you toward being remotely in tune. Sure, you could've splurged on those vocal lessons, but why not let the crowd realize you're a hack.

THE LEMMY

Unless you're a basketball camp reject, singing up at the mic will inevitably make you look like a runt. Bathtub crank and unfortunate facial moles don't help either.

THE WHITNEY

Although at one time considered to be 'decent' (that is, if you were lobotomized), Whitney Houston brought microphone holding to a new low. Please note that the three spare fingers roll and/or tap up and down the 'shaft' of the mic.

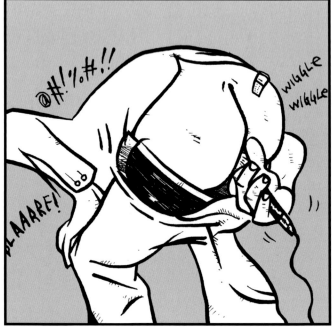

THE DOUBLE G

Fecalphiliacs, please take note: although not terribly sensible, letting "your little brown buddy" check the vocal mic usually provides both shock and chuckles. Note: take the foam mic windscreen off before pulling this stunt, dumbo.

THE MARS (RE)VOLTA

When all else has been done to death and you find yourself as the front man of the 20-something's version of Rush, what do you do? Make the mic stand your friend. Embrace it. Love it. Caress it. Why? Because there's no way anybody will buy your antics, ass captain.

THE LOOK AT ME! I CAN FLY LIKE AN EAGLE!

Sure, it might make the crowd think that their artist of choice is opening up, tearing down the walls and all that hullabaloo, but in actuality it's nothing a real man should do for fear of being clubbed on the way out of the club. Sound familiar, Moby? This method was used to a much wider critical acclaim by 60's pop dilletantes Shellaque from Evanston, Illinois.

THE SIMP

Nothing inspires contempt more than some British football hooligan trying to out-snark Johnny Rotten. It just ain't possible. Wanna treat the mic like it's the enemy? Go home, arsehole.

THE DARBY

Simple recipe for making a monster. Ahem. Take one mental derelict, add 2 cases of beer, add yet another case for good luck and then unleash on a crowd of equally simple-minded freaks. Stand back and watch the fireworks fly. Note to Boy Scouts: use a clove hitch to wrap the microphone cord repeatedly around said monster's arm to keep the hits a-comin'!

THE NESS

You know Mike Ness is allergic to metal, right? Neither do his fans! Or rather, his fan. This leads to various local crew guys having to hold the mic for him while he air guitars his 'hit.'

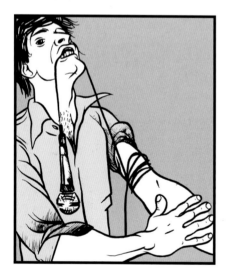

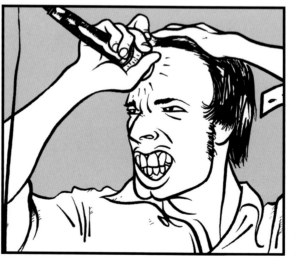

THE COBAIN

Done especially when a band is 'breakin' it down,' there's nothing that can amuse the fans more than givin' a shout out to Horse. I mean, who in their right mind doesn't think heroin is, like, the coolest thing ever?

THE BLOODY 58

We've all seen it before, 40 minutes on stage plus two cases of PBR yields a singer smashing a broken beer bottle into his forehead. The fear of scars would scare a mere mortal from this stunt, but true rockers (like Ted Leo) don't even blink.

SHOWCASE SHOWDOWN

A magic wand mic is hard enough to find, but you've got to be in a swing band in order for it to come off as even semi-legit. Here's a better idea, Chachi: use a megaphone.

THE XLR NOOSE

Some nights you might feel like hanging yourself, but what the heck, let the audience dream their little dreams. Perfect for ballads!

THE ENTWHISTLE

Only The Ox could come up with a method that was both British (read: not cool) and unquestionably cool at the same time. Not one to get his hands wet on a water bottle between songs, one cage would be mounted on each side of the mic stand for maximum liquid refreshment. In the left bottle? Water with a twist of lemon. In the right? Absinthe. John was nothing if not a total lush. God bless him. Or rather, may he rest in peace.

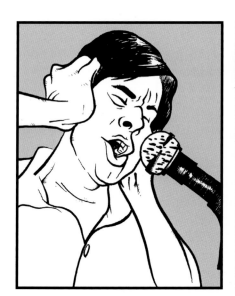

THE WE ARE THE WORLD

Cranking heart-felt takes in the studio is a bitch, but when cameras are filming your 'behind the scenes' reel, all bets are off. Made famous by legions of now C-grade 'vocalists' during the 80's, when feeding Africa was, like, totally important and stuff.

THE TURNER

Although under Ike's intimidating control 24-7 throughout the 60's and 70's, Tina never stopped treating the microphone like the honest-to-God phallic symbol that it truly is. To this day, her technique is often employed by Barbie Doll-esque divas on Top 40 radio. Classic? Absolutely!

THE BON

Mr. Scott's burly, larger-than-life stage persona which was larger than life was only rivalled by his throngs of imitators, with one Mr. Rollins leading the pack. Sorta like a longshoreman taking Fred Flintstone out on a blind date. Genius.

WE GIVE THANKS!

by Dag Luther Gooch with Steve Birmingham, Daniel Gill, Alan Jacobson, Amanda Nichols and Carrie Weston • illustration by Joe Peery

As we consider all of the bands that through the years have brought us great joy and inspiration, let us consider the following generation of bands that they have given us. Some carbon copies, some one-uppers, and in most cases, bastard spawns, side projects, and generally mutated versions of their ancestors, we give thanks this season to these icons for shooting their fertile seed into rock'n'roll only adding to an overpopulated mp3 wasteland.

Thanks to...	Thank you for....
Brian Wilson	The Elephant fucking 6003 (by my last count), Wilson Phillips, the rest of The Beach Boys and their tired efforts together and on their own, Pianosaurus, Modest Mouse, Flaming Lips, The Shins, Wondermints, Frank Black's solo career, The Polyphonic Spree, Danielson and my miserable birth.
Beastie Boys	Limp Bizkit, Rage Against the Machine, Eminem, The Spin Doctors, Insane Clown Posse, Beck, 311, Cypress Hill, The Roots, Kid Rock, the Bloodhound Gang, House of Pain /Everlast, Uncle Cracker and my ex-girlfriend's 6 DUIs.
Pixies	Nirvana (and all the Blink 182's and Sum 41's they let in "the year punk broke"), Weezer, Man...or Astro-Man?, The Toadies, Everclear, The Verve Pipe, or just so all of the bases are covered, the "quiet verse/loud chorus" formula, sci-fi surf rock, and geek punk. Also a big thanks to their next recording, born out of pride and greed, that will eventually usher in another generation of even shittier bands.
Dinosaur Jr.	Who begat Sebadoh, who begat Sentridoh and Folk Implosion, who begat a huge generation of CD baby-suckling mp3-desktop record producers, who begat myspace.com, who begat my inability to get any fucking work done. And also, for all the slow punk rock bands that can't sing and play guitar solos that span the length of an entire song.

Led Zeppelin	Aerosmith, Kiss, who begat Def Leppard, who begat Kings X, who begat The Darkness. Thank you for the clones: Great White, Kingdom Come, Whitesnake, Zebra; the cover bands: The Zeppelins (Ted & Dread); the revivalists: The Black Crowes, The Cult, Dream Theater, Faster Pussycat, Lenny Kravitz, Guns N' Roses, Jane's Addiction, The Mission UK, Soundgarden; the name droppers: Jeff Buckley, J Mascis, Let's Active, Beastie Boys; but mostly the mountain of shit like Zakk Wylde, Bon Jovi, 4 Non Blondes, Sammy Hagar/Van Halen, Michael Schenker, Living Colour, Joan Jett, Kix, as well as any other hair metal, nü-metal, speed metal or funk metal you can name. And thanks to the tour jet you flew in on.
U2	The Alarm, The Call, Coldplay, The Cranberries, Gene Loves Jezebel, The Church, The Cult, The Gloria Record, Hothouse Flowers, The Waterboys, The Ocean Blue, The Sundays, The Tragically Hip, Radiohead, Better Than Ezra, Sunny Day Real Estate, the last several Pink Floyd albums, Christian Rock, pseudo-Christian rock and Christian emo.
Lou Reed	Bruce Springsteen, Jackson Browne, Nico, Morrissey, Morphine, The Strokes, Radio 4, The Dandy Warhols, and your massive, crushing ego.
Syd Barrett	Jandek, Robyn Hitchcock, The Brian Jonestown Massacre, Roger Waters solo, Wesley Willis, Daniel Johnston, Robert Wyatt, Jad Fair, Jeff Mangum, The Legendary Stardust Cowboy, "outsider music," and that guy from The Manic Street Preachers.
Aerosmith	Guns'n'Roses, Bon Jovi, Whitesnake, Hootie & the Blowfish, The Calling, Nickelback, the evil Chad Kroeger effort, Evanescence, Dashboard Confessional, Hoobastank, Dave bloody Mathews Band, and bad God rock such as Creed.
The Beatles	Wings, Plastic Ono Band, The Jam, Paul Weller, Style Council, Oasis, Blur, Rembrandts, Bangles, Travelling Wilburys, Ocean Colour Scene, the whole sorry mess that was Britpop, Crowded House, The Vines, one hit wonder Liverpool bands like The La's.
The Velvet Underground	The Modern Fucking Lovers, The Ponys (and every other strumtastic garage band dressed in black turtlenecks these days), The Feelies, and all them self-serious college rock bands, and thank you specifically to Moe "After Hours" Tucker, for making every woman with a saccharin voice think it's acceptable to put her acid cuteness at the forefront...that's right, Moe, your drum majoring led this parade of 'tards: Donnellies, Hatfields and fucking Frente. Frente!
The Replacements	Soul Asylum, The Goo Goo Dolls, Gin Blossoms, Ryan Adams, Semisonic, Counting Crows, Wilco, The Bottle Rockets, Nirvana, Green Day, Paul Westerberg, and Grandpaboy.
Fugazi	Jawbox, Nation Of Ulysses and Bad Religion. We give thanks for the one-off polyp known as Pailhead. Yes, we will never stand in line. Bless you for Shudder To Think, Helmet, The Get Up Kids, Braid, Cursive, Ted Leo, and all the people who secretly want to thank U2, but owe it all to you.
Big Black	For transforming the miserable synth-pop careers of Ministry and Nine Inch Nails into the anger-filled industrial juggernauts that pulled the wool over the eyes of a bunch of 120 Minutes-loving college DJs. Thank you for Rapeman, Shellac, and all the direct fruit of thine loins. Also, thank you for Six Finger Satellite, Tar and the entire Hydrahead discography.
Suicide	Shellac, Chrome, Loop, Cabaret Voltaire, and Spaceman 3. And especially, for Skinny Puppy. They were blissfully fun to mock.
Neu!	The Silver Apples, Stereolab, Tortoise and Ui. Basically, thank you for the whole post-rock borefest that took 20 years to catch on.

Ten Steps To Get The Most Out Of Your Rock Show Experience by Brian Teasley

Diez pasos fáciles para conseguir el la mayoría de su experiencia de la demostración de la roca

10 einfache Schritte, zum die die meisten aus Ihrer Felsen-Erscheinen-Erfahrung herauszubekommen

Tien Gemakkelijke Stappen om de meesten uit Uw Rots te krijgen tonen Ervaring

Goal 1: Escape The Elements

Meta
Doel
Doel

Walk in the front door. Jesus, do we have to tell you to breathe?

Escape los elementos. Caminata en la puerta delantera. ¿Jesús, tenemos que decirle respirar?

Entgehen Sie den Elementen. Weg in der vorderen Tür. Jesus, müssen wir Ihnen erklären zu atmen?

Ontsnap de Elementen. Gang in de voordeur. Jesus, moeten wij u om te ademen vertellen?

Goal 2: Get In Free

Tell the door guy you're on the list. When he doesn't find your name, let him know you just talked to the band's press agent that afternoon, and said they'd fax it in. Preparation: The door guy most assuredly plays in some shitty band who has a single out. Find out the name of the b-side and tell him you really dig his stuff, especially that track, "_____," on the B-side. Next thing you know, you're wearing a laminate and drinking the band's Rolling Rock.

Consiga en libre. Diga a individuo de la puerta que usted está en la lista. Cuando él no encuentra su nombre, déjelo le conocen hablar con el agente de prensa de la venda esta tarde, y eso que él lo dijo lo enviaría por telefax adentro. Preparación: El individuo de la puerta lo ma's assuredly posible juega en alguna venda shitty que tenga un expediente de siete pulgadas hacia fuera. Descubra el nombre del B-lado y digalele realmente empuje su materia, especialmente esa pista "_____", en el B-lado. Cosa siguiente usted le conoce está usando un laminado y está bebiendo la roca del balanceo de la venda.

Erhalten Sie in freiem. Erklären Sie dem Türhalteseil, das Sie auf der Liste sind. Wenn er nicht Ihren Namen findet, lassen Sie ihn kennen Sie sprach gerade mit dem Pressemittel des Bandes heute nachmittag, und das, das sie sie sagten, würde es innen faxen. Vorbereitung: Das Türhalteseil spielt assuredly in irgendeinem shitty Band, das eine sieben-Zoll-Aufzeichnung heraus hat. Finden Sie den Namen der B-Seite heraus und erklären Sie ihm Ihnen wirklich Grabung sein Material, besonders diese Schiene "_____", auf der B-Seite. Folgende Sache kennen Sie Sie tragen ein Laminat und trinken Rollen-Felsen des Bandes.

Krijg in Vrij. Vertel de deurkerel u op de lijst bent. Wanneer hij uw naam niet vindt, laat hem het weten u enkel sprak aan de agent van de bandpers vanmiddag, en dat zij they'd fax het in zeiden. Voorbereiding: De deurkerel het meest zonder twijfel speelt in één of andere shitty band die een zeven duimverslag uit heeft. Kom de naam van de B-Kant te weten en vertel hem u graven werkelijk zijn materiaal, vooral die "_____" volgen, aan de B-Kant. Het volgende ding dat u u draagt een laminaat en drinkt de band Rolling Rots hebt geweten.

Goal 3: Get Free Alcohol

Let the bartender know that you're with the band that's about to play and you'll need to get a few shots of Jäger before they go on. Right before you finish asking, let them know how awesome everyone has been, and how you and the band are so excited to be back because a lot of the other shows have been really fucked up. Now it's time for you to become the drunk asshole we all know you really are. Warning: Watch out for Jaded Robot. He'll fuck your shit up.

Consiga El Alcohol Libre. Deje a camarero saber a que la venda alrededor el juego y ellos deseó a algunos individuos para Jaeger. Derecho antes de que usted acabe el pedir, déjelos saben cómo es impresionante ha sido cada uno y usted y la venda son así que excitado para estar detrás porque los muchos de las otras demostraciones realmente se han cogido para arriba. Ahora es hora para usted de sentir bien al asshole borracho nosotros que todo le conoce realmente está. Nota: Reloj hacia fuera para la robusteza de Jaded - él cogerá su mierda para arriba.

Erhalten Sie Freien Spiritus. Informieren Sie den Barmixer, daß das Band ungefähr zum Spiel und zu ihnen einige Halteseile für Jaeger wünschte. Recht, bevor Sie beenden zu bitten, lassen Sie sie können, wie ehrfürchtig jeder gewesen ist und Sie und das Band also sind, aufgeregt, um zurück zu sein, weil eine Menge anderen Erscheinen wirklich oben geburnst worden sind. Jetzt ist es Zeit für Sie, dem betrunkenen Arschloch zu stehen wir, die alle Sie sind wirklich kennen. Anmerkung: Bewachung heraus für Jaded Roboter. Er burnst Ihre Scheiße oben.

Krijg Vrije Alcohol. Laat de barman weten dat de te spelen band ongeveer en zij een paar kerels voor Jaeger wilden. Het recht alvorens u eindigt vragend, liet hen weten hoe ontzagwekkend iedereen is geweest en hoe u en de band zo achter opgewekt om bent te zijn omdat de heel wat andere shows werkelijk omhoog fucked zijn geweest. Nu is het tijd voor u dronken asshole te worden wij allen weten u werkelijk bent. Nota: Horloge uit voor Robot Jaded. Hij omhoog zal fuck uw shit.

Goal 4: Take A Leak

If you have to sit and shit, be prepared to have everyone to see what's inside the genie's bottle, that is unless you just happen to be at one of the three clubs that actually have doors on their stalls. Bonus: Try to flood the club by clogging the sink and then turning on the faucet.

Tome un escape. Si usted tiene que sentarse y la mierda esté preparada para tener cada uno para ver cuál está dentro de la botella de los genie, ése es a menos que usted apenas suceda estar a la una de los tres clubs que tienen realmente puertas en sus paradas. Prima: Intente inundar al club estorbando el fregadero y dando vuelta en el grifo.

Nehmen Sie eine Leckstelle. Wenn Sie sitzen müssen und Scheiße vorbereitet wird, um jeder zu haben, zum zu sehen, was innerhalb der Flasche der genies ist, ist das, es sei denn Sie gerade geschehen, bei einer der drei Vereine zu sein, die wirklich Türen auf ihren Ställen haben. Prämie: Versuchen Sie, die Verein zu überschwemmen, indem Sie die Wanne verstopfen und auf den Hahn sich drehen.

Neem een Lek. Als u moet zitten en shit voorbereidingen wordt getroffen om iedereen te hebben om te zien wat binnen de fles van het genie is, is dat tenzij u om enkel één van de drie clubs gebeurt te bedragen die eigenlijk deuren op hun boxen hebben. Bonus: Probeer om de club te overstromen door de gootsteen te belemmeren en de tapkraan aan te zetten.

Goal 5: Get Free Drinks Off Some Mild Acquaintances

Don't forget that every day is your birthday. Be sure to be stoic, yet sad, when relaying to them that you came to the show all alone. Guess what... Your dumb-ass friends are no smarter than Denny's employees, so drink up!

Consiga Las Bebidas Libres De Algunos Conocidos Suaves. No se olvide de él es su cumpleaños. Sea seguro ser stoic pero triste al retransmitir a ellos que usted vino a la demostración todo solamente. ¿Conjetura qué? ¡Sus amigos del mudo-asno son no más elegantes que los empleados de Denny, así que beba para arriba!

Erhalten Sie Freie Getränke Weg von Etwas Milden Bekannten. Vergessen Sie es nicht ist Ihr Geburtstag. Seien Sie sicher, stoic aber traurig zu sein beim Neu legen zu ihnen, daß Sie zum Erscheinen ganz alleine kamen. Vermutung was? Ihre Dumbesel Freunde sind nicht intelligenter als Angestellte Dennys, also trinken Sie oben!

Krijg Vrije Dranken van Sommige Milde Kennissen. Vergeet niet het uw verjaardag is. Ben zeker stoic maar droevig te zijn wanneer het aflossen aan hen dat u aan de show al alleen kwam. Gissing wat? Uw stom-ezelsvrienden zijn neen slimmer dan de werknemers van Denny, zo drank omhoog!

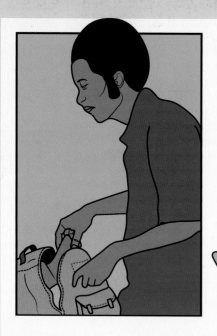

NO EAR PLUGS

Ningunos enchufes del oído

Keineohrbolzen

Geen oorstoppen

(1) # CORRECT HECKLING PROCEDURE
Procedimiento que interrumpe correcto / Korrektes hechelndes verfahren /
Correcte heckling procedure

(2) # BATHROOM PROTOCOL
Protocolo del cuarto de baño / Badezimmerprotokoll /
Het protocol van de badkamers

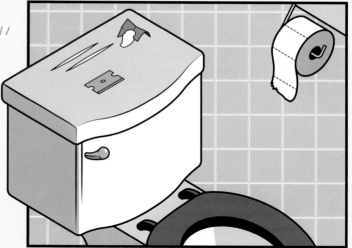

NO SOAP

Ningún jabón

Keine seife

Geen zeep

NO TOILET PAPER

Ningún papel de tocador

Kein toilettenpapier

Geen toilet document

NO ROCK DROPPING

El ningún caer de la roca

Kein felsenfallen

Geen rots het dalen

 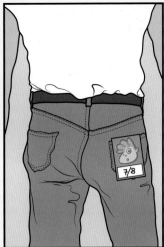  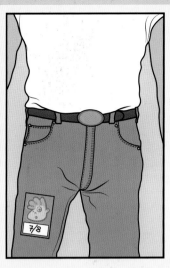

NO SHORTS OR CUT-OFFS

Ningunos cortocircuitos o atajos

Keine kurzschlüsse oder abkürzungen

Geen borrels of besnoeiing-offs-besnoeiing

3 **PROPER GUEST PASS PLACEMENT**
Colocación apropiada del paso de la huésped / Korrekte Gastdurchlaufplazierung / De juiste plaatsing van de gastpas

4 **THE HIPSTER "NOD"**
El cabeceo del hipster / Das hippie-kopfnicken / Het teken hipster

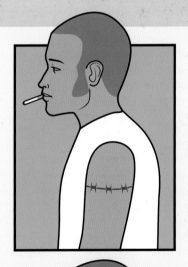

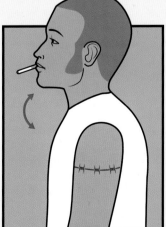

NO NOSE PICKING

Ninguna cosecha de la nariz

Kein nase sammeln

Geen neus het plukken

STANDARD CLUB LAYOUT
Disposición estándar del club
Standardvereinlayout
Standaard clublay-out

FOLLOW THE YELLOW ARROWS
Siga las flechas amarillas
Folgen Sie den gelben Pfeilen
Volg de gele pijlen

ROCK CLUB SAFETY INSTRUCTIONS

Instrucciones de seguridad del club de la roca

Felsenverein-Sicherheitsvorschriften

Van de de clubveiligheid van de rots de instructies

Concept: **HENRY H. OWINGS, GARTH JOHNSON & SETH JABOUR**   Illustrations: **SETH JABOUR**

5 IN CASE OF INTOXICATION
En caso de que de la intoxicación / Falls von der intoxikation /
In het geval van intoxicatie

If you see an unconscious patron lying on the floor, poke with foot. Whether it does or doesn't move, exit area immediately.

Si usted ve a patrón inconsciente el mentir en el piso, empuje con el pie. Si hace o no se mueve, área de salida inmediatamente.

Wenn Sie einen unbewußten Gönner sehen, auf dem Fußboden zu liegen, stoßen Sie mit Fuß. Wenn es tut oder nicht bewegt, Ausgabebereich sofort.

Als u een onbewuste patroon ziet liggend op de vloer, por met voet. Als het doet of zich niet beweegt, uitgang gebied onmiddellijk.

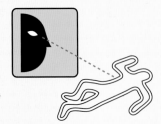

Be cautious of unidentified fluids on the floor.

Sea cauteloso de líquidos no identificados en el piso.

Seien Sie von nicht identifizierten Flüssigkeiten auf dem Fußboden vorsichtig.

Voorzichtig ben van niet geïdentificeerde vloeistoffen op de vloer.

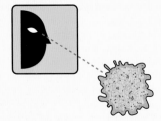

6 IN THE EVENT YOU ARE SHORT
En el acontecimiento usted es corto / Im falle sind sie kurz /
In de gebeurtenis bent u kort

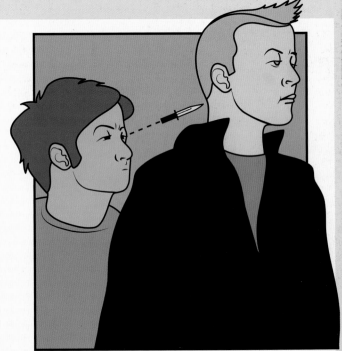

Caution! Big heavy feet in steel tipped boots overhead!

¡Precaución! ¡Los pies pesados grandes en acero inclinaron cargadores por encima!

Achtung! Grosse schwere füße im stahl spitzten matten obenliegend!

Voorzichtigheid! Grote zware voeten in staal getipte laarzenoverheadkosten!

Caution! Flying bottles!

¡Precaución! ¡Botellas del vuelo!

Achtung! Flugwesenflaschen!

Voorzichtigheid! Vliegende flessen!

Ten Steps To Get The Most Out Of Your Rock Show Experience (continued)

Goal 6: Record The Show For Bootlegging Purposes

Preparation: Have (insert on-line webzine here) cards printed up with your name. Show up right before band takes the stage. Apologize for being late, complain about a specific airline and how you'll never fly with them again. Let the sound man know how excited you are to not be recording some lame shit like Coldplay for once and how the band he's running sound for is the real deal. If you're lucky, the band will get temporarily popular like At The Drive-In and you can buy that 50" flat-screen you've been wanting with bootleg sales.

Registre La Demostración Para Los Propósitos De Bootlegging. Preparación: Tenga tarjetas en línea de piedra del balanceo impresas para arriba con su nombre. Demuestre para arriba a la derecha antes de que la venda tome la etapa. Discúlpese por ser atrasado, y quéjese por una línea aérea específica y cómo usted nunca volará con ellos otra vez. Déjelo saber excitada la es para una vez no registrar algo de mierda coja como Coldplay y cómo la venda el es corriente sonido para es el reparto verdadero. ¿Si usted es afortunado la venda conseguirá temporalmente popular como en la impulsión adentro y usted puede comprar que 50? plano-pantalla que usted ha estado deseando con ventas del bootleg del Internet.

Notieren Sie Das Erscheinen Zu den Bootlegging Zwecken. Vorbereitung: Haben Sie Digital Club Network-Karten oben gedruckt mit Ihrem Namen. Stellen Sie oben nach rechts dar, bevor Band das Stadium nimmt. Entschuldigen Sie sich für Sein spät, und beschweren Sie sich über eine spezifische Fluglinie und wie Sie nie mit ihnen wieder fliegen. Informieren Sie ihn, wie Ihnen für einmal, etwas lame Scheiße wie Coldplay nicht zu notieren aufgeregt sind und wie das Band er laufend ist, Ton für das reale Abkommen ist. Wenn Sie glücklich sind, erhält das Band vorübergehend wie am Antrieb innen populär und Sie können kaufen daß 50? Flachschirm, den Sie mit Internet bootleg Verkäufen gewünscht haben.

Registreer de Show voor het Smokkelen van Doeleinden. Voorbereiding: Heb de Digital Club Network online kaarten van de Steen die omhoog met uw naam worden gedrukt. Net toon omhoog alvorens de band het stadium neemt. Verontschuldig me voor het zijn laat, en klaag over een specifieke luchtvaartlijn en hoe u nooit met hen opnieuw zult vliegen. Laat hem weten hoe opgewekt u voor een keer wat lame shit zoals Coldplay niet moet registreren en hoe de band hij lopend geluid heeft voor de echte overeenkomst is. Als u gelukkig bent zal de band populair tijdelijk als bij de Aandrijving binnenkomen en kunt u dat 50 kopen? flat-screen u met Internet illegale verkoop hebt gewild.

Goal 7: Get Free Merch

Preparation: Find out bass player's name. During the set, go up to their merch guy and tell him that you're Dan ____ (have the same last name as the bass player) and that you are his cousin, but have to leave because you have to be at work at 6:00 a.m. Of course, your cousin (the bass player) told you to grab whatever you wanted, so feel free to get multiple copies to trade in later.

Consiga La Mercancía Libre. Preparación: Descubra a jugador bajo conocido. Durante el sistema, va hasta su individuo del merch y le dice que usted sea ____ de Dan (tenga el mismo nombre pasado que el jugador bajo) y que usted es su primo, pero tiene que dirigir encendido hacia fuera porque usted tiene que estar en el trabajo en 6:00 a. m. Por supuesto su primo el jugador bajo le dijo asir lo que usted deseó así que sensación libre conseguir copias múltiples para negociar adentro más adelante.

Erhalten Sie Freie Waren. Vorbereitung: Finden Sie des Baß-Spielers Namens heraus. Während des Satzes bis zu ihrem merch Halteseil und erklärt geht ihm, daß daß Sie Dan ____ sind (haben Sie den gleichen letzten Namen wie der Baß-Spieler) und daß Sie sein Vetter sind, aber müssen an heraus vorangehen, weil Sie an der Arbeit bei 6:00 a sein müssen. m. Selbstverständlich erklärte Ihr Vetter der Baß-Spieler Ihnen, zu ergreifen, was auch immer Sie wünschten, also das Gefühl frei, mehrfache Kopien zu erhalten, um innen später zu handeln.

Krijg Vrije Koopwaar. Voorbereiding: Kom de naam van de BasSpeler te weten. Tijdens de reeks, ga aan hun merchkerel uit en vertel hem dat u Dan ____ bent (hebben de zelfde laatste naam zoals de basspeler) en dat u zijn neef bent, maar moet uit leiden omdat u op het werk bij 6:00 a moet zijn. m. Natuurlijk vertelde uw neef de basspeler u om te grijpen wat u zo gevoel vrij wilde om veelvoudige exemplaren ertoe te brengen om later handel te drijven in.

Goal 8: Throw Band Off With Your Best Heckle

(See elsewhere in this book for more detailed instructions.)
Example: "Quit playing that homophobic hate shit!" Warning: Do not let the band see that the heckles are coming from you or the next steps will be <u>much</u> more difficult.

La Venda Del Tiro Apagado Con Su Mejor Interrumpe. Véase Chunklets 14 y 16 junto con lista del sabotaje de la demostración en esta edición para más instrucciones. ejemplo: ¡El jugar parado que homophobic odie la mierda! Advertencia: No deje la venda ver que interrumpe están viniendo de usted o los pasos siguientes serán mucho más difíciles.

Throw-Band Weg Mit Ihrem Besten Hecheln. Sehen Sie Chunklets 14 und 16 zusammen mit Erscheinensabotageliste in dieser Ausgabe für mehr Anweisungen. Beispiel: Beendigtes Spielen, daß homophobic Scheiße hassen Sie! Warnung: Lassen Sie das Band nicht sehen, daß kommen von Ihnen hechelt, oder die folgenden Schritte viel schwieriger sind.

Werp weg Band met Uw Beste Heckle. Zie Chunklets 14 en 16 samen met sabotagelijst in deze kwestie voor meer instructies tonen. Voorbeeld: Opgehouden met speel die homophobic haat shit! Het waarschuwen: Laat de band niet zien dat heckles uit u komen of de volgende stappen zullen veel moeilijker zijn.

Goal 9: Get Backstage

Preparation: Procure a water squirt bottle. Right after the band finishes their set, spray yourself down as if you had been sweating profusely. Snag one of the band's spare guitars and walk past the bouncer, watching the backstage door. Throw in something clever like, "Hey, would you make sure no one grabs any of our pedals?"

Consiga Entre bastidores. Preparación: El agua arroja a chorros la botella. Derecho después de que la venda acabe su sistema, aerosol usted mismo abajo como si usted hubiera estado sudando profusamente. Gancho uno las guitarras de repuesto del la venda y caminata más allá del bouncer que mira la puerta entre bastidores. Tiro adentro ¿Hey, usted se cercioraria de nadie ganchos agarradores de nuestros pedales?

Erhalten Sie Backstage. Vorbereitung: Wasser sprizt Flasche. Recht, nachdem das Band ihren Satz beendet, Spray sich unten, als ob Sie ausgiebig geschwitzt hatten. Baumstumpf einer des Ersatzder guitarren und des Wegs Bandes hinter dem bouncer, welches die backstage Tür aufpaßt. Throw innen "Hey, würden Sie keins Zupacken irgendwie unserer Pedale überprüfen? "

Krijg Coulisse. Voorbereiding: De fles van het water squirt. Het recht na de band neer beëindigt hun reeks, nevel zelf alsof u overvloedig had gezweet. Winkelhaak één van band extra guitars en de gang voorbij bouncer die op de coulissedeur let. Binnen werp "Hey, zou u ervoor zorgen niemand om het even welk van onze pedalen grijpt ?"

Goal 10: Hang With The Band

You already have the guitar with you, go up to the guitar player and tell him someone was trying to steal it. Tell them you're touring with whatever bad FM edge station band is playing the local enormodome that evening. They'll kiss your ass because secretly they'd love to be playing there themselves. Take advantage of whatever drugs, booze and groupies they have, and then get the hell out of there before anyone connects the dots.

Caída Con La Venda. Usted ya tiene la guitarra con usted, va hasta el jugador de la guitarra y le dice que alguien intentara robarla. Dígales que viajar con cualquier mala venda de la estación del borde de FM está jugando el Enormodome que tarde. Besarán su asno porque amarían secretamente jugar el Enormodome ellos mismos. Aprovéchese de cualesquiera drogas, licores y groupies tienen y después consiguen el infierno de allí antes de que cualquier persona conecte los puntos.

Fall Mit Dem Band. Sie bereits haben die Guitarre mit Ihnen, gehen bis zum Guitarre Spieler und erklären ihm, daß jemand versuchte, sie zu stehlen. Erklären Sie ihnen Ihr Reisen mit, was schlechtes FM Rand-Stationband das Enormodome spielt, das Abend. Sie küssen Ihren Esel, weil geheim sie das Enormodome würden spielen mögen selbst. Ziehen Sie Nutzen aus, was Drogen, Schnäpse und groupies sie haben und dann die Hölle aus dort herausbekommen, bevor jedermann die Punkte anschließt.

Hang met de Band. U reeds hebt guitar met u, gaat aan de guitar speler uit en vertelt hem iemand probeerde om het te stelen. Vertel hen uw het reizen met welk slechte band ook van de randcFm post Enormodome die avond speelt. Zij zullen uw ezel kussen omdat in het geheim van they'd houd Enormodome zelf te spelen. Haal voordeel uit welk drugs, booze en groupies zij ook daar hebben en dan de hel uit worden alvorens iedereen de punten verbindt.

Goal 11: Next Show – Repeat 1 Through 10

La Demostración Siguiente, Repita Los Pasos 1 A 10
Folgendes Erscheinen. Wiederholen Sie Schritte 1 Bis 10
Volgende toon. Herhaal Stappen 1 door 10

PROMOTER EXCUSES

For why people didn't show up to your show*
(a.k.a. Why you'll never hear "Your band sucks" or "I didn't do my fucking job")

by Brian Teasley • illustrations by Eryc Simmerer

1. People just aren't getting out after 9/11.

2. There have been too many good shows lately.

3. The old promoter quit and the new promoter didn't have time to really do anything.

4. No one comes to shows on ____day (usually Sunday through Wednesday, although I love "Yeah, Thursdays can be a weird one"), but I'll have you come back on a weekend with this really great local opener who draws a couple hundred people every time they play.

5. Everyone went to _____ (vacation spot—I love to get Ibiza whilst in Europe, just a personal fave) for holiday.

6. An unstoppable juggernaut of a draw (e.g. Modest Mouse, Le Tigre, or Pinback) is playing down the street.

7. The rain really stopped a lot of people from coming out.

8. Your opening band really pissed off some people last time you played, and I tried to tell the booking agent, but he/she wouldn't listen to me.

9. Complete mystery. I put up 400 posters, got advertising on the radio, and took out print ads, and I just can't figure out what happened.

10. (Feel free to do your best Alice Cooper.) "School's Out For Summer."

11. The new movie in a series of sequels and prequels opened tonight. Thanks, Keanu.

12. Report cards just came out, and a lot of kids got shitty grades.

13. There has been a rampant drug epidemic and people aren't spending money on anything except their "drug" habits.

14. A recent outbreak of multiple suicides has occurred and the scene is unraveling.

15. Everyone just went to the free in-store you played instead of actually paying money to come to the real show.

16. People were worried about some sort of natural disaster (brush fires, hurricanes, twisters, blizzards, a horde of locusts, etc.).

17. The Great White thing has parents freaked out about their kids going to shows.

18. There were a lot of kickin' house parties going on tonight.

19. Some huge sporting event is taking place on television (NBA playoffs, Super Bowl, World Series, College Bowl game, or World Cup).

20. There is a vigil being held for a local punk rock legend that just died in a "pit accident."

*All of these are based on actual lies, bullshit, and incoherent cocaine-speak stories that have been told to me. The lesson here is that when you were in school, if you were the person who didn't contribute shit to your group project and let everyone else do the work, then being a rock promoter is probably a solid career choice for an asshole like you.

KEEP SUCKING!

Truth, heckles & consequences

by Dag Luther Gooch with Robert Schriner • illustration by Joe Peery

On many different occassions, we at *Chunklet* have published tutorials on heckling. How-tos, When-tos, and Why-tos; all of them very informative. Yet, some of you still don't quite understand the pleasure of yelling "Fuck your boat, Blackbeard!" at June of '44, "Cap'n JAZZ!!" at Promise Ring, or "My balls, your mouth!" at Cat Power. These stolen moments will not only enrich your life, but the lives of others. So, as one final attempt to get our readership to take their heroes down a notch, here are twelve heckles and their consequences.

Repeatedly screamed "See No Evil" at **Matthew Sweet** show. Bitched out by guitarist Richard Lloyd. Girlfriend chimed in "You're an asshole who just bitched out one of the three people who bought your solo record." She would later buy a Television poster and put it up over my amplifier to keep me from playing guitar because she thought I was horrible.

Shouted "Play 'Cuts Like A Knife!'" at **Cracker**, standing next to guys in Antenna (Jake Smith, John Strohm, on tour with Cracker) who moved immediately. Yelled "Summer of '69" and had to jump out of the way before getting snatched bald.

"Aren't you gonna play some Big Star?" to **Alex Chilton**, countered by "I thought I might." No Big Star songs ever actually played. "The Letter" sufficed as show was basically free anyway due to door guy connection.

I once saw **The Delta 72** play in a record store. This was after their Man...or Astro-Man? tour and several other tours that had them playing clubs here in town. So the setting was small as I pushed my way to the front of the stage wearing sunglasses and played a harmonica through their entire set. I don't know if a harmonica really counts as a heckler's tool, but it was used in the spirit. No one in the band said anything; they all just sort of looked on in a sheepish kind of way, not sure what to do.

"I Wanna Destroy You" at the **Jazz Butcher**. Reply: "You've undoubtedly mixed us up with another group of middle-aged twats." This was followed by "Somewhere Over The Rainbow."

After Jeff Mangum of **Neutral Milk Hotel** at packed-to-hilt show said "We are Neutral Milk Hotel," I shouted "We know." Instantly followed by Mangum's head-drooping embarrassment, one "2-Headed Boy," several "Rock my shit"'s and "I love you, motherfuckin' bitch"'s, and later a big drunk bearhug.

I picked up a Garfield-in-a-rabbit-suit stuffed animal at a gas station on the way to San Diego to see Teengenerate. His name became Garbunny and looked completely absurd. I held it up to **Mary Lou Lord** as she was playing the opening spot. She took one look at it, stopped in the middle of a song, started crying and walked off the stage.

"You rock my fuckin' balls off" at **Modest Mouse**, countered with gibberish shouting that sounded vaguely like original heckle. Later invited by Isaac Brock to throw up in a bathroom with him. Invitation refused. After Brock's trip to the men's room, I had to look at, walk through, stand in, piss in, and not add, to said vomit.

"Play that song that I heard on MTV that one time" at **The Jack Rubies**. Song I heard on MTV was played, followed by "Play it again." Song not repeated.

Shouted "Turn the fuck up! I can't fucking hear you!" at **Belle and Sebastian**. 2,000 very quietly angry fans snarl at me, including some guys in Spoon. Then went to the sound guy who at first refused to turn it up until asked "How much did you pay to be here? How far did you fucking drive? There are no less than 50 speakers up there, and I can't hear a fucking thing!" After turning up the mains, he said "if anyone complains, I'll have to turn it back down." This added to the irony of an over-paid balding mullethead soundman who was wearing a Sex Pistols t-shirt.

Once again standing with guys in Antenna, shouted "Fat Bottom Girls," and "I Want To Ride My Bicycle" at **Jellyfish**. This time, Freda Boner (Love) was also in tow. "We have to tour with these guys," she says to us. One of them says, "We already gave up on trying to make him stop."

A friend of mine actually got on stage with this local band, and while facing them yelled the song title "Suicide is Painless" over and over for the entire set; during songs and after. He completely fucked them up as they tried to keep it together and ignore him.

DREAMO VERSUS EMO

Q: What do you get when you mix a dumb rock dude with a wanna-be art fag?

A: An Emo rocker.

by Henry H. Owings & Brian Teasley • illustration by Joe Peery

It is no surprise that a recent "Hot Topic" in emo-land is the idea that the genre is utterly sexist. Somewhere along the line, the generically dumb rock dude figured that he'd get way more coochie if he'd write aloof yet "smart" melodies, dress the lyrical content with star-crossed, forlorned relationships that he never actually had, and, most importantly, come up with some limp-dick name that reads like a bad haiku. Soon after, the newly-christened emo guy gets so much tail that the band van smells like a Tokyo fish market. But what's in the name, you say?

Think about it: sure, a cheap Mexican-made Strat can work well as a girl-fishing rod, but the best bait on this emo-pussy-hook-scheme is an arty, 3-word-to-sentence-long non sequitur name, such as Screaming Under A Sky Yet To Fall. The names are so goddamned innumerable, grossly predictable, and downright banal that if you've ever written bad poetry in high school, you can come up with 30 or so in under five minutes. Not a believer? Think emo is too pure to be so trite? Put your faith where your sleeve tattoos are and try to distinguish real-life from hastily written bullshit. Emo or Dreamo—we'll never listen to it either way.

1. Pass the Fiddle
2. 5 Minute Penalty
3. Pen and Paper
4. How The West Was Done
5. Black Without Blue
6. Give Up The Ghost
7. Mary, A Ship Won't Sink
8. Most Precious Blood
9. Rise Against
10. Murder By Death
11. A Static Lullaby
12. Feel The Stick
13. Eleven Years On
14. Sky Vs. Ground
15. Diet Commercial
16. Anti-Anti
17. Hey Mercedes
18. Growl or Grimmace
19. The Love Scene
20. Pound for Lb.
21. Mob Quota
22. Slump Revivalist
23. Last Place Winners
24. Hotwire
25. Slick Shoes
26. My Friendly Ghost
27. Eyes Wide As Saucers
28. Taking Back Sunday
29. The Starting Line
30. Chubby Drawn Grind
31. Snapshots of an Alive Ghost
32. Bedroom Tangle Jar
33. Year of the Rabbit
34. For Rodney Allen
35. Stun
36. Everytime I Die

37. Earlybird Story
38. Ferret Keeper
39. The Rocket Summer
40. Birthday Death Ray
41. Dead Guy
42. Kill Position
43. Clue To Kalo
44. Cult of Luna
45. The Letters Organize
46. A Faith Called Chaos
47. Nobody Wins
48. Ryan's Hope
49. Hot Rod Circuit
50. The Escape Engine
51. Anthym
52. The Beyond
53. Nova Scotia Spells Blood
54. Thousand Fool Crotch
55. Role Model Machine
56. Vaux
57. Pink Grease
58. Follow Her Surprise
59. Ultimate Fakebook
60. Bleeding Through
61. Daylight Darkness
62. Song In The Air
63. Pulled Out Of A Hat
64. Dead By July
65. The Long Baths
66. Personal Heart Ship
67. Sex on Saturday
68. All Night
69. Express to Ho Chi Minh
70. The Road Ahead
71. Point/Counterpoint
72. The New Photo Op

73. Red WaterBlood Water
74. Apple Dunk Shot
75. Saturday Looks Good To Me
76. Cold Hard Cash
77. Panic In Detroit
78. Fairview
79. Pelican
80. Mr. Oblivion
81. Feel The Silence
82. Fortress of Lonely Chairs
83. Winner of The Weak
84. Natural American Spirit
85. Save My Baby
86. Nerves of Steel
87. My Shadow's Shadow
88. Mark The Arrival
89. Boy Sets Fire
90. Ground or Gorilla
91. Blue-Eyed Boy Mister Death
92. Make-Out Closet
93. Last One In The Hole
94. The Last Lap Dance
95. Kind of Like Spitting
96. Mock Orange
97. Flash For Pants
98. The Stereo
99. Count The Stars
100. The Shiela Divide
101. Amish Buggy Accident
102. Hope Conspiracy
103. Avenue of the Strongest
104. Vendetta Red
105. AM Music
106. Cigarette Poltergeist
107. Hands at Ten and Two

THESE ARE THE BAND NAMES THAT ARE REAL, CHUMP: 6, 8, 9, 10, 11, 17, 19, 24, 28, 29, 33, 35, 36, 39, 41, 43, 44, 45, 46, 47, 48, 49, 50, 51, 52, 56, 57, 59, 60, 62, 64, 68, 75, 77, 78, 79, 89, 91, 95, 96, 98, 99, 100, 102, 103, 104, 105.

TIME IS RARELY KIND

118 acts that will never become retro-hip

by Jordan N. Mamone

I am constantly astounded by what passes for cool in the ironic sandbox in which we play. Every year, some emerging, faddish rock subculture generates renewed interest in another set of ghastly, washed-up groups from decades past. Never did I think I'd overhear some Terrastock casualty espousing the virtues of Hot Tuna and Moby Grape bootlegs. Or watch an idiot stoner dude comb eBay for Uriah Heep and Budgie albums. Or punch out a post-rocking Trans Am fanboy for trying to convince me of the merits of Ultravox and Dokken. Or endure the complete Walker Brothers catalog while brutally skullfucking a trio of malnourished, lollipop-licking Belle and Sebastian chicks. (Their androgynous boyfriends are away "on holiday" in the U.K., shopping for Momus imports and daydreaming of being sodomized by Nick Drake's corpse.) Christ, even emo-core has made a comeback! Spare me.

As of this writing, all of the aforementioned performers still suck. And they will always suck, no matter how many times they fall in and out of fashion. Miraculously, we are living in an age when Abba, Wings, Van Halen, Zapp, Gary Numan, OMD and the Carpenters are all respected names again—even considered god-damned classics in certain circles! But never fear, my misanthropic friend, the untouchable bands and solo artists listed below will never fetch collector's prices at the local snippy record boutique. Today's brightest stars will not drop their names as influences. Odious critics will not "rediscover" their "lost classics" from the cutout bins. Their songs will continue to spell nothing but disgust, bewilderment and misfortune for you and your precious peer group.

True iconoclasts must now embrace, worship and emulate the following 118 wretched relics, no matter how horrible their music may be. Open wide, hipster, and remember, shit smells rank no matter how much of it your friends enjoy eating.

Sheriff

Device

Goldfinger

BoDeans

Killer Dwarfs

Blues Image

Arzachel

Hipsway

An Emotional Fish

Life, Sex, and Death

The Brooklyn Bridge

Boris Grebenshikov

Collective Soul

Lone Justice

K7

Transvision Vamp

Flesh for Lulu

MC 900 Ft. Jesus

The Christians

Staff Sergeant Barry Sadler

Freaky Fuckin' Weirdos

Green Apple Quickstep

The Marshall Tucker Band

Shalamar

Mama's Pride

Ugly Kid Joe

Brand X

Jackyl

Nudeswirl

Moxy

McRad

Ambrosia

Vanilla Trainwreck

Bogshed

Little Caesar

The Toadies

Pig Bros

Dayglo Abortions

Roachford

Chokebore

Get Smart!

Al B. Sure!

Elvin Bishop

Melissa Manchester

Asleep at the Wheel

Disneyland After Dark

John Cafferty and the Beaver Brown Band

Giuffrea

DeBarge

Blodwyn Pig

Eddie Money

Ritual Tension

Gene Loves Jezebel

U.K.

Tonio K

Tora Tora

Great White

Curved Air

Exile

Green Jello/Green Jelly

Urban Dance Squad

Always August

The Woodentops

The Blue Nile

Kixx

Tangier

Jason and the Scorchers

Jobriath

Keith

Lindisfarne

Klaatu

Civ

Mr. Big

Winter Hours

Wishbone Ash

Webb Wilder

Stigmata A Go Go

Phillip Michael Thomas

My Life with the Thrill Kill Kult

Ready for the World

Fearless Iranians from Hell

World Domination Enterprises

The Jump in the Saddle Band

Naked Eyes

Robbie Neville

Pablo Cruise

Starcastle

Mr. Mister

GTR

SWA

The Jets

Glass Tiger

Pond

Starship

Point Blank

Blues Magoos

Blood Circus

Loose Ends

Gut Bank

PMS

L'Trimm

Charlie

Jermaine Stewart

Stikky

Shai

Nektar

Level 42

Eddie Rabbit

Johnny Hates Jazz

Musical Youth

Nelson

Kathy Mattea

Wet Wet Wet

Bang Tango

Shirts

Spoiler

Camel

Stinky Toys

Now add your own, genius...

OUT-OF-TOWN SLEEP OVER!

25 ways to make a touring band's stay at your house much more memorable

by Robert Schriner • illustration by Eryc Simmerer

We've all been in the position at some show where a band is desperate for a place to stay. Sometimes you end up being the guy that offers, and sometimes you're the guy who gets volunteered for the job. This has happened to me a number of times which inspired me to recommend a list of things you could do to a band that you don't particularly like, but somehow end up hosting.

1. Tell them they have to sleep in your yard because you already promised another band your living room.

2. Offer them dog food in an attractive serving dish.

3. Play a copy of their record repeatedly at a really loud volume.

4. Send them out to get beer, then turn all the lights out, lock the doors, and go to bed.

5. Set up an easel and draw each member of the band in a really insulting fashion, and then insist that they buy the drawings.

6. Walk around naked.

7. Walk around naked with a gun.

8. Walk around naked with a gun and a bottle of whiskey.

9. Walk around naked with a gun and a bottle of whiskey, and ask them why they don't like to party.

10. Leave the show before they can, and give them directions to someone else's house...like a cop.

11. Don't be afraid to show off your interpretive dance routine, especially when they're trying to sleep.

12. Tell them that *you're* sleeping in the van tonight.

13. If the band is Seam, tell them your girlfriend is coming over after work and that she likes to "get freaky."

14. Have their van towed from your house while they're sleeping.

15. Insist on jamming with them regardless of your total lack of musical talent.

16. Fake Tourette Syndrome.

17. Tear your house apart "looking for something," but do this in total silence.

18. Hold your index fingers straight up while holding your thumbs toward each other so your hands resemble what a movie director sees. Film the band through you fingers and thumbs and remain absolutely silent. Do this for a minimum of an hour.

19. Invite a member to try your very own homemade vodka. If you don't have any, use mustard.

20. Block their van in your driveway and deny any knowledge of whose car it is.

21. Steal their van's license plate to put on another band's van later.

22. Call the police and tell them you had a party and some sketchy uninvited guests showed up and won't leave.

23. Accuse them of being racists because of arty lyrics.

24. Order more pizza than any of you could possibly consume under the name of one of the band members.

25. Have a friend call your house as a promoter calling to cancel the show in the next town.

ROCK SHOW SABOTAGE!

35 surefire ways to ruin a show for the suckers who actually paid to get in

Partially attempted by Henry H. Owings and Brian Teasley • illustration by Eryc Simmerer

1. De-tune heads while band is eating dinner.

2. Hit power breaker during band's set. *[Classic]*

3. Find out guitar player's girlfriend's name and yell that she gives good head between songs.

4. Find out guitar player's mother's name and yell that she gives good head between songs.

5. Cover the back of one of their guitar necks with Vaseline.

6. Throw (lit or unlit) fireworks on stage.

7. Fake a fight with a friend during a ballad.

8. Open a jar of deer hunting urine musk on stage seconds before the band performs (note: also yell "Looks like the rut is starting early this year" during their set).

9. Put a bee's nest inside the kick drum microphone hole.

10. Pay ten girls to chant "Rapist!" at the lead singer.

11. Be in the opening band, and play the headlining band's set before them.

12. Get a job as the house sound guy and put flange on everything. After the band's set, tell them you used to be Tears for Fears touring sound guy.

13. Bring a megaphone, and repeat all the band's in between song chatter.

14. Convince local Nazi organizations that the band features former members of Skrewdriver.

15. Two words: pepper spray.

16. Hide an amp near the stage and play along in the bathroom via a wireless unit.

17. Spike band's water with LSD or Ecstasy.

18. Glue all the picks to the stage floor.

19. Throw $10,000 of fake money into the crowd seconds before the band's encore.

20. Set fire to a bag of leaves (or hair), and throw it on the soundboard.

21. Get a photo pass for the show, and bring an 1890's era (read: pull the hood over your head to take the picture) camera which must be set on stage in order for it to work.

22. Call all local radio stations and tell them the show is cancelled. (Extra points for rescheduling show for the next week at the local humane shelter and/or rival club.)

23. Hire a professional wrestler to challenge the singer to a match.

24. Help band load in early, telling the band you're part of the club staff. Then fifteen minutes into their set, give them the "pointing-at-your-watch-pissed-off" face, mouthing that they have one more song left.

25. Get all of your friend's to help throw 5,000 teabags at the drummer throughout the entire show. (Bonus: try to hit his water cup and make actual tea!)

26. Make fictitious pornographic video tape boxes featuring the band's logo and their faces on the actors/actresses. When the merch guy is gone for even a second, stuff the video tapes in the t-shirt box. Immediately call the cops and inform them that the band is distributing pornographic material to minors. Stand back and watch the drama unfold!

27. Lock band in dressing room as the crowd chants for an encore. *[Classic]*

28. Hook a CD player in the soundboard and play studio versions of the band's songs over the PA while they perform the exact same songs live.

29. Bring your dog to the show where the guitarist routinely jumps into the crowd (e.g. The Mooney Suzuki) and claim he kicked your dog. Cause as much of a ruckus as you can.

30. Put cooking grease on the stage prior to performance.

31. Pull fire alarm during band's set. *[Classic]*

32. Tell the soundman you're there from a webzine to record the show, and run an auxiliary out of the vocals to a harmonizer allowing you to detune anything in any fashion you see fit.

33. Have a banner rigged at the back of the stage that you can control to have pulled down and at height of performance, trigger the release of a "We Suck Dick For Crack" banner.

34. Pay the local pregnant crack whore to claim the bass player got her pregnant for "his mama's baby."

35. Just let the band suck on their own.

CLAP YO' HANDS AND SAY 'EH'

A handy guide to musicians' "mysterious" non-verbal gestures

by Henry H. Owings with Brian Teasley • illustrations by Adam Fuchs

Sometimes it takes us by surprise here at *Chunklet* HQ when we realize that many of our readers aren't the social creatures we fancy ourselves. More importantly, when thrust into a rock club with smoke in the air and PBR cans on the floor, most of the subtle hand gestures that musicians use to communicate both with each other and with the crowd in attendance seem to go underneath most people's radar. So, as per usual, we are here to explain for the as-yet ill-informed that these heretofore perplexing non-verbals are to rock'n'roll what Semaphore Code is to boats at sea. Soak it up, mateys!

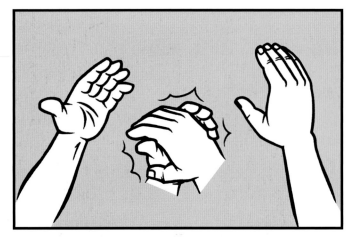

GET TO MINDLESSLY CLAPPING, YOU MONKEYS!

When a band is unable to motivate the crowd to clap along (typical), they make the drummer stand up with his hands over his head in an attempt to convince the crowd to get with it.

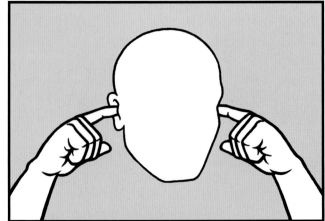

THE MONITORS ARE FEEDING BACK

For the first couple of songs of any given show, giving the soundman monitor instructions is acceptable. However, after that, all bets are off. Maybe he's ballin' some chick in the booth, but, regardless, this gesture ain't good news.

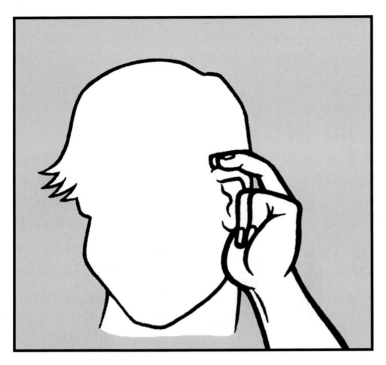

I CAN'T HEAR YA

The perfect gesture to defuse a potential heckling disaster! For added effect, do this in tandem with sheets of guitar distortion in the background for comedic bonus points.

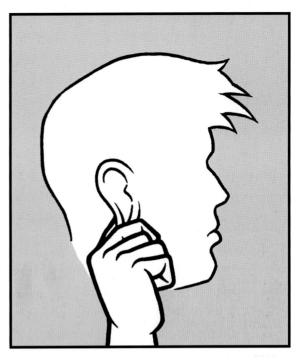

THE CAROL BURNETT

Baseball pitcher cues are entirely useless unless they're punctuated with some of the classics, like this one from early-80's television!

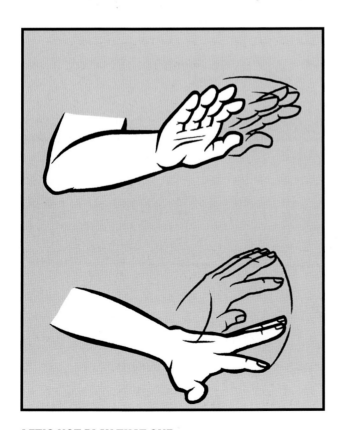

LET'S NOT PLAY THAT ONE

Even though the ink on the set list has dried, this gesture is an immediate cue to bail and move on to the next song.

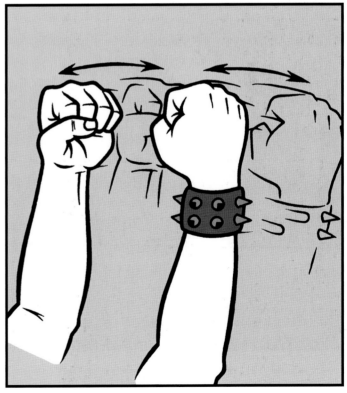

PUMP WITH ME, YA'LL!

This is usually a call-and-response thing where the singer starts and then the people closest to the stage join in. Cheesy? Oh, you bet.

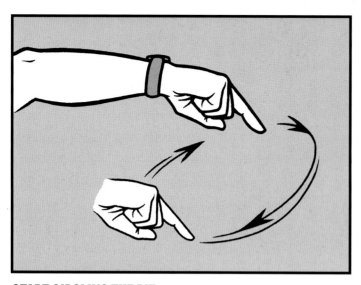

START CIRCLING THE PIT
Behold: I give you the hardcore equivalent to line dancing. Now bow to your partner, sucker! For shits and giggles, send the pit into a tizzy by shifting it counterclockwise!

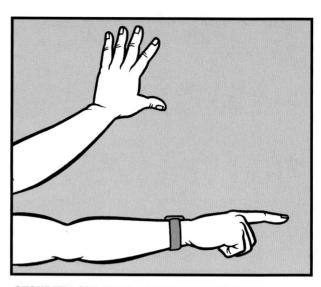

SECURITY, GET THAT ASSHOLE OUTTA HERE
Some shithammered fratboy jag bag cold-cocks his girlfriend during the band's ballad. Stop the show, and keelhaul that sucker mid-song!

STRAIGHT EDGE
Only a dogma as dense as "No Drink, No Drugs, No Sex" could have a rite of passage as banal as crossing your arms.

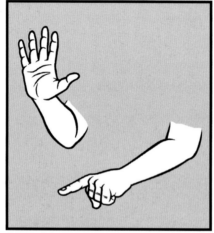

THAT'S $5 FOR FUCKIN' UP!
Be just like the Godfather of Soul and penalize band members for each infraction. I gotcha! That's $5!

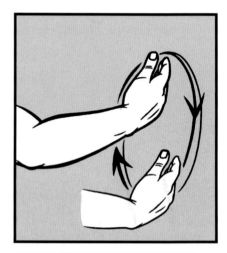

C'MON, WE'RE LOSING THE FLOW
The perfect set is never longer than 45 minutes, but, just remember, tuning can completely destroy momentum.

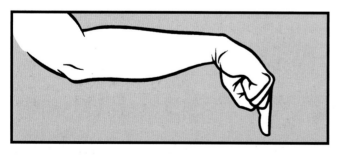

MONITORS DOWN
Too much tambourine in your mix? The singer's voice driving you insane? No sweat, my fair-haired musician-type amigo. When it's too much, don't get angry, just turn it down.

MONITORS UP
Can't hear yourself over the seven Marshall stacks on stage? Need to actually hear the drummer like you do in practice? This li'l move will do the trick nicely!

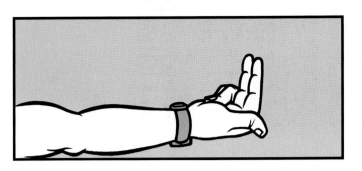

HEY SWEET THING, COME HERE

Immortalized by Gene Simmons but employed *ad nauseam* by horndogs masquerading as musicians all over the world. Hey baby, yeah, you! Let me show you my 'full' range! Backstage, 'natch.

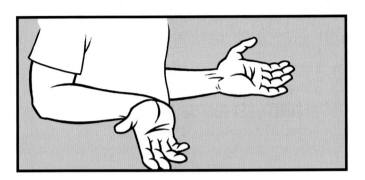

WHAT'S THE BIG HOLD UP?

Just when you think that everything's going smoothly on stage, the bass player breaks a string and shoves broken glass in his hand simultaneously! Smooth move.

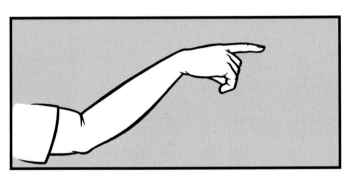

YEAH, YOU'RE BEING ROCKED

There's nothing quite as courteous as pointing into the crowd to remind them how much (or how little, as the case may be) they are being rocked. You! Oh yeah! You! Yeah, c'mon!

HAIL SATAN (IRONIC)

Heavy metal (primarily of The Effin' Champs/Early Man variety) has made this gesture entirely harmless. Run the other way? Only if they're ugly.

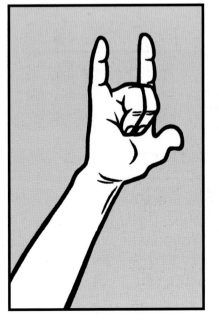

HAIL SATAN (NOT IRONIC)

Seeing this done can only mean one thing: the after-show will include drinking the blood of some dumb virgin.

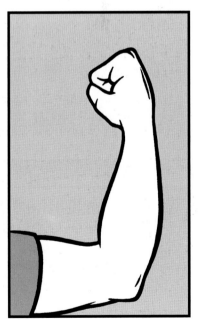

DUH REBEL YELL

Defiance isn't terribly English[*], so it's sorta pathetic that Billy Idol made this his signature move. Argh.

*Witness The Darkness' rise to fame

SUE EVERYBODY!

Our suggestion list for frivolous rock lawsuits

by Brian Teasley & Henry Owings • illustration by Joe Peery

Rich people of the world…unite and take over! Oh, double damn… I must have momentarily forgotten that you nad-bags already did that tens of thousands of years ago. Well then, consider this a kid's placement activity where your six-figure-plus money clip is the crayon! At worse, think of this as making a pledge to an NPR that doesn't play Tortoise/Godspeed pastel wall-sounding shit for every goddamn bumper.

If four suburban Illinois douche-juices can sue Creed for $1.8 million because Special Olympics Jesus-boy Scott Staff was too fucked out of his almond-sized brain to get through even one of Creed's want-to-be-secular Pearl Jam-lite-isms, then just think what we could do with a $550 an hour hot-shit lawyer! While the Creed case was dismissed, at least the band was forced to publicly apologize with their tails between their legs and their tall boys behind their backs, which is fine. Who wants to see man-snugglers who paid $60 to see Creed win anything?

Tit for tat. We'll give you laudable endeavors in the quest for impeccable music taste, and you give us the raw green cheeda so we can sue the boxer-briefs off some annoyingly shitty bands, sending them back to the local record store crap-house from whence they came. The following is a starter list of the targets at which our legal magic wand would be waved.

Fischerspooner	For copyright violation of *Cats*
The Mooney Suzuki	For continued use of Croakies in order to keep Ray-Bans intact while performing
Don Caballero	For false advertising
The Makers	For forcing male nipple exposure on audience
The Locust	For use of new polite political stage dogma to apologize for the fact they're just the new dude rock
Perry Farrell	For uniting adventure hippies everywhere again
Star Sailor	For wearing too much off-white
Enon	For making half (you know the "half" I'm talking about) of their new material sound like Stereolab karaoke
Nick Cave	For still not having a fucking chin
Sigur Rós	For murdering people through boredom
Andrew WK	For wringing the last drops of irony out of the word "party"
Kings of Leon	For wig abuse
David Grubbs	For raping Roget's Thesaurus
Junior Senior	For just being
Har Mar Superstar	For trying to smuggle plums into the country
Dead Meadow	For inventing the unnecessary term "Emo Stoner Rock"
Carlos D from Interpol	For environmental damage from excessive hair spray use
Nina Nastasia	For having the personality of a Social Security office ashtray
The Fleshtones	For leaving their retirement home recreational area
The Postal Service	For putting their name on an unreleased Lightning Seeds record
The Country of Wales	For never producing anything better than the Super Furry Animals
The Ramones	For self-necrophilia
The Cuts	For reviving Christopher Cross's career
Liz Phair	For being the world's most unsexy mommy
The Libertines' Peter Doherty	For not OD'ing
Daniel Johnston	For impersonating a mentally ill person
Metallica	For giving Robert Trujilo a career after Suicidal Tendencies
Trachtenberg Family Slideshow Players	For raising a future Dana Plato, home-schooled weirdo
Shangri-La Records	For naming their store after Steve Miller's worst song
Broken Social Scene	For being Canadian
Th' Legendary Shack*Shakers	For having the audacious stupidity of writing "The" as "Th'". Guys, let all that stupid Squirrel Nut Zippers shit die.
The Thorns	For being balding guy appreciation rock's Traveling Wilburys and for their planned "Thornbirds" rock opera
Joe Pernice	For making a drunken joke become reality: writing a novella based around The Smiths' *Meat Is Murder* album

We are the septic-ice samurais!

ALLOW US TO NAME YOUR SHITTY BAND

by Garth Johnson • illustrations by evildesign.com

You poor bastard.....

Perhaps you're in the process of forming a new shitty band. Perhaps you have been casting about for a name for your current shitty band. Are you being sued by some bullshit English band that thought up your band name years ago? Yet again, *Chunklet* comes to the rescue with the ultimate band-naming resource. Finally, you can create band names as generic as you sound. It's as easy as 1-2-3!

Simply choose a word from Column A, a word from Column B, and a word from Column C, add them together and... Voila! A perfect encapsulation of the way your band sounds. Maybe you're like Jeff Tweedy, Jim Thirwell or Stephin Merritt—creativity just spills out like Tad trying to squeeze into Beck's Prada chinos. Now you can have as many band names as you have shitty side projects!

Feeling classic? Try using the word 'The' and adding a word from column C. You can be The Factory or The Sponge. Reach up and feel your hair. Is it long? Is it matted? Does it smell like patchouli? Choose a word from column B and choose a word from column C that sort of rhymes. You could be Trout Mountain or Elastic Flashback. Are you in a Japanese noise band? Just pick a bunch of words from any column and go with it. You didn't even realize that you could now be known as MC Loco Intergalactic Funklord Meatmouth or Sister Furry Electric Kitten Mutants!

Do you have tattoos? Do you play through a distortion pedal? Just pick some badass words from any column, and string them together. Voila! Satan's Diesel Bucket or The Bastard Dick Daddies is born! Are you a retro-hipster? Make sure you pick words like Ultra, Deluxe, Hi-Fi, Stereo, Imperial or O-matic. Damn! You're now known as Stereomatic Deluxe! You'll be fighting off lunchbox-carrying groupies with a stick!

To make a long story short, you haven't shown any creativity yet. C'mon! Listen to your music. Choosing your band name is no time to start toying with something as volatile as imagination. With enough hard work and determination, in a few years *Chunklet* could be writing about how overrated *your* shitty band is!

COLUMN A	COLUMN B				COLUMN C		
Anal	'57	Burning	Ghost	Naked	Skankin'	[any number]	Engine	Nixon
DJ	Abstract	Butt	Goat	Necro	Skid	500	Eye	Ocean
Electric	Acid	Buzz	God	Neon	Sky	69	Face	O-Matic
Ex-	Acme	Candy	Golden	New	Slim	Aces	Factory	Orgy
Hydro	Acoustic	Captain	Grave	New	Small	Agenda	Faith	Pagans
Johnny	Action	Chemical	Gravel	New York	Smashing	Agents	Farm	Parade
Kid	Adrenaline	Clown	Green	Night	Smegma	Alcoholics	Filth	Penis
King	Adult	Cold	Groove	Nipple	Snatch	Alias	Flashback	Pigs
Loco	Aerial	Collective	Gutter	Nixon	Social	Alien	Flowers	Pimps
Los	Aero	Cowboy	Gypsy	Northern	Soft	All-Stars	Funk	Pork
MC	African	Crazy	Happy	Nuclear	Solid	Amp	Galaxy	Psycho
Mega	Afro	Crush	Hard	Nut	Sonic	Angels	Galore	Psychosis
Princess	Agenda	Cycle	Hate	Ocean	Soul	Animals	Ghosts	Puppets
Queen	Air	Dark	Heart	Ohio	Sound	Anyonymous	Girls	Pussy
Raging	Ajax	Dead	Heavy	Orange	Southern	Apocalypse	Goats	Quartet
Reverend	Alabama	Death	Hell	Orgy	Space	Apple	Gods	Queens
Satan's	Alcohol	Demon	High	Outrageous	Special	Army	Grass	Rage
Septic	Alcoholic	Detroit	Hog	Ozark	Spirit	Art	Grave	Rays
Sister	Alias	Dick	Hollywood	Pagan	Sponge	Asphalt	Guns	Ring
The	Alien	Diesel	Holy	Pain	Spoon	Ass	Hazard	Rodeo
Thee	Almighty	Dillinger	Horny	Panic	Static	Asshole	Head	Roses
Turbo	Alpha	Dirt	Hot	Penis	Stereo	Attack	Heads	Saints
Ultra	Altar	Dog	Hungry	Pimp	Stiff	Babies	Hearts	Samurai
	American	Doom	Hydro	Pink	Stone	Band	Hi-Fi	Satan
	Amp	Dope	Ice	Plastic	Strawberry	Bastards	Hogs	Scepter
	Anal	Down	Imperial	Pop	Sub	Biscuit	Holocaust	Scream
	Analog	Drag	Indigo	Pork	Sugar	Bitch	Honey	Seven
	Angel	Dream	Intergalactic	Power	Suicide	Bomb	Horses	Sheep
	Angry	Drive-by	Iron	Psychedelic	Super	Bombs	House	Sluts
	Animal	Drug	Jenny	Psycho	Swerve	Bone	Jam	Snakes
	Anonymous	Drunk	Jesus	Pussy	System	Booty	Jesus	Snatch
	Anti-	Dub	Karma	Quasi	Tar	Box	Jones	Sonic
	Apollo	Eat	Kid	Queen	Teenage	Boy	Juice	Soul
	Aqua	Echo	King	Radio	Terror	Boyfriends	Junkies	Sound
	Armored	Elastic	Kung-Fu	Rage	Thrash	Boys	Kids	South
	Art	Electra	Large	Ragin'	Tiger	Brothers	Kings	Spirit
	Ashtray	Electric	Left	Rain	Toilet	Bucket	Kings	Static
	Asphalt	Electronic	Lightning	Raven	Tokyo	Butt	Kitten	Stick
	Ass	Elvis	Lilac	Red	Tonic	Buzz	Lightning	Sticks
	Asshole	Evil	Loco	Retard	Train	Cadillacs	Lizards	Sugar
	Atari	Exploding	Loop	Revenge	Trash	Caesar	Loop	Suicide
	Audio	Fabulous	Lord	Road	Tree	Case	Lord	Sultans
	Automatic	Farm	Lounge	Rock	Trout	Cats	Love	System
	Average	Fart	Love	Rocket	Twin	Clowns	Machine	Team
	Baby	Fast	Lust	Rodeo	Twisted	Collective	Magnet	Teeth
	Bad	Filthy	Machine	Saliva	Ultimate	Cops	Man	Tigers
	Bastard	Flaming	Magic	Samurai	Uncle	Cowboys	Manson	Toilet
	Beef	Flash	Maximum	Satan	Vampire	Crank	Meat	Tones
	Bent	Flicker	Meat	Saw	Velvet	Crew	Men	Tongue
	Big	Floating	Meat	Scream	Walking	Crush	Messiahs	Tonic
	Bionic	Flower	Metal	Screamin'	Wasted	Daddies	Midgets	Train
	Bitch	Flying	Monkey	Septic	Wax	Daddy	Mob	Trash
	Black	Freakin'	Monster	Sex	Wedding	Day	Monkey	Tree
	Blind	Freaky	Morbid	Sexual	Wet	Dead	Monsters	Trio
	Blood	Free	Mother	Sexy	Whiskey	Deluxe	Mothers	Trout
	Bloody	Fucking	Motor	Shaved	White	Devils	Motor	Twins
	Blue	Funk	Mountain	Shot	Whore	Dick	Mountain	UK
	Bomb	Furry	Mouth	Sick	Wild	Diesel	Mouth	Vampires
	Bone	Fuzzy	Mud	Signal	Winged	Doctors	Mud	Volt
	Boogie	Galaxy	Murder	Silver	World	Dogs	Muffin	Warning
	Booty	Georgia	Mutant	Skank	Yankee	Dolls	Mutants	Wedding
						Dream	Nation	Whores
						Dreams	Nauts	World
						Drunks	Nights	Worms
						Elvis	Nipples	Youth

CHUNKLET
MAGAZINE

HARVEY P. CHUNKLET, PUBLISHER

We're All In This Together.

Except You. You're A Dick.

MEET THE STAFF

illustration by Terry White

Kraig Menetto (inadvertent proof-reader) - We're still trying to figure a way to legally prevent Kraig from getting a copy of this book.

Jason McCorkle (transportation for the tenth anniversary festivities) - Jason does multimedia installation work in the greater Georgia area when he's not driving around them high-falutin' comedy types for us.

Pat Murphy (rough sketch artist) - Athens' illustrative foot soldier gets little credit for drawing a lot of the embryonic ideas that are later sprinkled with pixie dust. I wish he'd quit asking why has to draw everything on my ass.

Dan Bajda (professional misanthrope) - Much of my hatred for humanity and its shit-stinkin' by-product, art, comes from long conversations with an inebriated Dan. God bless you, you sad sack of ass-fudge.

Chuck Short (research) - Okay, Chuck, stop sending us the now-uncovered vaults of the Ventura Blvd. Boys.

Matt Frediani (fact checkin' badass) - Matt was indispensable in his thorough Encyclopedia Brown-like proofing. He can spot a syntax error like the mechanical *Clash Of The Titans* owl bat targeting an escaped hamster. Thank God we ignore all his suggestions.

Mike Herrick (album reviewer) - Portland's own freelance rock critic laureate submits loads of great reviews that we don't use, which he then sells to "real" magazines for what might as well be monopoly money to us.

Shirley Maidt (fan art contest coordinator) - Shirley runs VELUX, one of the finest galleries this side of any direction from the Mississippi. I'm glad the "irreplaceable" images of our soon-to-be-published contest were documented by someone who wasn't me.

Jean Stisser (spiritual assistance) - No one is a better listener than my good friend, Jean. She is an invaluable confidant, especially in dark times, and has sat with me when I've been utterly in the pits. Strangely, her Christmas present for me this year was an SAR-1 Romanian AK semi-automatic assault rifle.

Mike Horgan (black metal consultant) - While no longer terrorizing the crowd as a guitar-demon in the Nightmare Manboy, Mike still keeps us up on the latest innovations in Black Metal.

"Black" Jason Watson (hip-hop editor) - Jason makes things seem almost off-white when he contributes what he calls "his flava" to the book.

Dana Washington (regional distribution) - In her career as a professional nurse, she gives hernia exams. This must explain why she's so damn good at getting *Chunklet* all over the South.

Wayne Connely (vending machine guy) - Wayne is just a cool old dude who knows a thing or two about the rock biz. He used to roadie for the Christian band, Truth, but now stocks our office snack machine like only a seasoned tour dog could.

Meagan Mather (curator of odds and ends) - While not fulfilling her commercial music studies at Georgia State University, Meagan interns two days a week, and is smarter than any whip that I've been smacked with.

William "Mike and the Mechanics" Teeter (keeper of "The Broadsword") - No one likes grudge work, but there is not a soul alive that can sharpen a battle-ax like this guy. Hey, Mikey, maybe one day we'll actually get to use those goddamned things in a real battle! Keep spittin' and shinin', bro.

Matthew Jungblut (accountant) - Matthew, are you sure we can't write off all that Planet Smoothie?

Terra Coleman (receptionist of the people) - After doing her own fanzine, *Talking Machine Company*, she's decided to come guard the doors at our H.Q. She is a queen bee in a hive of industry.

Helen Sundquist (gal Friday) - We actually have no idea what Helen does for *Chunklet*. We just enjoy watching her do it.

Johnny Paycheck (verbals) - Not to be confused with the recently deseased country singer, Johnny is a frequent contributor to *Home & Shelter Design Magazine*, *Electric Sox*, the electroclash journal, and *McSweeney's*.

Pepe Gilbert (professional microphone model) - Pepe posed for our illustrators in all the compromising, flexibility-testing microphone positions we conceptualized. After he did the G.G. Allin "internal pose," we let him keep the mic as a souvenir.

Mike "King Diamond" Adams (overseas distribution) - Mike helps get our little book in all kinds of places that ain't America. Did we mention that he likes that band King Diamond?

Janet Sykes (lost luggage finder) - Janet is one of Austin, Texas's finest ambassadors of happy-fun time. Thanks to her, a suitcase full of issue 17 didn't go forever bye-bye at the Houston airport.

Larry Schlagel (web consultation) - Larry is like the slimy brother I never disassociated myself from, who told me the web site "sucks" in the hope that I would pay him to redesign it.

Joyce Raddatz (transcription master ninja) - A top-shelf Williamsburg woman who is the wanton desire of every last male staffer.

Lyle Burgerson (perpetual hard-ass) - Although no longer an "official" member of the residents of The Residents, Lyle is a mother-fouler of unchallenged proportions and writes under "assumed" names. Oops…sorry dude.

Shecky Love (visual stimulation) - Shecky's tireless dedication to his craft has him consistently clocking in overtime in search of the perfect gummy product. He also is the world's foremost expert in the new genre of home design reality shows.

Bil Krisheimer (middle management) - Didn't contribute much to this issue because of TiVo.

Tony King (freelance writer and record label owner) - The inventor of uncomfortable silences and pregnant pauses, Tony is the guy you always manage to sit next to at a party when your boyfriend has disappeared.

Maya Alexandri (international distribution) - If you think *Chunklet* only appeals to white Southern males, speak to Maya, who has translated these esteemed pages into Greek, Inuit, and Esperanto.

Alfonso Ceglia (flag bearer) - One of our most loyal and seriously handicapped staff members, Alfonso has defended the *Chunklet* flag for five years now, shouting down naysayers, causing mall riots and biting when necessary.

Hashish Narval (online programmer) - This soft fudge mountain of a man came to *Chunklet* after a brief dot.com disaster. He is happy to recieve a paycheck, and no longer dreams of owning his own jet.

Gordon Tate (man of leisure) - This one time at a party, El Gordo got really messed up on apple Schnapps and ate an entire tub of Shedd's Spread on a dare. He spent the rest of the night telling everybody about it.

Nick DeWitt (advertising sales rep) - Nick is a handsome, cordial fella. Nick spends his afternoons chatting up the sales girls in trendy stores, and totally relating to whatever the store owners have to say about ad budgets. Snazzy dresser...for a heterosexual.

Yenory Yardley (junior assistant art director) - Yenory has been with the company for about six years. She is quick to give advice to the newer employees and hangs in there (although she's bitter as hell) waiting for the day when she might be "The Creative Director." She's been close, but passed up in the past. Chin up, Yenory!

Franklin Pierce (subscriptions manager) - When Franklin isn't bitching to management about stocking the drink machine with V8 Splash or looking online at Winger song lyrics, he is busy taking subscriptions. Franklin's hard work and dedication has jumped our subscription rate to almost 150,000!

Shep Masterson (jazz editor) - It has become apparent that Shep doesn't really know anything about jazz, but he got business cards printed and everything, so we figured we'd leave it alone for now. A Shep-penned career overview of Enoch Light and the Light Brigade is slated for our next issue.

Gina Guilardo (stylistic typist) - Gina has the inimitable ability to type at an average speed. Much like ancient medicine men using the ceremonial nonanchee root, we feel it is not our place to question the mysterious power with which she is endowed.

Jon Porter (deputy of PowerPoint posturing) - No one can bore a room full of hipsters like lackluster concept man, Jon P. He always has a plethora of ideas, and maybe one of these days there'll actually be a good one in the lot. Keep swingin', Jonboy; you're bound to hit the piñata one of these days.

Pat Bollinger (word and sperm counter) - Pat loves to count things; sort of like a Rain Man that doesn't mind getting his hand sticky. It's incredibly soothing to hear Pat prattle on, "…fifty-thousand nine-hundred twenty-three, fifty-thousand nine-hundred twenty four, fifty-thousand nine-hundred twenty five…"

Erika Miller (legal representation) - Erika has flawlessly defended the magazine against the various inane suit-jobs who have…oh, yeah, we're not supposed to talk about it.

Wayne Francis Leonard (ombudsman) - Kudos to Wayne for his tireless efforts in dealing with the biggest collection of humorless whiners to ever plague a publication.

D'arabian Hazelden (chaplain) -Reverend D gets mistaken for Aaron Neville, like, all the time. Seriously.

LaShawn de la Croix (fashion editor/style consultant) - With his youthful sass and his hotpants-clad ass, LaShawn keeps us all looking "fabulous" by being liaison for our sponsorship deal with Marc Jacobs. He aspires to be the RuPaul (or at least the Meshach Taylor) of his generation.

Yuki Kirby (intern) - After a brief internship frustrating the folks at *Ready Made*, Yuki headed south for the glamor that is cutting up boxes, feeding the dog and affixing address labels. Way to use that Mills B.A., Yuki!

Les Desiderio (collections overlord) - I have never seen anyone at all, particularly anyone whose job is to call people for money, enjoy their work as much as Les does. What a sadistic bastard. But he's *our* sadistic bastard.

William Welliver (sycophant) - "Man…that's awesome! *Chunklet* kicks *Magnet's* ass! What a layout! Hell, yeah, another illustration! You... fat? No way, them's just cushion for the pushin'."

Barbara Anne Josephstein (proofing) - A passionate real estate developer, Barbara Anne is busy converting *Chunklet* world headquarters into lofts. She has just finished writing a Benedictine chant to be performed by Lord of the Dance this fall, and she raises Percherons in a studio apartment off Bankhead Highway in Atlanta.

Harvey Coltrane (former AOR DJ, *Chunklet* uncle figure) - Harvey cut his teeth at KKOK playin' slabs of Yes and ELP. He hangs out 'cause his old lady is a pain. Boy, does he have some stories!

Scott Myer (head of keyboard crud production) - Though he has absolutely nothing to do with *Chunklet*, this recent NYC transplant was fine enough to get his Popeye's fried chicken spew all over one the office keyboards while checking his email. Who said that New England city boys had better manners than fine Southern gentlemen?

Mike "Why aren't there more girls gaming online?" Armstrong (network administrator/web designer) - Mike has tirelessly worked to keep us up and running, giving up nights, weekends, relationships, hygiene and just about everything else in his sad, lonely life.

Kimmie Weinstock (office manager) - Coffee, tea or death by a blunt object?

Joop Van der Beek (offshore accounts manager) - He's blonde, he's bad and, boy, does he know his way around the Caribbean! Despite his propensity for thrift, this Dutchman can party with the Titans, and keep the taxman off our ass in every hemisphere. Naturally, his job keeps him on the move, but we keep a cold jar of mayonnaise in the office fridge for that rare occasion in which he drops by for lunch.

Randy Saksman (systems administrator) - Randy's responsibilities are described in his contract as maintaining the Unix server, and administering security. Apparently, Randy's duties include only littering the server room floor with Taco Bell wrappers and indexing porn sites. Andy, you're fired. And take your light saber with you.

Dale Jesperson (estranged father figure) - We keep him around for laughs. He's 45, divorced, two kids, wears Fubu head to toe, and has frosted tips. His 20-year-old daughter calls him "extreme dad" and it's been overheard that he's looking forward to her next party in hopes of getting lucky and "snuffing the rooster."

Timmy Tilford (taste tester) - The T.T. man makes sure the king only gets the best of poisons. After becoming part of the Adopt-a-Gutter Punk plan (St. Louis division), his life smells as much like a bed of roses as it can for someone who slept covered only by mildewy bubble wrap under an interstate overpass for almost two years.

Ben Johnson (file clerk) - Ben does nothing all day.

Shane Cavalier (masseur) - He has magic hands. When he asks if you want him to "do the front," slip him a fiver. You won't regret it.

Willard Truffle (cock-n-bull story maker) - Once the pride and joy of the Myrtle Beach porn industry, Willy T., formerly our cock-and-ball story maker, now fabricates the most astounding half-truths we've ever seen. However, he still hasn't lost his ability to write some of the steamiest "true to life" smut this side of *Man-Docker Quarterly*. Hey, Will, remember when the Native American women who were protesting the Braves game gave everyone from the office a "freebie" behind that giant Coke bottle made out of baseball memorabilia?

Urian Barmund (second team coordinator) - Urian is kind of like my Mini Me sidekick, who somehow managed to grow to full size despite his three-pack a day Lucky Strike habit as a junior high hellion. Every good magazine has to have a sidekick, even if said sidekick isn't really a midget. Uri, you're still a little guy to us! Oh, yeah: Urian's favorite movie of all time is Cher's 1990 classic tale of tails, *Mermaids*.

Yedda Peony (slicer of life) - Yedda is all about the who, what, where, when and how of the here-and-now, as opposed to the then and there, for all of us him-and-hers, here at the you-know-where.

Wyndham Hill (bail bondsmen) - It's no big secret that the *Chunklet* staff likes to occasionally chug-a-lug a little of the old Cabbagetown Backdoor Tarnation Water, and when the staff has a sip or two, they like to fuck shit up real good. Thank the good Lord Satan that Wyndham is there to sneak miniature hacksaws into birthday cakes for everybody. Yo Wyndy, how about one of them conjugal visits once in a while?

Dr. Dave Spiegel (medical consultant) - When not prescribing Viagra to staff members, Dr. Dave and his head nurse Kathryn show us pictures of their insides and outs. He's now famous for the bumper sticker on his Beemer that screams "Doctors do it to you while you are unconscious."

Shecky Green (*Golden Girls* aficionado) - Known to expound on the genius of Sir Mix-a-Lot. Shecky started the dance crazes "The Windshield Wiper" and "The Stop, Drop and Roll."

Alex "Dusty" Broome (senior recombobulator) - Don't let her diminutive stature, disarming smile or lazy eye (the left one) fool you—Alex is a warrior queen and "Look at this place—it's a pigsty!" is her cry.

Rev. Jonathon Johnson-Janson III (religious fact-checker) - Died of a heart attack shortly after the table of contents. Boys formerly molested by the esteemed fact-checker revealed at his funeral that he was actually a second, not a third.

Morton Socks (ombudsman) - We're not exactly sure what Morton does, or what his title even means, for that matter, but he assured us that we need to have one of these "real bad." Morton's most recent claim to fame was that he was next in line to getting on *Queer Eye for the Straight Guy*, but got beat out by that accountant from Spokane.

Rick Scaglione (creepy guy who seems to be everywhere we go) - We don't know how, but he's there when we show up. He was at the grocery store today, and yesterday when we were picking up our dry cleaning, and Sunday at the flea market. No, we don't think we sound paranoid. Yes, it could be coincidence, but why do you have to invalidate everything we say? Listen, this isn't going to work out between us.

Debra Batrees (lazy English bird) - Keen as mustard, yet easily confused. Has confessed to a deep fascination with America and works at a sex clinic. Regularly buries bands alive with the aid of alcohol in dirty clubs where she can be found air drumming/guitaring with considerable expertise.

Sally Simmons (Freddie Mercury unitard model) - Thought the "GA" in Athens, GA was a fancy-pants way of abbreviating Greece. Boy, was she pissed when there weren't any naked statuesque men running around.

Mantis Goodbarger (Brit-pop fellatio) - Has an unhealthy fascination with all things Buffy. His last entry in log was titled "Whatever happened to my dreadlocks?" They were buried in the yard!

Wilbur Tyson (bloopers editor) - Wilbur... oh, God... here it comes... not again... wait... wait... look-it! Look-it... look... no... oh, Jesus... right smack in his own shit... aw, fuck... holy crap... rewind it... c'mon, just one more time!

Lydia Patton (fluffer) - I have always had a mental block regarding making my own bed. Unfortunately, I'm afraid that's never going to change with Lydia treating my fluffy stuffings with the gingerly delicate caress that only her dainty hands (which make my pillows look huge) can provide.

Leonie Cumstock (director of razzmatazz) - By day a singing Christian party clown, by night our one true inspiration. As she says, "Zizzle-fizzly-doo, spark in the dark, light this candle, sweet as a tart, roody-doody-dinkle!"

Buck Tennant (pyrotechnics technician) - Goddammit, Buck! You can't get anything right! We said "Whitesnake," not "Great White."

Scag Winesack (retired private investigator) - Semi-retired P.I., ex-FBI, ex-cop, ex-con. Eats over crime scenes, and has had triple-bypass surgery. Tries not to take a lot of cases these days, but sometimes he sees a photograph, and gets sucked in. He's pretty goddamned lonely. And plays sax.

Lil' Lil' (age 3, the world's youngest rapper) - His first record, titled *Lil' Politikin'* was a modest success, but his third album, *I Ain't Lil' No Mo* was his real breakthrough. After that record, he dropped the first Lil', only answering to "Lil'."

Chad Hitler (outside sales) - Yes, of the Barrington Hitlers. You wouldn't believe how many deals are leveraged by a famous name.

Reed Seville (consoler of extraordinary talent) - You have simply not lived until you hear this guy riff on "It is with sincere regret that I learned of your recent loss."

Tequila Lovely (recent ex-convict, unemployed) - TQ hangs out regularly and sweeps up for extra cash at his favorite childhood record store, Farly's. During his incarceration, the record store was purchased by a new owner, Randall Badeaux. Randall introduced him to the wonders of *Chunklet* to keep him from talking to customers. Why did TQ go to prison, you ask? Breaking and entering (kicking down door of Farly's), theft (stealing collectable records) and vandalism (leaving an "upper decker" or "top shelf" in the toilet).

Ahida Obeidat (proofer) - Ahida left her dying, widowed mother and six sisters in Jordan to study Molecular Physics at Harvard. When she contacted our offices about her desperate lack of street cred and begged to volunteer, we didn't have to deliberate for very long. Really, Ahida, it's no problem.

Jeri Ullrey (British wit and international distributor) - A sweet tart of knackered soul, whose swish attitude and wet snogs keep her in the hearts and pants of the *Chunklet* staff.

Chuck (AKA Lucky Chunk) Luciano (captain of the IT staff) - Chuck was born into money and soon lost it all with a failed investment buying up Interpol seven inches. He spends his days under desks and goes places few of us need to.

Smurfette (female Smurf) - You bitch! You gave it up to Handy! Even after I pulled you out of Azreal's ass I still couldn't get any. My balls are normally blue, but this just hurts.

Grover "Big Pepto" Wentworth (assistant caddy, gentleman of leisure) - "Big P" always brings back a receipt and correct change from Swap-O-Rama, so clearly, he can be trusted.

Lance Boyles (nutritionist) - When our Austin-based ace isn't incessantly ranting about essential fatty acids and probiotics, this former executive assistant to Donny Osmond's manager delights the staff to no end with his declarations that he's really quit smoking this time — for real.

Tony "Boomer" King (flashlight holder) - Also known as "Holy Shit!," Tony's duties at *Chunklet* consist of gluing every single letter of individual type to the page layouts by hand, band/comedian fluffing, writing soft-blow rejection letters for unsolicited poetry, listening to thousands of hours of Trail of the Dead studio outtakes and so on.

the meet the staff key

Thaddeus McPherson - (webmaster) - When not spouting off about all the great things Ohio has contributed to our culture, Thad is working hard to keep chunklet.com up to date and looking great!

Cagney Halden (mail room supervisor) - When someone asking you for a job lists their qualifications as being able to outdrink anybody and defeat any bike messenger at leg wrestling, do you really need to see a resumé?

Britney Hampton-Lewis (fashion choreographer) - Britney is an ex-model and ex-girlfriend of many of the staff. She personally revamped the *Chunklet* line of clothing, and is due to launch the much anticipated Chunk-Pharm in May.

Mitchell Kent (quality assurance) - Not that we get many unsatisfied customers in this business, but when we do Mitchell is just a generic form letter away from total placation.

Brent L. Stayner (legal counsel) - Without a doubt the most eloquent lawyer to ever drink milk from a jug at a deposition. Brent actually got an apology from the estate of Andy Griffith for what was initially a copyright infringement suit for *Chunklet's* "Son of What it Was, Was Football" DVD.

Willet Steinke (head of our quality control department's quality control division) - Vegetarian, barfly and workbench technician (20 bucks a pop) for our staff of bedroom guitarists.

Eugene "Genie" Forsythe (resident whiskey-dick) - Wants to know what the fuck you're looking at.

Louise Krum (moral barometer) - Proofreads articles to determine our standing with God. Wears long ugly dresses that only God would make you wear.

Troy Hagen (libel lawyer) - Knows the difference between slander and parody. Will say in court that a member of an obscure indie band with a full-time job is a public figure. Invaluable.

Fester Gob (old-school punk) - Keeps the staff informed on what retro punk scene/band is the most trendy at the moment. Right now it's the west Texas country-punk scene of 1981.

Anthony Carr (corporate consultant) - Cut company expenditures by 3% in 2004 by discontinuing use of child-safe bindery glue. Responsible for setting up Jamaican tax shelter.

Samantha Rooks (promotions) - Sam keeps track of all the CDs received and sends them to writers in lieu of payment. Saves tickets to death metal shows for herself.

Robert Masterson (high-profile guest columnist) - Also contributes to the *New Yorker* and *Rolling Stone.* He's expensive but keeps us viable in the high-brow literary circles. He refuses to step inside the *Chunklet* offices, but insists we keep a desk for his secretary.

Joanne Garrett (spelling guru) - Has to know how to spell every word used in the articles, including names of bands, weird drugs and the latest celebrity boyfriends.

Ted Pesker (bouncer) - Ted is stretched a little thin trying to keep out non-trendy musicians and comedians who want to be in the magazine. We might have to hire a second guy just to keep Patton Oswalt away.

David "Beep" Rodriguez (staff music historian) - Raised in the streets of Long Beach, this one time jazz fan, has succeeded his life to the electronica that the kids love today. His only regret is that he forgot how to rock.

Dr. Burgle Johansson (staff psychiatrist) - He helps promote inter-office over-the-counter drug-abuse.

Mayor McCheese (aftermarket analyst) - After his fall from grace during the Russian dressing riots of 1989, his honor took refuge inside the *Chunklet* supply closet. He has been helping out ever since hoping to vindicate himself in the eyes of his god.

Simon Levinson (workflow management) - You can lead a horse to water, but you can't get him off the damn internet when there's work to be done and you're not looking. Enter Mr. Levinson. Simon sets deadlines, checks hourly work logs, demands progress reports, and challenges your manhood (where applicable) when unsatisfied with the three former items. While consensus here at the office is that Simon's a motherfucker, Simon keeps ink on our pages and bathroom breaks to a minimum!

Conlon Vigga (intercom networking) - Conlon ensures that our elaborate in-house paging system works flawlessly even though many of us think that it's too goddamned loud.

LaQuandemetra Estevez-Jackson (shoe-sprayer) - Keepin' our shoes sanitized for our private bowling lanes (4 of 'em!) for 8 wonderful years.

Milt Hutto (consultant) - We pay Milt $5,000 a month to come in and "shake things up" like a good little consultant. He has a cache of business cards (expensive imported linen paper) and a framed business license...and that's about it. He's faking his way through it like every-fucking-body else in his chosen profession.

Richard Hoover (design/ layout) - Responsible for the majority of *Chunklet's* look and feel. Currently, he is the creative director for Abercrombie and Fitch and serves as the treasurer for the New York City branch of H.P.M.A. (Homos that Play Music and do Art). Before beginning his professional design career, Richard played drums briefly for Hole before joining the New Klezmer All Stars. He has also played drums for Hank III, Ravi Shankar, and Dionne Warwick, as well as playing lead bass on Bruce Campbell's forthcoming album: *Bubba Hotep, the Rock Opera*.

Jennifer Ferenz (assistant to the technical director) - Jennifer is in charge of complaining about everything as if she was the only person in the whole fucking world with problems. She's been known to say "this place would totally fall apart if it wasn't for me" while removing a staple. She doesn't actually work here.

Steve Warscyk (accounts receivable supervisor) - Last year Steve drank a whole bottle of Pepto-Bismol during tax time and then left this really crazy jet black turd in the toilet. It was fucking huge and shaped like a question mark, complete with a little floaty point at the end. We took a picture of it and Photoshopped it onto a picture of Steve in his Riddler costume from Halloween '95.

Mika "Mittens" Izakomu (student/artist) - Little is known about "Mittens" other than that she really can't speak English very well, loves "All-American rock and jam, biotch! Let's partay!" and apparently has decided that if she sends in enough lists of comparisons between seemingly unrelated things she'll get published. Her last list "Laser Tag Vs. Coffee Enema" was rejected for its two-point brevity. She is also super hot.

Joseph "Bud" Podlesny (writer/composer/drummer) - Bud was in-home incarcerated for quite a few years for public drunkenness that resulted in the molestation of several pets at a neighbor's party. He lived with his mother until this June when he was to be set free from house arrest. The Friday which marked the end of his sentence, he was found dead in his toolshed having fallen from a ladder onto a table saw. His claim to fame was being drummer for Apice (solo project of Vanilla Fudge guitarist Carmen Apice) and djembe player for the Dreadful Grapes.

William Harrisbourg (fact/ spell checker) - Ten-year-old home schooled son of unwed gutterpunk mom. William spends the early part of the day at a Montessori and the later part of the day listening to his mother bash Bush while he talks to strangers on message boards asking obscure questions, correcting their grammar, spelling and historical accuracy, and scolding them for misbehaving on the internet.

Cricket (commentator/sidekick) - Colorman to Tequila Lovely. Cricket will not speak to you unless TQ speaks first. Do not step to TQ unless you like to get fucked with. Do not step to Cricket either unless you like to get bruised. If you hate you will be "Denied! From way downtown!" Expect to be referred to by number or last name when dealing with Cricket: "Malkmus rolls out a smooth lay up to protect his status as the Mack and — DENIED! FROM WAY DOWN TOWN!! Bachman returns with fingers number ffffooooouuuurrr.... FRESH!"

Rick Duhon (combat journalist) - Rick is one of the "new breed" of punks: hardcore conservative "wor on terra" military punks. Didn't realize just how punk rock war was until his head was mounted with an M-40 so he could keep his hands free to manipulate the hand controls of his jet pack, and was ejected from an airplane sideways to surprise the enemy. That's what he says. Swear. I know, I know, but it sounds real coming in over an international phone line.

Richard T. Samuels (phone sex operator) - For intense, live, one-on-one phone action contact Richard and his velvety fog voice rolling over your phone line.

Grizzly "Gold Tooth" McMahon (criminal prospector) - Dude's a fucking *nut*. He's been living in this cave for like 40 years and mumbles to himself about all the gold he has stashed, and how smart he is because no one will ever find it. I could have sworn he's the same guy who stole Christmas that one year too.

James Burdyshaw (sex advocate) - Truth be known, we wouldn't have much sex if it weren't for James poking at the publisher saying, "Henry, go out and get yourself involved with some sex." Also, you may remember him as the guitar player in Sinister Six.

Claudia Mahoney (vice president of software marketing) - Claudia plans these events for software conventions where she has to have speakers talk about the products and all that shit. One year she hired Dana Gould from the Simpsons as the afternoon recess entertainment and he bombed. This year she hired The Capital Steps.

Carl Brodsky, M.D. (pill reviewer) - Takes samples constantly just to see what they'll do. Tell him something your doctor gave you for whatever. He'll tell you what he thinks of your doctor. Send him what the doctor gave you and he'll take it, no questions asked, even if you are taking medication to make your dick smaller. Not a real doctor.

John McCarthy-Martin (fireman) - He's a stand up guy in a sit down world. A favorite memory of mine is when John, in an act of unparalleled bravery, broke into a burning house to make fun of the voluntarily homeless teens who'd shacked up there for the night.

Greg "Breast Pump" Fitzsimmons (emergency medical technician) - I saw this comic talking about how his wife was breast feeding, but they went on vacation without the baby and her tits got all swollen up with out it. So the dude started sucking away. It was funny but gross, but kind of horny too.

Phil "In" Leblanc (accidental madlibber) - Suffers from anemia. Does assignments on time and is very thorough in his investigation, yet because of his neurological disorder all nouns proper and common are replaced with doohickey, thingamobbobbit, whatchadiddle, fuckity, thatband, whoever from thatotherband, whozit... You get the idea.

Derek "November Rain" Varnell (telesales captain) - Sells seashells on the seashore and likes to laugh and point when guitarists break strings. Has a heart of gold and a head like a sieve. Damn it! He's irreplaceable!

Franklin Garth Mohammed (technical advisor) - Works mainly out of the office, which is lucky as no one can really be sure of what he looks like. When he does come in, he affects a lusty "catalog pose" posture designed to get the ladies fruity. Without him, we would be strictly analog.

Jerry Fondren (deal scout) - Son of a used car dealer and nephew of famous '70s playmate Debra Jo same-last-name. Has only three topics of conversation: Porn, cars, and deals. If you can get through the details of the other two, the deals are incredible.

Hern Berford (air freshener) - If you smelt it, he dealt it. The foremost dealer in artificial olfactory enjoyment for over fifteen years, there isn't a stink cloud this man cannot tame. His contributions to the scene are unheralded, but he remains humble, saying only "Nice smells put people in a better mood."

Masta-Assif Omar (world beat) - Afghan battle rapper. Drops it tight it with damn near impossible to follow 7/4, 5/8, and 37.5/16 beats. Also bleats like a goat. He believes that the Afghans and their Muslim brothas are "truly kickin' it old school," and are the "original gangstas," and "fuck all those DIY punks 'cuz until they start learning to make they own squats, they own ride, and they own aspirin, ain't nothin' but a buncha pusseez."

Rajiv Escovar (reverse bench-press champion) - Mahoney can put down over 300 lbs. without even trying. Just, *bam*! And the shit will be lying on the ground. No strain, no puffing out and 100%-natural steroid-free.

Mack McGillicutty (apocalypse insurance broker) - As with all members of the gambling community, Mack doesn't hedge his bets when there's a certainty on hand. The world will end one day and...

Andrew Shitzenhand (criminal prosecutor) - Dude's a fucking *narc*! Look out when he's walking with another guy in a black hat. That means he's about to serve a warrant on your ass.

THANKS

Mexicans of Lorna Road and the new American slavery, Ann Coulter's small, yet obviously visible, penis, my special little dream of giving every child Herpes and a Slush Puppy, the Museum of Burnt Fur, the Branford Marsalis Quartet for letting me jam with them at the Alys Stephens Center, the janitorial staff at Dean and Co., all my dawgs up in the A to the R to the Bee's who got them mad grill skillz, my manservant, Tico Torres (not the Bon Jovi guy), Suicide Bomb Pop popsicles, the way vintage Sun britches make my cock look huge, the Bobby T. show and everyone at Señor Frog, Virginia Woolf and *The Cooter of the Gods: A Murder Mystery*, the Red Lobster on Hwy 31, the Strutting Duck crew circa '92, 202 E. Sanford (mothafucka!), O, Holy Shit! (Community Fecal Fetish Christmas Theater), aristocratic British butterfly hunters, the Karl Rove/Korla Pandit Blues Duo, what you call "pink lemonade," Graceland Too, my ability to have an orgasm while puking, 99 cent family order of hushpuppies at Taco Bell/Long John Silver's on Crestwood Boulevard, the Toilet Swiffer™, recent dialogues on anti-Semitism in heated Wiffle Ball games between Protestant and Jewish teams, Japanese rappers who use the "N" word in a country where the word strikes no chord of offense, Janet Jackson's wardrobe "malfunction," everyone who has sung along with Billy Joel's "Piano Man," did I mention South Worcestershire haggis? Let's see, colors synonymous with flavors, the Little Ambassador, banana puddin'-flavored IV packets, Mee-Maw for poppin' all the bumps on my back, the brunch detectives, my personal trainer Habu who screams, "Do one more for baby Jesus!," Utah — the town, not the state, the female staff at Wax N Facts (you make me feel like my ugly, bitchy, perennially PMS'd girlfriend ain't all that bad), bugs who are trapped in amber, my fleeting virginity, Burt & Kurt from 101.1FM The Source, Mexi-Cali vs. Tex-Mex Stratego Championship '01, Kobe Bryant's sperm (specifically sperm #2, #438 and #389), Plexiglass (y'all's shit is almost bulletproof, ya'll), my milkman André (how do you keep it so cold, dawg?), Mooney Suzuki brand Spray-On Bald Spot Camouflager, the 1979 Iranian hostage crisis (damn, the USA Olympic Hockey team beat Russia that year. In your face, commie bastards!), the idiosyncratic world of Klondike bars, staged debates, Par Par's Party of Four, Kikkoman naturally-brewed soy sauce, that Christian fish logo thing people put on their SUVs, sexy children who know they're sexy, homeless street people who know web design, your worst sexual performance, Long's Electronics' return policy, Midgie, the super chocolate brownie dwarf boy, Georgia Championship Wrestling, Blue Demon Y Las Invasadoras de Ass-Venom, Spike from G.N.P., W.A. 'Berry High School's 1988 undefeated Junior Varsity Baseball Team, rollerblade line dancing, all-you-can-shovel horse manure, the Econochrist '91 tour, the off-Broadway sex battles: *The Vagina Monologues vs. Puppetry of the Penis,* Optimus Prime, those bros who let me crash in their van outside of Rotterdam, custom amputation, the Sherman Oaks Chamber of Commerce, family of D. Boon's Minutemen laundry service, shitty, underpowered PAs at VFW halls, glory hole #6 at Famous Al's in Tuscumbia, Alabama, plants that you can hang, every double-digit prime number (except 17; you let me down at the roulette table, so you're dead to me!), old black bluesmen who don't have nicknames like Shoutin' Jeremiah, Asians, Mello T, the real life Chico and the Man, Peter W. Van Hoy, MD of Giving Love A Bad Name, hand robots, S&H Green Stamps, turnstile clickers, Shoney's All-You-Can-Eat breakfast bar refill servers, Jim Burke Used Cars, the Cliffs Notes version of any book by a Brontë sister, Scrub-claw penis pump cleaning brush, Dick Cheney's daughter (the gay one who brought on Lesbogate), Fermented Freddy and Da Drunk Playtime crew, Spicy Mike's Gopher Candies, Southminster Saints, Buzz, my lucky scarf, red dye #6, the new Chinatown, Bob's cat Skeletor, the starting outfield line-up of the 1979 Houston Astros (still "doin' it in the dome," César Cedeño?), the Durian fruit of Southeast Asia, virtualinsults.com, the new (and even zestier) taco-flavored Doritos, underwater polo, Coach Wayne Short, battered, breaded, and flame-broiled crustacean dippin' sticks, every bad, fake new wave British '80s band except Heaven 17 (remember, 17? You're dead to me!), Expressway South, Russian Bogies, all the cake-eatin' mothafuckas at the Clairmont Road Piggly Wiggly, moviefone.org (that's right!), the American Sanitary Plumbing Museum, chuckdcookies.com, Nicolas Cage's bald spot, The Pasta Pot, Today-Tomorrow-Always perfume by Avon, Dave Johnson and Dale Dave Johnson, everybody else on George W. Bush's college cheerleading team, classic Raid commercials with the cartoon spray can, Hardee's 100% Angus Beef Western Bacon Thickburger, uninsured Americans (you pathetic pussies), The Better Sex series, the much-improved Fox News graphics department (how can you make my dick hard *and* fuel my hatred of towelheads?), the monobrow, *The Ultimate Beginner Series: Rock Keyboards Step Two with David Garfield,* Gospelman, Sinclair Broadcasting and other crazy-ass right-wing Nazi media, Everlast boxing gloves (you're still #1, baby!), David Ortiz Snack Ems, the word "stoop," the Loose Douche Lesbian Bar in Rayville, Louisiana, the harmony vocals on Bruce Hornsby's "That's Just The Way It Is," Mach 3 replacement blades, "The Great Michelob Taste," Estrin-D, God's medicine (otherwise known as "Angels"), the Real March of Dimes, the 2004 presidential candidate for the Concerns of People (Prohibition) Party, Gene Amondson, Rocktoberfests everywhere, the 1984 Libertarian presidential candidate, Dave Bergland, the moustache of Koose Muniswamy Veerappan, Star Wars-themed gangsta rap, The Evil Eye, Mister Ed's Elephant Museum, my long-standing high school crush Jennifer Fuller, anyone whose last name is Culpepper, Chocolate-cherry-vanilla Dr. Pepper, the New Urine Nation, the unlikeliness of having a plane crash, the Rom Space Knight Marvel comic book series, Swedish Dutch meatballs, peeps from the 'hood, Bondage Boys Discount Gear, mystic visions of wolves that appear before you in three-dimensions, *Da Vinci Code* Scrabble, that Butthole Surfers side-project the Jack Officers, *Moxie: The Musical,* John Edwards and other phony psychics, Simon Bar Sinister, a future cure for ovarian cancer, Blue Parrot's Bike Day, Naked Rodeo - the band, *Shrek II: The Hot Dog,* bridges made of rainbows, life coaches, Gary Tatterson Pets Specialty Personal Check design, all the temps that work the night shift at the Emory Kinko's, vaginal lipstick, Milton Bradley's Simon, the Flat Earth Liberation Front, the Aluminum Foil Deflector Beanie, Underwear Boy, 24-Hour Church of Elvis, the Museum of Menstruation, sympathetic Martha Stewart banners, bloody juice from raw chickens, Bryan Ferry's smugness, Tijuana bibles, Cadillac wheels, Greg Ginn's solo work (on my yard), Navy grog, inglorious bastards, Starfleet Command, the Dracula myth, *Dr. Haggard's Disease,* my personal friend Rick Moody, victims of molestation by Mr. Wizard, Sgt. Fury and his howling commandos, Don Winslow from Old Navy, any sport the playing of which can kill you, Dr. Fate, *Red Sonja,* Parker Brothers French Card Game Craze, Mille Bornes, Golferino, burp guns, Kame Bazooka, the Mini Cake Museum, Kure Kure Takora, The Mack, garter belts for men, Beck's ex-girlfriend Leigh Limon, the Ford Ranchero, the Lift & Load Depot, Celtic Frost's *To Mega Therion*, people with sweaty feet, Mutt Lange for finally bringing the "Shania" sound to indie labels, the South of the Border stop in South Carolina (when can I move in? Hope y'all still got room!), sad, pathetic minor hipsters who think the Robert Tilton fart tape is funny, Guy Laroche (no, really, you keep it; it's your disease), the guitar player in VHS or Beta who got beat up by the door guy from that band King Horse at the U.S. Maple show August 8, 1998 at the Mercury Paw in Louisville (hope that shit healed, bro), Nutmeg Kemur-Jim, the polio scare of the 1920's, two-newspaper towns, the Leonard Nimoy Should Eat More Salsa Foundation, Giant Gold Buddhas, Herbal Essence, normal penises, my baby Beth, King Vitamin, the original two-member version of The Who, enclosed phone booths, yellow cornmeal, the spare eyeball of Sammy Davis Jr. that I won on eBay, the golfing skills of Alice Cooper, my souvenir toilet paper from Jandek's house, Attack Beaver, Roberto Wilson, my fast-twitch muscle trainer, Milan Kundera (you still got it; keep writing if you're alive), whoever came up with the cliché "Separate the sheep from the goats," Sex on the Beach (both the drink *and* party band), Blue Cheer's *Vincebus Eruptum*, jock itch remedies, Necrosadist and Necrophagist of East Atlanta, crosswinds.net, puppies in the tub (ain't whachoo thank, girl!), that dude from Dramarama who works on a backhoe, women who want waist-length hair, Otto Van Bismarck, porn magazines that overuse footnotes, Mr. Entertainment and a few other Caucasians from Hollywood, Florida, snowmen who aren't frosty, the infamous Audrey Tautou internet porn film (yeeowch!), the Puka, Levi's for feet, Crumb Munchkin - the band (not the soup), the pre-Raphaelite brotherhood, Pet Heaven, the Mannerists, Yves Klein (for giving us Yves Klein Bleu), Kara Walker (for keeping it real), whoever designs those godawful Smog Veil ads, the menopause taboo, the smell of burning brisket, Joseph M. Farley Nuclear Plant units 1 & 2, Dothan, Alabama, Cardamom, Keebler waffle cones that make tasty snack ideas, people who can fake playing the Theremin, Andrew Quinn's giant 4-foot inflatable giraffe toss set, Ice-T for producing David Hasselhoff, baby coffins, "Cannibal Holocaust," my peeps in Kurdistan, hairiness in women, Lester Holt and everyone at MSNBC (actually, daytime only—Chris Matthews can go suck some Hardballs), Michael O'Bannon (still owe you money for the Gastr' Del Sol *The Serpentine Similar* artwork), the recently reunited Shampoopoo, Tab (the cola and the hamster), anything that isn't a "Jesus is my homeboy" shirt, Joan of Arc-shaped S'mores, all you Sagittariuses ('cause I know I can fuck you), the Servant Girl Annihilator Tour in Austin, Texas, my retarded atheist friends who don't believe in God but still believe in ghosts, the Allah bobblehead doll, subconscious racism, "party" as an adverb, people who actually think "Weird News" columns are funny, belly button discharge, Gay Divorce Court, the bass player from Mercy Me who I did that drunk sorority girl with, Yoshitomo Nara (but get your own style, faggot), men who refuse to ever hit a woman (unless she's a rockabilly chick, of course!), any kind of flame that isn't real, people who have the Gun Club on their iPod (now, that's cool!), some people that use heroin, all my bitches that work the food court at Lenox Mall, the stroke of Ram Dass, the *Grill Skills* instruction video, NPR: The Beer, *The Total Nerd: A Comprehensive Handbook*, inspired by *Revenge of the Nerds* authors: Joan Wilen and Lydia Wilen, my wife, my family, my friends, and most importantly, God... and while I'm thanking God, I'd like to give a shout-out to The Holy Spirit, Jacob, Gideon, Abel, Seven Angels with seven plagues, promise names in Colosse, pain with a purpose Zophar, the rest of the Levites, the Widow's Oil, Abner, Joab's murder of Abner, Hebron, 2nd Thessalonians (you go, girl!), the stoning of Stephen, Philip and the Ethiopian, tax collectors everywhere, Ezekiel, Hosea and his adulterous wife — naughty ho'!, Paul and Silas in prison (bad boys, bad boys, what you gonna do...), Gideon and the Fleece, Peter's denial of Christ, all them plagues of Egypt, dudes with leprosy, paralyzed fucks, fig trees, sermonizing on the motherfuckin' mount, Herod (keep up the... bad work!), Sarah's infertility and worry-free sex, that crazy-ass Tower of Babel, Amorites in the 'hood, them spelling Rebecca "Rebekah," all that early fuckin' and begettin' (yo my boys!), sons of Leah: Reuben, Jacob, Simeon, Levi, Issacher and Zebulon (kick it, homies!), the revolt of Moab, 2nd Chronicles 4:18, Titus the Troubleshooter, the Sabbath – rest, you overachieving assholes!, the taming of the tongue, the great multitude in white robes, the Lamb and the 144,000 (fuck the rest of y'all), Shamgar, the song of Deborah, Rehoboam's family, the condemnation of Idolaters, leprosy (if I haven't thanked it enough already!), the son of Helig, the son of Matthat, the son of Levi, the son of Melki, the son of Jannai, the son of Joseph, the son of Matthias, the son of Amos, the son of Nahum, the son of Esli, the son of Naggai, the son of Maath, the son of Semein, the son of Josech, the son of Joda, the son of Joanan, the son of Rhesu, the son of Zerubbabel, the son of Sheaitiel, the son of Neri, the son of Melki, the son of Addi, the son of Cosam, the son of Addi, the son of Elmadam, the son of Er, the son of Joshua, the son of Eliezer, the son of Jorim, the son of Matthat, the son of Levi, the son of Simeon, the son of Judah, the other son of Judah, the son of Joseph, the son of Jonam, the son of Eliakim, the son of Melea, the son of Mattaha, the son of Nathan, the son of David, the son of Jesse, the son of Obea, the son of Boaz, the son of Solomon, the son of Nashon, the son of Amminadab, the son of Ram, the son of Hezron, the son of Perez, the son of Judah, the son of Jacob, the son of Isaac, the son of Nahor, the son of Serus, the son of Rev, the son of Peley, the son of Ebor, the son of Shelah, the son of Cainan, the son of Arphaxad, the son of Shen, the son of Noah, the son of Lamech, the son of Methuselah, the son of Enoch, the son of Jured, the son of Mahalalel, the son of Kenan, the son of Enosh, the son of Seth, the son of Adam, the son of God...oh, yeah, Caleb, the blood of Christ, Zachariah, Balaam, Hoshea (the last king of Israel), Hebrew servants (clean it up, bitch!), the defeat of the Amalekites, the Valley of Dry Bones, Jesus washing his disciples' feet (yo, Peter, get ya' some tough-actin' Tinactin, bro), the riot in Ephesus (y'all know how to fuck shit up), all of them archangels that be guarding over Israel, Habakkuk, the Battle of Jericho, Daniel getting his ass out of the Lion's Den, the stoning of Stephen (smoke up, Bible dude!), deaf mutes, ten virgins, the mustard seed parable and whatever the hell it's about, the jeering of Elisha, the Golden Calves at Bethel and Dan (bling bling Old Testament style), predestination, Eli's wicked sons, the death of Lazarus, Jeremiah 5:2, the Oracle against Damascus, the beheading of John the Baptist (Nick Berg, eat my dust...I mean since your head's already on the ground and everything), Paul's farewell to the Ephesian Elders, kicking the piss out of the Oxgods, that Festus asswipe, all nuggets of theology, all them broken-ass seals and scrolls, Old Testament God being wise, yet ruthless, Absalom's dirty little conspiracy, the Israelites throwin' down with the Benjamites, Achan's sin, the Covenant renewed at Mount Ebal, God's rejection of Zedekiah's request, the silly faith of the Centurion, Stephen's meaningful, but longwinded, speech to the Sanhedrin, new wine in old wineskins (bring on the wake-up juice), sheep and goats (especially the sexy ones), feeding of the 4,000 good-for-nothing fucks, man at the pool of Bethesda, Creationism, Jesus going ape-shit in the temple and all them unemployed demons everywhere, and of course my main man Zacchaeus.

AFTERWORD

FROM THE DESK OF
RONALD THOMAS CLONTLE
POST OFFICE BOX 23 LINCOLN NE 68583

Henry,

Thanks for sending the "Overrated" galleys. Seems we're in agreement on a lot of the entries, especially Television (Billy Ficca didn't really blossom until he joined the Waitresses, IMO) and Bright Eyes (although he has gotten me into wearing chokers). Can't say I'm with you on Metallica's 'St. Anger'...might have something to do with it being the album I lost my virginity to.

Word of warning: I hope you're ready for the torrent of vitriol this thing will undoubtedly unleash. When the first edition of my book, "Rock, Rot & Rule," came out in early '98, I had no idea how much hate mail I was going to receive. Earthlink cancelled my account after their mainframe got bombarded with thousands of missives from irate David Bowie fans who took exception to my placing their hero in the "rot" column. I stand behind my assessment that the guy's made too many changes over the years. Same goes for Neil Young. Don't get me started on all the jerks who disagreed with me on the whole "Madness invented ska" thing. It's like, go write your own book, you dicks.

But don't let all the complaints get you down, man. Just keep the following words of wisdom in mind and you'll be fine: "You're not a real music journalist until your life's been threatened by a member of Dillon Fence."

Best wishes,

Ronald Thomas Clontle

P.S.: Be on the lookout for a complimentary copy of my new book, "Irish Thunder: The Larry Mullen Jr. Story (Part One)." Word is that Fred Savage is VERY interested in playing L.M. Jr. in the film version. But that's just between you and me, OK? Fingers crossed!

FOR ONLY EIGHT DOLLARS
EACH ISSUE OF
CHUNKLET
TEARS ALL YOUR FAVORITES
A NEW ONE